Subjectivity, Citizenship and Belonging in Law

This collection of articles critically examines legal subjectivity and ideas of personhood and citizenship inherent in legal thought. The chapters offer novel perspectives on current debates in this area by exploring the connections between public and political issues as they intersect with more intimate sets of relations and private identities. Covering issues as diverse as autonomy, vulnerability and care, family and work, immigration control, the institution of speech, and electoral qualifications and the right to vote, they provide a broader canvas upon which to comprehend more complex notions of citizenship, personhood, identity and belonging in law, in their various ramifications.

Anne Griffiths is Professor of Anthropology of Law at the University of Edinburgh, UK.

Sanna Mustasaari is based at the University of Helsinki, Finland, and **Anna Mäki-Petäjä-Leinonen** at the University of Eastern Finland, Finland.

Subjectivity, Citizenship and Belonging in Law

Identities and Intersections

Edited by Anne Griffiths,
Sanna Mustasaari and
Anna Mäki-Petäjä-Leinonen

LONDON AND NEW YORK

First published 2017
by Routledge

2 Park Square, Milton Park, Abingdon, Oxfordshire OX14 4RN
711 Third Avenue, New York, NY 10017

a Glasshouse book

Routledge is an imprint of the Taylor & Francis Group, an informa business

First issued in paperback 2018

Copyright © 2017 selection and editorial matter, Anne Griffiths, Sanna Mustasaari and Anna Mäki-Petäjä-Leinonen; individual chapters, the contributors

The right of Anne Griffiths, Sanna Mustasaari and Anna Mäki-Petäjä-Leinonen to be identified as the authors of the editorial material, and of the authors for their individual chapters, has been asserted in accordance with sections 77 and 78 of the Copyright, Designs and Patents Act 1988.

All rights reserved. No part of this book may be reprinted or reproduced or utilised in any form or by any electronic, mechanical, or other means, now known or hereafter invented, including photocopying and recording, or in any information storage or retrieval system, without permission in writing from the publishers.

Notice:
Product or corporate names may be trademarks or registered trademarks, and are used only for identification and explanation without intent to infringe.

British Library Cataloguing in Publication Data
A catalogue record for this book is available from the British Library

Library of Congress Cataloging-in-Publication Data
Names: Griffiths, Anne M. O., editor. | Mustasaari, Sanna, editor. | Mäki-Petäjä-Leinonen, Anna, editor.
Title: Subjectivity, citizenship and belonging in law : identities and intersections / Edited by Anne Griffiths, Sanna Mustasaari and Anna Mäki-Petäjä-Leinonen.
Description: New York, NY : Routledge, 2016. | Includes bibliographical references and index.
Identifiers: LCCN 2016022537 | ISBN 9781138121720 (hbk) | ISBN 9781315650807 (ebk)
Subjects: LCSH: Persons (Law) | Identity (Psychology)—Social aspects. | Citizenship—Social aspects
Classification: LCC K3224 .S83 2016 | DDC 346.01/2—dc23
LC record available at https://lccn.loc.gov/2016022537

ISBN: 978-1-138-12172-0 (hbk)
ISBN: 978-1-138-59089-2 (pbk)

Typeset in NewBaskerville
by Apex CoVantage, LLC

Contents

Notes on contributors vii
Acknowledgements ix
Preface xi

Introduction 1

1 **Identities and intersections: critical perspectives on the person of the law** 3
SANNA MUSTASAARI, ANNA MÄKI-PETÄJÄ-LEINONEN, ANNE GRIFFITHS

PART I
Politics, power and subjectivity 27

2 **The ancient subject of speech** 29
SAMULI HURRI

3 **Disenfranchisement and political capacity** 53
PABLO MARSHALL

4 **'Electoral shenanigans': the constituted electorate, the constituent people, and the porous state** 72
PANU MINKKINEN

5 **Who belongs? The Turkish citizen subject in turmoil** 84
KATI NIEMINEN

PART II
Recognising 'the different' subject 103

6 The genderqueer in UK law: why current laws
   are insufficient 105
   CAROLYNN GRAY

7 Best interests of the child in family reunification – a
   citizenship test disguised? 123
   SANNA MUSTASAARI

8 Protecting a person with dementia through restrictions of
   freedom? Notions of autonomy in the theory and practice
   of elder care 146
   ANNA MÄKI-PETÄJÄ-LEINONEN

9 What to do with the other in human rights law? Ethics of
   alterity versus ethics of care 171
   DOROTA GOZDECKA AND SANNA KOULU

PART III
Personhood, property and contribution 191

10 Families, identity and belonging: rethinking personhood
   and property in Botswana 193
   ANNE GRIFFITHS

11 The breadwinner, the homemaker and the worker/carer:
   new stereotypes for old? 214
   JANE MAIR

12 From obedience to initiative? Precarious work and
   changing subjectivities in labour law discourse 232
   MARJO YLHÄINEN

13 Human dignity mediated: personhood, humanity, and the
   logic of property in law and bioethics 253
   UKRI SOIRILA

   Index 271

Notes on contributors

Dorota Gozdecka, LL.D., is Senior Lecturer at the Australian National University. Her primary research area focuses on legal theoretical aspects related to the accommodation of cultural diversity. She has the title of a Docent (Adjunct Professor) of Jurisprudence from the University of Helsinki.

Carolynn Gray is Senior Lecturer and Programme Leader for Law at the University of the West of Scotland. Her research centres on the rights of LGBT individuals, in particular the right to legal recognition of gender identity and the role of third parties, such as medical professionals, in this process.

Anne Griffiths is Professor of Anthropology of Law at the School of Law, University of Edinburgh. Her research focuses on anthropology of law, comparative and family law, African law, gender, culture and rights. Her work has explored the study of law through an anthropological perspective based on ethnography grounded in detailed field studies.

Samuli Hurri, LL.D., is a fellow at the Helsinki Collegium for Advanced Studies at the University of Helsinki. His chapter in this book is produced as part of his research project on The Legal Language of Moral Struggles, funded by the University of Helsinki.

Sanna Koulu, LL.D., is Senior Lecturer at the University of Lapland. Her research focuses on the field of family law, specifically child law. Currently her main research interests are the relations between the family and the nation state and the challenges they pose to transnational regulation.

Jane Mair is Professor of Private Law at the University of Glasgow. Her research concentrates on research and teaching in the areas of employment law and family law. Unifying factors include her interests in the legal regulation of personal relationships; the interaction of work and family and the influence of gender in both areas.

Pablo Marshall is a lecturer at the Law School of the Universidad Austral de Chile and chief editor of the academic journal Derecho y Crítica Social. He completed his PhD in Law at the University of Glasgow. His current research interests focus on the relations between constitutional theory and voting rights.

Panu Minkkinen is Professor of Jurisprudence at the University of Helsinki, Finland. His numerous publications cover themes ranging from the critique of the neo-Kantian remnants of legal thinking to the legal dimensions of contemporary critical theory. Currently his two main research interests are political constitutional theory and the various intersections of law and the humanities.

Sanna Mustasaari is a doctoral candidate at the University of Helsinki. Her research focuses on transnational processes and family relations, culture, gender, generation, and rights. She is a member of the research projects 'Legal Language of Moral Struggles' and 'Transnational Muslim Marriages: Wellbeing, Law and Gender'.

Anna Mäki-Petäjä-Leinonen, LL.D., is a Senior Researcher at the University of Eastern Finland. Her research area focuses on elder law combining jurisprudence with social and medical sciences. She is Docent in family law at the University of Helsinki and Docent in elder law at the University of Lapland.

Kati Nieminen is a doctoral candidate at the University of Helsinki, Faculty of Law. Her research interests are legal theory, law and culture, human rights, and resistance. Kati is a member of the research project 'The Legal Language of Moral Struggles'.

Ukri Soirila is a doctoral candidate at the University of Helsinki, and an affiliated researcher at the Erik Castrén Institute of International Law and Human Rights. His research focuses on international law, human rights, and critical legal theory. Ukri is a member of the research project 'The Legal Language of Moral Struggles'.

Marjo Ylhäinen, LL.D., is Senior Lecturer on Labour Law at the University of Eastern Finland. Her research area focuses on the differentiation of work, precarious work, and its regulation. She is also interested in multidisciplinary research, especially sociology of law and critical discourse analysis.

Acknowledgements

The editors would like to acknowledge the work done by Dr Sanna Koulu, who was part of the editorial team at the early stages of this project.

We owe gratitude to Professor Niklas Bruun, Dr Massimo Fichera, Dr Sarah Garlington, Dr Linda Hart, Dr Hanna-Kaisa Hoppania, Professor Urpo Kangas, Ms Sanna Karhu, Professor Emeritus Simo Knuuttila, Dr Susanna Lindroos-Hovinheimo, Dr Saara Pellander, Professor Jan R. Stenger and Dr Andreja Zevnik, as well as the anonymous reviewers for their invaluable comments and critique on the individual chapters.

Preface

This book originated in a growing awareness that something is wrong with the way that law perceives its subjects. Approaches to legal inquiry springing from analytical and doctrinal jurisprudence could neither recognise nor respond to the calls for social justice hailing from the margins of social experience, and in fact these margins were growing wider so that the experience of exclusion might concern a considerable number of people. Moreover, as researchers of family law interested in issues of care, cultural diversity and legal phenomena that may not reach courts but take place in the various sites of everyday life, we constantly felt the need to justify academic endeavours in these areas. To ponder upon these issues an informal research group was established at the Faculty of Law of the University of Helsinki in 2012 with the focus on what could somewhat vaguely be described as 'soft family law' and which later networked with the University of Edinburgh Law School.

The impetus for this book emerged out of a workshop on identity and belonging, at the University of Edinburgh in May 2013. We would like to thank all participants to the inspiring workshop, who in addition to the editors included Jennifer Corrin, Dianne Gove, Dorota Godzecka, Carolynn Gray, Katja Kahlina, Katja Karjalainen, Magdalena Kmak, Sanna Koulu, Jane Mair, Pablo Marshall, Nina Miller, Kati Nieminen, Henna Pajulammi, Ann Stewart and Marjo Ylhäinen. For taking part in the discussions during the seminar and more broadly on topics that this book concerns we would like to thank Ed Wilmsen. The workshop was organised by the Universities of Edinburgh and Helsinki, in conjunction with the Global Justice Academy at the University of Edinburgh. We owe gratitude to these institutions and would in particular like to thank Professor Christine Bell, the Director of the Global Justice Academy at the University of Edinburgh. We would also like to thank the Finnish Foundation for Municipal Development (KAKS) for their financial support.

For the support and encouragement to pull through this publication we would like to thank Dean Kimmo Nuotio from the Faculty of Law at the University of Helsinki. Also others, especially Professor Urpo Kangas and

Professor Panu Minkkinen, have been generous in providing their support and advice during the project. John Calton MA, lecturer in English, helped us to improve the language and structure of several chapters, often with a rather tight schedule.

The intersections between relational theory, law and social research continue to fascinate and inspire research. In Finland these interdisciplinary efforts have lately been happening within the framework of the 'Relations and Law' research group, moderated by Linda Hart. Thank you RELA, especially Hanna-Kaisa and Linda!

Introduction

Chapter 1

Identities and intersections
Critical perspectives on the person of the law

Sanna Mustasaari, Anna Mäki-Petäjä-Leinonen, Anne Griffiths

The fictive bearer of rights

> From one perspective, being a 'person' in our constitutional system does not take you very far... You are on the field, but your place in the game is an entirely different matter. Being recognized as a person guarantees very little in the way of substantive social protection, rights and responsibilities, and entails virtually no democratic voice at all. It is common in political theory to hear the claim that citizenship is overly-thin and formalistic, yet arguably, personhood is far thinner and more formal still.
>
> Linda Bosniak[1]

This book offers an excursus on legal subjectivity and citizenship in law, both underpinned by various notions of personhood, identity and belonging. The themes of personhood and subjectivity, long the subject of debates within the humanities,[2] are approached in this volume from the perspective of law; each chapter asks how a person is constructed in law and what it means to be 'a legal person'. While the contributors are, by no means, the first to consider these questions,[3] the volume engages with a legacy of critical theory which warns against taking the objective foundations of law and rights for granted and ignoring questions that have to do with subjectivity.

---

1 Linda Bosniak, 'Human Rights within one state: Dilemmas of personhood in liberal constitutional thought,' in *Are Human Rights for Migrants? Critical Reflections on the Status of Irregular Migrants in Europe and the United States*, Marie-Bénédicte Dembour and Tobias Kelly (eds.) (London: Routledge, 2011), 207–8.
2 For instance *Ortner* has noted that social and cultural theory owe much in their progression to the struggle over the role of the social being. Sherry B. Ortner, 'Subjectivity and Cultural Critique,' *Anthropological Theory* 5:1 (2005), 31–52.
3 See, for example, the work by Ngaire Naffine, *Law's Meaning of Life: Philosophy, Religion, Darwin and the Legal Person* (Oxford: Hart Publishing, 2008); 'The Legal Presumption of Reason: Noble Truth, Useful Fiction, Ignoble Lie,' *Cleveland State Law Review* 53 (2005), 1–10; and 'Who are Law's Persons? From Cheshire Cats to Responsible Subjects,' *Modern Law Review* 66:3 (2003), 346–67.

This book challenges the notion of a particular form of reason that has come to stand for *all* reason in its universal applicability to multiple contexts and sites of study. It also questions conventional approaches to the ways in which the subject of rights is constructed in law, highlighting their exclusionary power in terms of who gets to be acknowledged as a rights bearer, and who does not, resulting in those who are excluded finding their rights' claims rejected because of their ascribed lack of legitimacy.[4] In undertaking this project our purpose has not been to reconstruct a generic category of the person of the law or indeed to lay claim to any such category. On the contrary, we accept the fact that the law often constructs its subjects inconsistently. The 'subject' is a fiction constituted by a variety of underlying assumptions about the properties that constitute 'the person'. These assumptions relate to the capacities of the subject as well as to the situation-specific structures that shape realms or forms of social action.

The main thread running through the book is an examination of how personhood is constructed as legal subjectivity and how this may be transformed as it both shapes and is shaped by the everyday life of individuals, and political and social institutions. What this highlights are the many ways in which meanings of personhood are configured in time and space through particular processes that shape their specificity and application. Drawing on a theoretically rich and wide-ranging assortment of literature, the chapters in this volume provide an important and novel perspective on current debates in this area by bringing together the public and private dimensions that construct personhood and people's experiences of it. They explore the connections between public and political issues as they intersect with more intimate sets of relations and private identities, providing a broader canvas upon which to comprehend more complex notions of citizenship, personhood, identity and belonging in law, in all their various ramifications.

Attributes of personhood and belonging in legal thought

Looked at from these varying perspectives, personhood and belonging not only vary across cultures but also manifest themselves in different ways in different contexts within the same culture.[5] It seems illogical therefore to assume that any metaphysical concept of personhood would hold true across the variety of legal contexts and discourses. For instance, according

---

4 See, for example, Siobhan Mullally, *Gender, Culture and Human Rights: Reclaiming Universalism* (Portland, OR: Hart Publishing, 2006). See also James Boyle on the critique of objectivity and phenomenology of alienated subjectivity; 'Is Subjectivity Possible? The Post-Modern Subject in Legal Theory,' *University of Colorado Law Review* 62 (1991), 489–524.
5 Susan Rasmussen, 'Personhood, Self, Difference, and Dialogue (Commentary on Chaudhary),' *International Journal for Dialogical Studies* 3:1 (2008), 32.

to *Naffine*, there are three different ways in which the relationship between legal and metaphysical persons may be perceived.[6] It is, firstly, possible to insist that the legal person is a purely legal construct and that no necessary connection exists between the legal and metaphysical persons. The other two approaches to personhood in law view it as either 'any reasonable creature in being' or the 'responsible subject'. The first takes humanity as the decisive attribute of personhood and relies on both biological determinats as well as metaphysical ideas about what it means to be a human, influenced by cultural and religious ideas about what it means to be a person.[7] This humanity is taken to be natural and is based on individuality and autonomy; the person is taken to be separate, distinct and self-possessing. The third approach to legal personhood is to view it as something that is essentially concerned with social agency. Legal personality, according to this line of thinking, requires agency that involves the ability to initiate and take part in legal actions. In this context the legal agent needs to be rational and responsible, a morally and rationally capable being; the biological human being is only the beginning of development towards full personality, one that demonstrates rational capacity.

The chapters in this volume contest all these constitutive elements of legal personhood and the ways in which they construct rationality. Let us now examine the key concepts on which both legal and political theory draw in discourses on subjectivity, citizenship and belonging in slightly more detail.

Subjectivity

> *Agency is not some natural or originary will; it takes shape as specific desires and intentions within a matrix of subjectivity – of (culturally constituted) feelings, thoughts, and meanings.*
>
> Sherry B. Ortner[8]

'Subjectivity' is an ambiguous and existentially complex term. It refers both to the inner states of acting subjects, such as modes of thought or affect,

---

6 Naffine, 'Who are Law's Persons?' In her more recent work she introduces four schools of thought: *legalism*, which holds that the law's concept of 'person' has no determinate content; *rationalism*, which holds that the constitutive trait of legal persons is the capacity to reason; *religionism*, which holds that membership of the human species is the constitutive trait of legal persons; and *naturalism*, which points to the evolutionary continuity between species and argues for extending legal personality to non-human animals. Naffine, *Law's Meaning of Life*.
7 Ngaire, 'Who are Law's Persons?'
8 Ortner, 'Subjectivity and Cultural Critique,' 34.

and to the cultural and social formations that give rise to and shape those inner states.[9] Under these conditions, 'subjectivity' in law may refer both to the condition of being a legal subject as well as to the selfhood and experience of the relational person.[10] The subject is thus a constitutive legal concept, encompassing identity and lived experience. Subjectivity can also represent, as *Biehl, Good & Kleinman* have observed, both an empirical reality and an analytic category that not only embraces the remaking of culture (in terms of transformations associated with forms of social organisation and institutional domains) but also captures the inner reflections and experiences of human subjects.[11]

Ortner has emphasised the analytical importance of distinguishing between cultural anthropology of subjectivity (a theoretical tradition oriented towards interpretation of the formation of subjectivities) and other theorisations of subjectivities as social positions or locations formed by particular political discourses. The diverse forms of politically oriented analyses of 'subject-making' focus not so much on the experiencing subject as an end in herself, but the workings of power that are evident in her constitution. Contemporary critical theorisations on subjectivity owe much to the French philosopher *Foucault*, whose studies on power place a central emphasis on how human beings are made subjects as well as the process of 'subjectivation', by which he refers to the ways in which people are invited to recognise their moral obligations.[12] Foucault's theoretical framework has had a profound influence also in the fields of jurisprudence and legal philosophy.[13]

'Subjectivity', produced through practices in particular social fields, is an outcome of a particular interplay of intersecting discourses formed around social practices. These discourses are cultural and both reflect and organise

---

9 Ortner, 'Subjectivity and Cultural Critique'.
10 The question of subjectivity has played a significant role also in philosophy. The diverging approaches to subjectivity is one of the dividing lines between the transcendental and the metaphysical traditions of philosophy. See David Carr, *The Paradox of Subjectivity: The Self in Transcendental Tradition* (Oxford: Oxford University Press, 1999).
11 Joao Biehl, Byron Good and Arthur Kleinman (eds.), *Subjectivity: Ethnographic Investigation* (Berkeley: University of California Press, 2007).
12 See, for instance, Michel Foucault, 'The Subject and Power', *Critical Inquiry* 8 (1982), 777–95; and Paul Rabinow (ed.) *The Essential Works of Michel Foucault Vol. 1, Ethics: Subjectivity and Truth* (London: Allen Lane, 1997), specifically 'On the Genealogy of Ethics: An Overview of Work in Progress', 264.
13 Foucault's ideas on power, knowledge and subjectivity have been utilised, for instance, by *Samuli Hurri* in his outline of a theory of legal practice. Undertaking this project Hurri has studied in particular how legal and extra-legal powers operate productively to make particular kinds of human beings, and, in the process, create venues for resistance. See Samuli Hurri, *Birth of the European Individual: Law, Security, Economy* (Abingdon: Routledge, 2014).

forms of subjectivity.¹⁴ In this volume, the chapters by *Mustasaari*, *Nieminen* and *Ylhäinen* examine the legal and political processes by which subjectivities are produced. For instance, in her chapter, Ylhäinen analyses legal texts from Finnish judicial bodies to critically interrogate the representations of work and shows how the employer and the employee emerge as a particular pair of subjects, informed and shaped by the images attached to the conditions of business and the mode of production. From a very different perspective, *Soirila* argues in his chapter that biotechnology and new theoretical innovations have opened the possibility to push us to think of legal categories and legal subjectivity in new ways by challenging the notion of the human subject as an autonomous flesh-and-blood individual.

Cultural anthropology, being holistically oriented, seeks to understand complex forms of consciousness, such as structures of thought, reflection and affect, where social agents are always more than the particular social locations they occupy. Thus, subjectivity may be viewed as the basis of 'agency', a necessary part of understanding how people (try to) act on the world even as they are acted upon.¹⁵ This leads to subjectivity embracing forms of specific cultural and historical consciousness as well as various unconscious dynamics. In addition, actors, both individually and collectively, may be assumed to have some degree of reflexivity about themselves and their desires, as they have, at least to some extent, the ability to understand how their circumstances form them. This relationship between an individual and community, structure and agency, is present in the inquiries this volume contains. In this volume, the chapter by *Griffiths* adopts an ethnographic approach to investigating the shifting inheritance norms and how these changes reflect women's evolving roles and their recognition as subjects. From a different perspective, that of ancient texts, *Hurri* discusses the role of moral language as constitutive of us as human beings and as making us moral subjects in diverse societal contexts.

In practice, however, these types of analysis overlap, coincide and mutually inform one another. For instance, discussing the precariousness of work in contemporary societies, Ylhäinen particularly draws on Ehrenberg's analysis on the significant shift in the contemporary Western mindset towards an understanding of social action first and foremost through the ideal and imperative of individual autonomy.¹⁶ Within this structure of thought and reflection, government through the central norm of guilt, discipline and obedience is replaced by government through the ideal of responsibility and initiative. Thus, instead of merely being situated in particular positions

---

14 Ortner, 'Subjectivity and Cultural Critique,' 36.
15 Ortner, 'Subjectivity and Cultural Critique,' 33.
16 Alain Ehrenberg, *The Weariness of the Self: Diagnosing the History of Depression in the Contemporary Age* (Montreal, Ithaca: McGill-Queen's University Press, 2010).

in the social, political, economic or religious matrix, subjectivity is governed by a complex sets of feelings and fears, such as the fear of conceptual chaos. Conceptual chaos here refers not just to a lack of interpretation but of interpretability, emerging either as the limits of capacity to understand (bafflement), limits to one's power of endurance (suffering) or limits of moral insight (intractable ethical paradox).[17]

Citizenship

> Nevertheless it is true that citizenship, even in its early forms, was a principle of equality, and that during this period it was a developing institution. Starting at the point where all men were free and, in theory, capable of enjoying rights, it grew by enriching the body of rights which they were capable of enjoying. But these rights did not conflict with the inequalities of capitalist society; they were, on the contrary, necessary to the maintenance of that particular form of inequality.
>
> T. H. Marshall[18]

Questions of personhood, citizenship and legal subjectivity are related to the ways in which we recognise, protect and control human agency that is both individual and collective. Thus, they are also inevitably present in inquiries about the nature of law and rights – and indeed, of political institutions. As *Minkkinen* demonstrates in his chapter, in this relationship the constituent people form part of the constituted institutions, lying 'dormant within the constituted electorate until one day it awakens and chooses to call into question one or another constituted institution, including the role of the electorate that it has given itself'.[19] The unpredictable nature of the relationship between the citizen and her community – the porous state – thus carries radical potential to change the ruling regime.

Legal scholars associate citizenship with rights and participation, placing emphasis on the right to be treated equally before the law, political rights and the entitlement and obligation to participate as a full and equal member within the economy and the polity.[20] Conceptually, citizenship is closely connected to social inclusion, equality and access to justice; for even when citizenship is understood primarily as a matter of legal status, its dimensions of membership and participation point towards an understanding of rights and legal subjectivity as a form of agency. Such an understanding is

---

17 Ortner, 'Subjectivity and Cultural Critique,' 40.
18 T.H. Marshall, *Citizenship and Social Class and Other Essays* (Cambridge: Cambridge University Press, 1950), 33.
19 Minkkinen, Chapter 4 in this volume.
20 See, for example, Richard Bellamy, 'Evaluating Union Citizenship: Belonging, Rights and Participation Within the EU,' *Citizenship Studies* 12:6 (2008), 597–611.

underpinned by an intrinsic respect regarding a person's autonomy as a critical agent.[21]

In his chapter, *Marshall* discusses criminal disenfranchisement on the basis of offenders' lack of political capacity and notes that to consider civic virtue as a requirement of voting implies something more substantial than a mere regulation of such a right. It implies not just the denial of the vote for offenders but the denial of their public personality; the capacity to participate in collective government. The practice of excluding offenders from the right to vote thus implies their reduction and degradation to a second class of citizens.

One way of conceiving citizenship, suggested for example by *Turner*, connects citizenship to participation in different social arenas, such as work, war and reproduction. According to Turner, these forms of participation used to result in three types of social identity: worker-citizens, warrior-citizens and parent-citizens. As citizenship based on the nation-state becomes challenged or weakened, the rights presented in classical theorisations over citizenship are being supplemented with rights of a more global nature.[22] Cultural rights (to language, to a share in the cultural heritage of a community, and to religious identity) have become central to the modern politics of identity, but these cultural rights have neither precise nor necessary connections with membership of the nation-state. The concept of 'cultural citizenship' extends the scope of citizenship to cover intimate and cultural dimensions. As *Horsti* and *Pellander* note, discussing public debates on family migration, the 'broader social and cultural discourses and practices create the conditions within which a more narrow entitlement to political rights emerges. This broader understanding of citizenship recognises not only legal documentation and access to social services, but also the sense of belonging and the right to practice one's culture'.[23] The chapter by Mustasaari in this volume engages with this discussion by looking at how citizenship of second generation children becomes defined by their family constellation and transnational family ties and by markers of identity as manifestations of their otherness and non-belonging.

The 'transnational element' is a defining feature not only of the law but also of the social relations and communication flows of our time. On the one hand, in legal studies the concept of transnationalism has been invoked as a response to the facts of fragmentation and inter-legality. It has

---

21 Ruth Lister, 'Unpacking Children's Citizenship,' in *Children and Citizenship*, Antonella Invernizzi and Jane Williams (eds.) (Los Angeles, London, New Delhi and Singapore: Sage Publications, 2008); and 'Why Citizenship: Where, When and How Children?,' *Theoretical Inquiries in Law* 8 (2007), 693–718.
22 Bryan S. Turner, 'The Erosion of Citizenship,' *British Journal of Sociology* 52:2 (2001), 189–209.
23 Karina Horsti and Saara Pellander, 'Conditions of Cultural Citizenship: Intersections of Gender, Race and Age in Public Debates on Family Migration,' *Citizenship Studies* 19:6–7 (2015), 752.

also been used as a means of highlighting the inadequacies of municipal and international law that arise from a regulatory framework premised on the nation-state. For this approach fails to take account of the broader normative frameworks and legal processes that are at work here, that fundamentally affect many fields of public and private law.[24] On the other hand, studies in transnationalism also observe a shift away from the national society paradigm and towards rearrangements of geosocial spaces.[25] What is important for the socio-legal constructions of personhood and subjectivity, is the interrelatedness of global, national and local that transnationalism studies address.[26] Globalisation also takes place in the social sites of everyday life, but the norms that it espouses, such as international human rights, are translated and negotiated to meet the particular contexts – the process referred to as the vernacularisation of human rights.[27]

Belonging and identity

> *Returning to the Kentucky landscape of my childhood and most importantly to the hills, I am able to reclaim a sublime understanding that living in harmony with the earth renews the spirit. Coming home to live in Kentucky was for me a journey back to a place where I felt I belonged. But it was also returning to a place that I felt needed me and my resources, a place where I as a citizen could be in community with other folk seeking to revive and renew our local environment, seeking to have fidelity to a place.*
>
> bell hooks[28]

Subjectivity includes notions of belonging that, in contemporary theorisations, have come to encompass both citizenship (covering the participatory dimension of belonging), and identity (that articulates the diverse ways in which people define themselves and others and the relations between them). *Yuval-Davis et al* argue 'that it is impossible to understand the ways individual people and groupings relate to and are being treated by both state and society these days just by being related to as either citizens and/or having specific ethnic, national or racial identities. The politics of belonging encompass and relate both citizenship and identity, adding an emotional dimension which

---

24 Miguel Maduro, Kaarlo Tuori and Suvi Sankari (eds.), *Transnational Law: Rethinking European Law and Legal Thinking* (Cambridge: Cambridge University Press, 2014).
25 Anne Hellum, Shaheen Sardar Ali and Anne Griffiths (eds.), *From Transnational Relations to Transnational Laws: Northern European Laws at the Crossroads* (Farnham and Burlington: Ashgate, 2011).
26 See, for instance, the discussions in Kate Nash (ed.), *Transnationalizing the Public Sphere: Nancy Fraser et al.* (Cambridge and Malden: Polity Press, 2014).
27 Sally Engle Merry, 'Constructing a Global Law – Violence against Women and the Human Rights System,' *Law and Social Inquiry*, 28:4 (2003), 941–77.
28 bell hooks, *Belonging: A Culture of Place* (New York: Routledge, 2009), 65.

is central to notions of belonging'.[29] Conversely, the notion of subjectivity also gives rise to exclusion where a person is deemed not to belong to the group that he or she lays claim to. The power of the law to produce subjectivities through projects of belonging is discussed in this volume, for instance by *Nieminen*, as she studies the fundamental conflict over the citizen subject in Turkey. She shows how this conflict was traditionally located in the dispute over the roles of religion and ethnicity in relation to the Kemalist subject but that, during the Gezi protests in 2013, the citizen subject was revealed as fragmented and diverse far beyond the familiar axes of ethnicity and religion.

The idea of belonging is central to our understanding of the self, of what it means to be an individual embedded in social relations.[30] For *Carillo Rowe*, belonging means longing for the other, an affect that is spatially situated.[31] Unsurprisingly, family remains one of the most important sites of belonging.[32] Since intimate and affective ties are a key component in belonging, family is central to the individual's perceptions of identity and belonging. In her chapter, *Griffiths* studies both the cultural markers of personhood and belonging as well as the ways in which individuals perceive themselves and their place within society through looking at the value and recognition of caring relationships within the family. But it is also about attachment or loyalty to a place,[33] be that a physical, territorial place like the hills of Kentucky or a social space that comes into being through the representations of members of a community who invest it with their own forms of meaning. For as *Khan* observes, belonging is about 'spaces (literal and metaphorical), traditions, and culture'.[34] Thus *Bohlin* has defined belonging as the position of subjective participants, of being included in the category of an 'authorised "we" '.[35] In this sense, belonging may also be perceived as a moral claim to recognition.

---

29 Nira Yuval-Davis, Kalpana Kannabiran and Ulrike M. Vieten, 'Introduction,' in *The Situated Politics of Belonging*, Nira Yuval-Davis, Kalpana Kannabiran and Ulrike M. Vieten (eds.), (London: SAGE Publications, 2006), 1–14.
30 Aimee Carillo Rowe, 'Be Longing: Toward a Feminist Politics of Relation,' *NWSA Journal* 17:2 (2005), 16.
31 Ibid. 26.
32 Belonging, Research report by the Social Issues Research Centre, 2007, www.sirc.org/publik/belonging.pdf (accessed 14 February 2016). The report mapping belonging in 21st-century British society identified six key social identities in which people most frequently anchor their sense of belonging. According to the report, family remained the most important site of belonging, 'despite public debate about the decline of the family in modern society' (p. 4). The other five identities were related to friendship, lifestyle choices, nationality, professional interests, and team spirit and shared interests.
33 Nadia Lovell, 'Introduction: Belonging in Need of Emplacement?' in *Locality and Belonging*, Nadia Lovell (ed.) (London: Routledge, 1998), 1–22.
34 Anoosh W. Khan, 'Citizenship and Belonging: A Socio-Political Paradigm Shift,' *PUTAJ – Humanities and Social Sciences* 20 (2013), 81–92.
35 Anna Bohlin, 'The Politics of Locality: Memories of District Six in Cape Town,' in *Locality and Belonging*, Nadia Lovell (ed.) (New York: Routledge, 1998), 175.

Questions relating to recognition of 'identity' have become a central feature of political struggles of our time. The play between structure and agency has been noted in critiques of universal subjectivity that maintain that the symbolic order of subjectivity is, in fact, an ideological project of gendered and colonial domination.[36] In a world where social categories are significant social markers, the impact of the law is far from the same for everyone. In legal thought, 'identity' debates have emerged as questions of recognition of identities that contest dominant paradigms. The essential question remains: which identities form part of the legal subject and what are the consequences that ensue from this? In other words, how are we to decide which differences should be acknowledged in law and what kind of concept of equality should underpin our efforts to eliminate discriminatory structures that are premised on the basis of difference? In some cases, the recognition of identities is directly defined in legal texts, as *Gray*'s chapter on the genderqueer definition of personhood demonstrates. Personhood as legal subjectivity appears to be restricted by the lens of law, so that legal categories in fact reinforce patterns of recognition already existing in legal structures. As Gray shows, in these cases equality is not achieved by merely expanding the scope of the problematic category.

Distinguishing between various aspects of belonging, such as spatial, ritual and emotional dimensions, Khan has showed that 'along with the legalistic definitions of citizenship and belonging, the geographical space, imagined space, and cyberspace also play a role in certifying the notions of belonging'.[37] Hence, the embeddedness and relationality of the self makes the notion of identity crucial to the concept of belonging. Instead of being understood as properties or fixed traits of personality, identities are better perceived as narratives of self, founded on and emerging in social interactions which bid us take part in communicative practices based on shared beliefs and values. Identities may be perceived, as for example by *Yuval-Davis, Kannabiran and Vieten*, as narratives 'clustered around some hegemonic constructions of boundaries between "self" and "other" and "us" and "them" that are closely related to political processes'.[38] In discussing a variety of these political projects of belonging, *Yuval-Davis* notes that identity narratives can be individual or collective reflecting situations where collective identity narratives often reinforce those of individuals.[39] The identities are formed in the mundane practices of day-to-day life, such as practices of care. These relationships and practices that are often perceived as having

---

36 Ortner, 'Subjectivity and Cultural Critique,' 32.
37 Ibid. 89.
38 Yuval-Davis, Kannabiran and Vieten, 'Introduction', 1–14. See also Nira Yuval-Davis, *The Politics of Belonging: Intersectional Contestations* (London: SAGE Publications, 2011).
39 Yuval-Davis, *The Politics of Belonging*, 14.

little political significance are, in fact, powerful sites of subject-making. Several chapters in this volume discuss personhood, citizenship and subjectivity in the context of interpersonal relationships and care.

Caring relations

> *Unless there is caring there is no possibility for justice, yet we need justice so that we can care. Without justice care can become abuse and without care justice loses its heart.*
>
> Jonathan Herring[40]

Several chapters in this volume address care, caring relations or ethics of care. Ethics of care, as it was first articulated by *Gilligan*,[41] focuses on the ethical reasoning that springs from the condition of relationality. Instead of being about abstract rules and universal principles, ethics of care maintains that ethical decision-making is better conceived as attentiveness, trust, responsiveness to need, and other such dimensions. Rather than abstract decision-making processes, which require impartiality and universal rules, even abstract ethical solutions unravel through nuanced narratives that engage with caring relations from the perspective of carers and the cared-for, whose interests clearly have much in common.[42] Thus the ethics of care is about an approach to morality that rests on relationality and responsiveness to the dependent other in their terms.

Instead of being only about an 'other' who is particularly close to 'self', ethics of care views what is morally urgent from the perspective of the one who is in a vulnerable position in a relationship. Care theory thus emphasises that focusing on care relations requires paying more attention to interactions among unequals; relations which actually dominate our social life. Ideally these relations are good care relations, but they can also be abusive and exploitative. Hence the *role of power* in care relations should be acknowledged, so that measures against the possibility for exploitation and neglect can also be developed.[43] Oppressive relationships of this nature may also be harmful for a person's ability to make autonomous decisions.

---

40 Jonathan Herring, *Caring and the Law* (Oxford and Portland: Hart Publishing, 2013), 68.
41 Carol Gilligan, *In a Different Voice. Psychological Theory and Women's Development* (Cambridge, MA: Harvard University Press, 1982).
42 Virginia Held, *The Ethics of Care: Personal, Political, Global* (Oxford: Oxford University Press, 2006).
43 See, for instance, Annemieke van Drenth and Francisca de Haan, *The Rise of Caring Power. Elizabeth Fry and Josephine Butler in Britain and the Netherlands* (Amsterdam: Amsterdam University Press, 1999) and Eva Feder Kittay and Ellen K. Feder, 'Introduction' in *The Subject of Care: Feminist Perspectives on Dependency*, Eva Feder Kittay and Ellen K. Feder (eds.) (Lanham: Rowan & Littlefield, 2002), 2.

The importance of ethics of care has been acknowledged by numerous theorists and researchers working in a variety of fields, including economics, education, sociology, philosophy, social policy, politics and law. With regard to the latter, *Herring* has explained how the law can powerfully utilise an ethic of care in many legal arenas.[44] The question of the relationship between an ethics of care and an ethics of justice[45] has been controversial but most care ethicists today agree that care and justice should go hand in hand.[46] In their chapter, *Gozdecka* and *Koulu* analyse three cases from the European Court of Human Rights and argue that by bringing together the ethics of care and ethics of alterity, the shortcomings of the logic which seeks to universalise the ethics of justice might be remedied.

While most caring relationships are informal and based on intimate and familial relationships, care is also a site of policy-making. Instead of being merely about private activity of no interest to the state, the state is in fact a powerful actor, shaping the ways in which caring is managed within families as well as the institutions of the state.[47] The questions relating to the recognition and management of care within the political process have attracted scholarly attention in many disciplines as they continue to be at the heart of the political and legal struggles of the declining welfare society.[48] In her chapter *Mäki-Petäjä-Leinonen* reviews the forthcoming Finnish Autonomy Act and explores how the legislation has adopted the principles of person-centred care in order to support the autonomy of a person in institutionalised care.

When it comes to the ways families function, 'no family is an island'.[49] As the chapter by *Mair* points out, the way caring is understood in families and valued by society is in fact greatly influenced by other societal structures, such as the structures of working life. Indeed, childcare and domestic work remain undervalued and often invisible within economic policy and political debate. This is due partly to the moral value attached to caring that takes

---

44　Herring, *Caring and the Law*.
45　Ethics of justice focuses on questions of fairness, equality, individual rights, abstract principles and their consistent application. It seeks a fair solution between competing individual interests and rights. See for instance Held, *The Ethics of Care*, 15.
46　See, for instance, Annemarie Mol, *The Logic of Care: Health and the Problem of Patient Choice* (London: Routledge, 2008), 75 and Selma Sevenhuijsen, *Citizenship and the Ethics of Care: Feminist Considerations on Justice, Moralty and Politics* (New York: Routledge, 1998), 145.
47　Herring, *Caring and the Law*, 3.
48　For instance Joan Tronto, *Moral Boundaries. A Political Argument for an Ethic of Care* (New York: Routledge, 1993). See also Hanna-Kaisa Hoppania in her academic dissertation which investigates the politics of care and analyses the enacting process of the Act on Care Services for Older People. Hanna-Kaisa Hoppania, *Care as a site of a political struggle* (University of Helsinki: Academic dissertation, 2015, available at https://helda.helsinki.fi/handle/10138/157561 (accessed 15 April 2016)).
49　Maxine Eichner, 'Families, human dignity, and state support for caretaking: Why the United States' failure to ameliorate the work-family conflict is a dereliction of the government's basic responsibilities,' *North Carolina Law Review* 88:5 (2010), 1619.

for granted who the person performing such care should be. In a societal context which is very different from that of Mair, *Griffiths* looks at the roles in the family as well as understandings of personhood and how they serve to symbolise other constructs and roles, such as gender, age or dependence.[50]

The question of value and visibility of caring is closely connected to the attributes we attach to personhood. To be able to assess responsibilities in interpersonal relations changes the way we view personality and what it means to be a person. This focus on relations and reciprocity forces us to critically revisit some of the concepts underlying the liberal rights discourse, such as the concepts of autonomy, capacity and rationality.

Autonomy and relationality

> *Autonomy is a mode of interacting with others. Relations, including those with collectivities of all sorts, become not just potential threats to autonomy but its source.*
> Jennifer Nedelsky[51]

The concept of autonomy is pivotal to liberal rights discourse. Liberalism views autonomy as a sphere of personal freedom as well as responsibility to shape one's life according to one's own coherent or incoherent and distinctive personality.[52] Thus autonomy is central to the integrity of the person and forms the interrelationship of the individual and the community within a liberal scheme where everyone is entitled to a personal sphere of freedom protected from interference by fellow citizens or the community as a whole.[53] This account of autonomy presumes that in order to be recognised as an autonomous person one has to be capable of making rational decisions. In law, this capacity is usually understood as an ability to understand and assess information relevant to the decision and to communicate the decision reached.

The problem here is that law assumes that after having reached certain milestones of capability, principally maturity or adulthood, we are equally capable. When we are considered capable, our competence is not affected by how others judge the rationality of our decisions.[54] Capacity is thus interlinked with the expectation of rationality, for as Naffine observes, 'law

---

50 On the questions that a convincing inquiry should ask, see the discussion in Rasmussen, 'Personhood, Self, Difference, and Dialogue,' 37.
51 Jennifer Nedelsky, *Law's Relations: A Relational Theory of Self, Autonomy, and Law* (New York: Oxford University Press, 2011), 55.
52 See, for instance, Joseph Raz's account of autonomy in *The Morality of Freedom* (Oxford: Clarendon Press, 1986), 369 and as described by Ronald Dworkin in *Life's Dominion: An Argument about Abortion and Euthanasia* (New York: Knopf, 1993), 224.
53 Ronald Dworkin, 'Autonomy and the Demented Self,' *The Milbank Quarterly* 64 (1986), 4–16.
54 Jonathan Herring, 'Losing it? Losing what? The Law and Dementia,' *Child and Family Law Quarterly* 21:1 (2009), 5–6.

works with an overarching presumption of reason: a presumption that we are rational subjects'.[55] Law is for rational human subjects, for sane rational adults who, because of their capacity to reason, can assume moral as well as legal responsibility for their actions. As such they can enter into moral and legal community with others of a similarly rational nature.[56] Thus the rational legal subject has the capacity to understand the difference between right and wrong along with the ability to bear the consequences of unwise decisions. However, the arguments based on capacity may be justified in arbitrary ways based on political considerations that, as the chapter by Marshall illustrates in the case of criminal disenfranchisement, highlight the 'differences between moral and jural personhood'.[57]

According to *Dworkin* it is the capacity to bear the consequences that allows people to have inconsistent values and to make inconsistent choices.[58] Yet, at the same time, law has to regulate and provide protection for citizens who do not conform to the ideal of an objective, rational person. When a person is deemed to lack or have diminished capacity, the question arises how such persons are to be treated in legal contexts. The issue of incapacity poses interesting challenges for our understandings of autonomy and personhood. Are all aspects of autonomy equally important and all interests of the individual on a par? How and by whom should these be evaluated? Various answers may be offered. Dworkin, for one, has suggested that we distinguish between critical interests, such as those related to the development of life goals, and experiential interests, such as the capacity to experience enjoyment and pleasure. According to him, the critical interests are more important to the autonomy of a person and should, consequently, be taken to survive incapacity.[59]

Dworkin has been criticised for placing too much weight on 'critical interests' with the result that the current individual is positioned as a mere subject of control, treatment, or restraint.[60] The way we approach changes in capacity is revealing of the ways in which we understand personhood as it forces us to pose the question as to whether the person remains the same or becomes different. Some consider an affirmative answer more empowering and argue that a person with incapacity continues to be the same person although that person now may have different values and goals than

---

55 Naffine, 'The legal presumption of reason,' 1–2.
56 Naffine, *Law's Meaning of Life*.
57 Rasmussen, 'Personhood, Self, Difference, and Dialogue,' 37.
58 Dworkin, *Life's Dominion*, 224.
59 Ibid. 201–2 and 224–9. Similarly for Meyers, the autonomous self is the 'true self' found through critical reflection, which distinguishes it from the apparent self. Meyers further divides the concept of autonomy to local (situation specific) autonomy and programmatic (major life decisions) autonomy. Diana T. Meyers, 'Personal Autonomy and the Paradox of Feminine Socialization,' *Journal of Philosophy* 84:11 (1987), 619.
60 Herring, 'Losing it? Losing what?', 20.

previously.⁶¹ In Herring's view, there are senses in which the person is the same as the person they were. For instance, the person remains the same in a bodily sense as well as in the context of their relationships with others. In another sense, however, the person may cease to be the same, and what once was important about a person may have completely vanished, leaving only the most tenuous link between the past and present person.⁶² The question here is about the ways in which personal experience may be used to legitimate authority as well as about the possibilities to challenge such powers.⁶³ The chapter by *Mäki-Petäjä-Leinonen* asks how much rationality is to be expected in decision-making of a person with dementia and argues that certain leeway should be given for some irrationality, also when dealing with persons without full legal capacity.

In addition to liberal views of autonomy, nuanced accounts of autonomy and personhood have been developed in the fields of biomedical ethics and care theory.⁶⁴ These debates have considerably added to our understanding of the social ontology of personhood and social relations. In his chapter, *Soirila* examines the concept of human dignity, which in contemporary legal thought has been presented as a solution to the challenges brought about by the developments in biotechnology. He describes how the concept of dignity has been used in two contradictory senses: as something from which the freedom of choice can be derived from (rights-founding usage) and as something that limits the scope of those choices by reference to values of more communal nature (obligation-creating usage). In this discussion, *Soirila* in fact deals with themes that have been prevalent in debates over the concept of autonomy, such as whether autonomy should be perceived as inherently value-laden (substantive or weakly substantive views) or approached in neutral terms (procedural views).

Relational theorists have been critical of liberal approaches to autonomy on the basis that they fail to recognise its inherently social nature, which

---

61 See, for instance, Allen Buchanan, 'Advance Directives and the Personal Identity Problem,' *Philosophy & Public Affairs* 17:4 (1988), 277–302; Rebecka Dresser, 'Missing Persons: Legal Perceptions of Incompetent Patients,' *Rutgers Law Review* 46:2 (1994), 609; and Agnieszka Jaworska, 'Respecting the Margins of Agency: Alzheimer's Patients and the Capacity to Value,' *Philosophy and Public Affairs*, 28:2 (1998), 105–38.
62 Herring, 'Losing it? Losing what?', 22.
63 Rasmussen, 'Personhood, Self, Difference, and Dialogue,' 37.
64 See, for instance, the influential work by authors such as Thomas Beauchamp and James Childress in the field of biomedical ethics (Thomas Beauchamp and James Childress, *Principles of Biomedical Ethics*, 6th edn, Oxford: Oxford University Press, 2008) and authors such as Martha Fineman, Jonathan Herring, Jennifer Nedelsky, Catrione MacKenzie, and Natalie Stoljar in the fields of political and legal theory (Martha Fineman, *The Autonomy Myth: A Theory of Dependency* (New York: The New Press, 2004); Jonathan Herring, *Relational Autonomy and Family Law* (London: Springer, 2014); Jennifer Nedelsky, *Law's Relations: A Relational Theory of Self, Autonomy, and Law* (New York: Oxford University Press, 2011); Catrione MacKenzie and Natalie Stoljar, (eds.), *Relational Autonomy: Feminist Perspectives on Autonomy, Agency and the Social Self* (Oxford: Oxford University Press, 2000)).

requires autonomy to be reconceived as relational. *Nedelsky* has noted that, rather than considering persons as atomistic individuals, we should consider autonomy as created by, dependent upon, and exercised through relationships with other people.[65] Consequently, legal inquiry should focus primarily on supporting the relationships that best promote these core values, as opposed to focusing solely on the claims of the individuals.[66] This means that in dealing with personhood a relational perspective must take account of the fact that identities and interests, as well as account of 'self' and 'other', are intertwined. We are all embedded in social relationships and all our decisions are affected by responsibilities towards those others who are significant to us.[67] In emerging legal fields such as elder law, relational theory proved to offer theoretically convincing as well as practically useful approaches to questions concerning personhood and autonomy.[68] As *Mäki-Petäjä-Leinonen*'s chapter illustrates, both the individual and the relational approach of autonomy can be seen as important when promoting the autonomy of a person with dementia.

The concept of autonomy also underpins constructions of rights and responsibilities in the allocation of economic advantage and burdens both within economic relationships in the market and intimate relationships between family members. The emerging debates in the fields of labour law and feminist theories address the changes in the market, such as the increasing commodification of 'body work'[69], which results from the contradictory trends of the individualisation of work and, simultaneously, its standardisation.[70] As the chapters by Mair and Ylhäinen point out, autonomy as the sphere of private choice is firmly connected to economic value and capacity to profit and shapes the ways in which we allocate risk and added value. These chapters contribute to the research on the changing social organisation of labour, addressing both the discussions on the value of paid work and unpaid care work as well as the inadequacy of current distributive and protective measures available in both family law and labour law.

---

65 Jennifer Nedelsky 'Reconceiving Autonomy: Sources, Thoughts, Possibilities,' *Yale Journal of Law & Feminism* 1:1 (1989), 21. See also, Linda Hart, *Relational Subjects: Family Relations, Law and Gender in the European Court of Human Rights* (Helsinki: University of Helsinki, 2016).
66 Nedelsky, *Law's Relations*, 238.
67 Herring, *Caring and the Law*, 71–3.
68 See, for instance, Rosie Harding on legal constructions of dementia, 'Legal Constructions of Dementia: Discourses of Autonomy at the Margins of Capacity,' *Journal of Social Welfare & Family Law* 34:4 (2012), 427.
69 See, for instance, Ann Stewart, *Gender, Law and Justice in a Global Market* (Cambridge: Cambridge University Press, 2011), 193–226.
70 See, for instance, R. L. Cohen, K. Hardy, T. Sanders, and C. Wolkowitz, 'The Body/Sex/Work Nexus: A Critical Perspective on Body Work and Sex Work', in *Body/Sex/Work – Intimate, Embodied and Sexualised Labour*, Carol Wolkowitz, Rachel Lara Cohen, Teela Sanders and Kate Hardy (eds.) (London: Palgrave Macmillan, 2013), 3–27.

Summary of the individual chapters

Many chapters in this book combine the traditional approach of legal inquiry either with a philosophical critique (Gray; Marshall), or alternative accounts of ethics such as care theory and an ethics of alterity (Mair; Mäki-Petäjä-Leinonen; Gozdecka and Koulu), or additional methodological approaches such as intersectionality (Mustasaari) or critical discourse analysis (Ylhäinen). However, many chapters adopt a perspective on legal phenomena that differs altogether from traditional or doctrinal forms of legal inquiry. Some of them approach the questions of citizenship through contemporary philosophical thinking, and the works of authors such as *Jacques Rancière* (Nieminen) and *Roberto Esposito* (Soirila), while others revisit ancient texts (Hurri); some read contemporary literature to better understand the founding issues of law (Minkkinen), and some offer analysis firmly rooted in an anthropological research tradition (Griffiths). The chapters are grouped under three broad themes, which are central to the quest to tease out the various discursive traits of citizenship, subjectivity and belonging in contemporary law.

I: Politics, power and subjectivity

Samuli Hurri: 'The Ancient Subject of Speech'. Hurri examines the role of language as constitutive of us as human beings by exploring the social institution of speaking. The chapter begins with an observation of the problems of free speech as they emerge in the various online media in diverse forms of hate speech. In order to understand these phenomena, Hurri takes us back in time to the archaic world of Hesiod and Homer to provide us with two forms of criticism of the institution of speech. In Hesiod's *Works and Days*, the nature of the critique towards the institution of speech is social, whereas in Homer's *Iliad*, the nature of this critique is ethical. Moving on to the classical period, Hurri discusses how language is conceived by Aristotle as inevitably connected to man's nature as a political animal. He sets out from Aristotle's famous postulation that indeed language and speech are what make human beings human: distinct from animals and capable of political life.

Pablo Marshall: 'Criminal Disenfranchisement and Political Capacity'. Marshall both introduces and argues against the claim that criminal offenders should lose their voting rights because of their lack of civic virtue. It is firstly argued that this proposition is subject to the same kind of problems as the argument that offenders may vote disruptively. Comparing the issue with the reasons given for excluding children from the franchise, it is then argued that offenders do not present a case of either cognitive or moral impairment and that their exclusion does not serve to protect any relevant interest in democracy. The author argues that the denying of criminals' citizenship rights to criminals implies a denial of some important aspects of personality. Consequently, Marshall argues that the explanation for the current practice of criminal disenfranchisement must be found in other, perhaps undemocratic, ideas and that these can be associated with a type of disrespect that may constitute some form of subaltern subjectivity.

Panu Minkkinen: '"Electoral Shenanigans": The Constituted Electorate, the Constituent People, and the Porous State'. Through his insightful reading of Jose Saramago's extraordinary novel Seeing, Minkkinen discusses certain peculiarities inherent in constitutional institutions. In the novel, the vast majority of citizens of an unnamed city cast a blank ballot on voting day, causing dismay and disarray in the bureaucracy. The tacit refusal of the novel's citizens to go on playing the ceremonial role of legitimators of political power leads Minkkinen to examine the role of the 'people' as the popular sovereign as well as what he calls 'constituent interventions in constituted institutions'. He analyses how episodes similar to the scene depicted in the novel can radically change relationships between constitutional institutions, even when they are not brought about by changes in the constitutional law.

Kati Nieminen: 'Who Belongs? The Turkish Citizen Subject in Turmoil'. Nieminen discusses the role of law in constructing the Turkish citizen subject. To make sense of how the law participates in this process, Nieminen draws upon Rancière's conceptualisations of police and politics. The role of law is discussed with three examples: political party dissolution cases (the court), the Kurdish peace process (the cabinets) and the Gezi protests (the streets). The main argument is that, while claims for recognition of ethnic and religious identities have been increasingly successful and so have lost some of their radical political potential, a new unpredictable subject emerged during the Gezi protests, making the full diversity of identities irreversibly visible.

II: Recognising 'the different' subject

Carolynn Gray: 'The GenderQueer in UK Law: Why Current Laws are Insufficient'. This chapter explores the way in which UK law provides for legal recognition of one's gender identity and for protection from discrimination on the basis of the same characteristic. It is argued in the chapter that provisions contained in the Gender Recognition Act 2004 and in the Equality Act 2010 are inadequate because they provide recognition of, and protection for, a very limited experience of gender which is based wholly on the perception of gender as a binary category. Those who experience gender as other than binary, who could be called non-binary or genderqueer, are excluded from these legislative provisions.

Sanna Mustasaari: 'Best Interests of the Child in Family Reunification – A Citizenship Test Disguised?'. Mustasaari discusses citizenship and belonging of second generation children through a close reading of an immigrant family reunification case from the Finnish Supreme Administrative Court.

She uses the theoretical framework of intersectionality to understand what discursively takes place within the decision, as the evaluation of the best interests of the children is used to define and legitimise accounts of belonging. The review provided in this chapter suggests that citizenship, specifically the citizenship of a child, is a discontinuous legal construction, determined not solely by citizenship as a formal status derived from nationality but by a plethora of identity factors marking the belonging of a person both in the family and in the jurisdiction of a nation state.

Anna Mäki-Petäjä-Leinonen: 'Protecting a Person with Dementia through Restrictions of Freedom? Notions of Autonomy in the Theory and Practice of Elder Care'. Mäki-Petäjä-Leinonen presents the individual and relational approaches to autonomy arguing that although these two approaches are often contradictory, both are needed to support the autonomy of people with dementia. She scrutinises autonomy throughout the progression of dementia and over the three levels of capacity: A person with dementia may make a decision with full capacity; a person with dementia with borderline capacity may make a decision with support or participate in a decision-making process; and finally, the decisions of a person with incapacity may be made by either respecting the person's prior instructions or by a substituted decision-maker. Finally, Mäki-Petäjä-Leinonen considers whether a genuine respect for autonomy at all levels of capacity will reduce the need to use restrictive measures when caring for people with dementia. She concludes with an examination of the forthcoming Finnish Autonomy Act and its outcomes.

Dorota Gozdecka and Sanna Koulu: 'What to do with the Other in Human Rights Law? Ethics of Alterity versus Ethics of Care'. Gozdecka and Koulu note that in the realm of human rights, a universalistic ethics of law has been criticised for too abstract rules and lack of concern for nuances of interpersonal relations. The authors consider the relevance of ethics for human rights with a focus on two alternative accounts of ethics: an ethics of alterity, springing from the Levinasian responsibility for meeting the Other, and an ethics of care that tries to recognise and respect our responsibilities for specific others. These accounts are not an easy fit with the traditional logic of legal human rights, but they offer new possibilities for law to recognise subjects who are in relationships with others. The authors examine the juxtaposition of these two accounts of ethics and argues that the existence of both is valuable for human rights, as their difference itself offers a site for reflection on the place of otherness in law.

III: Personhood, property and contribution

Anne Griffiths: 'Families, Identity and Belonging: Rethinking Personhood and Property in Botswana'. In Botswana the family is at the centre of individuals' perceptions of identity and belonging. Griffiths' article explores these dimensions that embrace personhood by examining shifts in the customary law of inheritance in relation to land. Based on ongoing ethnographic research from the 1980s, and 2009–2010, Griffiths investigates the shifting norms that have transformed the way in which gender relations in families are perceived and how these have played out in terms of the allocation of customary land certificates by Kweneng Land Board that provide evidence of women acquiring greater access to and control over land. Focusing on everyday life and uncontested transmissions of property, rather than disputes, Griffiths explores the changing notions of personhood. What emerges are the ways in which the circulation of property among a more nucleated family group, rather than among more extended kin, operates to place women within a more advantageous position when it comes to dealing with land as their roles within family life come to be re-evaluated.

Jane Mair: 'The Breadwinner, the Homemaker and the Worker/Carer: New Stereotypes for Old?'. Mair considers the value of caring work in families and the 'right to care' in the two contexts of working life and family life. Care is a complex concept that often eludes the structures of the legal, and even in late modern welfare states families remain one of the primary sites for caring work. As such it is often dichotomous: care within the family is intimate and non-legal, a question of interpersonal relations, while care in institutions or by paid workers is viewed in terms of labour law, which rejects the intimate and personal dimensions of care. Mair argues that one reason for challenging the divide between public and private is to facilitate greater movement between the two: individual men and women can be both public employees and private family members. This is an ideal which informs policy in respect of employment law where the discourse has moved from maternity rights through family-friendly provision to the vision of a modern workplace.

Marjo Ylhäinen: 'From Obedience to Initiative? Precarious Work and Changing Subjectivities in Labour Law Discourse'. Ylhäinen explores the contradictory assumptions embedded in the legal discipline of labour law. Legal texts, mostly judgments, are analysed in order to find out what kind of subjectivity is attached to the employee as the counterpart of the other subject to feature in these texts, the employer. The construction of the employment relation is created in the surroundings of business and normal work. This discourse, constructed in the legal arena, not only reflects legal regulation and its interpretation but also reinstates the idea of the protection of the normal employee. It is argued that the employee's identity is closely connected to an understanding of the manner of protection as well as to the way in which the identity of the employer is constructed.

Ukri Soirila: 'Human Dignity Mediated: Personhood, Humanity, and the Logic of Property in Law and Bioethics'. In this final chapter Soirila examines the concept of human dignity as a solution to novel bioethical questions, raised by recent scientific developments which have radically challenged many of our basic assumptions about human ontology and subjectivity. Even though human dignity has no doubt been used as a balancing tool vis-à-vis some of the threats posed by biotechnology, Soirila argues that it tends to block opportunities to think about legal subjectivity in new, creative ways. This is especially so when the paradigmatic references to human dignity fall back on the logic of property that Roberto Esposito claims dominates philosophical and legal thought.

Towards new conceptions of personhood

In addressing diverse domains this collection offers a kaleidoscopic take on the question of who is the person inhabiting the law. Yet central to all the chapters is a concern that represents one of the eternal questions in social sciences: the relationship between the individual and the community. For in one way or another, each chapter addresses the concept of the person and the attributes of autonomy, rationality and morality that constitute the person, as well as the relationship of that autonomous person to other social agents and communities. As *Rasmussen* notes, 'ideologies of personhood prevalent within any culture predispose specific [ways] of approaching relationships with self and others and with action'.[71] The chapters reveal, in their different ways, the relationship that exists between the individual and the community, and how this is perceived and enacted through various accounts of identity and belonging that adhere to different kinds of national, transnational and cultural communities.

While seemingly at odds with one another, the relational views promoted by Mäki-Petäjä-Leinonen, and the conceptions of freedom and moral agency as examined by Hurri in the opening chapter of this book, bear more points of resemblance to one another than is at first apparent. For sure, the free man inhabiting the Aristotelian polis was not the earner-carer that Mair in this volume addresses. Nevertheless, listening to a 'different voice',[72] we might say that, in today's welfare state, to be free and autonomous stands for having the ability and agency to govern care and to understand caring relations from the perspective of those in subordinate or dependent positions.

Taken together, the chapters in this book testify to the continuing importance of theorising on these themes. The alliance of subjectivity, citizenship and rights necessarily carries both inclusionary and exclusionary powers. Yet, as *Nash* has noted, 'the ideal of the public sphere, if it is invariably concretised in exclusionary ways, always also gestures beyond itself, to ideas of genuine participation in establishing the common good'.[73] We suggest that

---

71 Rasmussen, 'Personhood, Self, Difference, and Dialogue,' 33.
72 Refers here to Gilligan's *In a Different Voice*.
73 Kate Nash, 'Introduction,' in *Transnationalizing the Public Sphere*, Nancy Fraser et al, (Cambridge and Malden: Polity Press, 2014), 1–7.

critical debates on subjectivity, citizenship and legal personhood, as well as identities and belonging, offer routes towards a more legitimate and justified order of inclusion and exclusion. We hope this book takes this project one step further.

Bibliography

Beauchamp, Thomas and James Childress. *Principles of Biomedical Ethics*, 6th edn. Oxford: Oxford University Press, 2008.
Bellamy, Richard. 'Evaluating Union Citizenship: Belonging, Rights and Participation within the EU,' *Citizenship Studies* 12:6 (2008), 597–611.
Biehl, Joao, Byron Good and Arthur Kleinman (eds.). *Subjectivity: Ethnographic Investigation*. Berkeley: University of California Press, 2007.
Bohlin, Anna. 'The Politics of Locality: Memories of District Six in Cape Town.' In Nadia Lovell (ed.), *Locality and Belonging*. New York: Routledge, 1998, 163–82.
Bosniak, Linda. 'Human Rights within One State: Dilemmas of Personhood in Liberal Constitutional Thought.' In Marie-Bénédicte Dembour and Tobias Kelly (eds.), *Are Human Rights for Migrants? Critical Reflections on the Status of Irregular Migrants in Europe and the United States*. London: Routledge, 2011, 201–21.
Boyle, James. 'Is Subjectivity Possible? The Post-Modern Subject in Legal Theory,' *University of Colorado Law Review* 62 (1991), 489–524.
Buchanan, Allen. 'Advance Directives and the Personal Identity Problem,' *Philosophy & Public Affairs* 17:4 (1988), 277–302.
Carillo Rowe, Aimee. 'Be Longing: Toward a Feminist Politics of Relation,' *NWSA Journal* 17:2 (2005), 15–46.
Carr, David. *The Paradox of Subjectivity: The Self in Transcendental Tradition*. Oxford: Oxford University Press, 1999.
Cohen, Rachel Lara, Kate Hardy, Teela Sanders and Carol Wolkowitz. 'The Body/Sex/Work Nexus: A Critical Perspective on Body Work and Sex Work.' In Carol Wolkowitz, Rachel Lara Cohen, Teela Sanders and Kate Hardy (eds.) *Body/Sex/Work – Intimate, Embodied and Sexualised Labour*. London: Palgrave Macmillan, 2013, 3–27.
Drenth, Annemieke van and Francisca de Haan. *The Rise of Caring Power. Elizabeth Fry and Josephine Butler in Britain and the Netherlands*. Amsterdam: Amsterdam University Press, 1999.
Dresser, Rebecka. 'Missing Persons: Legal Perceptions of Incompetent Patients,' *Rutgers Law Review* 46:2 (1994), 609–719.
Dworkin, Ronald. *Life's Dominion: An Argument about Abortion and Euthanasia*. New York: Knopf, 1993.
Dworkin, Ronald. 'Autonomy and the Demented Self,' *The Milbank Quarterly*, 64:S2 (1986), 4–16.
Ehrenberg, Alain. *The Weariness of the Self: Diagnosing the History of Depression in the Contemporary Age*. Montreal, Ithaca: McGill-Queen's University Press, 2010.
Eichner, Maxine. 'Families, Human Dignity, and State Support for Caretaking: Why the United States' Failure to Ameliorate the Work-family Conflict is a Dereliction of the Government's Basic Responsibilities.' *North Carolina Law Review* 88:5 (2010) 1593–626.

Feder Kittay, Eva and Ellen K. Feder. 'Introduction.' In Eva Feder Kittay and Ellen K. Feder (eds.), *The Subject of Care: Feminist Perspectives on Dependency*. Lanham: Rowan & Littlefield, 2002, 1–13.

Fineman, Martha. *The Autonomy Myth: A Theory of Dependency*. New York: The New Press, 2004.

Foucault, Michel. 'The Subject and Power'. *Critical Inquiry* 8:4 (1982), 777–95.

Gilligan, Carol. *In a Different Voice. Psychological Theory and Women's Development*. Cambridge, MA: Harvard University Press, 1982.

Harding, Rosie. 'Legal Constructions of Dementia: Discourses of Autonomy at the Margins of Capacity'. *Journal of Social Welfare & Family Law* 34:4 (2012), 425–42.

Hart, Linda. *Relational Subjects: Family Relations, Law and Gender in the European Court of Human Rights*. Helsinki: University of Helsinki, 2016.

Held, Virginia. *The Ethics of Care: Personal, Political, Global.* Oxford: Oxford University Press, 2006.

Hellum, Anne, Shaheen Sardar Ali and Anne Griffiths (eds.). *From Transnational Relations to Transnational Laws: Northern European Laws at the Crossroads*. Farnham and Burlington: Ashgate, 2011.

Herring, Jonathan. *Relational Autonomy and Family Law*. London: Springer, 2014.

Herring, Jonathan. *Caring and the Law*. Oxford and Portland: Hart Publishing, 2013.

Herring, Jonathan, 'Losing it? Losing What? The Law and Dementia,' *Child and Family Law Quarterly* 21:1 (2009), 3–29.

hooks, bell. *Belonging: A Culture of Place*. New York: Routledge, 2009.

Hoppania, Hanna-Kaisa. *Care as a Site of a Political Struggle*. University of Helsinki: Academic dissertation, 2015). Available at https://helda.helsinki.fi/handle/10138/157561 (accessed 15 April 2016).

Horsti, Karina and Saara Pellander. 'Conditions of Cultural Citizenship: Intersections of Gender, Race and Age in Public Debates on Family Migration,' *Citizenship Studies* 19:6–7 (2015), 751–67.

Hurri, Samuli. *Birth of the European Individual: Law, Security, Economy*. Abingdon: Routledge, 2014.

Jaworska, Agnieszka, 'Respecting the Margins of Agency: Alzheimer's Patients and the Capacity to Value,' *Philosophy and Public Affairs* 28:2 (1998), 105–38.

Khan, Anoosh W. 'Citizenship and Belonging: A Socio-Political Paradigm Shift,' *PUTAJ – Humanities and Social Sciences* 20 (2013), 81–92.

Lister, Ruth. 'Unpacking Children's Citizenship.' In Antonella Invernizzi and Jane Williams (eds.), *Children and Citizenship*. Los Angeles, London, New Delhi and Singapore: Sage Publications, 2008, 9–19.

Lister, Ruth. 'Why Citizenship: Where, When and How Children?' *Theoretical Inquiries in Law* 8:2 (2007), 693–718.

Lovell, Nadia. 'Introduction: Belonging in Need of Emplacement?'. In Nadia Lovell (ed.), *Locality and Belonging*. London: Routledge, 1998, 1–22.

MacKenzie, Catrione and Natalie Stoljar (eds.), *Relational Autonomy: Feminist Perspectives on Autonomy, Agency and the Social Self*. Oxford: Oxford University Press, 2000.

Maduro, Miguel, Kaarlo Tuori and Suvi Sankari (eds.), *Transnational Law: Rethinking European Law and Legal Thinking*. Cambridge: Cambridge University Press, 2014.

Marshall, T.H. *Citizenship and Social Class and Other Essays*. Cambridge: Cambridge University Press, 1950.

Merry, Sally Engle. 'Constructing a Global Law – Violence against Women and the Human Rights System,' *Law and Social Inquiry* 28:4 (2003), 941–77.

Meyers, Diana T. 'Personal Autonomy and the Paradox of Feminine Socialization,' *Journal of Philosophy* 84:11 (1987), 619–28.

Mol, Annemarie. *The Logic of Care: Health and the Problem of Patient Choice*. London: Routledge, 2008.

Mullally, Siobhan. *Gender, Culture and Human Rights: Reclaiming Universalism*. Oxford and Portland, OR: Hart Publishing, 2006.

Naffine, Ngaire. *Law's Meaning of Life: Philosophy, Religion, Darwin and the Legal Person*. Oxford: Hart Publishing, 2008.

Naffine, Ngaire. 'The Legal Presumption of Reason: Noble Truth, Useful Fiction, Ignoble Lie,' *Cleveland State Law Review* 53:1 (2005), 1–10.

Naffine, Ngaire. 'Who are Law's Persons? From Cheshire Cats to Responsible Subjects,' *Modern Law Review* 66:3 (2003), 346–67.

Nash, Kate (ed.). *Transnationalizing the Public Sphere: Nancy Fraser et al.* Cambridge and Malden: Polity Press, 2014.

Nash, Kate. 'Introduction.' In Kate Nash (ed.), *Transnationalizing the Public Sphere: Nancy Fraser et al.* Cambridge and Malden: Polity Press, 2014, 1–7.

Nedelsky, Jennifer. *Law's Relations: A Relational Theory of Self, Autonomy, and Law*. New York: Oxford University Press, 2011.

Nedelsky, Jennifer. 'Reconceiving Autonomy: Sources, Thoughts, Possibilities,' *Yale Journal of Law & Feminism* 1:1 (1989), 7–36.

Ortner, Sherry B. 'Subjectivity and Cultural Critique,' *Anthropological Theory* 5:1 (2005), 31–52.

Rabinow, Paul (ed.). *The Essential Works of Michel Foucault Vol. 1, Ethics: Subjectivity and Truth*. London: Allen Lane, 1997.

Rasmussen, Susan. 'Personhood, Self, Difference, and Dialogue (Commentary on Chaudhary).' *International Journal for Dialogical Studies* 3:1 (2008), 31–54.

Raz, Joseph. *The Morality of Freedom*. Oxford: Clarendon Press, 1986.

Sevenhuijsen, Selma. *Citizenship and the Ethics of Care: Feminist Considerations on Justice, Moralty and Politics*. New York: Routledge, 1998.

Social Issues Research Centre. *Belonging, Research report by the Social Issues Research Centre*, 2007. Available at www.sirc.org/publik/belonging.pdf (accessed 14 February 2016).

Stewart, Ann. *Gender, Law and Justice in a Global Market*. Cambridge: Cambridge University Press, 2011.

Tronto, Joan. *Moral Boundaries. A Political Argument for an Ethic of Care*. New York: Routledge, 1993.

Turner, Bryan S. 'The Erosion of Citizenship,' *British Journal of Sociology* 52:2 (2001), 189–209.

Yuval-Davis, Nira. *The Politics of Belonging: Intersectional Contestations*. London: SAGE Publications, 2011.

Yuval-Davis, Nira, Kalpana Kannabiran and Ulrike M. Vieten. 'Introduction.' In Nira Yuval-Davis, Kalpana Kannabiran and Ulrike M. Vieten (eds.), *The Situated Politics of Belonging*. London: SAGE Publications, 2006, 1–14.

Part I

Politics, power and subjectivity

Chapter 2

The ancient subject of speech

Samuli Hurri[1]

What is wrong with speech?

This book is about ourselves (subjectivity, citizenship and belonging) in modern society. However, this chapter is situated in ancient Greece, which makes it seem somewhat and somehow the odd one out. But in this case going back in time is an element in an effort to understand one's own time, an effort that recalls the anecdote about the 'anthropologist fish', which would never find out about water. Things near at hand stay out of sight because they disappear in self-evidence. Historical critique may be useful for dissipating the self-evidence around one's own time by showing that things were not always as they are now.

As the topic of this chapter is speech, let me start from what has become self-evident about speech today. Speech, the practice of language, has since Aristotle been considered constitutive of what we are as human beings. This practice gives us the primary method of articulating our experiences and communicating with others. It can hardly be avoided. And why avoid it anyway? Speech is a great asset: Information disseminates through networks of communication, which enhances progress and enlightenment. Reading books, writing down our thoughts and engaging in conversations with friends; these are the ways in which we find out who we are as individuals. Speech is fundamental, invaluable.

Legal systems put freedom of speech high up among civil and political rights. The freedom of speech responds not only to a fundamental human need for speech, but also to certain other needs that are equally fundamental. Public discussion breaks ignorance and allows for truth to come to light. Unconstrained expression allows people the possibility of self-fulfilment as individuals. Participation by citizens in debating affairs of general interest is essential to the functioning of democracy. Alert and critical public attention

---

1 The author is grateful to Professor Simo Knuuttila and Professor Jan Stenger for their critical comments and overall support. However, they are not responsible for any of the interpretations made in this chapter, or its mistakes.

checks the spread of arbitrary power and corruption.² Finally, insofar as the legal system itself is based on democratic legitimacy, that system would undermine its own conditions of existence if it did not guarantee freedom of speech.

On the one hand, the fact that people may speak freely defines a free society. On the other hand, a free society is more rational, efficient and comfortable for people to live in. No doubts about this should exist, either in fact or in principle. Nevertheless, a gnawing feeling has started to grow recently that something grievous may be swelling. Strange things are happening, not outside, but within the ramparts of the free society. People have started to speak about weird things in a weird way. I will offer a couple of examples.

The first example: A female blogger uploaded a piece where, from the point of view of gender equality, she criticised the way in which a department store marketed its products. In response, a misogynist rage broke out in the social media, where fantasies were disseminated about raping the blogger and killing her children. The second example: A ship-owning company re-organised its transportation services between the mainland and offshore islands so that winter-time ice roads for cars could no longer be used. The company's majority shareholder, Mr. L., was attacked on the Internet by a wave of hate. 'Burn in your own ship, sick Jew', someone told him, while another was putting him 'into the oven'. But then, one of the commentators also presented some interesting reflections:

> Paper and internet can stand everything; and just for my own fun (really the state and [L] do not care about people's opinion) ... just for fun, with no greed for money – I pee into [L's] ear and then I also shit onto his head.³

I will not offer further examples. The last citation makes me wonder about a few things, however. The commentator says that paper and Internet can stand everything, in other words, that no standards exist but perfect freedom. In so far as people's opinion really is irrelevant, as our commentator also suggests, is the irrelevance perhaps the cause or the consequence of perfect freedom? Another set of wonders emerges from the latter part of the comment cited, where excrement is made fun of. Looking at that, one may ask what the source of speech truly is, what really generates it. Is it reason ultimately, or rather some ghastly, giggling, mad underside? If the latter is the case, is gross libertinage in this area unequivocally good for society?

---

2 See Eric Barendt, *Freedom of Speech* (Oxford: Oxford University Press, 2007), 6–23.
3 European Court of Human Rights, judgment of 16 June 2015, in *Delfi As v Estonia*, Application no. 64569/09, para. 18.

Finally, is it good for ourselves (for our purposes of self-fulfilment) that all that goes on within ourselves can be placed in the open air?

These concerns indicate a worry that something may somehow be wrong in current conditions for speaking. Thus far nobody has managed to thoroughly analyse what is happening: the free society is unprepared and surprised. For the practice of law, these problems may turn out to be just normal business. As a principle, freedom of speech will be taken for granted in the future too, but the new realities, notably on the Internet, will generate some new balancing between the right of free speech and responsibilities to be borne by its exercise. The literature, however, contains suggestions of a need for more fundamental reconsiderations relative to speech. For example Jeremy Waldron in his book on *The Harm in Hate Speech* has called attention to the fact that a large part of the social reality in which people live is produced and upheld by speech.[4] In turn, Judith Butler in her discussion of hate speech has pointed out that practices of speech generate people's experience of themselves, their own reality as individuals.[5]

With these present-day worries and puzzles in mind, this chapter goes back in time in order to find out about the subject of speech in ancient times. Although at the beginning it was said that speech has been considered constitutive of human beings since Aristotle, it will transpire that the problem of speech is much older. In the classical period (roughly, the fifth century BC that preceded Aristotle's century) Greece saw an unprecedented idea coming true: a polity based on speech and centred on the agora, the famous place of public debate about common affairs. For us today, the notion of an agora bears the image of a polity where power is exercised through the practices of speaking, and where the social status of individuals depends on their skills in speaking. We look back to speaking Greeks as the source of their polity's strength and as the guarantor of their freedom as citizens.[6]

So it is commonplace for us to think that speech flourished in the classical Greek city-state, at least in Athens at the time of Pericles.[7] It became

---

4 Jeremy Waldron, *The Harm in Hate Speech* (Cambridge, Mass. and London: Harvard University Press, 2012).
5 Judith Butler, *Excitable Speech: A Politics of the Performative* (New York and London: Routledge, 1977).
6 Christian Meier, *A Culture of Freedom. Ancient Greece and the Origins of Europe* (Oxford: Oxford University Press, 2012); Jean-Pierre Vernant, *The Origins of Greek Thought* (Ithaca and New York: Cornell University Press, 1982).
7 Athenian democracy was of course an object not only of admiration, but also of stern criticism, both in its own time and over the following centuries. See Elizabeth Rawson, *The Spartan Tradition in European Thought* (Oxford: Clarendon Press, 1969); Jennifer Tolbert Roberts, *Athens on Trial. The Antidemocratic Tradition in Western Thought* (Princeton, New Jersey: Princeton University Press, 1994); and Michel Foucault, *The Government of Self and Others. Lectures at the Collège de France 1982–1983* (Basingstoke and New York: Palgrave Macmillan, 2010).

a form of life at least for the wealthy, male upper stratum of that society. By contrast, we have a much vaguer idea of the place of speech in Greece before the classical era. In so far as the archaic period (roughly, 700–500 BC) created the conditions for the rise of the culture of speech, it is probable that at the very start of that period this culture was not so prominent. Should we know what the situation at that time was (let us say, at the turn of the eighth century BC) then we could perhaps find out how the rise of speech occurred. Against this backdrop, the following will be my attempt at posing this problem, that of the ancient subject of speech.[8]

Hesiod's *Works and Days*: social criticism of speech

At least two trustworthy literary sources exist for the seeds of an idea about the place of speech in the Greek spiritual universe just before the archaic period or at its start. The first source is of course the Homeric epic, *The Iliad* and *The Odyssey*, written down in the eighth century. A small section of the *Iliad* will be analysed, but before that another source will be taken up. This is Hesiod's *Works and Days*, which dates back to the same century as Homer. In the light of present knowledge, Homer and Hesiod are the first written works in the West. Starting from Hesiod, let us see what these texts say about speech.

In the background to Hesiod's *Works and Days* stands a legal case between him and his brother Perses. Perses is planning to contest their earlier distribution of their father's estate before a court of law. Hesiod is extremely annoyed and in this mood he addresses *Works and Days* to his brother. Perses needs a lesson in the manners of an honourable peasant. Hesiod's message to his brother is that he should stay away from the company of idle socialites who gather in downtown marketplaces. Perses should focus on work. A farmer like him has a task to do every day, throughout the year, on his own property.

Works and Days sets out as criticism of the intrigues and trickery conducted in the form of judicial speeches,[9] but it quickly becomes clear that Hesiod has nothing good to say about the entire world of words. This town life of talebearers and agitators is governed by what he calls the bad *Eris* (Strife), a malicious divinity who disseminates anger, disunity and quarrels among people. A good *Eris* also exists, the demigod of competition. The good *Eris* of competition is rooted in the culture of the soil and influences people

---

8 For the reader interested more generally in the subject, I suggest the collection of articles edited by Ineke Sluiter and Ralph Rosen, *Free Speech in Classical Antiquity* (Leiden and Boston: Brill 2004).
9 On this point, see Michel Foucault, *Wrong-doing, Truth-telling. The Function of Avowal in Justice* (Chicago: The University of Chicago Press, 2014), 45–6.

to make harder efforts through their desire to excel their neighbours.¹⁰ Perses is under the spell of the bad *Eris* and Hesiod urges him to turn to the good one:

> Perses, lay up these things in your heart, and do not let that Strife (*Eris*) who delights in mischief hold your heart back from work, while you peep and peer and listen to the wrangles of the court-house. Little concern has he with quarrels and courts who has not a year's victuals laid up betimes, even that which the earth bears, Demeter's grain.¹¹

In Hesiod's worldview, the culture of speaking is a social plague for it takes people's time away from useful work. Lured by the 'wrangles of the court house' and plunged into thoughtless frenzy that only the idleness of the agora may generate, people forget not only about what is necessary but also what is truly valuable in life. Indeed, *Works and Days* does not consider work as a mere troublesome necessity; it puts forward a notion of a good life where work is of the highest value, it is the meaning of life. Curiously, with his beneficial divinity of competition, and his ethics of minding one's own business, the agrarian Hesiod appears to be anti-political in a way that recalls the neoliberals of our own day.

Having explained what the purpose of his writing is, and before going into the yearly routines regulating the peasant life, Hesiod inserts two mythical sections into his text. The first of these is about the curse that Zeus sent to humans in the form of an adorable woman, Pandora. The second, about human generations, follows the first as if it were the story of the evolution of the curse up until his own time. In Hesiod's own period, mortals are endlessly tormented by misfortune, and he laments that he has to live at this miserable time and with these miserable people.

Hesiod envisions, however, that the future may be even harder to bear: the curse will take a particularly vicious form in the coming generation. This next generation will be completely overtaken by the bad *Eris*: 'The father will not agree with his children, nor the children with their father, nor guest with his host, nor comrade with comrade; nor will brother be dear to brother as aforetime'.¹² The future will hold no place for honesty and justice, rogues and ruthless arrogance will take over. Curiously, it also

---

10 According to Foucault, *The Government of Self and Others*, 166, this type of opposition between the agora and the *gê* (cultivated land) is constant in ancient Greek culture. More generally, see Ineke Sluiter and Ralph Rosen (eds.), *City, Countryside, and the Spatial Organization of Value in Classical Antiquity* (Leiden and Boston: Brill 2006).
11 *Works and Days*, verses 27–32.
12 Verses 182–4.

appears that the future will be a time of words – bitter, painful words spat on everything that used to be venerable. In the world to come,

> [...] the wicked will hurt the worthy man, speaking false words against him, and will swear an oath upon them. Envy, foul-mouthed, delighting in evil, with scowling face, will go along with wretched men one and all.[13]

In the future, speech will be a means in the hands of wicked people, who would employ words for committing wrongs. The coming world is indeed the world of 'false words' (μύθοισιν σκολιοῖς, *muthoisin skoliois*). Twisted discourses will penetrate the social body, bending its moral backbone out of shape, and speech will stand unequivocally for injustice. Having thus clarified his standpoint, Hesiod then moves on to explain that to work – in peace, every day – is a better way for a man to gain a share in prosperity. If 'he steals it through his tongue',[14] by telling lies before courts of law, it will not last for long.

The rest of *Works and Days* consists mostly of explaining the daily routines of a farmer at every season of the year. Towards the end, however, Hesiod returns to the issue of speech, elucidating once again the reasons why he thinks that the ethos of the man of few words is also the ethos of the wise man. 'The best treasure a man can have', says Hesiod, 'is a sparing tongue, and the greatest pleasure, one that moves orderly; for if you speak evil, you yourself will soon be worse spoken of'.[15] The wisdom of the man of few words springs from his in-depth understanding of what may be called the economy of evil speaking.

The economical use of words, or the sparing 'tongue' (γλῶσσα, *glôssa*), is accompanied by an idea of measurement. A tongue that moves 'orderly', as Hesiod's English translator says, is in the original a tongue that moves 'κατὰ μέτρον' (*kata metron*), that is, 'according to a measure'. A wise man measures up his words in silence before speaking them out, not because it is better to hide one's thoughts, but because words always come with consequences. If you speak, you will be spoken of, says Hesiod. The eternal circuit of chatter (in Greek γλωσσός, *glôssos*) informs the economy of words: speaking (εἴπω, *eipô*) will always be followed by hearing (ἀκούω, *akouô*). Like capital invested in production, speech will also be amassed in the process by some mysterious logic: what you will hear is going to be 'more' (μεῖζον, *meizon*) than what you have said yourself. A wise man always thinks twice before thrusting the great wheel of talk into movement.

---

13 Verses 193–9.
14 Verse 322.
15 Verses 720–2.

Almost done with everything, Hesiod gives his final warning about the devious world of speech that is his most important lesson to Perses: 'Avoid the talk of men. For Talk is mischievous, light, and easily raised, but hard to bear and difficult to be rid of. Talk never wholly dies away when many people voice her: even Talk is in some ways divine'.[16] The word Hesiod uses for Talk is φήμη (*phêmê*), which has a double meaning. On the one hand, it means the word on the street that goes around in society, a rumour that travels from mouth to mouth. On the other hand, it means someone's fame or reputation. Fame is of the same nature as rumour, and they both live on the nosiness of a society of gossipers.

Hesiod's conclusion is that Talk is a divinity. Together with the bad *Eris*, it sovereignly governs the town-life of rumours and fame. We might say today that talk is a dodgy social fact beyond anyone's control. The wise man in any case stays away from talk: this is the precept resulting from Hesiod's sociological analysis of speech. At the time when the agora was about to be born, and when the busy centuries of intensive parliament were just ahead of him, Hesiod's criticism was crushing: speaking is an addiction that takes people's time away from useful work; words are weapons in the hands of evil-doers; the economy of evil talk is a dangerous game. All of this goes on in the town, so stay as far from it as possible.

Homer's *Iliad*: ethical criticism of speech

According to its opening line, *The Iliad* is a story about the wrath of Achilles. The story begins by Agamemnon depriving Achilles of the beautiful maiden Briseis, which is an unbearable offence. From then onwards, the insulted and humiliated Achilles stands back from fighting and starts storing up resentful, destructive virulence in him. At the end of the story, Achilles returns to the battlefield, transforms into a sort of divine monster,[17] and finally pours out his mad rage on the leader of the Trojan troops, Hector. The way in which Achilles treats Hector's corpse terrifies even the gods. Reading the story from beginning to end, it seems that because Achilles could not destroy Agamemnon, he redirected his fury to Hector, so that *The Iliad* is like a bridge spanning these two wraths. Whereas *Works and Days* is about the frugal ethos of small peasants, *The Iliad* is about the horrifying vigour that underlies the warrior ethos.

Hesiod's peasant and Homer's warrior certainly represent the remotest possible value systems, but nevertheless something is common to them. Like *Works and Days*, *The Iliad* also offers a strong critical perspective on

---

16 Verses 760–4.
17 The high point of this is in Book 21 of *The Iliad*, where Achilles engages in a highly symbolic battle with the river Xanthus.

speech. While standing far apart from each other in Greek cultural space, both will later, in the classical era, provide their own, traditionalist type of support for conservatives. The traditional value systems of Hesiod and Homer will be means in the hands of conservatives who would resist the more or less radical democrats and their reshaped value system of the agora.[18] Whereas in *Works and Days* the nature of criticism of speech is social, in *The Iliad* this criticism is 'ethical' in the archaic sense of the word.[19] The Homeric problem in this respect is the place that the psychic system of an ancient warrior has for speech.

The piece of text to be looked at next appears in a scene known as 'The Embassy to Achilles' (Book 9 of *The Iliad*). Some background is needed to understand what is going on. Achilles has stayed away from fighting because of Agamemnon's offence. Meanwhile, the Trojans have almost crushed the Achaean army. Agamemnon is in despair; he tells everyone to flee and sail home. Appalled by this, the other warlords urge Agamemnon to send negotiators to Achilles and to beg him to join in the fight again. Agamemnon agrees and Odysseus, Phoenix and Ajax agree to undertake the mission. What follows is a staging of three discourses by these men, each trying to persuade Achilles in their own way, and of three negative responses by Achilles. The first who tries to bring him round is Odysseus, and when his talk is done, Achilles starts his reply in the following way:

> Son of Laertes, sprung from Zeus, resourceful Odysseus,
> I must speak the word bluntly,
> How I will act and how I think it shall be accomplished,
> For as hateful to me as the gates of Hades
> Is he who hides one thing in his mind, and says another.
> As for me, I will speak as it shall also be accomplished.[20]

---

18 This contestation, let's say, between Sparta and Athens has formed Western political thought throughout its history. See e.g. Roberts, *Athens on Trial*; Rawson, *The Spartan Tradition in European Thought*; and Foucault, *The Government of Self and Others*.

19 The notion 'ethical' needs to be understood in the context of the archaic culture of shame and honour that informs Achillean warrior behaviour. A classic study in this regard is Arthur W.H. Adkins, *Merit and Responsibility: A Study in Greek Values* (Chicago and London: The University of Chicago Press, 1975).

20 *The Iliad* 9.308–10, 12–14. The version given above is cited in Plato's *Lesser Hippias* 365a–b, which is not exactly the same as in *The Iliad*. I want to cite the *Lesser Hippias* anyway, because for the centuries to come that dialogue lays bare the parameters for reading into this encounter between Achilles and Odysseus a wider confrontation between the two as models of man. It may also make us aware of the ways in which these two paragons still affect our ideas about what we should be like, despite the fact that they are buried beneath thousands of years of historical sedimentation.

The first thing to be pointed out is the way in which Achilles addresses his interlocutor: 'resourceful Odysseus'. In Greek that is πολυμήχαν' Ὀδυσσεῦ, (*polymêchan' Odysseu*). A more verbatim way to render this in English would be: 'Odysseus, the man of many means' (πολυ+ μηχανή, *poly + mêchanê*). The Greek word *mêchanê* stands for 'means' and 'machines', but also for 'wiles' and 'tricks'. That is why some translators have put the address in English as 'Odysseus of many wiles',[21] or 'Odysseus, great tactician'.[22] '*Polymêchan' Odysseu*' is one of the formulaic epithets of Odysseus in the Homeric epic. For example, in Book 2 of *The Iliad*, Pallas Athene addresses Odysseus in exactly the same line as Achilles in the embassy scene.[23] Other epithets for Odysseus (for example πολύμητις, *polymêtis*[24] and πολύτροπος, *polytropos*[25]) depict him as a man of many plans and counsels (*mêtis*) or many turns and ways (*tropos*), equally implying an intention to deceive.

The great fame of Odysseus as a speaker was testified by the Trojan lord Antenor: 'But when [Odysseus] let loose that great voice from his chest and the words came piling on like a driving winter blizzard – then no man alive could rival Odysseus!'[26] Helen's account of Odysseus is also a telling one: 'he's quick at every treachery under the sun – the man of twists and turns'.[27] In *The Odyssey*, the hero himself tells the Phaecians that he is 'known to the world for every kind of craft'. The word translated as 'craft' here is δόλος (*dolos*). This word properly means 'a bait' (for trapping fish) or, more generally, 'any cunning contrivance for deceiving or catching'.[28] The legendary wooden horse, for example, was a *dolos* meant for Trojans (needless to say, the horse was Odysseus's idea).[29] So Odysseus had a reputation, and very much so in the eyes of Achilles, too. This is definitively confirmed in the scene of *The Odyssey* where the son of Laertes visits the underworld (Hades), which very much surprises the ghost of his late comrade, Achilles:

> Royal son of Laertes, Odysseus, man of tactics (πολυμήχαν' Ὀδυσσεῦ, *polymêchan' Odysseu*), reckless friend, what next? What Greater feat can

---

21 By A.T. Murray.
22 By Robert Fagles.
23 In Greek: 'διογενὲς Λαερτιάδη πολυμήχαν' Ὀδυσσεῦ' (*diogenes laertiadê polymêchan' Odysseu*) *The Iliad*, Fagles translation, 2.201–202: 'Royal son of Laertes, Odysseus, great tactician (*polymekhan' Odysseu*)'; Murray translation, 2.173–174: 'Son of Laërtes, sprung from Zeus, Odysseus of many wiles'.
24 See, e.g., *The Iliad*, Murray translation, 1.311, 3.200–201 and 8.474.
25 In the opening line of *The Odyssey*.
26 *The Iliad*, Fagles translation, 3.266–8.
27 *The Iliad*, Fagles translation, 3.243–4.
28 As defined in Liddell and Scott's *Greek–English Lexicon*.
29 *The Odyssey*, Murray translation, 8.494; Fagles translation, 8.553.

that cunning head contrive? What daring brought you down to the House of Death?[30]

However, returning to the embassy scene of *The Iliad*, the point is that Achilles's depiction of Odysseus as *polymêchanos* enables Achilles to present himself as the opposite of Odysseus. Right below the address, Achilles says of himself: 'I must speak the word bluntly'. In Greek, again, 'speaking bluntly' is ἀπηλεγέως ἀποειπεῖν (*apêlegeôs apoeipein*). The meaning of that expression is 'speaking out without caring for the consequences'. Unlike the schemer Odysseus, who constantly makes plans and sets up traps by way of speaking, Achilles does not think about the effects of what he says at all. Calculation with words is next to holding something in concealment, and this is what Achilles hates more than anything: hiding one thing and saying another. This way Achilles presents himself as a person who hides nothing, or who never hides behind words. Odysseus, in turn, stands for speech as a means of concealing oneself, obscuring one's plans from others and leading them astray.

So Achilles speaks without a care for the consequences and hides nothing in speech. Ultimately this attitude seems to result from the fact that speech is a minor matter to a warrior. What matters, instead, is that his thoughts will come true, that they will lead to action. Words may be said on the way, but they may not meddle with the warrior's path to action. The psychic system of a warrior should be as straightforward as possible, which makes speaking necessarily marginal. The less a fighter has to speak, the greater will be his valour. Achilles stands for an immediate materialisation of one's will. Any discursive mediation is at best a regrettable delay, and at worst a sign of indecision.[31]

Nevertheless, situations arise when even a warrior must speak, and it is in one of these that Achilles finds himself when the embassy of the other great warriors comes to talk to him. Knowing perfectly well what storm of words will be blasted at him, he has clearly decided to stay firm no matter what happens. This test will be much more critical for him than any of his physical combats; now he needs to excel in the practice of speaking. In response, Achilles gives Odysseus and the others a discursive hammering that contains 'the longest stretch of continuous argument in the *Iliad*', as Bryan Hainsworth points out.[32] Apropos of exactly this particular scene, Michel

---

30 *The Odyssey*, Fagles translation, 11.536–9.
31 See John Heath's discussion of Achilles as a speaker in Chapter 3, 'Talking through the Heroic Code: Achilles learns to tell tales', of his book *The Talking Greeks: Speech, Animals, and the Other in Homer, Aeschylus, and Plato* (Cambridge: Cambridge University Press, 2005); and more generally Adkins, *Merit and Responsibility*.
32 Bryan Hainsworth, *The Iliad: A Commentary. Volume III, books 9–12.* General editor G.S. Kirk. (Cambridge: Cambridge University Press, 1993), 100.

Foucault had a remarkably sharp perception of the principle behind Achilles's presentation of himself as a speaking warrior. It is useful to cite him at length:

> Between what [Achilles] thinks and what he says, between what he says and what he wants to do, between what he wants to do and what he will in actual fact do, there is no concealment, no deviation, nothing which hides the reality of what he thinks and what will be the reality of what he does.[33]

A warrior's words are the direct opposite of the words of a tactician. Words will bring visible to others the connection between his thought and action, but words will not play any other role in his system. Like the Trojan Aeneas says in *The Iliad*, only small boys quarrel by way of words, whereas the men's way is deeds.[34] This general scorn of speech appears also to be at work in the background to the embassy scene: Achilles speaks bluntly, 'so you won't crowd around me, one after another, coaxing like a murmuring clutch of doves'.[35] At the end of the scene, however, something peculiar happens as regards that background. Whereas the starting point was that thoughts and deeds should always be superior to words, the end result of the embassy to Achilles is that all this is turned on its head: Achilles will be trapped by his own words.

The person who first perceives the treacherous thing that had just happened is Ajax. Returning to their camp from the failed mission of negotiating with Achilles, Ajax gives his analysis to Agamemnon.[36] It was entirely wrong to try to beg Achilles. Agamemnon should not have sent the embassy to him, with promises of great gifts and honours. Their purpose was to appease the rage of Achilles, but what happened was exactly the opposite. He became even angrier than before: 'He's a proud man at the best of times, and now you've only plunged him deeper in his pride', says Ajax to Agamemnon.[37] Achilles was not ready for a real parley, but only used the situation to vent his spleen. In fact, the negotiations put him in such fervour

---

33 Michel Foucault, *The Courage of Truth. Lectures at the Collège de France 1983–1984* (Basingstoke and New York: Palgrave Macmillan, 2011), 222.
34 *The Iliad*, Murray translation, 20.200–203: 'Son of Peleus, think not with words to afright me, as I were a child'. Fagles translation, at 20.233–235: 'But Aeneas, taking a long deep breath, replied, "don't think for a moment, Achilles, son of Peleus, you can frighten me with words like a child, a fool [...]"'.
35 *The Iliad*, Fagles translation, at 9.376–7. Murray translation, at 9.310: 'that ye sit not by me here on this side and on that and prate endlessly'.
36 *The Iliad*, Book 9 *in fine*.
37 *The Iliad*, Fagles translation, at 9.853–4; Murray translation, at 9.699–700: 'haughty is he even of himself, and now hast thou yet far more set him amid haughtinesses'.

that, as a final point, he swore that he would not join the war before the Trojan army reaches his own ships.

This was of course not a promise that the embassy was expecting or aiming to get. So there was no verbal pact made between Achilles and the party of lords that visited him. Achilles rather made a pact with himself. With that, things changed considerably for the worse as this type of pact is more binding for a Homeric warrior than his pact with someone else. The warrior will always have to be true to himself; words may not deviate from 'what will be the reality of what he does', as Foucault observed. Should Achilles break his promise to himself, this would at once break the continuum between his thoughts, words and action, a continuum that defines the warrior attitude towards speaking. What one speaks at the present moment may not deviate from what one will do in the future. But once this is said, things turn on their head. What will be done now may not deviate from what has been said before.

Relative to deeds, words were supposed to be always second-rate for Achilles, but strangely they end up dominating his deeds. What happens seven books later in the story (in Book 16 of *The Iliad*) shows that Ajax was entirely right in his analysis: the oath that Achilles gave, despite the fact that nobody wanted it, will operate on him from then onwards. At a tragic turning point, Achilles would have been finally ready to forget his rage, but he is no longer free to enter the battlefield. This is because of the regrettable words that had slipped out of his mouth earlier. Now as the Achaean army stands on the brink of breakdown, what Achilles tells Patroclus is this:

> Enough.
> Let bygones be bygones now. Done is done.
> How on earth can a man rage on forever?
> Still, by god, I said I would not relax my anger,
> not till the cries and carnage reached my own ships.[38]

Achilles cannot fight. To compensate this, he and his closest friend Patroclus end up contriving a bluff together, which later turns out to be a fatal mistake. Patroclus wears the armour of his friend, and then goes to battle as if he was Achilles. This make-believe should hearten the Achaean troops and strike fear into their enemy. At first, the plan seems to work well: the Achaeans regain their strength and the Trojan onslaught is put to a halt. At the sad end, however, Patroclus forgets the strict order of Achilles not to

---

38 *The Iliad*, Fagles translation, at 16.68–72; Murray translation, at 16.61–3: 'Howbeit these things will we let be, as past and done. In no wise, meseems, was I to be filled with ceaseless wrath at heart; yet verily I deemed that I should not make an end of mine anger, until the hour when unto mine own ships should come the war-cry and the battle.'

proceed on the plain, but to come back at the moment when the enemy has been forced away from the ships. In its place, Patroclus moves from defence to attack. Eventually Patroclus confronts Hector, loses the combat, and dies with Hector's spear in his chest.

This plot by Achilles and Patroclus admittedly weakens somewhat the image of Achilles as a truthful warrior. Did his self-portrayal (at the beginning of his response to Odysseus) not imply that such wiles and tricks belong to Odysseus the tactician, not to Achilles the warrior? True, the trick was not made in the form of speech. In this regard, however, a famous ancient critic went so far as to claim that Achilles was really a liar just like Odysseus. In one of Plato's dialogues, Socrates himself makes this radical claim.[39] Looking at the scene that we have just analysed, Socrates points out that while telling the men of the embassy that he was just about to sail home and leave everything, Achilles had nothing of the sort in mind. Was he not clearly just waiting for the right moment to re-enter the battle? In any case, Achilles never intended to leave, but was so clever that even Odysseus did not realise that he was bluffing all the time.

In his own way, however, Plato confirms what the traditional view was, still at the end of the classical period. Whereas Socrates's interpretation was critical and against the canon, that interpretation will only make sense as against the traditional or archaic interpretation. In Plato's dialogue, the archaic interpretation is represented by Hippias, and therefore what he says is more interesting to us. Hippias says that Achilles is better than Odysseus, because Achilles is 'truthful and simple', whereas Odysseus is 'wily and a liar'.[40] Plato's literary criticism reveals that Achilles was neither simple nor truthful, but it also reveals that the traditional view of Achilles was the opposite.

The traditional interpretation of Homer appears to have been that speech is a dubious practice. Certainly, there are many occasions in *The Iliad*, where the capacity for speech is not only a sign of wit, but of nobility as well. From time to time, warriors assemble and practice rhetoric, trying to persuade, judge or praise other warriors. Strangely enough, even in the midst of the fiercest fighting heroes may suddenly address long oratories to their opponents, to themselves, or to gods. Book 23 contains judicial argumentation between Menelaus and Antilochus, both trying to prove their right to the prize after a chariot race, which shows that a Homeric hero very much appreciated skilful use of words.

Nevertheless, at the points studied above a certain ethical shadiness seems always to accompany speech. On the one hand, speakers like Odysseus may generally be well-respected characters, but they are also full of

---

39 *Lesser Hippias* 370a ff.
40 *Lesser Hippias* 365b.

schemes. Potentially, some secret plan is always lurking behind their words. Admirable people like Achilles speak their mind freely and without a care for the consequences. On the other hand, even a man like Achilles must be careful with his words. Achilles's promise shows that words are invested with peculiar might: a truthful speaker will be bound by his words. While talking, he is wrapped in his own words without even noticing it. The spiders of discourse weave their webs behind his back.

Aristotle's *Politics*: humans are defined by speech

The above glimpse of Hesiod and Homer showed that speaking was not charged with positive value only at the beginning of the archaic period. Nevertheless, from then onwards speech started to make its way to the centre of Greek life. The culmination of this development took place in classical, fifth century Athens. For the moment, however, I will jump over that high point of the culture of speech, the classical period, and focus on a time when it was already approaching its disappearance.

Towards the end of the fourth century BC, democratic ways of governing and the political system of the agora lost their vitality in Athens. Their pulse had recovered the aftershock that the Peloponnesian war aroused in Athens, but the Macedonian triumph at the Battle of Chaeronea in 338 BC turned out to be deadly, not only for the system of independent city-states, albeit 'immortalized in the speeches of Demosthenes' exactly at that time,[41] but also for the belief in democratic and republican values. With Alexander's succession to the throne of Macedonia in 336 BC, the Greeks left behind four prodigious centuries of constitutional experimentation in independent city-states and colonies. The nascent political structures of empire would shortly come in their place.

Situated in that historical moment of sea change is Aristotle, Alexander's illustrious tutor, and his book on *Politics*. A small passage of that book, still echoing the sounds of a free society, will be examined next. What Aristotle says in the passage is this: Speech (λόγος *logos*) is a gift of nature that places human life apart from merely animal life. Humans alone possess speech, other animals possess mere voice (φωνὴ, *phône*). In other words, humans are defined by speech.

It should be noted that Aristotle makes his statement in a special argumentative context. He turns to speech because he wants to argue that humans are political by nature. The unique capacity of humans for speech is taken for granted, and Aristotle takes it up in order to validate his claim

---

41 Werner Jaeger, *Paideia: the Ideals of Greek Culture, Vol III: The Conflict of Cultural Ideals in the Age of Plato* (New York and Oxford: Oxford University Press 1986), 289.

that humans are meant to live in political society, in a city.⁴² Therefore, in Aristotle's mind a seamless connection exists between political life, speech and humanity. To lay this connection bare, let us examine the passage at length:

> Now, that man is more of a political animal than bees or any other gregarious animals is evident. Nature, as we often say, makes nothing in vain, and man is the only animal who has the gift of speech. [...] The power of speech is intended to set forth the expedient and inexpedient, and therefore likewise the just and the unjust. And it is characteristic of man that he alone has any sense of good and evil, or just and unjust, and the like, and the association of living beings who have this sense makes a family and a state.⁴³

Evident from this passage is that not just any kind of speech defines humanity; Aristotle has something specific in mind. To begin with, what Aristotle calls speech (*logos*) at this point, is designed to indicate *moral* qualities: the advantageous and the harmful, the right and the wrong, the good and the bad. Humans are those who would talk about these things. Moreover, Aristotle clearly focuses on a sphere that goes beyond mere talk, a sphere we may call *language* because a system of universal concepts operates there.⁴⁴ *Logos* is still predominantly a 'thing said', but with an important extension to quite another semantic field. *Logos* is also a word for 'rational principle', 'reason', 'rule', 'argument', 'calculation', and so on.⁴⁵ Appearing as a rational language, moral speech will be subjected to certain regulation – to certain requirements of structure, to say the least – and therefore also to the critical review of listeners.

The moral qualities borne by language may stand as certain norms of rationality imposed on speaking; this is something one understands without difficulty. However, the problem is not the inherent norms of language,

---

42 It is conceivable that, during and after the strife ensuing from the defeat in the Peloponnesian war, in Athens some people were reverting to peasant virtues, to Hesiod's precepts, one might even say preferring rural life to city life. This is at least Foucault's view; for him, the growth of anti-urban, anti-democratic and anti-rhetorical sentiments was apparent, for example, in the court trial scene in Euripides's play *Orestes* (New York: Oxford University Press, 1995) lines 818–20. See Foucault, *The Government of Self and Others*, 166–8.
43 *Politics* I.1, 1253a10–17.
44 This may be understood even in terms of the famous *langue/parole* distinction by Ferdinand de Saussure in his *Course in General Linguistics* (Glasgow: Fontana and Collins, 1978), 9–17. Language (*langue*) is an underlying system, a social structure, whereas speaking (*parole*) consists of individual acts that make use of the underlying system of language.
45 See C.C.W. Taylor's comments to his translation of *Nicomachean Ethics* (Oxford: Oxford University Press, 2006), 65–6.

but the claim that these norms amount to defining human beings.[46] The problem is whether the moral qualities borne by moral language impose themselves as the norms of humanity. If they have this much power, then how does it come about? The above quote tells that the power of speech is intended to 'set forth' these moral qualities. Aristotle's word for the operation of 'setting forth' is δηλοῦν (*dêloun*). *Dêloun* means: to 'make something visible or known' or 'clear to the mind'. Hence, moral language has the power to make moral qualities (the good and the bad, the right and the wrong, the useful and the harmful) visible and clear to the human mind.[47]

But then, is it Aristotle's view that the ensuing moral visibility and clarity is enough to make us humans? Is this the essence of what humans are, some sort of sobriety in moral matters? This question is not minor, and only a modest outline of a response may be provided here. Even that modest outline requires a moment to view Aristotle's broader ethico-political system.

Something to start with is provided in Book III of *Politics*, where three interconnected elements describe a citizen living in an Aristotelian republic. The first element is that he will participate (*metechô*) in the public exercise of power.[48] Participation is his right and obligation at once. The second element is a special ability (*dunamis*) required of him: he needs to be able to rule, and to be ruled, in turns.[49] Moreover, these two positions of the free citizen are intertwined, so that one is able to rule only if one is able to be ruled as well.

From the first and the second element, a third concerning knowledge follows. A citizen needs to know (*epistamai*) the exercise of political power from both ends of the relation: from the governor's end and from the subject's end. In other words, a citizen 'should know how to govern like a freeman, and obey like a freeman'.[50] This knowledge is two-part (governing and obeying) but it is nevertheless the same, undivided knowledge of a freeman.

---

46 This appears to be the view of Thomas Aquinas and his *Commentary on Aristotle's Politics*: 'if nature gives to a being something that of itself is ordered to some end, it follows that this end is given to this being by nature' (book I, lecture I, paragraph 37). The end of language will by the same token signify the end of humans.
47 It may sound strange to make so much of a standard word such as *dêloun*. However, in the passage in question this word defines what human *logos* can do, whereas the passage employs the words σημεῖον (*sêmeion*, 'function as a sign') and σημαίνειν (*sêmainein*, 'show by a sign') for what the animal *phônê* can do. Be that as it may, the point is that moral qualities appear to be properties internal to the system of language, so that *logos* essentially makes known to humans something pertaining to itself. By contrast, *phônê* functions as a sign of things existing externally to language. These extra-linguistic things, in turn, are the pains and the pleasures that all animals feel and may communicate to each other with a roar, whine, purr, and so on.
48 *Politics* III.1, 1275a22–23, 30, 1275b15–20.
49 *Politics* 1277a26–28.
50 *Politics* 1277b14–15.

Incorporating all these elements – participation, ability and knowledge – the citizen generally speaking is the 'one who shares in governing and being governed'.[51]

The above system of exchange of roles stands at the heart of Aristotle's republic, but it should be observed that this system is meant only for the free.[52] Only those men who are their own masters may participate in governing the polity. As Aristotle explains in the first book of *Politics*, being one's own master is not really a question of legal status.[53] Freedom, like slavery, is a condition of one's soul. Clearly, freedom is neither absence of externally imposed obstacles, nor an individual's right that prohibits the interference of others in the sphere of their autonomy. Instead, freedom is the touchstone of the quality of a citizen; freedom is a quality standard: a citizen must prove himself worthy of his title by acting in a certain, self-controlled way. To be counted among the free, a citizen must show he is his own master. One cannot contribute to the governing of public affairs if one is not able to govern one's self first. This way of understanding the question of freedom leads to the domain of ethics, where the moral constitution of a free citizen may be further expounded.

Knowing now that Aristotle's *Politics* requires freedom of citizens, *Nicomachean Ethics* could in turn be read as a book explaining what it means to be free ethically, to be one's own master. In outline, such a reading begins with three basic notions: *praxis*, *êthos* and *hexis*. A free person would be someone who first of all recognises that the ultimate goal of his life, happiness, is borne at every moment of his life by his actions (*praxis*).[54] Accordingly, the final end of each of his actions should be good conduct (*eupraxia*), not so much their external effects.[55] Instead of external effects, his practice of ethics has an internal effect: it generates virtuosity in him. He will carefully fashion his character (*êthos*) in his actions; every one of them must be fit for a free man.[56] Practical knowledge of ethical virtues, for example of courage and temperance, is helpful for him, but not enough. As a courageous and temperate man, he is not only the person who has figured things right in his mind, but the person who is ready to act.[57] When the moment comes, he will do so too. Being thus disposed, finally, is a matter of habit, *hexis* (state of character, disposition). In the end, all these notions tie together in a single weft: *hexis* solidifies into *êthos* through *praxis*.

---

51 *Politics* 1283b42–1284a1.
52 So that 'a state is a community of freemen'; *Politics* 1279a21. The word for the free is ἐλεύθερος, *eleutheros*.
53 *Politics* I.4–6.
54 *Nicomachean Ethics* 1098b15–23.
55 *Nicomachean Ethics* 1139b3, 1140b5–10.
56 *Nicomachean Ethics* 1103a31–1103b25, 1103b30–31, 1114a7–11.
57 *Nicomachean Ethics* 1103b25–31, 1105b2–4.

The above sketch must be the briefest possible introduction to Aristotle's ethico-political system. Nevertheless, it must suffice for our purposes of responding to Aristotle's problematic definition of humanity. Let us start by considering the effects of the republican system – a system where everyone exercises power in turns – on society. In Aristotle's mind, two important effects ensue from it. The first feature of the practice of exchanging positions is that it will uphold *equality* between citizens: no one will rise above or sink below the others.[58] Secondly, in a society governed this way, power tends not to be abused but exercised for the *common good*. This tendency is explained by the fact that everyone knows, while in power, that they will soon have to step down and be subjects again.[59]

Equality and the common good may be considered as social and political effects of a system where citizens conduct public tasks in turns. Yet the mere conduct of tasks is not all there is; something more is involved, something whose effects are more immediate and inherent to the practice of exchanging roles. In a republic, says Aristotle, 'the one party rules and the others are ruled in turn, as if they were no longer the same persons'.[60] The last sentence about a person *not remaining the same* (as he is 'coming into other states of being' or 'coming into the state of being of others')[61] may look like a mere figure of speech.[62] Moreover, in so far as the main idea of this passage is merely about changing political roles, one's personality is not altered in reality. Nevertheless, the suggestion of a shift in the mode of being, effect by political conversation, seems promising as regards our puzzle concerning Aristotle's idea about people turning into humans through moral language.[63] By a flight of imagination, let us therefore presume that conversation with others brings about a third, psychic type of effect: people turn into other persons while participating in the political life of the republic.

So how would the last-mentioned idea, the psychic effect, match up with our question about humanity and moral language? One way to interpret Aristotle is that his moral language, as employed in political arenas, results in a metamorphosis or conversion in people: 'We' constantly turn into 'others' when we speak to them. Seen from this perspective, the work of language appears to be not only the theoretical clarity it sets forth (*dêloun*) in the mind about moral principles, but also a practical and moral broadening

---

58 *Politics* 1259b5.
59 *Politics* 1279a8–13.
60 *Politics* 1261b4–5.
61 In Greek: 'ἂν ἄλλοι γενόμενοι', (*an alloi genomenoi*), where ἄλλοι (*alloi*) is the plural of ἄλλος (*allos*), 'other', and 'γενόμενοι' (*genomenoi*) derives from γίγνομαι (*gignomai*), 'to be born', 'to come into being', or 'to come into a state of being'.
62 Aristotle's text gives it as a figure of speech, using the word ὥσπερ (*hôper*), meaning 'as if'.
63 Especially so, if this passage is read together with what Aristotle says about the need of some good friends to talk to. See *Nicomachean Ethics* IX.9.

of the mind. In the process of speaking, the mind breaks free from its egocentric confines. Moral language is the medium that tends to make us see even ourselves in the eyes of other persons, at the same time as it is the medium through which republican government comes to pass. In other words, moral language allows us to understand the other's point of view.[64] Perhaps Aristotle's definition of humanity suggests this type of effort.

This is fine as far as it goes. Turning to ethics next, what may the self-mastery of a free person have to do with our problem? The above brief sketch for a reading of *Nicomachean Ethics* concluded that through ethical practices something is solidified into the character of the person. This 'something' is going to be his *hexis*. What, at the end of the day, is *hexis* and has it got something to do with moral language? Were *hexis* simply about inculcation of the moral qualities borne by moral language (the good, the just and the useful), then the problem would perhaps be solved as simply as this: humans are rational about moral matters and language may be credited for this fact.

The solution does not seem to be as simple as that, however. *Hexis* is more complicated, and moreover turns out to be not in the first place about reason and rationality. The second Book of *Nicomachean Ethics* is quite clear about it. In the first place, *hexis* is the relation one habitually maintains towards feelings. Rather than with the rational part of the soul, *hexis* deals with the irrational part. *Hexeis* are the ways in which we confront our fears and manage our desires.[65] *Hexis* defines the extent to which we may resist pleasure and endure pain.[66] What has language got to do with that?

Not much, suggests Aristotle's vocabulary. The 'irrational' part of the soul is named the ἄλογος (*alogos*), that is, the 'speechless'. The rational part, in turn, is τῆς ψυχῆς τὸ λόγον ἔχον (*tês psyches to logon ekhon*), that is, 'the soul that has speech'.[67] Whatever the irrational part of the soul may be otherwise, language seems definitely to have nothing to do with it. Reason is defined as that which has language; the other part is that which has no language. In a roundabout way, however, language has got everything to do

---

64 Drawing on Kant's Critique of Judgment, Hannah Arendt has called this effect of political life on the mind of the people the 'enlarged mentality'. See Hannah Arendt, 'Truth and Politics', in Arendt, *Between Past and Future: Eight Exercises in Political Thought*, 227–64 (New York: Penguin Books, 1977), at 241–2.
65 *Nicomachean Ethics* 1104a10–25; 1104b4–29; 1105a5–17; 1105b2; Chapter 5 of Book II; 1106b25, 1152b1–5.
66 *Nicomachean Ethics* 1104a26–1104b2. The themes of resistance and endurance reappear in Book VII. Book X returns to the theme of pleasure.
67 The more usual reading of the word *logos* in the context of Aristotle's theory of the soul is not 'speech' but 'reason'. However, I think it would be wrong to consider their relation a mere homonymy, so that it would just happen to be the case that the same word *logos* stands for both of these entirely different things. In my mind, the polysemy of the word *logos* brings together its two meanings, 'reason' and 'speech', suggesting that they have something important to do with each other.

with both parts. This other way may be found in what Aristotle says about the *nature* of this entire division, about the *sense* in which he speaks about the soul as divided into rational and irrational.

To begin with, Aristotle tells that the soul's compartmentalisation is ἐξωτερικοὶ λόγοι (*eksoterikoi logoi*, usually understood to mean 'someone else's doctrine').[68] So it does not genuinely belong to Aristotle's own discourse, at least not the one that he is presently conducting. At the same time, this more or less foreign idea is very important, irremovable, in his own system: 'No doubt, however, we must none the less suppose that in the soul too there is something beside reason, resisting and opposing it'.[69] It transpires that with the division comes a particular view of the psychic life: this is depicted as an internal struggle between these two elements, rational and irrational. At any rate, Aristotle endorses this *eksoterikos* view and creates his theory of ethics on it. Turning to the main question, finally, what is the nature of this view, according to which 'one element in the soul is irrational (*alogos*) and one has reason (*logon ekhon*)'?[70] This is what Aristotle says:

> Whether these are separated as the parts of the body or [as the parts] of anything divisible are, or [whether these] are *distinct by definition*[71] but by nature inseparable, like convex and concave in the circumference of a circle, does not affect the present question.[72]

Aristotle makes this remark only in passing, as it were. After a while, he returns to the issue, but only in order to hush it up: 'In what sense [the one element] is distinct from the other elements does not concern us', he says tersely and stops.[73] Whatever this implies, in the above passage he nevertheless indicates that the irrational and the rational are possibly 'distinct by definition' only. The effect of this is that these parts may very well be distinguishable merely in thought. Generally speaking, I am sure that no one doubts the enormous significance of the distinction between rational and irrational for posterity. Without it, we could not possibly be the kind of beings we are today: we have learned to look into ourselves this way, and could not think any other way. Tracing it back to Aristotle, however, we have one of its main progenitors leaving us with an ambiguous impression that it does not have to have so much to do with reality.

But then, what has it to do with, if not reality? Looking at this passage together with the earlier passage – that defines humans as subjects of speech – at

---

68 The division of the soul is one of Plato's central doctrines. See *Republic*, Book IV.
69 *Nicomachean Ethics*, Ross & Brown translation, 1102b20–25.
70 *Nicomachean Ethics* 1102a29.
71 Emphasis added.
72 *Nicomachean Ethics*, Ross & Brown translation, 1102a29–33.
73 *Nicomachean Ethics* 1102b16–17.

least one answer seems to be readily available. Whatever else it may be, the division is at the very least a structure of moral language. Or rather, it is not merely a structure of moral language, but the very staging of it. In so far as the soul is a theatre of morality, every single drama there is fundamentally about the 'rational part' trying to make the 'irrational part' follow its direction. The opposition between these two characters is not just the work of moral language, but something without which that language does not work.

Let me conclude these somewhat over-long, but even so, over-hasty remarks on Aristotle. What, at the end of the day, is the resulting outline for a response to the problem of speech and humanity? Where we started, the view of Aristotle was that human beings consummate their nature by endorsing a system of moral language. Nature has given us speech, so that we may clarify moral qualities to ourselves (the good, the right, and the useful) and form communities with others. We went beyond those things, where we ended, as two things appeared to be implied by moral language. Employing it in political life, we constantly 'become other persons' by including the perspectives of others in our own. That would be the first theme of a prospective response to the Aristotelian problem of speech and humanity. Employing it in our ethical life, we enact an inner conversation and struggle between the irrational (speechless) and the rational (speaking) parts of ourselves. That would be the second theme of the response.

Conclusion: the ancient subjects of speech today

Like everything else that Aristotle said, his passage on speech, as the defining quality of human beings, has also had a tremendous impact on our understanding of ourselves. We have a strong tradition of thinking about ourselves, not only as speakers of languages, but somehow more fundamentally as subjects of language. This is not only about our power over language, but about the power of language over us. Subjectivity is erected, upheld and ordered according to systems we call languages, by which we mean all kinds of symbolic orders. Should we believe in 'nature's purpose', it must have been to make people talk to each other, and thereby form bonds and communities. Language, however, is more than a mere medium of communication for us; rather, it is more like water is to fish.

No point in history can precisely be given at which humans invented language, entered into the world of conversation, and finally became subjects of language. It is more plausible to agree with Émile Benveniste that 'it is a speaking man whom we find in the world, a man speaking to another man, and language provides the very definition of man'.[74] Accordingly, it would be

---

74 Émile Benveniste, *Problems in General Linguistics* (Coral Gables, Florida: University of Miami Press, 1975), 224.

a silly misunderstanding to start making historical excursions, not to mention readings of Hesiod and Homer, with a view of some time where speech supposedly did not exist – and then compare it with some Aristotelian, fully developed discourse, a language that is capable even of reflecting itself.

Instead of origins, the previous sections point at the variation and shifts between different periods in people's attitudes towards speaking. Hesiod thought about it as a social plague and for Homer at least one kind of speaking was an ethically dubious practice. Crossing over to the Aristotelian epilogue of the classical era, one finds a completely different view of speech, where reason and rationality have entirely overrun the previous suspicion towards rumour and the talk that goes around in the streets, on the one hand, and towards tricks and wiles contrived in the form of speech, on the other hand. There was not only one ancient subject of speech, but many.

Some would say that the things that I have discussed above are completely different matters. Aristotle was no longer speaking about Hesiod's world of speech, as by *logos* he meant reason. Instead of *Politics* and *Nicomachean Ethics*, his book on *Rhetoric* would have come closer to the themes I have just dealt with by way of reading Hesiod and Homer. This is very much true, and in some ways this alteration of meaning of the word 'logos' may well be the final key to the riddle of speech. Nevertheless, my modest response to this criticism would still be that Aristotle nevertheless was *speaking* about reason, so that even the reader of Aristotle cannot but remain signposted to the world of words.

Finally, I want to return to the present-day problems I started with. Against the self-evidence of the blessings of free speech, I juxtaposed recent unpleasant experiences of what is known as hate speech. Is a relevant lesson to be learned from my ancient excursions? I am not sure. It is certainly not that now, enlightened by Hesiod, we should finally break the Aristotelian spell, and do away with the constitutional and human right to free speech. What I have in mind in this regard is rather that, as in ancient times, today the subject of speech is also not a singular position.

For centuries and millennia, humans have explored their own words, trying to discover the universal truth about themselves. But perhaps every speaker harbours their own unique truth, and this may be the whole point. Speakers of today would naturally include liars and swindlers who would not mind one second about other people's point of view. They also include charlatans who cannot control themselves and keep polluting the Internet with all kinds of licentious drivel. Finally, they would also include the serious and the straight who would just go on, stubbornly trying to make sense to others – and make themselves understood.

Bibliography

Adkins, Arthur W.H. *Merit and Responsibility: A Study in Greek Values*. Chicago and London: The University of Chicago Press, 1975.

Arendt, Hannah. 'Truth and Politics'. In H. Arendt: *Between Past and Future. Eight Exercises in Political Thought*, 227–64. New York: Penguin Books, 1977.
Aristotle. *The Politics*. Translation by Benjamin Jowett, revised by Jonathan Barnes. Edited by Stephen Everson. Cambridge: Cambridge University Press, 1988.
Aristotle. *Nicomachean Ethics, Books II—IV*. Translated with an Introduction and Commentary by C.C.W. Taylor. Oxford: Oxford University Press, 2006.
Aristotle. *The Nicomachean Ethics*. Translated by D. Ross, revised by L. Brown. Oxford: Oxford University Press, 2009.
Barendt, Eric. *Freedom of Speech*. Oxford: Oxford University Press, 2007.
Benveniste, Émile. *Problems in General Linguistics*. Translated by M.E. Meek. Coral Gables, Florida: University of Miami Press, 1975.
Butler, Judith. *Excitable Speech. A Politics of the Performative*. New York and London: Routledge, 1977.
Euripides. *Orestes*. Translated by John Peck and Frank Nisetich. New York: Oxford University Press, 1995.
Foucault, Michel. *Wrong-doing, Truth-telling. The function of Avowal in Justice*. Edited by F. Brion and B.E. Harcourt. Translated by S.W. Sawyer. Chicago: The University of Chicago Press, 2014.
Foucault, Michel. *The Courage of Truth. Lectures at the Collège de France 1983–1984*. Basingstoke and New York: Palgrave Macmillan, 2011.
Foucault, Michel. *The Government of Self and Others. Lectures at the Collège de France 1982–1983*. Basingstoke and New York: Palgrave Macmillan, 2010.
Hainsworth, Bryan. *The Iliad: A Commentary*. General editor G.S. Kirk. Volume III, books 9–12. Cambridge: Cambridge University Press, 1993.
Heath, John. *The Talking Greeks. Speech, Animals, and the Other in Homer, Aeschylus, and Plato*. Cambridge: Cambridge University Press, 2005.
Hesiod. 'Works and Days'. In *The Homeric Hymns and Homerica / Hesiod*. With an English Translation by Hugh G. Evelyn-White. Cambridge, MA: Harvard University Press; London: William Heinemann, Ltd., 1914.
Homer. *The Iliad*. Translated by R. Fagles. New York: Penguin Books, 1990.
Homer. *The Iliad*. With an English translation by A.T. Murray, in two volumes. Cambridge, MA: Harvard University Press; London: William Heinemann, Ltd., 1924.
Homer. *The Odyssey*. Translated by R. Fagles. New York: Penguin Books, 1996.
Homer. *The Odyssey*. With an English translation by A.T. Murray, in two volumes. Cambridge, MA: Harvard University Press; London: William Heinemann, Ltd., 1919.
Jaeger, Werner. *Paideia: the Ideals of Greek Culture, Vol III: The Conflict of Cultural Ideals in the Age of Plato*. New York and Oxford: Oxford University press 1986.
Meier, Christian. *A Culture of Freedom. Ancient Greece and the Origins of Europe*. Oxford: Oxford University Press, 2012.
Plato. *Complete Works*. Edited by John M. Cooper. Indianapolis/Cambridge: Hackett Publishing Company, 1997.
Rawson, Elizabeth. *The Spartan Tradition in European Thought*. Oxford: Clarendon Press, 1969.
Roberts, Jennifer Tolbert. *Athens on Trial. The Antidemocratic Tradition in Western Thought*. Princeton, New Jersey: Princeton University Press, 1994.
Saussure, Ferdinand de. *Course in General Linguistics*. Edited by C. Bally and A. Sechehaye with A. Reidlinger. Glasgow: Fontana and Collins, 1978.

Sluiter, Ineke and Ralph Rosen (eds.). *City, Countryside, and the Spatial Organization of Value in Classical Antiquity.* Leiden and Boston: Brill 2006.

Sluiter, Ineke and Ralph Rosen (eds.). *Free Speech in Classical Antiquity.* Leiden and Boston: Brill 2004.

Thomas Aquinas. 'Commentary on Aristotle's Politics'. Translated by Ernest Fortin and Peter O'Neill. In *Medieval Political Philosophy: A Sourcebook.* Edited by Ralph Lerner. New York: Free Press of Glencoe, 1963.

Vernant, Jean-Pierre. *The Origins of Greek Thought.* Ithaca and New York: Cornell University Press, 1982.

Waldron, Jeremy. *The Harm in Hate Speech.* Cambridge, MA and London: Harvard University Press, 2012.

Chapter 3

Disenfranchisement and political capacity

Pablo Marshall[1]

Introduction

Many convicted offenders around the world do not vote in elections because they have been legally deprived of their voting rights. This is the case in countries such as Australia, Brazil, France, Italy, France, Russia, the United States and the United Kingdom. Offenders belong to one of the few categories of electoral exclusions that remain generally in force from the time prior to the principle of universal suffrage. Even though the legal regulation of elections is considerably diverse, there is a considerable continuity in the exclusion of criminal offenders. The other categories that are commonly excluded are children, people with mental disabilities, and foreign citizens.[2] All these categories of exclusion are the object of analysis and debate.[3]

During the last decade, the issue of criminal disenfranchisement (CD) has come to be recognised as a significant problem and, accordingly, laws in different countries have increasingly been examined under human rights standards. This recent process of judicial review has generally found that CD contravenes basic agreements of respecting fundamental rights and extending democracy. Furthermore, there is a growing academic consensus that CD degrades offenders to the status of second-class citizens, diminishing their dignity by means of denial of suffrage, and treating them unfairly by impeding their ability to express their interests in the rule-making process.[4]

---

1 I would like to thank Guillermo Jimenez, Paz Irarrazabal, Steve Collins, Beth Pearson and Emilios Christodoulidis for their comments to a previous version of this chapter.
2 An overview of electoral exclusions in comparative law can be found in André Blais, Louis Massicotte and Antoine Yoshinaka, 'Deciding who has the right to vote: a comparative analysis of election laws,' *Electoral Studies* 20 (2001), 41–62.
3 See, e.g. Ludvig Beckman, *The Frontiers of Democracy. The Right to Vote and its Limits* (London: Palgrave Macmillan, 2009).
4 The literature is extensive. An overview of legal and political problems can be seen in Alec Ewald and Brandon Rottinghaus (eds.), *Criminal Disenfranchisement in an International Perspective* (New York: Cambridge University Press, 2009).

The governments in these cases have justified CD by appealing to the abstract aims of punishing offenders and promoting civic responsibility and respect for the rule of law.[5] The literature has primarily focused upon the punitive argument for CD. However, underlying popular support for CD can also be found in the idea that the franchise is tied to some degree of *civic virtue*. This chapter engages with this latter idea, which is linked to the idea of a *regulative disenfranchisement* – the role of which is to negatively determine the scope of the electorate. According to this idea, which has gained support in the American debate about CD, it might be permissible for a democratic government to exclude offenders from the franchise for reasons grounded in their lack of *political capacity*. A well-known example of this kind of exclusion concerns children. Tracking the similarities between CD and the exclusion of children sustains a line of argument usually implied in discourses supporting the exclusion of offenders: they lack the capacity needed to engage in elections. Structuring this argument in a manner compatible with democratic principles requires the elaboration of a concept of political capacity sufficiently thin to avoid any suspicion of an *ideological use* of the franchise, but thick enough to include elements linked to the commission of a criminal offence.

However, this approach is flawed for the following reasons, which are developed in this chapter and have not yet been considered in the debate on regulative disenfranchisement. In a democracy, those who are subject to the law must also be considered as law-makers and the right to vote is a form of recognition that plays a fundamental role in the process of legitimation of the law.[6] Disenfranchising offenders with full cognitive capacity denies the character of deliberative persons in the political sphere (law-making process) while simultaneously affirming it in the legal realm (as subjects of the law). This denial cannot be explained in democratic terms; rather, it affirms, on the one hand, an exclusionary republican ambition, and on the other, an opportunity for the ideological use of the franchise requirements to exclude, disempower and marginalise certain citizens. In the terminology used by this volume, denying *citizenship* rights to criminals implies a denial of some important aspects of *personhood* and can be associated to a type of disrespect that may constitute some form of subaltern *subjectivity*.

The argument in this chapter follows the following structure. The first section reconstructs a civic virtue case for CD, discarding weaker arguments and focusing upon what can be called a Rawlsian argument for CD. The second section briefly reviews the reasons for the exclusion of children and

---

5 See, e.g., Ruvi Ziegler, 'Legal Outlier, Again? U.S. Felon Suffrage: Comparative and International Human Rights Perspectives,' *Boston University International Law Journal* 29 (2011), 221–38.
6 See Jürgen Habermas, *Between Facts and Norms* (Cambridge: The MIT Press, 1996).

argues that the case for children's electoral exclusion is only based upon the maintenance of the integrity of the election and not on their lack of capacity to vote. The third section criticises the civic virtue argument for CD on the grounds that criminals are even less vulnerable to an argument of regulative disenfranchisement based on civic virtue and concludes that reasons for disenfranchisement must therefore be located outside of a democratic framework.

The purity of the ballot box: between self-interest and civic virtue

One of the most historically important reasons for the justification of CD argues that the community holds a right to maintain *the purity of the ballot box*. This notion involves the belief that elections, as part of the general democratic process, are an extremely important aspect of community life, and therefore must not be contaminated by the lack of responsibility of unworthy or morally unsuitable elements of society.[7] This argument can assume two main forms. The first marks a concern with the way in which convicted offenders are going to vote. It is the *disruptive voting* argument. The second argument is drawn from *civic virtue* and focuses instead on offenders' lack of moral qualifications to undertake such an important civic duty. These will now be considered in turn.

Disruptive voting

Disruptive voting is an argument concerned with the impact of offender voting on the outcomes of the electoral process based on the expression of their political preferences. CD thus seeks to avoid disruptive voting by excluding those elements of the electorate that could erode and damage the current institutional configuration of the common good. They are natural candidates to be excluded because the way in which they intend to vote is presumed to be against the rule of law and democracy, selfish and factional, or with the aim of altering and weakening the content and administration of criminal law. It is also claimed that offenders would be diluting the vote of those law-abiding citizens, thereby disrespecting law-abiding citizens and cheapening the franchise, and that this might even call into question the moral authority of the electoral outcome.[8] Based on these

---

7 See John Kleining and Kevin Murtagh, 'Disenfranchising Felons,' *Journal of Applied Philosophy* 22 (2005), 225–6.
8 See, generally, Alec Ewald, 'An "Agenda for Demolition": The Fallacy and the Danger of the "Subversive Voting" Argument for Felony Disenfranchisement,' *Columbia Human Rights Law Review* 36 (2004) 109–43.

premises, CD is construed as a measure against the *abuse* of democracy, with the objective of protecting the rule of law.

This argument encounters three important problems, as presented by Alex Ewald: First, it depends on assumptions that are unlikely to be demonstrated. For example, the argument is premised upon the feasibility of rational, self-interested and instrumental political behaviour of offenders. Furthermore, it requires that they can collectively pursue an agenda around candidates and parties that are supportive of offenders' interests. Second, given that apathy is the major democratic illness, the act of casting the ballot has a deeply conservative meaning, which contributes to the renewal of the commitment of the individual to the legitimacy of the political system. Therefore, the exercise of the right to vote cannot be disruptive but can only contribute to guaranteeing the legitimacy of the law and, in doing so essentially work in the opposite direction to disruption. Third, there is wide agreement that the way in which a potential elector might vote cannot determine their participation in the political process. The prerogative of the electorate to select the relevant reasons to vote for the option of their preference is generally recognised.[9] As the participation of individuals in the law-making process is structured in terms of rights of participation, this prerogative can be reconstructed as a consequence of the legal nature of the right to vote. As legal rights, these rights are free of communicative obligations, because '[u]nlike morality, law cannot obligate its addressees to use individual rights in ways oriented to reaching understanding, even if political rights call for precisely this kind of public use'.[10] This formal character of the rights of political participation protects a person's autonomy against arbitrary interventions at the cost of making impossible any accountability of its orientation towards the common good. This is not necessarily opposed to the perspective that voting must be oriented by the use of public reason[11] but nevertheless restricts the implementation of that objective. We recognise a *right* to vote as belonging to our fellow citizens because one of the most important premises of democracy is that people disagree about the way in which we should organise society. Elections and voting are mechanisms designed to contribute to settling such disagreements,[12] and nobody should be excluded from the franchise because they hold different opinions.

Disenfranchisement, political capacity and civic virtue

If excluding offenders from elections cannot be justified based on the way in which they are going to vote, other justifications must explore different

---

9 Ibid. 124–32.
10 Habermas, *Between Facts and Norms*, 130.
11 See John Rawls, *Political Liberalism* (New York: Columbia University Press), 215, 219.
12 See John Rawls, *A Theory of Justice* (Oxford: Oxford University Press, 1999), 360.

routes. Observing the current system of electoral exclusions reveals that children and people with mental disabilities are not excluded from the franchise for that reason. The exclusion of these groups of people mainly focuses on their input to the electoral process rather than on any electoral outcome.[13] In other words, they are not excluded because of the way in which they are going to vote but because they cannot vote with the level of engagement the community expects. The concept of political capacity used to justify these exclusions rests upon the lack of some *cognitive* ability that is underdeveloped or in the process of being fully developed.[14] This constitutes a considerably *thin* concept of political capacity when compared with previous exclusionary requirements associated with wealth, character and social status, whose ideological use was directed to exclude minorities and marginal groups from access to political power.

However, there is no evidence that offenders are unable to act as rationally and autonomously as other adult individuals. In order to explore this issue, it is illuminating to compare the electoral capability rules and the criminal liability rules. One of the conditions for the justification of criminal punishment rests upon the capacity of adults to avoid committing criminal offences. This capacity is absent (or attenuated) in the case of children, which in turn explains their lack (or attenuation) of criminal liability. Whilst it may be affirmed that a lack of understanding of what is at stake in their conduct underlies both electoral and criminal incapacitation of children, this is evidently not the case with regard to adult offenders. There must be some symmetry regarding these capacities.[15] If offenders were not rational and autonomous, 'it would be irrational for us to hold them responsible for their criminal conduct in the first place'.[16] Therefore, cognitive capacity is not a sufficient justification for CD.

Another possibility for the justification of CD is to formulate a *thicker* concept of political capacity. An argument for such a conception of political capacity must disregard cognitive demands and instead focus on moral aspects of personality.[17] The natural candidate for this is the concept of *civic virtue*. This concept is normally linked to the republican idea of the virtuous citizen.[18] From this perspective, participation in public affairs is a fundamental responsibility of citizens. The common concern for the *res publica* is what

---

13 See Mhairi Cowden, 'Capacity, claims and children's rights,' *Contemporary Political Theory* 11:4 (2012) 362–7.
14 See Joanne Lau, 'Two Arguments for Child Enfranchisement,' *Political Studies* 60 (2012) 862.
15 See, e.g., Nicholas Munn, 'Reconciling the Criminal and Participatory Responsibilities of the Youth,' *Social Theory and Practice* 38:1 (2012) 139–59.
16 Michael Cholbi, 'A Felon's Right to Vote,' *Law and Philosophy* 21:4/5 (2002) 563.
17 See, e.g., Roger Clegg, 'Who Should Vote?' *Texas Review of Law and Politics* 6 (2002) 159–78.
18 See Judith Shklar, *American Citizenship: The Quest for Inclusion* (Cambridge, MA: Harvard University Press, 1991), 3–19.

permits the maintenance of liberty and pursuit of the common good. In these terms, the importance of politics correlates with the requirements to engage in it. This is the basis on which public participation is conceived 'not as rights but as a privilege attached to the satisfaction of a necessary responsibility'.[19] However, such a demanding conception is considerably problematic because it might require the disenfranchisement of a broader group of citizens. Moreover, a republican conception has been historically predisposed to justify an ideological use of the franchise. A civic republican concept of civic virtue was associated 'with the exclusion of blacks, women and the poor from the political process. In each of these cases, ascriptions of political incompetence rationalized the lines that were drawn'.[20]

In an effort to justify CD, Christopher Manfredi articulates a link between the character of offenders and some personality traits considered to display a lack of virtue. He argues that offenders have a character that is predominantly self-regarding, oriented towards the present moment and impulsive, and on the whole less empathetic than would be typical of other citizens. Criminal behaviour is associated with '1) rapid time discounting; 2) minimal internal verbal mediation; and 3) shallowly ingrained standards of behaviour'. This supposed character outline contrasts with the idea that political capacity involves a minimal civic virtue element as a component, which consists of 'empathy ("a willingness to take importantly into account the rights, needs, and feelings of others") and self-control ("a willingness to take importantly into account the more distant consequences of present actions")'.[21] The inability to develop behaviour displaying minimal civic virtue is, therefore, attributed to a psychological cause.

From a systematic perspective, this account gives shape to a twofold concept of political capacity, including cognitive and moral elements. The first, the incapacity to understand politics and act autonomously in elections, operates in the exclusion of children and people with severe mental disabilities. The second, related to civic virtue, might operate in the exclusion of adolescents and offenders. According to Manfredi, 'both groups generally exhibit unusually impulsive and self-centred behaviour that renders them temporarily unfit to exercise the political rights and responsibilities of citizenship'.[22] Adolescents, however, display similar levels of rationality and autonomy as the adult population. In addition to explaining CD, therefore, this two-fold conception of political capacity has the additional advantage

---

19 See John Deigh, 'On Rights and Responsibilities,' *Law and Philosophy* 7 (1988) 147–78.
20 Note, 'The Disenfranchisement of Ex-felons: Citizenship, Criminality, and "the Purity of the Ballot Box",' *Harvard Law Review* 102 (1989) 1308.
21 Christopher Manfredi, 'In Defence of Prisoner Disenfranchisement.' In Alec Ewald and Bryan Rottinghaus (eds.), *Criminal Disenfranchisement in an International Perspective* (New York: Cambridge University Press, 2009), 274–5.
22 Ibid. 275.

of articulating an argument to explain the denial of the right to vote to adolescents.[23] This proposal might sound unconvincing, especially in so far as it regards the empirically unproven psychological profile of offenders as integral to explaining their lack of civic virtue. It has, however, the quality of distinguishing between cognitive and moral aspects in the concept of political capacity.

A perhaps more solid philosophical foundation for this idea can be found within liberal ranks, in particular, in the Rawlsian concept of a sense of justice. He describes this notion as:

> the capacity to understand, to apply, and to act from the public conception of justice which characterizes the fair terms of social cooperation. [...] also express a willingness, if not the desire, to act in relation to others on terms that they also can publicly endorse.[24]

This capacity is what defines the status of an individual as a moral being and, as a consequence, gives grounds for a duty of mutual respect.[25] Rawls clearly maintains that different individuals might have varying capacities for a sense of justice and 'this fact is not a reason for depriving those with a lesser capacity of the full protection of justice'.[26] But what happens to those who do not qualify for that minimum? Rawls observes the anomaly of crime and punishment in a just society:

> It is true that in a reasonable well-ordered society those who are punished for violating just laws have normally done something wrong. This is because the purpose of the criminal law is to uphold basic natural duties [...] and punishments are to serve this end.[27]

When these cases of dissonance arise, Rawls insists upon approaching them as individual deviations rather than social problems: 'a propensity to commit such [criminal] acts is a mark of bad character'.[28] The contempt that some crimes express for the basic values of mutual respect upon which our societies are based calls for the evaluation of the moral status of those engaged in such behaviour. Rawls insists that the absence of a sense of justice would struggle to be compatible with certain fundamental attitudes

---

23 See, e.g., Daniel Hart and Robert Atkins, 'American Sixteen and Seventeen year olds are Ready to Vote,' *The Annals of the American Academy of Political and Social Science* (2011) 201–22.
24 Rawls, *Political Liberalism*, 19.
25 See Rawls, *A Theory of Justice*, 337.
26 Ibid. 443.
27 Ibid. 276.
28 Ibid. 277.

and capacities included under the notion of humanity.[29] This statement has a solid exclusionary implication when it is linked to his acknowledgment that certain individuals act in a manner that is not compatible with the principles of reciprocity with which reasonable people can easily identify. The conclusion that Rawls offers in relation to those who are not willing to act according to the principles of justice is revealing in this respect:

> It is, of course, true that in their case just arrangements do not fully answer to their *nature*, and therefore, other things equal, they will be less happy than they would be if they could affirm their sense of justice. But here one can only say: *their nature is their misfortune*.[30]

In sum, the commission of an offence shows that offenders lack the sense of justice normally associated with reasonable people. This is not, however, sufficient to justify CD from a Rawlsian perspective. Evidently, Rawls himself never endorsed it. Moreover, he shows an explicit commitment to a concept of participation that has the role of enhancing the self-esteem and sense of political competence of citizens.[31] However, what is at stake is not whether Rawls himself endorsed CD but rather how his ideas are supportive of it.[32]

Jesse Furman has critically sketched a Rawlsian case for CD by associating the aforementioned attribution of bad character with Rawls' express commitment to participation and civic virtue. Rawls agreed that 'if the citizens of a democratic society are to preserve their basic rights and liberties [...] they must also have to a sufficient degree the "political virtues" [...] and be willing to take part in the public life'.[33] Furman's argument contrasts a commitment to the civic virtues of citizens in a democracy with an understanding of the offender as a defectively motivated subject. He suggests that disenfranchising those who have openly shown themselves to lack a sense of justice and the motivation to respect their fellow citizens would not be a suppressive measure. Rather, it would be a step towards democratic self-protection, or in Rawlsian terminology, towards 'the stability and welfare of a just order'.[34]

---

29 Ibid. 488.
30 Ibid. 504 (emphasis added).
31 Ibid. 1999: 203–6.
32 See, e.g., Mary Sigler, 'Defensible Disenfranchisement,' *Iowa Law Review* 99 (2014) 1725–44.
33 Rawls, *Political Liberalism*, 205.
34 Jason Furman, 'Political Illiberalism: The Paradox of Disenfranchisement and the Ambivalences of Rawlsian Justice,' *Yale Law Journal* 106 (1997) 1225.

Disenfranchisement as (electoral) incapacitation

It is certainly difficult to reconcile Rawls' moral argument regarding the lack of a sense of justice with that of Manfredi describing the self-regarding, impulsive, less empathetic psychological profile of offenders. Despite their differences, however, a connection can be traced between these ideas: those who have committed a criminal offence are understood as defective and that defect is related to their (in)capacity to understand social relations in just terms, a proven defect in (psychological or moral) motivation for the respect of fellow citizens and their rights.

A concept of civic virtue such as this might avoid: (i) the problems of output regarding issues presented by disruptive voting; (ii) a thicker concept of republican civic responsibility, proven to be prone to an ideological abuse of the franchise; and (iii) an expansive concept of cognitive capacity which explains CD by assimilating offenders and children. This concept, according to its defenders, might be able to begin from the premise of universal suffrage and offers an exception to it that satisfies both a requirement of universality (the exception is applied to everyone independently of any irrelevant personal feature such as wealth or birth) and that of the burden of proof (relevant reasons must be offered to justify the exclusion).[35] The exclusion is based on an abstract and universal standard of political capacity applied to everybody; law-abiding citizens have passed the test that offenders have failed.[36]

If the rationale of CD is purely regulative, its institutional characteristics might be importantly influenced by that fact. First, the lack of civic virtue can more easily be argued by appealing to a general unwillingness to respect the law rather than to the commission of a single crime. Therefore, it would be advisable to limit its application only to convicted recidivists. Second, it also seems easier to argue that civic virtue is lacking in cases involving more serious crimes, those that 'cast greater doubt on an offender's commitment to a community's public values',[37] as opposed to more common and minor crimes.[38] These two elements might make CD completely independent of the fact of imprisonment.[39] Third, regarding the restoration process, this should not be automatic after a certain period of time. As CD performs an incapacitating role, the political capacity which originally justified exclusion from the franchise 'should require an affirmative effort on the part

---

35 See Manfredi, 'In Defence of Prisoner Disenfranchisement,' 272.
36 cf Susan Easton, 'The Prisoner's Right to Vote and Civic Responsibility: Reaffirming the Social Contract?,' *Probation Journal* 56 (2009) 226–7.
37 Sigler, 'Defensible Disenfranchisement,' 1741.
38 See Beckman, *The Frontiers of Democracy*, 139.
39 cf Sigler, 'Defensible Disenfranchisement,' 1741–3.

of offenders',[40] for example, 'by conforming their conduct to the law for a period of time'.[41] Explaining CD in terms of incapacitation certainly requires that the standard of capacity in turn fits the institutional design of a measure of incapacitation.

Children voting

As just described, any argument based upon civic virtue is unsatisfactory from the point of view of democracy as a justification for CD, even when the noted institutional restrictions are in place. This is so because civic virtue cannot be a requirement for participation in a democracy, if democracy is understood as a project of self-government. Those disenfranchised offenders are treated merely as subjects of the law but with no participation in the law-making process. For the purpose of exposing the problems affecting the argument of civic virtue as a special case of the requirements for political capacity, it may be illustrative to begin with a comparison with the electoral exclusion of children.

The electoral exclusion of children

The widely held idea that children must be excluded from the franchise due to their lack of political capacity has been challenged by the literature in recent years, producing an exhaustive analysis. The exclusion of children can be approached from two perspectives. The first approach questions the universality of the standard by which children are excluded. The presumption of capacity for adults and incapacity for minors evidently leads to the inclusion of people that do not satisfy those standards and the exclusion of people fully prepared to carry out electoral tasks.[42] In the case of offenders, problems of under- and over-inclusiveness are especially in evidence.[43]

A second perspective observes that when other rules concerning the legal capacity of children are implemented, it is apparent that their incapacity only becomes relevant when either children themselves or a third party are in danger of being harmed by the children's conduct. Legal capacity rules are protective measures. From this perspective, the argument concerning the political capacity of children, as for that of offenders, lacks precision regarding what kind of harm must be prevented by electoral exclusion, instead focusing on other aspects of their incapacities.

---

40 Ibid. 1743.
41 Ibid. 1742.
42 See, e.g., Lau, 'Two Arguments for Child Enfranchisement'.
43 See, e.g., Heather Lardy, 'Prisoner Disenfranchisement: Constitutional Rights and Wrongs,' *Public Law* (2002) 532.

Capacity and harm in children's voting

Those activities from which children are excluded are not generally forbidden to adults because it is presumed that adults understand what is at stake in their conduct and therefore can deal with serious and dangerous activities responsibly. However, for a child to be legally excluded from certain activities both requirements must be satisfied: the activities must be potentially harmful and the subject must show that he is incapable of understanding what is really at stake in his conduct.[44] This two-fold approach to children's capacity rules enables us to consider their exclusion from the ballot box by setting out two questions: first, can children understand what is at stake in elections? Second, what is protected by the exclusion of people that do not understand what is at stake in an election?

The first question can lead to endless inquiry if considered in empirical terms. Experts have not reached agreement regarding the capacity of children. For example, following Hart and Atkins, it can be observed that contemporary discussions on children's capacity reveal a plurality of views: some suggest that it is not clear that adults have a rational capacity superior to that of children, especially adolescents,[45] or that the cognitive development of children concludes at age 16;[46] others suggest that the differences between adolescents and adults reside in discrete spheres such as pair relations and risky activities which do not allow one to justify differences in political capacity, or that children can identify principles of justice as early as six years old.[47] Conceiving capacity in empirical terms implies that the *fairness* of the requirements is achieved if they apply equally to the entire universe of subjects that *empirically* show similar levels of relevant understanding. It seeks to avoid over- and under-inclusiveness. It is evident that a two-year-old child does not have the cognitive capacity to, for example, understand politics and what is at stake in elections. However, nor does anything exceptional occur in relation to knowledge and reasoning when people turn 18 and therefore are qualified to vote. The cognitive capacity to understand voting is acquired at some point during development and it is acquired differently and at different times by different subjects. To be

---

44 According to this reasoning, children are usually permitted to engage in complex activities even if they are not equipped to understand their significance so long as no harm can be caused. At the same time, adults cannot generally be impeded from performing harmful activities for reasons related to their capacity. The legal rules of capacity commonly account for these effects as they differ between infants and adolescents, the former being completely prevented from carrying out dangerous activities and the latter being authorised to conduct activities involving a certain degree of danger due to a major development in their capacity to understand.
45 See Hart and Atkins, 'American Sixteen'.
46 Ibid. 218.
47 Ibid. 206.

sure, there is significant disagreement about exactly *when* this happens, to a great extent due to the fact that there is also significant disagreement about *what* is being investigated. However, this is not the only way to approach capacity requirements.

In normative terms, capacity requirements are a way of setting expectations and distributing responsibilities by recognising legal personality. When approached normatively, the *fairness* of the regulation is not achieved by demonstrating the coincidence of people's empirical and normative status but through the coherent treatment of people in all aspects of their legal personality. Somebody cannot be treated as capable of some affairs and incapable of other affairs which involve similar skills, degrees of understanding or the exercise of similar kinds of mental processes. For example, it is completely anomalous that subjects who are fully criminally liable – that is, whose conduct can form the object of condemnation – do not also possess the legal capacity to conduct their private business or get married. It is also anomalous that somebody who is allowed to work and earn a salary cannot be granted the right to financial independence. From that perspective, if the recognition of political capacity is tied to the recognition of other aspects of deliberative personality, the exclusion of children from elections might be coherent with their position within the legal system. Accordingly, it seems that the main argument supporting the reduction of the voting age is not based on empirical studies but on the corresponding attribution of legal responsibilities to minors, a fact that can be observed in private law and criminal and labour spheres.[48] To put it briefly, the expectation of morally autonomous behaviour cannot be directed solely at the constitution of minors as subjects of the law, but must also have a correlation in the construction of minors as responsible individuals, citizens and legal persons. Private and public spheres of autonomy are based on the same moral status and therefore cannot be radically dissociated.

What is the problem with children voting?

Nevertheless, the question remains with regard to the reason behind the exclusion of children from the political process. Even if they are not recognised as capable, their exclusion can only be justified on the basis of a potential harm. Arguments that only point out their incapacity miss this point. For example, to sustain that 'children and insane adults ought not in general have voting rights', because 'they are not able, through participation, to advance [their] interests',[49] fails to explain the problem generated

---

48 See Munn, 'Reconciling the Criminal'.
49 Thomas Christiano, *The Constitution of Equality* (Oxford: Oxford University Press, 2008), 129 note 33.

by their participation. Three responses have been offered to explain this problem.

First, it has been argued that children's electoral exclusion is for their own benefit: the best interests of the child require electoral exclusion because political participation would be harmful for them. The right to vote would involve the need to assume important responsibilities, which could in turn bring about stress and psychological costs that it is in their best interests to avoid. If the converse were true, they would be able to develop activities appropriate to their age, such as play and study.[50] This argument seems unconvincing unless the right to vote is conceived of as a legal obligation, as is the case in some jurisdictions. The argument appears more relevant when applied to the exercise of other political rights that children must exercise that may be more demanding than that of the right to vote.[51]

A second line of reasoning suggests that the exclusion of children protects the public from their political incompetence. The participation of incompetent electors would compromise the electoral outcome and therefore must be avoided.[52] This is also unconvincing: on the one hand, because the rationality of elections is given by the electoral offer, and not by the electoral demand. An incompetent electorate would not necessarily harm the outcome of elections through arbitrarily affecting a political option because this would presuppose a consistent vote from those regarded incompetent and whose exclusion is defensible solely on the basis that they lack a rational capacity to be consistent. Hence, this is a self-defeating reason. On the other hand, even if children are assumed to vote randomly, their participation would not alter the outcome of a real election in a relevant manner unless the majority of the voters were also incompetent.[53] Summing up, even including people with little or no political knowledge, a precarious rationality or impulsive behaviour does not affect electoral results in any way which is relevant.[54]

The third reason for excluding children from elections is more abstract. It holds that excluding children is a requirement for protecting political equality, as expressed through the equal value of the vote. Claudio López-Guerra has suggested this idea by affirming that the exclusion of children is not demanded by the *justice of allocation* of the right to vote, according to which 'all members of the polity who have the capacity to enjoy the

---

50 See Beckman, *The Frontiers of Democracy*, 114–9.
51 See Claudio López-Guerra, 'Enfranchising Minors and the Mentally Impaired,' *Social Theory and Practice* 38:1 (2010), 130–1.
52 See, e.g., Jason Brennan, 'The Right to a Competent Electorate,' *The Philosophical Quarterly* 61 (2011), 700–24.
53 See Robert Goodin and Joanne Lau. 'Enfranchising Incompetents: Suretyship and the Joint Authorship of Law.' *Ratio* (new series) 24 (2011) 154–66.
54 See López–Guerra, 'Enfranchising Minors,' 117–23.

benefits of enfranchisement (or experience the harm of disenfranchisement) should have the right to an equal vote', and 'the exclusion of those who lack the said capacity is *permitted but not necessary*'.[55] Instead, the necessity of their exclusion is a demand of the *operation* of the electoral process. Children, whose participation is not necessary but not prohibited, could damage the integrity of elections and the principle of political equality because they can be *instructed* by a third party, and therefore, like buying a vote, their vote could grant somebody more votes than their due share.[56]

The previous observations allow an understanding of the relevance of the exclusion of children, albeit *only* to some of them, not as a guarantee of good quality in the outcome of elections but as a way of maintaining the integrity of the election. These observations, at the same time, will contribute to an appreciation of the specific position of the demands of civic virtue as a justification for offenders' exclusion.

Civic virtue under examination

The theory of *disruptive voting* must be regarded as a case of the ideological use or abuse of the requirements of the franchise. What remains from it is the construction of a power-relation. It will be argued in this section that the demand for civic virtue as an eligibility requirement is no different. That is, when its premises are examined carefully, we find the same kind of impermissible argument. To demonstrate this, the scheme of analysis for the exclusion of children can be used to analyse the case of CD. The first question is therefore related to capacity, while the second is related to the harm that could be caused.

Do offenders really lack political capacity?

It has already been noted that defenders of this argument accept that offenders possess the cognitive capacity to understand what is at stake in elections and therefore are in a different position, in this regard, to children. It was also claimed that someone's political intentions, or the way in which he or she intends to vote, belongs to the sphere of protected autonomy and therefore cannot be used as a reason for exclusion. Contrary to these cases, what is alleged here is not that the vote is rationally outcome-motivated, in the sense of being aimed at furthering criminal interests, but that the vote is morally defective. For example, Mary Sigler's argument for CD is based on the presumption that by the commission of a serious offence, offenders unveil their lack of compromise with the 'public values that constitute the

---

55 López–Guerra, 'Enfranchising Minors,' 124 (emphasis added).
56 Ibid. 131–3.

political community'.⁵⁷ It serves as a test to connect the moral wrong of the crime and the expectation that such person would not vote in a morally motivated way according to a *public use of reason*. Thus, in a society that values virtuous participation, offenders must be excluded from voting.

The principal weakness of this argument is the clear inconsistency between the claim of responsibility implied by the punishment and the contradictory attribution of a lack of capacity in relation to elections. If the criminal conviction is an act of condemnation, the subject to which the crime is attributed must be recognised as holding the powers of a moral person. This responsibility constitutes recognition of the expectation of law-abidingness on the person's part, rooted in the inclusion of that person *qua* citizen in the democratic process. A criminal offence, in contrast, is constitutive of a disappointment of this normative expectation.

If what is expressed through a criminal conviction is condemnation, it must be acknowledged that offenders possess the moral capacity to be challenged by such a condemnation. Offenders are recognised by the criminal law, and by the legal system as a whole, as equipped with these kinds of moral capacities. Even during the time an offender is serving a prison sentence, the legal system continues to consider him a legal person, maintaining its expectation that the subject will conform his behaviour to the law. Offenders are recognised and treated, through their status as legal persons, as moral persons. Otherwise, total incapacitation, isolation or surveillance would be the only response to the commission of a serious offence. Notice the contrast with those individuals who lack *cognitive* capacities, in which case the commission of a serious offence is followed not by a punishment but by incapacitation measures, such as those provided by mental institutions.⁵⁸

Given that an offender is deemed responsible for not acting according to a sense of justice for which he is cognitively and morally equipped, it follows that he must be deemed cognitively and morally equipped to make political choices. This is so because what guarantees the fairness of capacity requirements is a certain coherent treatment of people in every aspect of their legal personalities.⁵⁹ As a result of their exclusion from the franchise, offenders are regarded as autonomous persons in the legal sphere, according to which they can be held legally accountable, but they are not considered autonomous in the political sphere. This provokes a serious democratic problem. Those affected by CD are not in the position to understand their

---

57 Sigler, 'Defensible Disenfranchisement,' 1735.
58 See Andrew Von Hirsch and Martin Wasik, 'Civil Disqualifications Attending Conviction: A Suggested Conceptual Framework,' *Cambridge Law Journal* 56:3 (1997) 599–626.
59 cf Cholbi, 'A Felon's Right to Vote,' 561.

duty to follow the law as a result of a process of production of democratic legitimacy, but their reasons are reduced to threat of punishment.

What is the problem with offenders voting?

Even if it is accepted that civic virtue is a requirement to vote that sets different standards of participation compared to those which apply to persons exercising their right of autonomy, excluding offenders on the grounds of their lack of political capacity is still not sufficient. It must be demonstrated that there is a harm to be avoided by their exclusion. Due to their similarities, it is useful to compare the presumptive harm of offenders voting with the reasons offered for excluding children.

First, to be sure, there is nothing in CD that can further the interests of offenders, even when it is claimed that it could facilitate their process of rehabilitation.[60] Second, the putative damage to the outcome of the election must be also discarded.[61] Offenders are not incompetent voters, and even if they are considered as such, that would not justify their exclusion. The remaining option is that the outcome might be compromised because offenders will consistently vote in support of some of the electoral offers. In that case, there are two possibilities: First, that their exclusion is based on the presumption that they vote rationally and motivated by self-interest, which might lead us back to the problems facing disruptive voting. Second, the idea that their morally defective vote must be linked to a moral judgment of the political options they support is also difficult to defend; it cannot be argued that allowing offenders to vote would transmit their criminality, for example, the contempt they have shown for the victims, to the law-making process.[62] In this way, it can be seen how the demands of civic virtue is expelled by the democratic logic. Third, it could be affirmed that offender voting affects the integrity of the elections or the principle of political equality. This would lead back to some primitive versions of *the purity of the ballot box* in which CD is justified as preventive of the commission of electoral offences or conflicts of interests between elected authorities and organised crime structures.[63] Indeed, the opposite seems to be the case. Political equality is affected not by offenders voting but by governments that unfairly exclude offenders from the franchise.

---

60 See, e.g., Sigler, 'Defensible Disenfranchisement,' 1738–40. Jeff Manza and Christopher Uggen, *Locked Out: Felon Disenfranchisement and American Democracy* (New York: Oxford University Press, 2006), 124ff.
61 See Claudio López-Guerra, *Democracy and Disenfranchisement: The Morality of Electoral Exclusions* (New York: Oxford University Press, 2014), 112.
62 Ibid. 114.
63 See, e.g., Ewald, 'An "Agenda for Demolition",' 117–8.

Concluding remarks

This chapter has observed that the idea of civic virtue, even when presented in a minimal version and apparently compatible with other current electoral exclusions, cannot successfully explain CD as a form of electoral incapacitation – at least not in a manner that is compatible with democracy as self-government. Against the constitutive democratic importance of the right to vote, the practice of CD presents a serious democratic problem: it conflicts with the central democratic principle that the addressees of the law must have rights to participate in the process of law-making. That is why we are granted a fundamental right to vote. It was demonstrated that children and offenders stand as separate groups with regard to arguments for excluding them from the franchise. The exclusion of children is justified on the basis of the protection of the electoral process, while the exclusion of offenders cannot be justified on any reasonable ground linked to political capacity.

But considering civic virtue as a requirement of voting implies something more substantial than a mere regulation of such a right. It implies not just the denial of the vote for offenders but the denial of their public personality; the capacity to participate in collective government. CD thus implies their reduction and degradation to a second class of citizens. The exclusion of those who lack the necessary value, moral authority or worthiness might contribute to *elevate* democratic politics in the eyes of the law-abiding citizens, expressing the value of the activity of public participation. Serving as a reminder of the *privilege* and *the moral character* involved in democratic activities, it highlights the meaning of the vote and a dimension of the franchise that is hidden by the universalisation of political rights. Behind these advantages, however, lurk more sinister exclusionary dimensions: CD defenders might 'think, talk and act as if those who commit crimes [...] should not be seen and treated as our fellow citizens [...] but form a distinct and lower class or category of being'[64] from whom they must distinguish themselves and protect against. This is a kind of social dynamic, latent in every democracy, which has the power to change the character of our communities if we do not fight against it.[65]

Bibliography

Beckman, Ludvig. *The Frontiers of Democracy. The Right to Vote and its Limits*. London: Palgrave Macmillan, 2009.
Blais, André, Massicotte, Louis and Yoshinaka, Antoine. 'Deciding who has the Right to Vote: A Comparative Analysis of Election Laws,' *Electoral Studies* 20 (2001) 41–62.

---

64 Anthony Duff, 'Punishment, Dignity and Degradation,' *Oxford Journal of Legal Studies* 25:1 (2005), 154.
65 See Pablo Marshall, *Criminal Disenfranchisement: A Debate on Punishment Citizenship and Democracy* (PhD Dissertation, University of Glasgow, 2015), 222–81.

Brennan, Jason. 'The Right to a Competent Electorate,' *The Philosophical Quarterly* 61 (2011) 700–24.
Cholbi, Michael. 'A Felon's Right to Vote,' *Law and Philosophy* 21:4/5 (2002) 543–65.
Christiano, Thomas. *The Constitution of Equality*. Oxford: Oxford University Press, 2008.
Clegg, Roger. 'Who Should Vote?' *Texas Review of Law and Politics* 6 (2002) 159–78.
Cowden, Mhairi. 'Capacity, Claims and Children's Rights,' *Contemporary Political Theory* 11:4 (2012) 362–80.
Deigh, John. 'On Rights and Responsibilities.' *Law and Philosophy* 7 (1988) 147–78.
Duff, Anthony. 'Punishment, Dignity and Degradation,' *Oxford Journal of Legal Studies* 25:1 (2005) 141–55.
Easton, Susan. 'The Prisoner's Right to Vote and Civic Responsibility: Reaffirming the Social Contract?' *Probation Journal* 56 (2009) 224–37.
Ewald, Alec 'An "Agenda for Demolition": The Fallacy and the Danger of the "Subversive Voting" Argument for Felony Disenfranchisement,' *Columbia Human Rights Law Review* 36 (2004) 109–43.
Ewald, Alec, and Bryan Rottinghaus (eds.). *Criminal Disenfranchisement in an International Perspective*. New York: Cambridge University Press, 2009.
Furman, Jason. 'Political Illiberalism: The Paradox of Disenfranchisement and the Ambivalences of Rawlsian Justice,' *Yale Law Journal* 106 (1997) 1197–231.
Goodin, Robert and Joanne Lau. 'Enfranchising Incompetents: Suretyship and the Joint Authorship of Law,' *Ratio* (new series) 24 (2011) 154–66.
Habermas, Jürgen. *Between Facts and Norms*. Cambridge, MA: The MIT Press, 1996.
Hart, Daniel, and Robert Atkins. 'American Sixteen and Seventeen year olds are Ready to Vote,' *The Annals of the American Academy of Political and Social Science* (2011) 201–22.
Kleining, John, and Kevin Murtagh. 'Disenfranchising Felons,' *Journal of Applied Philosophy* 22 (2005) 217–39.
Lardy, Heather. 'Prisoner Disenfranchisement: Constitutional Rights and Wrongs,' *Public Law* (2002) 524–45.
Lau, Joanne. 'Two Arguments for Child Enfranchisement,' *Political Studies* 60 (2012) 860–76.
López-Guerra, Claudio. 'Enfranchising Minors and the Mentally Impaired.' *Social Theory and Practice* 38:1 (2010) 115–38.
López-Guerra, Claudio. *Democracy and Disenfranchisement: The Morality of Electoral Exclusions*. New York: Oxford University Press, 2014.
Manfredi, Christopher. 'In Defence of Prisoner Disenfranchisement.' In A. Ewald and B. Rottinghaus (eds.), *Criminal Disenfranchisement in an International Perspective*. New York: Cambridge University Press, 2009, 259–80.
Manza, Jeff and Christopher Uggen. *Locked Out: Felon Disenfranchisement and American Democracy*. New York: Oxford University Press, 2006.
Marshall, Pablo. *Criminal Disenfranchisement: A Debate on Punishment Citizenship and Democracy* (PhD Dissertation, University of Glasgow, 2015).
Munn, Nicholas. 'Reconciling the Criminal and Participatory Responsibilities of the Youth,' *Social Theory and Practice* 38:1 (2012) 139–59.
Note. 'The Disenfranchisement of Ex-felons: Citizenship, Criminality, and "the Purity of the Ballot Box",' *Harvard Law Review* 102 (1989) 1300–17.
Rawls, John. *Political Liberalism*. New York: Columbia University Press, 1996.

Rawls, John. *A Theory of Justice.* Oxford: Oxford University Press, 1999.
Shklar, Judith. N. *American Citizenship: The Quest for Inclusion.* Cambridge, MA: Harvard University Press, 1991.
Sigler, Mary. 'Defensible Disenfranchisement,' *Iowa Law Review* 99 (2014) 1725–44.
Von Hirsch, Andrew and Martin Wasik. 'Civil Disqualifications Attending Conviction: A Suggested Conceptual Framework,' *Cambridge Law Journal* 56:3 (1997) 599–626.
Ziegler, Ruvi. 'Legal Outlier, Again? U.S. Felon Suffrage: Comparative and International Human Rights Perspectives.' *Boston University International Law Journal* 29 (2011) 197–266.

Chapter 4

'Electoral shenanigans'
The constituted electorate, the constituent people, and the porous state

Panu Minkkinen

Introduction

A 'constitutional moment',[1] to borrow the term coined by the American constitutional lawyer Bruce Ackerman, is a historical rupture in the continuity of a constitutional tradition when the constituted relationships between institutions change without the conventional lawmaking process. So a 'moment' understood as an individual episode may, for example, weaken the legislature in relation to the executive, or vice versa. This short chapter focuses on such moments in so far as they can be understood as constituent interventions into constituted institutions. The essay will focus on the role of 'the people' as the popular sovereign and its ability to exercise its democratic powers free of the restraints imposed by its constituted competence as the electorate. The argument will be illuminated by a reading of the novel *Seeing* by the Portuguese Nobel laureate José Saramago.[2] Although the novel is well known, I will recapitulate its opening scene here in so far as it is relevant for the main argument of this short essay.[3]

---

1 Bruce A. Ackerman, *We the People. Vol 1. Foundations* (Cambridge, MA: Belknap Press, 1991).
2 The novel was first published in 2004. For this chapter, the English translation by Margaret Jull Costa is used: Saramago, *Seeing*, London: Harvill Secker, 2006.
3 On Saramago and the law, see also Joana Aguiar e Silva, 'Is Justice for Sale? Further Readings on Saramago and the Law', *No Foundations: An Interdisciplinary Journal of Law and Justice*, 11 (2014), 94–115; Maria Aristodemou, 'Democracy or Your Life! Knowledge, Ignorance and the Politics of Atheism in Saramago's Blindness and Seeing', *Law, Culture and the Humanities*, 9:1 (2013), 169–87; Sandra M. Wierzba, 'Saramago's *Death with Interruptions*: A Path to Reconsider Essential Dilemmas Linked to Health Law', *Oñati Socio-legal Series*, 4:6 (2014), 1241–53. On constitutional theory and literature, see also Panu Minkkinen, 'The Juridical Romanticism of Friedrich Dürrenmatt's *The Execution of Justice*', in Matilda Arvidsson, Leila Brännström and Panu Minkkinen (eds.) *The Contemporary Relevance of Carl Schmitt. Law, Politics, Theology* (Abingdon: Routledge, 2016) 78–90.

The narrative

The author of the novel does not disclose the name of the country in which his story is set. But from the hyperbolically detailed and idiósyncratically punctuated description of the events, the reader might well be persuaded to infer that we are in some kind of pseudo-democracy not too unlike Saramago's native Portugal, or the *Estado Novo*, before the 1974 Carnation Revolution. The military is continuously present in the background as an ally of the right-wing government, and the hierarchic nature of the country's political institutions is made obvious by the culture of fear and formality that seems to permeate all government business.

The narrative begins on a Sunday when municipal elections are held in the country. The opening scenes take place early in the morning at number 14 of the capital's 44 polling stations where government appointed officials are preparing for their task of organising the elections. These electoral officials include the presiding officer, his deputy, a secretary, a number of poll clerks, and representatives from the three political parties that are running for office in these elections. The representatives from 'the party on the right', 'the party on the left' and 'the party in the middle', barely distinguishable from each other, are caricatured as being more concerned with the ideological appropriateness of the empty phraseology that they use than with politics itself.

The one thing that has made this particular election day special is the weather. It has namely been raining unusually heavily. It had started to rain already the previous day, and it has even caused floods and landslips. And so a high 'abstention rate'[4] – meaning presumably low turnout in this case – is to be expected even if the representative of the governing right-wing party is sure that a 'high sense of civic duty'[5] will eventually get the electorate on its feet even in such horrendous weather. When the doors of the polling station are opened, not a single voter is there to witness how the presiding officer, in accordance with the law and to prevent all 'electoral shenanigans',[6] opens the ballot box to confirm and to verify that it is empty. After this the presiding officer and his colleagues all vote. But still no one else is in sight.

An hour has passed, and by now the presiding officer has grown anxious about the no-show. At the suggestion of his secretary he calls the ministry of the interior to enquire about the situation at other polling stations because not a single voter has shown up here. The ministry confirms in response that the situation is similar all over the capital city, whereas elsewhere elections

---

4 Saramago, *Seeing*, 2.
5 Ibid. 2.
6 Ibid. 3.

have begun normally, strangely enough even in parts of the country where the weather is just as bad as it is here. So something odd is clearly happening. Once again at the initiative of the rather practically minded secretary, one by one the electoral officials call their nearest and dearest to make sure that at least they would be coming to fulfil their civic duty.

An hour later the first voter finally arrives, and then ten minutes or so later a second, and a third, and so on. Although voters are now beginning to arrive, there are never enough of them to form any kind of queue even if the electoral officials deliberately take their time to verify identities and to make the required notes on the electoral rolls. By midday the clouds are beginning to break up, but even when it finally stops raining, the very modest flow of voters does not seem to change. And so:

> nothing seemed to indicate that the civic hopes of the presiding officer would be satisfactorily fulfilled by a ballot box in which, so far, the votes barely covered the bottom. All those present were thinking the same thing, the election so far had been a terrible political failure.[7]

So at this point we are still talking about the embarrassment of a low electoral turnout that would rid the government of the formal legitimation that it needs to pursue its policies. Saramago clearly depicts these as sham elections in the sense that they have no real substantive meaning even though the formal procedures guaranteeing the integrity of the electoral process itself are vigilantly observed. Whoever wins, the three parties all prioritise self-interest above everything else, and the only thing that sets them apart is the delusive rhetoric that they use to justify their partisan self-interest. On the other hand, in the rhetoric used by all supposedly non-political government officials, these factually meaningless and formal elections are coupled with the pomp of representative democracy depicting participation as a 'civic duty'. In other words, voting in meaningless elections is the normative obligation of every eligible citizen, and so a low turnout, which is what seems to be happening here, can always be blamed on a morally suspect electorate.

Suddenly, at 4pm, 'an hour which is neither late nor early, neither fish nor fowl',[8] all those voters who have for whatever reason stayed at home up until then begin arriving at the polling stations of the capital city. They arrive in swarms. A sigh of relief is let out by the officials both at polling station number 14 and at other government offices where the situation has been followed with some unease. In fact, by the time that voting is supposed to end, there are still so many people queueing outside the polling stations that the ministry must extend the official deadline, first by two hours, and

---

7 Ibid. 12.
8 Ibid. 13.

later by a further half an hour in order to allow everyone who had made it inside by then to exercise their right to vote.

And so 'democracy had every reason to celebrate'.[9] Or so it at least seems. After the doors are closed, the officials at polling station number 14 begin doing what officials at every polling station are required to do by law. They empty the ballot papers from their boxes and begin the arduous task of counting the votes. The counting only finishes past midnight. And the results are quite astonishing:

> The number of valid votes did not quite reach twenty-five percent, with the party on the right winning thirteen percent, the party in the middle nine percent and the party on the left two and a half percent. There were very few spoiled ballots and very few abstentions. All the others, more than seventy percent of the total votes cast, were blank.[10]

Although voting has gone normally in other parts of the country, this unprecedented result is repeated at all polling stations in the capital city. The inexplicable voting anomaly triggers at least three different types of reactions. First, because the anomaly is limited to the capital city, the announcement of the results is immediately followed by scornful glee from the country's peripheries, not necessarily ridiculing the citizens who had cast blank votes, but more jeering at the central government that had begun celebrating the sudden turn in the electoral turnout too soon. Second, all three political parties begin to feverishly explain how and why the freak phenomenon can be interpreted as a mandate from the electorate especially to them and as a victory for the policies that they specifically represent. Third, the uneasiness that the result causes in the government, and the political machinery more generally, produces wild speculation as to what will and should follow: an annulment of the results and new elections, this time carefully orchestrated with media campaigns and the like so as to prevent anything like this happening again, or the suspension of all constitutional guarantees through a state of emergency in order to just wait until the dust settles, or simply to bite the bullet and do nothing.

Broadly interpreting a law on how to proceed when natural disasters hinder elections, the government opts for new elections in the capital city to be held eight days after the first. In announcing the new elections, the prime minister added that:

> the government was sure that the capital's population, when called upon to vote again, would exercise their civic duty with the dignity and decorum they had always shown in the past, thus declaring null and

9 Ibid. 15.
10 Ibid. 16.

void the regrettable event during which, for reasons that have yet to be clarified, but into which investigations are already fairly well advanced, the usual clear judgement of the city's electorate had become unexpectedly confused and distorted.[11]

'Electoral shenanigans', indeed!

Come Sunday, and the weather is excellent. Voters begin queueing up at the polling stations already early in the morning even before the doors are opened. But the results of the previous elections have made the government uneasy. So each queue is infiltrated by spies trying to uncover the reasons behind the odd electoral behaviour as well as the individuals responsible for it. But nothing out of the ordinary is detected. The government authorities are worried, about two things in particular. First, even if a seemingly good turnout this time around would be welcome, one would, all the same, also hope to see a decent percentage of abstentions. An overly enthusiastic electorate would simply be exchanging one anomaly for another. What is desperately needed is a return to normality. Second, and perhaps more worryingly, the voters are unusually unresponsive to the questions presented to them at exit polls. Not only is there a clearly detectable unwillingness to disclose how one has voted, but this behaviour is oddly uniform in different parts of the city even though the likelihood of someone being able to coordinate something like this is practically speaking non-existent.

Later that evening after the votes of this second election have been counted, a resigned prime minister appears on television to announce how his greatest fears have materialised with 'the party on the right, eight percent, the party in the middle, eight percent, the party on the left, one percent, abstentions, none, spoiled votes, none, blank votes, eighty-three percent'[12]. And he continues:

> those blank votes which have struck a brutal blow against the democratic normality of our personal and collective lives did not fall from the skies or rise up from the bowels of the earth, they were in the pockets of eighty-three out of every one hundred voters in this city, who placed them in the ballot boxes with their own unpatriotic hands.[13]

The analysis

Saramago's story continues with an unsuccessful attempt at normalising the situation with a state of emergency, and later with the spectacular exit of the country's political and legal elites from the capital with the aim of

---

11 Ibid. 19–20.
12 Ibid. 27.
13 Ibid. 27–28.

establishing a new seat of government outside the city limits. But for our purposes this initial starting point of the elections is enough.

The first worry of the presiding officer is a familiar one: electoral participation is a prerequisite for the perceived legitimacy of any given democratic system. And low turnout rates will often be interpreted as a challenge to its credibility.[14] This is clearly the case in, for example, the European Union. In the European elections of 2014, the final turnout rate was 42.61%, the lowest since the first direct elections in 1979,[15] and the continuously diminishing turnouts are regarded as a reflection of the popular resentment felt towards the so-called 'democratic deficit' of the Union.[16] Saramago's presiding officer and his colleagues are worried about the adverse effects that the bad weather might have on the turnout.[17] Clearly voter apathy is a familiar phenomenon here, too. These are, after all, mock elections, at least to the extent that no one seems to genuinely believe that the results, whatever they might end up being, could introduce any kind of major political change. The electoral officials are worried simply because they have a hard time convincing the electorate to participate even in good weather. Hence the 'civic duty' that may hopefully prompt an otherwise disinclined voter to find her way to the polling station even if she feels that it is a useless gesture.

When the weather improves and the voters finally start to arrive, there is an initial wave of relief. If the turnout ends up being at least acceptable, then the political system can be said to have received its blessing from the democratic electorate. But the realisation that such an overwhelming percentage of the cast votes are blank changes the situation. A blank vote is not the same thing as a no-show or even an abstention (i.e. arriving at the polling station but declining to vote). And the anxious response that the result receives from the government changes the status of the electorate radically.

We might say that such a result, painfully confirmed in a second election a week later, has the all makings of a *political crisis* similar to that of an unusually low turnout rate in any representative democracy.[18] Voting blank is, however, not apathy. A political crisis, as inconvenient as it may be, does

---

14 See e.g. Martin Rosema, 'Low Turnout: Threat to Democracy or Blessing in Disguise? Consequences of Citizens' Varying Tendencies to Vote', *Electoral Studies*, 26:3 (2007), 612–23.
15 See European Parliament, *Results of the 2014 European elections. 2014 opening session (01/07/2014)*. Available at www.europarl.europa.eu/elections2014-results/en/election-results-2014.html (accessed 26 August 2016).
16 For a discussion, see e.g. Jürgen Habermas, 'Democracy in Europe: Why the Development of the EU into a Transnational Democracy Is Necessary and How It Is Possible', *European Law Journal*, 21:4 (2015), 546–57.
17 On how realistic these worries are, see Mikael Persson, Anders Sundell and Richard Öhrvall, 'Does Election Day Weather Affect Voter Turnout? Evidence from Swedish Elections', *Electoral Studies*, 33 (2014), 335–42.
18 According to e.g. EIU (2016), 'apathy and abstention are enemies of democracy'. *Democracy Index 2015. Democracy in an age of anxiety. A Report by The Economist Intelligence Unit*, at 11.

not have the ability to destabilise the foundations of a political system. So even more than an inconvenience, the blank votes represent a *constitutional crisis*[19] to the extent that they put into question the established relations between those who rule and those who are ruled. By casting the blank votes, the individuals involved in the act reject the role of the electorate that the constitution offers them and take it upon themselves to employ a democratic power more radical than the institutions of the constitution itself. It is a moment when a *constituted* representative democracy and its institutions are unexpectedly called into question by a *constituent* popular sovereign.[20]

So we are dealing with two different power positions here: the electorate understood as the body of eligible voters, and, for want of a better term, 'the people'.[21] The democratic actor plays both roles at once. In normal constitutional and political circumstances, the actor may only display the former role by, for example, participating in elections and other forms of constituted political life. But because membership in the body of eligible voters is a constituted power position – someone or something still has the power to define those terms of eligibility – it must also be based on a mandate awarded by some other more 'fundamental' actor capable of constituting. Such a democratic actor is 'the people' as the popular sovereign.[22]

Every constitution includes a set of constituted institutions and practices that are incapable of constituting themselves. The ultimate justification for their existence must, then, rest on something more fundamental than the constituted institutions themselves. If we reserve the term 'the electorate' to depict the body of potential voters in a representative democracy whose eligibility to participate is determined in terms of nationality, age, mental capacity, and sometimes even status as inmate,[23] then it is clearly a constituted institution that cannot, within its criteria of eligibility, decide on those criteria themselves. So strictly speaking the electorate cannot decide in a valid way on its own eligibility to vote. Even if the representatives of the electorate can facilitate the decision by, for example, voting for a political programme that includes a change in those criteria, we use the fiction

---

19 Sanford Levinson and Jack M. Balkin, 'Constitutional Crises', *University of Pennsylvania Law Review*, 157:3 (2009), 707–53.
20 On constituent and constituted power, see Emmanuel-Joseph Sieyès, 'What is the Third Estate?' [1789], 92–162, in Emmanuel-Joseph Sieyès, *Political Writings. Including the Debate between Sieyès and Tom Paine in 1791*. Trans. Michael Sonenscher (Indiana, IN: Hackett Publishing, 2004); Martin Loughlin and Neil Walker (ed.), *The Paradox of Constitutionalism. Constituent Power and Constitutional Form* (Oxford: Oxford University Press, 2007).
21 See Andreas Kalyvas, 'Popular Sovereignty, Democracy, and the Constituent Power', *Constellations*, 12:2 (2005), 223–44.
22 See for instance Jerome Frank, *Constituent Moments. Enacting the People in Postrevolutionary America* (Durham, NC: Duke University Press, 2010).
23 See *Hirst v the United Kingdom [no. 2]* [GC], no. 74025/01, ECHR 2005-IX; see also Chapter 3 by Marshall in this volume.

of popular sovereignty to legitimise it: the ultimate democratic decision-maker must be 'the people'.[24]

But the electorate is a curious institution. While we may argue that by deciding on those criteria of eligibility the constituent people restricts itself into a constituted role as the electorate, and while we could also claim that such a self-restriction relinquishes the popular sovereign of its ultimate democratic power, constituted institutions can never quite domesticate the constituent power to which they owe their existence. So even if the democratic actor acts mainly as a constituted electorate by, for example, participating in elections, there is always a remnant of the constituent people in every constituted democratic institution. The constituent people lies dormant within the constituted electorate until one day it awakens and chooses to call into question one or another constituted institution, including the role of the electorate that it has given itself.

This seems to be happening in Saramago's novel, as well. The eligible citizens of the unnamed state have participated in both national and municipal elections before in ways that the government representatives identify as 'normal'. As readers we are led to believe that 'normality' in this particular case includes a more or less open admission of the less-than-optimal democratic value of these elections, and the admission will always include an acceptable amount of voter apathy. But such a democratic 'normality' is always frail. In this particular case the anomaly that breaks through the political routines is the anxiety caused by the possibility of a critical abstention rate seemingly caused by the bad weather. Once voters do start showing up, there is an unfounded sigh of relief that is made even more unfounded by the 'shameful spectacle'[25] of the empty votes.

The American constitutional lawyer Bruce Ackerman has coined the term 'constitutional moment' to depict historical turning points at which a given state of affairs – or a 'regime' – that has hitherto been considered unconstitutional becomes constitutional through the effective exercise of an exception.[26] Ackerman's idea of such turning points refers to judicial lawmaking through constitutional interpretation and so mainly applies to the democratic functions of the courts. So a Supreme Court 'landmark' decision that legitimises same-sex marriages[27] could, if successful, impose such a regime change. But we can expand Ackerman's idea of constitutional moments as higher lawmaking and regime shifts to include other institutions, as well. From the perspective adopted here, Ackerman's courts use a constituent

---

24 For a more nuanced notion of popular sovereignty, see Simone Chambers, 'Democracy, Popular Sovereignty, and Constitutional Legitimacy', *Constellations*, 11:2 (2004), 153–73.
25 Saramago, *Seeing*, 19.
26 Ackerman, *We the People. Vol 1. Foundations*.
27 *Obergefell v Hodges*, 576 U.S. ___ (2015).

power, exceptional in nature, to modify existing constituted arrangements. If successful, the exception then gels into a new constituted regime. This same relationship between what is constituted and the constituent power that executes the exception and solidifies it into a new constituted arrangement can be used to describe the democratic power of Saramago's electorate, as well. By exercising the residual constituent power that no constituted frameworks can quite contain, 'the people' put into effect a change of regime the political details of which the novel leaves open.

A final question remains. What makes such 'moments' possible? Do they simply follow from the overwhelming 'revolutionary' power of 'the people' as the popular sovereign? Saramago's novel hardly justifies such a reading, for blank votes are not the same thing as overthrowing a government through a popular uprising. And yet the effect of those empty ballots seems much greater than the gesture itself would suggest. So what makes the state vulnerable to such gestures? Saramago gives one hint in the way in which he positions himself as a narrator in the novel. Although there is no doubt about where the author's political sympathies lie, Saramago is, nevertheless, only able to recount the inner thoughts of the government officials. The motivations of the voters remain a mystery for the author just as much as they do for the officials. This quality of mystery suggests that the voters remain inappropriable and therefore also a politically autonomous 'multitude'.[28]

But perhaps there is something to be said of the state itself, as well. In the discussion on the rather unique constitutional developments of Bolivia,[29] one explanation that has been put forward claims that the unusual political alliances between the peasant movement and the indigenous peoples[30] that led to the 2009 'plurinational' constitution were only possible because Bolivia is neither a strong nor a weak state in the conventional senses but, rather, a 'state with holes',[31] that is, a state in a gradual and ever-continuing process of being constructed.[32] Although this pluralistic notion of a 'state with holes' has been specifically tailored for the Bolivian situation, and although it is heavily indebted to the Argentine political scientist Guillermo O'Donnell's theory of transitional democracies especially

---

28 Michael Hardt and Antonio Negri, *Multitude. War and Democracy in the Age of Empire* (London et al: Penguin Books, 2006).
29 E.g. Donna Lee Van Cott, *From Movements to Parties in Latin America. The Evolution of Ethnic Politics* (Cambridge: Cambridge University Press, 2005), 49–98.
30 E.g. Nicole Fabricant, *Mobilizing Bolivia's Displaced. Indigenous Politics and the Struggle over Land* (Chapel Hill, NC: University of North Carolina Press, 2012).
31 UNDP, *El estado del Estado en Bolivia. Informe Nacional sobre Desarrollo Humano 2007.* [s.l.]: (UNDP Bolivia, 2007), 99–100.
32 George Gray Molina, (2008) 'State-Society Relations in Bolivia: The Strength of Weakness', in John Crabtree and Laurence Whitehead (eds.), *Unresolved Tensions. Bolivia Past and Present* (Pittsburgh, PA: University of Pittsburgh Press, 2008), 110–11. I would like to thank María Paula Barrantes Reynolds for bringing this discussion to my attention.

in Latin America,[33] one might well argue that all states are, at least to a certain extent, 'with holes', 'porous'. This becomes evident during those individual 'moments' when a constituent power breaks through the constituted arrangements that the state refers to as its established framework and succeeds in implementing change.

My aim in this short chapter has been to illustrate how, contrary to what the positivistic legal tradition suggests, namely that at least ideally a state is a closed legal system, all states are by necessity 'with holes', 'porous', 'unfinished', 'transitory'. All states lead a supposedly settled political existence within well-contained competences that we assume to be a permanent state of affairs. But only until something unsettling and out of the ordinary happens. The state of Saramago's novel is no different from most representative democracies in the sense that its settled existence includes regular elections in which 'the people', normally contained as the electorate, have a particular role to play, a role the main function of which is to legitimise an existing regime. But in these specific elections, at this particular 'moment', 'the people' broke away from that containment and reassumed its position as the constituent popular sovereign calling that legitimacy into question. It could do so only because the state that offered the containment was never impermeable to begin with.

One might ask why such 'moments' do not happen more often than they do in the real world. Well, perhaps they do. An important strain of contemporary research has begun to reassess the relationship between 'populism' and democracy.[34] Seen from this perspective, populist episodes that may take the form of, for example, abnormal electoral behaviour would no longer be regarded as incidental 'pathologies' in a well-working democracy but, rather, as one reaction among others towards the growing disaffection arising from the democratic shortcomings of political liberalism. So Saramago's narrative of blank votes may also be read as a parable about political disillusionment, or perhaps even as a cautionary tale about what might happen when those blank ballots begin to be filled out.[35]

Bibliography

Ackerman, Bruce A. *We the People. Vol 1. Foundations.* Cambridge, MA: Belknap Press, 1991.

Aguiar e Silva, Joana. 'Is Justice for Sale? Further Readings on Saramago and the Law,' *No Foundations: An Interdisciplinary Journal of Law and Justice* 11 (2014), 94–115.

---

[33] E.g. Guillermo A. O'Donnell and Philippe C. Schmitter, *Transitions from Authoritarian Rule. Prospects for Democracy* [1986] (Baltimore, MA: Johns Hopkins University Press, 2013).

[34] E.g. Francisco Panizza (ed.), *Populism and the Mirror of Democracy* (London: Verso, 2005); Benjamin Arditi, *Politics on the Edges of Liberalism. Difference, Populism, Revolution, Agitation.* (Edinburgh: Edinburgh University Press, 2007).

[35] Cas Mudde, *Populist Radical Right Parties in Europe* (Cambridge: Cambridge University Press, 2007).

Arditi, Benjamin. *Politics on the Edges of Liberalism. Difference, Populism, Revolution, Agitation.* Edinburgh: Edinburgh University Press, 2007.

Aristodemou, Maria. 'Democracy or Your Life! Knowledge, Ignorance and the Politics of Atheism in Saramago's Blindness and Seeing,' *Law, Culture and the Humanities* 9:1 (2013), 169–87.

Chambers, Simone. 'Democracy, Popular Sovereignty, and Constitutional Legitimacy,' *Constellations* 11:2 (2004), 153–73.

EIU (2016) *Democracy Index 2015. Democracy in an age of anxiety. A report by The Economist Intelligence Unit.* Available at www.eiu.com/Handlers/WhitepaperHandler.ashx?fi=EIU-Democracy-Index-2015.pdf&mode=wp&campaignid=DemocracyIndex2015 (accessed 26 August 2016) (requires registration).

European Parliament (2014) *Results of the 2014 European elections. 2014 opening session (01/07/2014).* Available at www.europarl.europa.eu/elections2014-results/en/election-results-2014.html (accessed 26 August 2016).

Fabricant, Nicole. *Mobilizing Bolivia's Displaced. Indigenous Politics and the Struggle over Land.* Chapel Hill, NC: University of North Carolina Press, 2012.

Frank, Jerome. *Constituent Moments. Enacting the People in Postrevolutionary America.* Durham, NC: Duke University Press, 2010.

Gray Molina, George (2008) 'State-Society Relations in Bolivia: The Strength of Weakness'. In *Unresolved Tensions. Bolivia Past and Present*, edited by John Crabtree and Laurence Whitehead, 109–24. Pittsburgh, PA: University of Pittsburgh Press, 2008.

Habermas, Jürgen. 'Democracy in Europe: Why the Development of the EU into a Transnational Democracy Is Necessary and How It Is Possible,' *European Law Journal* 21:4 (2015), 546–57.

Hardt, Michael and Antonio Negri. *Multitude. War and Democracy in the Age of Empire.* London et al: Penguin Books, 2006.

Kalyvas, Andreas. 'Popular Sovereignty, Democracy, and the Constituent Power,' *Constellations* 12:2 (2005), 223–44.

Levinson, Sanford and Jack M. Balkin. 'Constitutional Crises,' *University of Pennsylvania Law Review* 157:3 (2009), 707–53.

Loughlin, Martin and Neil Walker (eds.). *The Paradox of Constitutionalism. Constituent Power and Constitutional Form.* Oxford: Oxford University Press, 2007.

Minkkinen, Panu. 'The Juridical Romanticism of Friedrich Dürrenmatt's *The Execution of Justice*'. In *The Contemporary Relevance of Carl Schmitt. Law, Politics, Theology*, edited by Matilda Arvidsson, Leila Brännstrom and Panu Minkkinen, 78–90. Abingdon: Routledge, 2016.

Mudde, Cas. *Populist Radical Right Parties in Europe.* Cambridge: Cambridge University Press, 2007.

O'Donnell, Guillermo A. and Philippe C. Schmitter. *Transitions from Authoritarian Rule. Prospects for Democracy* [1986]. Baltimore, MA: Johns Hopkins University Press, 2013.

Panizza, Francisco (ed.). *Populism and the Mirror of Democracy.* London: Verso, 2005.

Persson, Mikael, Anders Sundell and Richard Öhrvall. 'Does Election Day Weather Affect Voter Turnout? Evidence from Swedish Elections,' *Electoral Studies* 33 (2014), 335–42.

Rosema, Martin. 'Low Turnout: Threat to Democracy or Blessing in Disguise? Consequences of Citizens' Varying Tendencies to Vote,' *Electoral Studies* 26:3 (2007), 612–23.

Saramago, José. *Seeing*. Trans. Margaret Jull Costa. London: Harvill Secker, 2006.
Sieyès, Emmanuel-Joseph. 'What is the Third Estate?' [1789], 92–162, in Emmanuel-Joseph Sieyès, *Political Writings. Including the Debate between Sieyès and Tom Paine in 1791*. Trans. Michael Sonenscher. Indiana, IN: Hackett Publishing, 2003.
UNDP (2007) *El estado del Estado en Bolivia. Informe Nacional sobre Desarrollo Humano 2007*. [s.l.]: UNDP Bolivia. Available at www.undp.org/content/dam/bolivia/docs/informe2007elestadoestado.pdf (accessed 26 August 2016).
Van Cott, Donna Lee. *From Movements to Parties in Latin America. The Evolution of Ethnic Politics*. Cambridge: Cambridge University Press, 2005.
Wierzba, Sandra M. 'Saramago's *Death with Interruptions*: A Path to Reconsider Essential Dilemmas Linked to Health Law,' *Oñati Socio-legal Series*, 4:6 (2014), 1241–53.

Chapter 5

Who belongs? The Turkish citizen subject in turmoil

Kati Nieminen

Introduction

In this chapter I discuss the struggle over the Turkish citizen subject and how law interacts with parliamentary politics in the subject production process. The notion of law adopted here is diffuse and strained: law is inseparably intertwined with politics, morals and power struggles; the law is what(ever) the law does. I ask what else, besides providing solutions to legally formulated problems, does the law do? For this purpose, I explore the actual workings of law by following its lead to three sites of struggle: the courts (party dissolution cases), the cabinets (the Kurdish peace process) and the streets (the Gezi protests), in order to determine how the law shapes our lived world and specifically political subjectivity in Turkey.

I explore the role of law in the constant process of establishing and contesting official subjectivities. In making sense of the complex ways that law is part of the subject-making process, I utilise Rancière's conceptualisations of police and politics and discuss the possibilities and the potential of law in both contexts. For Rancière, politics is a battle over what and who is visible, and therefore his thinking is well suited to analysing the battle over subjectivities.

Politics, according to Rancière, is dissensus over what is political in the first place, and political subjectivity equals the capacity to create scenes of dissensus. Dissensus is not a dispute over interests or opinions, but a more fundamental disagreement over what is visible and speakable, over the seemingly self-evident.[1] The essence of politics, according to Rancière, is to disturb the apparent self-evidence; it is 'an intervention upon what is visible and sayable'.[2]

---

1 Jacques Rancière, 'Ten Theses on Politics,' *Theory & Event* 5:3 (2001), 1. See also Jacques Rancière, 'Who is the Subject of the Rights of Man?', *South Atlantic Quarterly* 103:2–3 (2004), 304; Jacques Rancière, *Disagreement: Politics and Philosophy*, trans. Julie Rose (Minneapolis, London: University of Minnesota Press 1999), 36.
2 Rancière, 'Ten Theses on Politics,' 21; Rancière, *Disagreement: Politics and Philosophy*, 36.

The police, in contrast, is the apparent self-evidence of the established social order. The police is what makes the distinctions between visible and invisible, belonging and separation, speakable and unspeakable, possible and impossible. Thus, the police does not equate with the police force or state violence. Neither does politics equate with parliamentarism or elections or with representative, communicative or deliberative democracy. For Rancière, these in fact belong to the realm of the police – hence, the distinction made between politics and parliamentary politics in this article. In the distinction between the police and politics, law is located in the sphere of the police, because law is a central mode of maintaining the prevailing notion of self-evidence.[3] Politics, when successful in opening the public space to what it excludes, easily turns into a police order establishing the new self-evident, again creating a basis for new political action. This is the incessant cycle on which I wish to elaborate in the following sections.

The struggle over the Turkish subjectivity can, on the one hand, be seen as a battle over the acceptable qualities of the citizen subject, i.e. as a battle between inclusion and exclusion. On the other hand, the struggle can be seen, especially in the light of the Gezi protests, as a battle for more fundamental transformation.[4] Resulting from shifts in the political power balance, the citizen subject is currently undergoing a transformation in Turkey and thus provides an intriguing opportunity to observe this process.

I begin my analysis by discussing the features attached to the subject position of a good citizen in Turkey from the beginning of the country's independence in 1923. I then move on to explore the ways in which the citizen subject is currently transforming, paying particular attention to the role of law in the process. The first site of exploration is the courtroom: analysing party dissolution cases from the perspective of subjectivation reveals the ways in which the law serves as a medium for contesting and maintaining the Turkish citizen subject and for the claims of recognition for different identities. The second site of inquiry is the cabinets of parliamentary politics: here the focus is on the Kurdish peace process, another example of a people demanding recognition for ethnic identity, even national identity. The third and last scene is the streets, where the struggle over political subjectivity in Turkey took place in the summer of 2013 in the form of large-scale protests during which, I argue, the prevailing notion of the citizen subject was challenged in a more radical sense.

---

3 Ari Hirvonen, 'Tasa-arvon demokratia – Jacques Rancière, erimielisyyden ajattelija,' in Toomas Kotkas and Susanna Lindroos-Hovinheimo (eds.), *Yhteiskuntateorioiden Oikeus*, (Helsinki: Tutkijaliitto, 2010), 356.
4 See Judith Butler, 'A Response to Ali, Beckford, Bhatt, Modood and Woodhead,' *The British Journal of Sociology* 59:2 (2008), 257.

Creating the citizen

Recent contributions to the academic study of ethnicity contest the reification of such concepts as ethnicity, nation, race and class, and their treatment as coherent, homogeneous and natural agents. Rogers Brubaker, for instance, argues that such groupness should be treated as an event, as something that happens, rather than as a fixed and given phenomenon.[5] In a similar vein Thomas H. Eriksen criticises essentialist tendencies and stresses the existence of an infinite number of versions of each culture, none of which is truer than others. For him, ethnicity is 'an aspect of a relationship, not a property of a group'.[6]

If agency and interests cannot be attributed to ethnic entities as such, then how should the struggle for recognition, e.g. for ethnic, religious or sexual identity or for specific minority interests, be understood? Indisputably, there can be shared interests and experiences, a sense of belonging and a sense of shared origins and history on which such claims for recognition are based. According to Brubaker, the tendency to partition the social world into quasi-natural intrinsic kinds 'is a key part of what we want to explain, not what we want to explain things with; it belongs to our empirical data, not to our analytical toolkit'.[7] Following Pierre Bourdieu's thinking, Brubaker suggests that participants' accounts often have a performative character; by invoking groups, they seek to summon them into being.

In social anthropology ethnicity is used to refer to aspects of relationships between groups 'which consider themselves, and are regarded by others, as being culturally distinctive'.[8] Therefore, it is easy to understand that the recognition of shared ethnic identity is crucial in becoming a distinctive ethnic group. The tension between the 'Turks' and the 'Kurds' springs precisely from this source: for the Turkish state the constructing of the unified, homogenous people has been essential in the nation building process, whereas the Kurdish minority has resisted the assimilationist policies of the state, striving instead to establish their own ethnic identity.[9]

---

5 Rogers Brubaker, 'Ethnicity without Groups,' in Montserrat Guibernau and John Rex (eds.), *The Ethnicity Reader: Nationalism, Multiculturalism and Migration*, 2nd ed. (Cambridge: Polity, 2010), 37.
6 Thomas Hylland Eriksen, 'Ethnicity, Race and Nation,' in Montserrat Guibernau and John Rex (eds.), *The Ethnicity Reader: Nationalism, Multiculturalism and Migration*, (Cambridge: Polity, 2010), 50.
7 Brubaker, 'Ethnicity without Groups,' 35.
8 Eriksen, 'Ethnicity, Race and Nation,' 46.
9 For an extensive analysis of the origins of the Kurdish nationalist movement, see M.R. Izady, 'The Kurds in Iraq and Iran,' in Montserrat Guibernau and John Rex (eds.), *The Ethnicity Reader: Nationalism, Multiculturalism and Migration*, (Cambridge: Polity, 2010), 198–210.

After becoming independent in 1923, the citizen subject in Turkey was constructed in opposition to the diversity of subjectivities in the Ottoman Empire. The modern national identity was built on the basis of homogeneity, unity and the notion of the common good.[10] The pluralistic model of the Empire was abandoned in favour of an all-embracing nation. In fact, before the Tanzimat reforms during the years 1839 to1876 there were no citizens (*vatandaş*) in the Empire; rather there were believers (*mümin*); there were no people (*millet*); rather there was the Muslim community (*umma*).[11] As the subject position of the citizen began to form, the relationship between the people and the state changed as well: the new subject was required to be loyal to the state and to show primary allegiance to it – to be not only a citizen, but indeed a good one.

During the first years of independence the challenge for the establishment was to bring together the diverse population.[12] For the purpose of creating unity and harmony, the official state ideology, Kemalism, named after Mustafa Kemal Atatürk, endorsed the idea that the people should share the same culture and ideals. National unity, or even uniformity, was one of the most frequently used concepts in the speeches of Atatürk and other leading party figures.[13] The Kemalist legacy particularly emphasises nationalism, secularism and a unitary, highly centralised state, as well as territorial and national integrity.[14] Atatürk's party, the Republican People's Party CHP (Cumhuriyet Halk Partisi) treasures the Kemalist legacy in modern Turkey.

Constructing a modern, secular national identity required re-forming the bodies of the people, especially the bodies of women, who were invited to adopt a new form of subjectivity by giving up the Islamic headscarf.[15] In

---

10 E. F. Keyman and Tuba Kanci, 'A Tale of Ambiguity: Citizenship, Nationalism and Democracy in Turkey,' *Nations & Nationalism* 17:2 (2011), 324–8.
11 Esengül Ayyildiz, 'Talkootöistä Kansalaistottelemattomuuteen,' in Leinonen, Anu, *et al.*(eds.), *Turkki Euroopan Rajalla?* (Helsinki: Gaudeamus, 2007), 323; Ergun Özbudun, 'Turkey – Plural Society and Monolithic State,' in Ahmet T. Kuru and Alfred Stepan (eds.), *Democracy, Islam, and Democracy in Turkey* (New York: Columbia University Press, 2012), 61–6.
12 The population, however, was not as diverse as it was in the Empire owing to territorial reasons after the First World War, the deportation of Armenians in 1915 and the exchange of populations with Greece in 1924.
13 Ergun Özbudun, 'Turkey – Plural Society and Monolithic State,' in Ahmet T. Kuru and Alfred Stepan (eds.), *Democracy, Islam, and Secularism in Turkey* (New York: Columbia University Press, 2012), 74.
14 Ergun Özbudun, 'The Turkish Constitutional Court and Political Crisis,' in Ahmet T. Kuru and Alfred Stepan (eds.), *Democracy, Islam, and Secularism in Turkey* (New York: Columbia University Press, 2012), 150.
15 Mary Lou O'Neil, 'You Are what You Wear: Clothing/Appearance Laws and the Construction of the Public Citizen in Turkey,' *Fashion Theory: The Journal of Dress, Body & Culture* 14:1 (2010), 65; Valorie K. Vojdik, 'Politics of the Headscarf in Turkey: Masculinities, Feminism, and the Construction of Collective Identities,' *Harvard Journal of Law and Gender* 33 (2010), 661.

bringing up the youth of the nation, the school curriculum played a key role in transmitting the officially selected and organised knowledge: in the 1920s the emphasis was on territorial issues; Islam was replaced by a republican morality, and ethnic diversity was suppressed in favour of emphasising sameness and togetherness. During the 1980s, Turkey began to be affected by globalisation and free market discourse and faced both reviving Islamism and escalating tension with the Kurdish population. Schoolbooks continued to highlight self-sacrifice as a central feature of a good citizen, but at the same time the societal changes were reflected in the introduction for the first time of the concept of a minority in textbooks. However, the concept of minority was accompanied by the concept of national security and references to enemies within. Since then, individual identity, rights and diversity have gained somewhat more weight in school textbooks.[16]

Throughout its history the major sources of diversity in Turkey have been ethnicity and religion. While the non-Muslim population is less than one percent, the Muslim majority itself is diverse, there being various Muslim minority groups. The state has tried to create unity among the Muslims by favouring Sunni Islam at the expense of Muslim minorities, who have been repressed by various interferences in their practices and organisational structures.[17] More importantly however, expressing religious affiliations in public has been restricted in order to create a universal standpoint for all citizens. From the beginning the key element of Kemalism was secularism (*laiklik*), and religion became a matter belonging to the private sphere, while simultaneously Islam was acknowledged as the official religion of Turkish society.[18] This change would not have been possible without creating a new subject position for the people, and so the citizen was created. The ideal subject of the state shows loyalty to the nation, both in deeds and in appearance.

Kurds constitute Turkey's largest ethnic and linguistic minority.[19] The current wave of Kurdish political activism in Turkey is generally traced back to the early 1960s, when the articulation of Kurdish identity grew stronger.[20] From the beginning, the Kurdish national movement challenged Kemalism and its notion of national unity and homogeneity. During the 1970s and

---

16 Keyman and Kanci, 'A Tale of Ambiguity: Citizenship, Nationalism and Democracy in Turkey,' 318; Basak Ince, 'Citizenship Education in Turkey: Inclusive or Exclusive,' *Oxford Review of Education* 38:2 (2012), 115–31.
17 Derya Bayir, *Minorities and Nationalism in Turkish Law* (Surrey: Ashgate, 2013), 112–15.
18 Seyla Benhabib, 'The Return of Political Theology,' *Philosophy & Social Criticism* 36:3–4 (2010), 453.
19 Özbudun, 'Turkey – Plural Society and Monolithic State,' 67–8.
20 On the diversity and politicisation of Kurdish identity, see M. H. Yavuz, 'A Preamble to the Kurdish Question: The Politics of Kurdish Identity,' *Journal of Muslim Minority Affairs* 18:1 (1998), 9.

1980s the Kurdish national liberation discourse, in which the Kurds were represented as a colonised people, intensified.[21]

Still today Turkey officially recognises only three minority groups, namely the Greeks, the Armenian Christians and the Jews. Recognition of official minority groups is outlined in the Lausanne Peace Treaty of 1923.[22] The Turkish Constitutional Court has defined the concept of minority in such a way that Turkey has been able to avoid acknowledging other minorities in its population.[23] Moreover, the Constitutional Court has explicitly stated that recognition of a minority status based on race or language is incompatible with the notion of territorial and national integrity, thus recreating and reinforcing the dichotomy and incompatibility of national unity and a pluralist society.[24]

The dominant feature of the battle over the Turkish citizen subject has been the claim for recognition of a specific kind of diversity based on ethnicity and religion. Pushing for recognition in the public as well as in the private sphere, religious and ethnic minorities have unsettled the 'self-evident' boundary between the private and the public in Turkey. Whereas recognition theories presuppose a subject of recognition, Rancière's starting point is that subjects do not pre-exist politics.[25] Following Rancière, it is thus possible to understand the challenge of the boundary between political and non-political as politics in its own right, instead of stressing the importance of identity and interest claims; for Rancière, the political does not belong to the public sphere; instead the political contests the division between public and private.

Battling over the citizen subject: the court, the cabinets and the streets

The court

> Political activity is whatever shifts a body from the place assigned to it or changes a place's destination. It makes visible what had no business being seen, and makes heard a discourse where once there was only place for noise; it makes understood a discourse what was once only heard as noise.[26]

---

21 See Cengiz Gunes, *The Kurdish National Movement in Turkey: From Protest to Resistance* (2012), 247–8, 250–1.
22 *Treaty of Peace with Turkey Signed at Lausanne, July 24, 1923*: III Protection of Minorities.
23 Bayir, *Minorities and Nationalism in Turkish Law*, 203. According to the Court, a minority is a group that is distinct from the majority in terms of language, religion, race etc. and is internationally recognised as a minority.
24 Constitutional Court of Turkey decision E. 1993/3, K. 1994/2, 16 June 1994; *Anayasa Mahkemesi Kararlar Dergisi (AMDK)* (Constitutional Court Reports) 30.3:1201, 1199, as cited in Özbudun, 'The Turkish Constitutional Court and Political Crisis,' 157.
25 Rancière, 'Ten Theses on Politics,' 4.
26 Rancière, *Disagreement: Politics and Philosophy*, 30.

In light of the ideal of a unified, secular citizen subject, it is understandable that to claim minority identity for the Kurds has been regarded as a threat to the state and to the status quo; according to the Constitutional Court, being part of the nation and being a minority group are mutually exclusive. Interestingly, the case law of the Constitutional Court concerning parties which were dissolved owing due to their position on the political, linguistic and cultural rights of Kurds are basically the only cases in which the Court has explicitly discussed minority issues and the concept of minority.[27]

The most recent party to be dissolved was the pro-Kurdish Democratic Society Party (Partiya Civaka Demokratîk, Demokratik Toplum Partisi), banned in 2009. The Constitutional Court unanimously argued that the party had become the centre of activities aimed at annihilating the unity of the state by its support of the PKK (Partiya Karkerên Kurdistan, the Kurdistan Workers Party), which is listed as a terrorist organisation by NATO, the EU and the US. According to the Court, the Party had attempted to obtain a number of rights and acquisitions by manipulating antidemocratic statements and actions and had used terrorism for political means.[28]

Besides the pro-Kurdish parties, the Islamic parties have been under close scrutiny by the Constitutional Court. The dissolution in 1997 of the predecessor to the current Justice and Development Party (AKP, Adalet ve Kalkınma Partisi), namely the Welfare Party (RP, Refah Partisi), has sometimes been described as a post-modern coup, placed on the same level as the military coups of 1960, 1971 and 1980, which were initiated by the idea that the military is the guardian of the secular Kemalist legacy.[29] The new coup strategy involved a radical change in the country's National Military Defence Concept, which declared Kurdish separatism and forms of Islamic activism to be internal threats to the fundamental characteristics of the Turkish state. Again, the ethnic and religious components were deemed the most dangerous forms of diversity for the unity of the nation.[30] The culmination of the post-modern coup was dissolving the RP. The case was ultimately referred to the European Court of Human Rights, which readily accepted the national Court's identification of Islam with totalitarian movements

---

27 Bayir, *Minorities and Nationalism in Turkish Law*, 191–3.
28 Bülent Algan, 'Dissolution of Political Parties by the Constitutional Court in Turkey: An Everlasting Conflict between the Court and the Parliament?' *Ankara Üniversitesi Hukuk Fakültesi Dergisi* 60:4 (2011), 822, 828.
29 M. Hakan Yavuz, 'A Preamble to the Kurdish Question: The Politics of Kurdish Identity,' 133.
30 Ümit Cizre, 'A New Politics of Engagement: The Turkish Military, Society and the AKP,' in Ahmet T. Kuru and Alfred Stepan (eds.), *Democracy, Islam, and Secularism in Turkey*, (New York: Columbia University Press, 2012), 132–4.

threatening democracy.³¹ The AKP itself was under threat of being dissolved in 2008.³² This time the Court did not agree with dissolution.³³

Although clearly sprouting from religious grounds, the AKP was, at least originally, described as a more moderate and pragmatic version of its predecessors. In 2005 Prime Minister Erdoğan (currently Turkey's president) strongly rejected defining the AKP in religious terms and denied that it was an Islamic party. Instead, he identified the organisation as a conservative democratic party. Erdoğan's statement did not reassure opponents, and the Kemalists grew increasingly suspicious that the AKP had a hidden agenda.

Dissolving political parties as a means of gaining political power and maintaining the status quo of political power relations seems to have come to an end. During 2002–2015, the AKP-led government introduced a set of constitutional reforms that contributed to this development. While some of the amendments were widely accepted as necessary for consolidating the liberal democracy in Turkey, such as affirmative action for women and the disabled, establishing public ombudsmen and expanding the protection of personal privacy and labour union rights, others caused serious debate. On the more disputed side there was, among other things, weakening the power of the Constitutional Court to ban political parties.³⁴ The most controversial revision concerned the composition of the higher organs of judicial authorities, such as the Supreme Board of Prosecutors and Judges, which makes judicial appointments. The reform potentially allows active government interference in this body. This stirred fears amongst the secularist opposition and government critics that the AKP was slowly institutionalising itself as a hegemonic party across the executive, legislative and judicial branches and thereby circumventing the checks and balances of the democratic system.³⁵

The Constitutional Court's role as the guardian of the Kemalist legacy is perhaps coming to an end as well, thanks to revisions introduced by the AKP.³⁶ The same thing is happening to the second protector of the Kemalist order, namely the military. In the summer of 2013 high military officials were on trial for conspiring once again to overthrow the government. In

---

31 *Case of Refah Partisi (The Welfare Party) and Others v Turkey [GC]*, app. nos 41340/98, 41342/98, 41343/98, 41344/98, ECHR 2003-II (13 February 2003).
32 See Algan, 'Dissolution of Political Parties by the Constitutional Court in Turkey: An Everlasting Conflict between the Court and the Parliament?'
33 Özbudun, 'The Turkish Constitutional Court and Political Crisis,' 160.
34 Mark Herzog, *FCP Briefing: Analysing Turkey's 2010 constitutional referendum*. The Foreign Policy Centre, 2010. Available at http://fpc.org.uk/fsblob/1269.pdf (accessed 16 September 2013).
35 Herzog, *FPC Briefing: Analysing Turkey's 2010 constitutional referendum*; Özbudun, 'The Turkish Constitutional Court and Political Crisis,' 162.
36 Özbudun, 'The Turkish Constitutional Court and Political Crisis,' 156.

the so-called Ergenekon trials the defendants faced charges ranging from membership in an illegal criminal network (Ergenekon) to illegal possession of weapons and instigating an armed uprising against the AKP. The first round of trials resulted in life sentences for a number of defendants of military background and lengthy sentences for others, including journalists, lawyers and academics.[37] The Ergenekon investigations reflect the dividing lines in Turkish society: according to some, the investigation of the alleged 'deep state' was long overdue and a move in the direction of democracy; in the view of others, it was a plot to overturn once and for all the legacy of Atatürk and an attempt to establish an Islamic state.[38] These two opposing sides can be seen as manifestations of the struggle over what is 'self-evident' in Turkish society, i.e. the question of the place of the Kemalist legacy in the present power plays and the meaning of this legacy: is it a remnant of the past or a fundamental building block for the democratic order?

The recent phases in the court battle over the Turkish citizen subject seem to indicate that the structures protecting the Kemalist subject have become vulnerable. The parties based on ethnic or religious identity contest the self-evidence of the organisation of the private and public in Turkish society, in which religion is a private matter and ethnicity does not really exist at all. Despite the state's successes in the cases discussed here, the parties based on a minority identity have persisted and gained more and more ground in the Turkish political landscape. At the same time, however, they have reinforced the perception that religion and ethnicity are the main, if not the only, sources of diversity and dissensus among the Turkish people. Thus, while the apparent self-evidence of the dividing lines between private and public has been made visible and has been questioned, the place of religion and ethnicity has remained 'self-evident'.

---

37 See Daren Butler, 'Turkish court to announce verdicts in Ergenekon conspiracy case,' *Reuters*, last modified 4 August 2013, www.reuters.com/article/2013/08/04/turkey-ergenekon-idUSL6N0G50AI20130804 (accessed 16 September 2013); Justin Vela, 'Features Analysis: Turkey's divisive Ergenekon trial: Conviction of alleged coup plotters seen by many as Islamists' revenge against the army,' *Al Jazeera*, last modified 12 August 2013, www.aljazeera.com/indepth/features/2013/08/201381175743430360.html (accessed 16 September 2013); James Reynolds, 'Turkey Ergenekon case: Ex-army chief Basbug gets life,' *BBC News Europe*, last modified 5 August 2013, www.bbc.co.uk/news/world-europe-23571739 (accessed 16 September 2013); Hasnain Kazim, 'Ergenekon Verdicts: Erdogan Silences Dissent in Divided Turkey,' *Spiegel Online International*, last modified 5 August 2013, www.spiegel.de/international/world/verdicts-in-turkish-ergenekon-trial-reflect-deep-divisions-a-914924.html (accessed 16 September 2013).
38 Butler, 'Turkish court to announce verdicts in Ergenekon conspiracy case'; Vela, 'Features Analysis: Turkey's divisive Ergenekon trial Conviction of alleged coup plotters seen by many as Islamists' revenge against the army'; James Reynolds, 'Turkey Ergenekon case: Ex-army chief Basbug gets life'; Kazim, 'Ergenekon Verdicts: Erdogan Silences Dissent in Divided Turkey.'

The cabinets

> The police can procure all sorts of good, and one kind of police may be infinitely preferable to another. This does not change the nature of the police [...].³⁹

Besides the courtroom, the battle over the citizen subject is taking place in the cabinets of parliamentary politics, where the law can be used for legislative bargaining. Legal reforms are currency in diplomatic negotiations over the so-called Kurdish question. As discussed above, during its early years the Republic embraced the unity of the people and sought to subdue all sources of diversity. As a result, the state refused to recognise the existence of all ethnic groups, including the Kurds, and it banned their languages and pursued other assimilationist policies. From the Kurds' perspective the state became an oppressive regime where there was no room for expressing their ethnic identity or their interests as a minority group, leading to violent protests. The state in turn responded to the rebellion with violence and forced migration. The Kurdish question has its roots in the minority issue in general, but it has long been reduced to a security question by the Turkish government; the question has become a problem of terrorism – a problem which has been violently responded to by the state.⁴⁰

The first attempts to find a peaceful solution to the Kurdish question were initiated in the early 1990s. The current attempts can be traced back to the AKP's rise to power in 2002 and the negotiations for Turkey's membership in the European Union. In this context the government introduced a series of reforms intended to meet the so-called Copenhagen criteria, which was the requirement for the membership negotiations to start. The reforms included among other things abolishing the state of emergency, decreased detention periods pending trial, abolishing the State Security Courts and eliminating legal restrictions on the use of the Kurdish language. However, by 2009 there had been little progress, and from the Kurds' perspective most of the reforms were merely empty gestures: launching Kurdish-language broadcasting and permitting limited instruction of Kurdish as an elective subject did not meet the goals of mainstreaming the use of the Kurdish language or introducing education in Kurdish.⁴¹

---

39 Rancière, *Disagreement: Politics and Philosophy*, 31.
40 Yılmaz Ensaroğlu, 'Turkey's Kurdish Question and the Peace Process,' *Insight Turkey* 15:2 (2013), 8–9. http://file.insightturkey.com/Files/Pdf/20130415155719_15_2_2013_ensaroglu.pdf (accessed 16 September 2013).
41 Joseph Logan, 'In Search of the Building Blocks of Opposition in Turkey,' *Middle East Research and Information Project*, last modified 10 June 2013, www.merip.org/mero/mero061013 (accessed 16 September 2013).

Still, the peace process took a promising turn with the ceasefire and the withdrawal and disarmament of the PKK fighters in 2013. However, by September 2013 the Kurdish rebels halted the withdrawal of their fighters from Turkey's Kurdish territory as had been agreed under a peace plan, and accused the government of not abiding by the deal's terms and failing to adopt the democratic reforms designed to reinforce the rights of the Kurdish minority. According to the Kurdish Communities Union, the PKK announced that it would maintain the truce, but halt the withdrawal of fighters.[42] In practice, the peace process was halted altogether as the 2015 elections approached. According to Kardas, 'many Kurds who viewed [the] AK party as the agent of change came to question its commitment to the resolution of the Kurdish issue'.[43]

Regardless of the ultimate result, the state-initiated peace process explicitly favouring peaceful solution was a unique and significant opening in itself in Turkish history. The Kurdish side also welcomed the initiative, and according to the incarcerated PKK leader Abdullah Öcalan, the Kurds 'have now reached a point where guns must go silent and ideas and politics must speak'.[44] In this setting law represented a promise of the recognition and institutionalisation of Kurdish identity. For a while it seemed to have become possible to establish a new 'self-evidence' in which the Turkish and Kurdish opposition would dissolve.

After the Kurdish People's Democratic Party (HDP, Halkların Demokratik Partisi) gained seats in the Turkish parliament in the elections of June 2015, the debates over the so-called Kurdish question once more audibly entered the public debates. Turkey headed towards new elections in November 2015, as the attempts to form a new government failed. What is particularly interesting, assuming that the HDP stays in parliament, is the way it will address its non-Kurdish voters: during the campaign, the HDP invoked the support of such groups as women and sexual minorities. This, according to Kardas, may emerge as the main challenge for HDP, as its core constituency remains ethnically mobilised.[45] Kurds might be heading for a position to form their own relationship with other, still marginalised groups, such as sexual and gender minorities.

The peace process on the other hand has come to an end, as Turkey, after some procrastination, joined the US in combatting ISIS in Iraq and Syria.

---

42 *EKurd Daily*, 'Kurdish PKK rebels stop withdrawing forces from Turkey,' last modified 9 September 2013, www.ekurd.net/mismas/articles/misc2013/9/turkey4777.htm (accessed 16 September 2013); Ensaroğlu, 'Turkey's Kurdish Question and the Peace Process'.
43 Saban Kardas, 'What Now for the Kurdish Peace Process?' *Al Jazeera*, last modified 8 June 2015, www.aljazeera.com/indepth/opinion/2015/06/kurdish-peace-process-turkey-election-erdogan-150608053456502.html (accessed 8 June 2015).
44 Ensaroglu, 'Turkey's Kurdish Question and the Peace Process.'
45 Kardas, 'What Now for the Kurdish Peace Process?'

Along with ISIS, Turkey has also targeted the Kurdish rebels.[46] The Iraqi and Syrian Kurds have been on the front line in combatting ISIS, and it is likely that the newly erupted fight against the PKK has its roots in Turkish parliamentary politics: it has been speculated that President Erdoğan was referring to the HDP when he called on the Parliament to strip those politicians with links to terrorist organisation of their immunity to prosecution, once again resorting to the rhetoric of national unity, this time using law and legal action as threats.[47] It remains to be seen whether the AKP will make a full circle from being under threat of being dissolved to initiating the dissolution of the HDP or prosecuting its members under the terrorism laws.

The recent twist in the peace process illustrates the way in which identity politics and legal recognition are subordinate to parliamentary power politics. The Kurds' claim of existence and equality has had to give way to power plays, and the situation has reverted back to the old juxtaposition of a unified Turkish nation wherein ethnic minorities claim recognition. It even seems that the Kemalist, Islamic and Kurdish identities are interdependent in Turkey: without one another they would be meaningless, while together they form the 'self-evidence' of the Turkish citizen subject.

The streets

> Genuine participation is the invention of that unpredictable subject which momentarily occupies the street, the invention of a movement born of nothing but democracy itself. The guarantee of permanent democracy is not the filling up of all the dead times and empty spaces by the forms of participation or of counterpower; it is the continual renewal of the actors and of the forms of their actions, the ever-open possibility of the fresh emergence of this fleeting subject.[48]

The protests in the summer of 2013 started on 31 May with police intervention in a peaceful demonstration in Gezi Park in Istanbul, an event

---

46 See e.g. Ceylan Yeginsu, 'Turkish Troops Enter Iraq in Pursuit of Kurdish Rebels,' *The New York Times*, last modified 8 September 2015. Available at www.nytimes.com/2015/09/09/world/europe/turkey-pkk-bombing-police.html?_r=0 (accessed 8 September 2015).
47 Anne Barnard, 'Turkey's Focus on Crushing Kurdish Separatists Complicates the Fight Against ISIS,' *The New York Times*, last modified 28 July 2015. Available at www.nytimes.com/2015/07/29/world/turkeys-focus-on-crushing-kurd-extremists-complicates-isis-efforts.html?_r=0 (accessed 28 July 2015); Leo Canrowicz and Zia Weise, 'Turkey – Kurdish conflict: President Erdogan's double-edged war against the PKK and Isis brings accusations of electioneering,' *The Independent*, last modified 28 July 2015. Available at www.independent.co.uk/news/world/middle-east/turkeykurdish-conflict-president-erdogans-doubleedged-war-against-the-pkk-and-isis-brings-accusations-of-electioneering-10422726.html (accessed 29 July 2015).
48 Jacques Rancière, *On the Shores of Politics*, trans. Liz Heron (London: Verso, 2007), 61.

organised to oppose government plans to raze a park in Istanbul's Taksim Square as part of an urban renewal project that included significant commercial development featuring Ottoman-style barracks. The demonstrations eventually spread from Istanbul and to 60 cities across Turkey. Ultimately, the fate of Gezi Park was no longer the central issue.[49] It has been pointed out that institutional lack of support for functioning political opposition was one of the underlying reasons for the Gezi protests. Despite campaigning for a pluralist democracy, the enshrinement of individual rights and liberties and a new era in Turkish history altogether, the AKP, after its third consecutive electoral victory in 2011, was giving signals about a new form of absolutist government.

According to Amnesty International, the Turkish authorities committed serious human rights violations on a massive scale during the protests. The police used live ammunition, tear gas, water cannons, plastic bullets and beatings of the protestors, resulting in three deaths and thousands of injured. It is likely that the majority of extensive police abuse will go unpunished, while the protestors and their supporters face charges, threats and harassment. In many cases the suspects are being investigated under the anti-terrorism legislation.[50] It might be tempting to accuse the AKP government alone for their exaggerated reaction to the protests, but that would be an oversimplification. The Turkish government has always protected itself from initiatives for change by identifying criticism with the threat of terrorism, and it has successfully used the law to protect the status quo.

From the state's perspective, the people, the citizens themselves, can become a threat to the existence of the state and to the existing police order, and the law can become a tool in the hands of the powerful. The state's use of police violence against the Gezi Park protestors, who made the population's diversity highly visible, indicates that the state perceived the protestors as a threat to itself and to the unified citizen subject. The excessive use of force cannot be dismissed as individual cases of police officers overstepping their authority. Instead, perhaps one of the most important functions of the state law is to provide backing for the restoration of public order and, in certain circumstances, authorising the use of violence

---

49 Scott Harris, 'Pent-up Grievances against Authoritarian Rule Explode into Angry Protests across Turkey: Interview with Asli Bali, assistant professor at the UCLA School of Law,' *Between the Lines*, last modified 12 June 2013. Available at www.btlonline.org/2013/seg/130621bf-btl-bali.html (accessed 16 September 2013).
50 Amnesty International, *Gezi Park Protests – Brutal Denial of the Right to Peaceful Assembly in Turkey* (London: Peter Benenson House, 2013). Available at www.amnesty.org/download/Documents/12000/eur440222013en.pdf (accessed 15 December 2013); see also *Al Jazeera*, 'Turkey Passes a Controversial Medical Aid Bill,' last modified 19 January 2014. Available at www.aljazeera.com/news/europe/2014/01/turkey-passes-controversial-medical-aid-bill-2014118135840694702.html (accessed 19 January 2014).

by the state against its own citizens. In the streets the law dressed up as police and military officers tried to forcibly suppress the occurrence of the unpredictable subject.[51]

The Gezi Park protests have been identified with the Occupy movement and even called Occupy Gezi. The Occupy protests began in September of 2011 on Wall Street in New York City and spread to almost 100 cities in more than 80 countries. The Occupy movement consciously distanced itself from party politics, identity politics and other traditional modes of revolutionary politics. The lack of alternative notions to the prevailing economic and social system has raised criticism of the movement. For some, it was inconceivable that the protesters did not have a clear, shared idea of what they were protesting against or of what they wanted instead. Others in turn have argued that the lack of unity is precisely the point of the Occupy movement.[52]

According to Asli Bali, two models of democracy were at the heart of the Gezi protests: the majoritarian and authoritarian claims of the Prime Minister and the AK party versus the participatory ethos of the younger generation, which, in turn, opposes both the AKP and the republican ethos of traditional Kemalism. In Gezi Park the protesters brought to the surface something that had always been there: the lack of a unified citizen subject in all its variety, irreducible simply to religion and ethnicity. The protests did not endorse or seek recognition for a new identity group with a shared set of interests. On the other hand, neither were the protests simply a temporary strategic coalition of different identity or interest groups. Rather the occupations were often seen by the participants themselves as a process of creating new subjects and subjectivities and deconstructing old ones.[53] This, in fact, is the powerful message of the Gezi protests. It is crucial to contest continuously the legitimacy of any established order and to promote a disruptive and fractured notion of community, because institutionalising such communities incorporates dissent into police order in the Rancièrian sense.[54] Any attempt to set the communities and subjectivities in stone would transform the politics into the police.

---

51 Rancière, *On the Shores of Politics*, 61.
52 See e.g. David Graeber, 'Occupy Wall Street's Anarchist Roots: The Occupy Movement is one of several in American History to be based on Anarchist Principles,' *Al Jazeera*, last modified 30 November 2011. Available at www.aljazeera.com/indepth/opinion/2011/11/2011112872835904508.html (accessed 16 September 2013); Lorey, Isabell, 'Non-Representationist, Presentist Democracy,' Lecture given at the *Autonomy Project Symposium* Van Abbemuseum Eindhoven, 7–9 October 2011, last retrieved 28 January 2014. Available at http://eipcp.net/transversal/1011/lorey/en (accessed 28 January 2014).
53 Keith Bassett, 'Rancière, Politics, and the Occupy Movement,' *Environment and Planning D: Society and Space* 32 (2014), 886–901; see also Lorey, 'Non-Representationist, Presentist Democracy.'
54 Bassett, 'Rancière, Politics, and the Occupy Movement,' 889.

Conclusion

Law, in this chapter, is understood as diffuse. Legislating and bargaining on the position and the rights of minorities, legitimating violence with terrorism-related laws, judging the legality of political parties and clearing the streets of protestors in the name of the law are all examples of the inseparable relation between the law, parliamentary politics and power. The examples discussed in this chapter of law's interaction with parliamentary politics in the process of subject production in Turkey illustrate that the fundamental conflict over the citizen subject has traditionally been located in the dispute over the roles of religion and ethnicity, even to the point of these factors constituting the Kemalist subject. Traditionally in courtrooms, law has backed up the ideal of a secular and ethnically homogeneous Kemalist subject, but as the place of religion in the public sphere was altered with the AKP's rise to power, the place of ethnicity changed as well, illustrated by the peace process and the results of the recent parliamentary elections in Turkey. Here, legal reforms were used as bargaining and campaign tools for institutionalising the more inclusive notion of the citizen subject. In the Gezi protests the fragmented nature of the citizen subject became irreversibly visible, and it is no longer possible to reduce the diversity of the Turkish people to ethnicity and religion. It may not be too farfetched to claim that during the Gezi protests, at least for a brief moment, a Rancièrian unpredictable subject occupied the streets again.

Reflecting on the role of law in the construction of the citizen subject and using Rancière's concepts of police and politics, it seems obvious, perhaps somewhat inevitable, that law is deeply embedded in the police order. With the three examples discussed in this article of the workings of the law in the world, I do not claim that this is all that the law is capable of. Despite law being inseparably intertwined with the police, events of Rancière's politics can and do take place within the law: every time that political parties based on minority identity have challenged or been challenged by the state in a court of law, an 'impossible' subject has existed, regardless of the verdict. Good examples of such an impossible subject emerging for a brief moment are the well-known, albeit usually unsuccessful, headscarf cases in Turkey and the European Court of Human Rights in which the impossible subjectivities of a Muslim woman devoted both to her religion and to secularist rule, feminism, and Western values, have been lived. Whilst law operates in dichotomies, either providing recognition or not, law also constitutes an arena in which unpredictable subjects can *be*, regardless of whether or not they *become* recognised.

To summarise the battle over subjectivities discussed in this article, I argue that while the claims for recognition of ethnic and religious identities have been increasingly successful in altering the seemingly self-evident distinction between private and public, they have also lost their radical political potential. During the Gezi protests, however, a new, unpredictable subject emerged for a short while. This subject was not reducible to religion, ethnicity or to the age-old tension between secularism and religion in Turkish parliamentary politics.

According to Rancière, any subjectification is dis-identification:[55] as subjectification is a process rather than an entity, the process is about dis-identifying from, as much as it is about identifying with. The Gezi protesters, in their refusal to make specific claims or to appear as a unified group, dis-identified themselves from the existing divisions between the unified Turkish people and the ethnic and religious minorities. It can be said, returning to Brubaker, that for a moment they succeeded in summoning into being another kind of subjectivity, fragmented and irreducible.

Bibliography

Al Jazeera. 'Turkey Passes a Controversial Medical Aid Bill', last modified 19 January 2014. Available at www.aljazeera.com/news/europe/2014/01/turkey-passes-controversial-medical-aid-bill-2014118135840694702.html (accessed 19 January 2014).

Algan, Bülent. 'Dissolution of Political Parties by the Constitutional Court in Turkey: An Everlasting Conflict between the Court and the Parliament?' *Ankara Üniversitesi Hukuk Fakültesi Dergisi* 60:4 (2011): 809–36.

Amnesty International. *Gezi Park Protests – Brutal Denial of the Right to Peaceful Assembly in Turkey*. London: Peter Benenson House, 2013. Available at www.amnesty.org/download/Documents/12000/eur440222013en.pdf (accessed 15 December 2013).

Ayyildiz, Esengül. 'Talkootöistä Kansalaistottelemattomuuteen.' In *Turkki Euroopan Rajalla?*, edited by Anu Leinonen, Tuula Kojo, Mervi Nousiainen, Sampsa Peltonen and Lauri Tainio, 319–36. Helsinki: Gaudeamus, 2007.

Barnard, Anne. 'Turkey's Focus on Crushing Kurdish Separatists Complicates the Fight against ISIS.' *The New York Times*, last modified 28 July 2015. Available at www.nytimes.com/2015/07/29/world/turkeys-focus-on-crushing-kurd-extremists-complicates-isis-efforts.html?_r=0 (accessed 28 July 2015).

Bassett, Keith. 'Rancière, Politics, and the Occupy Movement,' *Environment & Planning D: Society & Space* 32:5 (2014), 886–901.

Bayir, Derya. *Minorities and Nationalism in Turkish Law*. Surrey: Ashgate, 2013.

Benhabib, Seyla. 'The Return of Political Theology,' *Philosophy & Social Criticism* 36:3–4 (2010), 451–71.

Brubaker, Rogers. 'Ethnicity without Groups.' In *The Ethnicity Reader. Nationalism, Multiculturalism and Migration*. 2nd edn., edited by Guibernau Montserrat and John Rex, 33–46. Cambridge: Polity, 2010.

Butler, Daren. 'Turkish court to announce verdicts in Ergenekon conspiracy case,' *Reuters*, last modified 4 August 2013. Available at www.reuters.com/article/2013/08/04/turkey-ergenekon-idUSL6N0G50AI20130804 (accessed 16 September 2013).

---

55 Rancière, *Disagreement: Politics and Philosophy*, 36.

Butler, Judith. 'A Response to Ali, Beckford, Bhatt, Modood and Woodhead,' *The British Journal of Sociology* 59:2 (2008), 255–60.
Canrowicz, Leo. 'Turkey-Kurdish conflict: President Erdogan's double-edged war against the PKK and Isis brings accusations of electioneering.' *Independent*, last modified 28 July 2015. Available at www.independent.co.uk/news/world/middle-east/turkeykurdish-conflict-president-erdogans-doubleedged-war-against-the-pkk-and-isis-brings-accusations-of-electioneering-10422726.html (accessed 28 July 2015).
Cizre, Ümit. 'A New Politics of Engagement. The Turkish Military, Society and the AKP.' In *Democracy, Islam, and Secularism in Turkey*, edited by Ahmet T. Kuru and Alfred Stepan, 122–48. New York: Columbia University Press, 2012.
EKurd Daily. 'Kurdish PKK rebels stop withdrawing forces from Turkey.' *KurdNet*, last modified 9 September 2013. Available at www.ekurd.net/mismas/articles/misc2013/9/turkey4777.htm (accessed 16 September 2013).
Ensaroğlu, Yilmaz. 'Turkey's Kurdish Question and the Peace Process,' *Insight Turkey* 15:2 (2013), 7–17. Available at http://file.insightturkey.com/Files/Pdf/20130415155719_15_2_2013_ensaroglu.pdf (accessed 22 August 2014).
Eriksen, Thomas Hylland. 'Ethnicity, Race and Nation.' In *The Ethnicity Reader. Nationalism, Multiculturalism and Migration*, 2nd edn., edited by Guibernau Montserrat and John Rex, 46–53. Cambridge: Polity, 2010.
Graeber, David. 'Occupy Wall Street's Anarchist Roots. The Occupy Movement is one of several in American History to be based on Anarchist Principles.' *Al Jazeera*, last modified 30 November 2011. Available at www.aljazeera.com/indepth/opinion/2011/11/2011112872835904508.html (accessed 16 September 2013).
Gunes, Cengiz. *Kurdish National Movement in Turkey: From Protest to Resistance*. London: Taylor & Francis, 2012.
Harris, Scott. 'Pent-up Grievances against Authoritarian Rule Explode into Angry Protests across Turkey. Interview with Asli Bali, assistant professor at the UCLA School of Law.' *Between the Lines*, last modified 12 June 2013. Available at www.btlonline.org/2013/seg/130621bf-btl-bali.html (accessed 16 September 2013).
Herzog, Mark. *FCP Briefing: Analysing Turkey's 2010 constitutional referendum*. The Foreign Policy Centre, 2010. Available at http://fpc.org.uk/fsblob/1269.pdf. Last retrieved 16 September 2013 (accessed 16 September 2013).
Hirvonen, Ari. 'Tasa-arvon demokratia – Jacques Rancière, erimielisyyden ajattelija.' In *Yhteiskuntateorioiden oikeus*, edited by Toomas Kotkas and Susanna Lindroos-Hovinheimo, 327–76. Helsinki: Tutkijaliitto, 2010.
Ince, Basak. 'Citizenship Education in Turkey: Inclusive or Exclusive,' *Oxford Review of Education* 38:2 (2012), 115–31.
Izady, M.R. 'The Kurds in Iraq and Iran.' In *The Ethnicity Reader. Nationalism, Multiculturalism and Migration*, 2nd edn., edited by Guibernau Montserrat and John Rex, 198–210. Cambridge: Polity, 2010.
Kardas, Seban. 'What Now for the Kurdish Peace Process?' *Al Jazeera*, last modified 8 June 2015. Available at www.Al Jazeera.com/indepth/opinion/2015/06/kurdish-peace-process-turkey-election-erdogan-150608053456502.html (accessed 8 June 2015).
Kazim, Hasnain. 'Ergenekon Verdicts: Erdogan Silences Dissent in Divided Turkey,' *Spiegel Online International*, last modified 5 August 2013. Available at www.spiegel.de/international/world/verdicts-in-turkish-ergenekon-trial-reflect-deep-divisions-a-914924.html (accessed 16 September 2013).

Keyman, E.F. and Tuba Kanci. 'A Tale of Ambiguity: Citizenship, Nationalism and Democracy in Turkey,' *Nations & Nationalism* 17:2 (2011), 318–36.

Logan, Joseph. 'In Search of the Building Blocks of Opposition in Turkey,' *Middle East Research and Information Project*, last modified 10 June 2013. Available at www.merip.org/mero/mero061013?ip_login_no_cache=303c323c4b550725d3f23ce15aac9078.

Lorey, Isabell. 'Non-Representationist, Presentist Democracy.' Lecture given at the *Autonomy Project Symposium*, 7–9 October 2011, Van Abbemuseum Eindhoven. Available at http://eipcp.net/transversal/1011/lorey/en (accessed 28 January 2014).

O'Neil, Mary Lou. 'You are what You Wear: Clothing/Appearance Laws and the Construction of the Public Citizen in Turkey,' *Fashion Theory: The Journal of Dress, Body & Culture* 14:1 (2010), 65–81.

Özbudun, Ergun. 'Turkey – Plural Society and Monolithic State.' In *Democracy, Islam, and Secularism in Turkey*, edited by Ahmet T. Kuru and Alfred Stepan, 61–94. New York: Columbia University Press, 2012.

Özbudun, Ergun. 'The Turkish Constitutional Court and Political Crisis.' In *Democracy, Islam, and Secularism in Turkey*, edited by Ahmet T. Kuru and Alfred Stepan, 149–165. New York: Columbia University Press, 2012.

Rancière, Jacques. 'Who is the Subject of the Rights of Man?' *South Atlantic Quarterly* 103:2-3 (2004), 297–310.

Rancière, Jacques. 'Ten Theses on Politics,' *Theory & Event* 5:3 (2001), 1–33.

Rancière, Jacques. *Disagreement: Politics and Philosophy*, trans. Julie Rose. Minneapolis: University of Minnesota Press, 1999.

Rancière, Jacques. *On the Shores of Politics*, trans. Liz Heron. London, New York: Verso, 2007.

Reynolds, James. 'Turkey Ergenekon case: Ex-army chief Basbug gets life.' *BBC News Europe*, last modified 5 August 2013. Available at www.bbc.co.uk/news/world-europe-23571739 (accessed 16 September 2013).

Vela, Justin. 'Features Analysis: Turkey's divisive Ergenekon trial Conviction of alleged coup plotters seen by many as Islamists' revenge against the army.' *Al Jazeera*, last modified 12 August 2013. Available at www.Al Jazeera.com/indepth/features/2013/08/201381175743430360.html (accessed 16 September 2013).

Vojdik, Valorie K. 'Politics of the Headscarf in Turkey: Masculinities, Feminism, and the Construction of Collective Identities,' *Harvard Journal of Law and Gender* 33:2 (2010), 661–86.

Yavuz, M.H. 'A Preamble to the Kurdish Question: The Politics of Kurdish Identity,' *Journal of Muslim Minority Affairs* 18:1 (1998), 9–18.

Yeginsu, Ceylan. 'Turkish Troops Enter Iraq in Pursuit of Kurdish Rebels,' *The New York Times*, last modified 8 September 2015. Available at www.nytimes.com/2015/09/09/world/europe/turkey-pkk-bombing-police.html?_r=0 (accessed 8 September 2015).

Cases

Case of Refah Partisi (The Welfare Party) and Others v Turkey [GC], app. nos 41340/98, 41342/98, 41343/98, 41344/98, ECHR 2003-II (13 February 2003)

Constitutional Court of Turkey decision E. 1993/3, K. 1994/2, 16 June 1994; *Anayasa Mahkemesi Kararlar Dergisi (AMDK)* (Constitutional Court Reports) 30.3:1201, 1199

Part II

Recognising 'the different' subject

Chapter 6

The genderqueer in UK law
Why current laws are insufficient

Carolynn Gray

Introduction

The issue of trans*[1] rights have continued to be a focus in the UK since the enactment of the Gender Recognition Act 2004 (GRA 2004). However, the reforms, at least initially, centred on ensuring the rights of those who sought to live as members of the sex opposite to that registered on birth; the rights of the wider trans* community were largely ignored. However, on 6 January 2014 an Early Day Motion (EDM) was tabled in the UK House of Commons. The intention behind this EDM was to force a debate on the issue of providing legal recognition to those individuals who do not associate with a particular gender. Although it is very unlikely that a debate will be held on the subject matter of the EDM the fact that it was tabled shows that the plight of those individuals who do not associate with a particular gender is being noticed by those involved in the law-making process and should be welcomed for its symbolic function if nothing else. Indeed the EDM preceded other important developments in this area such as the recent campaigns for the rights of non-binary people by campaign groups[2] and the recommendations of the UK parliament's Women and Equalities Committee report into transgender equality which called for the UK government to make provisions for those whose gender identity lies outwith the binary system of male and female.[3] In addition to the work being carried out in the UK, the Council of

---

1 Trans* (with the accompanying asterisk) is used in this context to mean the broad spectrum of individuals who do not identify as the gender assigned to them at birth. It is therefore an umbrella term encompassing a variety of identities along the gender identity spectrum. For example it covers at one end *transsexuals* (those who seek to live fully as members of the sex opposite to that assigned to them at birth) but it also covers all other non-cisgendered identities such as gender outlaw, genderqueer, agender, third gender etc. Cisgender is the commonly accepted term used to denote those whose gender identity accords with that assigned to them at birth i.e. non-trans* people. For more on this see Avery Tompkins, 'Asterisk,' *TSQ: Transgender Studies Quarterly* 1:1–2 (2014), 26–7.
2 Such as that by the Scottish Transgender Alliance.
3 Women and Equalities Committee, 'Transgender Equality' HMSO 2016.

Europe further called for the rights of non-binary people in Resolution 2048 (2015) by stating that Member States must 'consider including a third gender option in identity documents for those who seek it'[4] thereby opening the possibility of non-binary individuals being able to move beyond the legally recognised system of binary gender and begin to develop alternative ways of being legally recognised gendered individuals. So, it is clear that there are moves towards obtaining legal recognition for non-binary gender identities; however, it is also clear that UK law is very far behind on this.

The purpose of this chapter is to show how, despite the recent advances towards recognising the rights of trans* people, noted above, the law remains insufficient as it places limits on who can access such protection and recognition. The calls for non-binary recognition, perhaps unwittingly, highlight the restrictions inherent within the existing protective legislation. In exploring the restrictions in the current legislation this chapter will utilise the work of Judith Butler to examine the UK laws in relation to recognition and protection of trans* individuals. It will be shown in this chapter that the particular poststructural critique developed by Butler enables those of us who seek to develop more inclusive and transformative laws to begin to debate the limits of the current laws by offering alternative ways of conceptualising the sex/gender dichotomy and of understanding the power of law in regulating acceptable sex/gender presentations in public space.[5]

Gender variant individuals in UK law

In the UK the two main pieces of legislation purporting to give protection to those whose gender identity differs somewhat from the norm are the GRA 2004 and the Equality Act 2010 (EA 2010). Section 9(1) of the GRA 2004 provides that:

> [w]here a full gender recognition certificate is issued to a person, the person's gender becomes for all purposes the acquired gender (so that, if the acquired gender is the male gender, the person's sex becomes that of a man and, if it is the female gender, the person's sex becomes that of a woman).

Section 7(1) of the EA 2010 provides that:

> [a] person has the protected characteristic of gender reassignment if the person is proposing to undergo, is undergoing or has undergone

---

4 Council of Europe Resolution 2048 (2015) [6.2.4].
5 Notwithstanding that the issue of utilising law to achieve these aims is problematic as will be discussed throughout this chapter.

a process (or part of a process) for the purpose of reassigning the person's sex by changing physiological or other attributes of sex.

The GRA 2004 in particular has been hailed as being a 'milestone in the recognition of transgender rights'[6] which is considered to be a piece of radical legislation[7] and groundbreaking reform[8] which located 'the UK at the forefront of global transgender law reform'.[9] The purpose of this chapter is not to challenge the undoubted benefit of having legislation such as this in place because clearly enabling individuals to obtain legal recognition of their gender identity and to be protected in the public sphere from discrimination on the basis of gender identity is a huge step forward for the UK. To show the benefit of such pieces of legislation for enabling the protection of one's identity it is important to contextualise the reforms contained in s.7 of the EA 2010 and s.9 of the GRA 2004. These reforms are the culmination of decades of sexing bodies in UK law and of UK law defining the identities of UK citizens which began in Scotland in 1957 with the case of *X, Petitioner*.[10] This case was concerned with whether or not one's sex registered at birth could be subsequently changed on one's birth certificate. In analysing the question the court determined that birth certificates could only be altered if a mistake had been made on initially registering the child's sex: subsequent sex reassignment surgery did not mean that the child had been wrongly sexed at birth therefore the birth certificate entry was an accurate record of historical fact. Shortly following *X, Petitioner*[11] was the English case of *Corbett v Corbett*[12] which is arguably one of the most famous cases in a UK court concerning the legal sex of an individual. The outcome of *Corbett* was that legal sex was to be determined by consideration of four factors: (i)

---

6 *R (B) v Secretary of State for Justice* [2009] EWHC 2220 (Admin); [2009] HRLR 35 at [30] as per David Elvin QC.
7 Sheila Jeffreys, 'They Know It When They See It: The UK Gender Recognition Act 2004,' *British Journal of Politics and International Relations* 10:2 (2008), 328.
8 Sharon Cowan, 'Looking Back (to)wards the Body: Medicalization and the GRA,' *Social and Legal Studies* 18:2 (2009), 247.
9 Andrew Sharpe, 'A Critique of the Gender Recognition Act 2004,' *Journal of Bioethical Inquiry* 4:1 (2007), 37.
10 1957 SLT (Sh. Ct.) 61. However five years previous to the decision in *X, Petitioner* the Scottish courts were asked to consider whether Elizabeth Forbes-Sempill was male or female. The Forbes-Sempill case was unreported. However a discussion is provided by Forbes in the Institutes of the Law of Scotland 1 1, 1, 18. In this case Elizabeth Forbes-Sempill had been born and registered as female but sought to live as a man: Ewan Forbes-Sempill. The court, in determining which sex Elizabeth belonged to, followed the accepted Roman Law practice which 'regarded the hermaphrodite as belonging to the [sex] he or she more closely resembled and, in cases of doubt, to be male.' (Elaine Sutherland, *Child and Family Law* (Edinburgh: T & T Clark, 1999)).
11 1957 SLT (Sh. Ct.) 61.
12 [1971] P 83.

chromosomes, (ii) gonads, (iii) genitalia and (iv) psychology.[13] However Ormrod, J stated that if the first three criteria are congruent then the person is legally sexed accordingly notwithstanding their psychological identification as male or female.

The *Corbett* judgment had long lasting consequences for those individuals who sought to have their physical sex reassignment recognised by UK law. For example in *Rees v United Kingdom*,[14] *Cossey v United Kingdom*[15] and *Sheffield and Horsham v United Kingdom*[16] the European Court of Human Rights (ECtHR) held that English matrimony law which restricted marriage to opposite sex couples was not incompatible with post-operative transsexuals' rights to marry and found a family as contained in Article 12 of the European Convention on Human Rights (ECHR) nor was refusal of the UK to recognise post-operative transsexuals a violation of Article 8 ECHR.[17] The ECtHR also held in *X, Y & Z v United Kingdom*[18] that non-recognition of a female-to-male transsexual as the father of children conceived via AID[19] did not amount to a breach of the children's rights under Article 8. The *Corbett* decision also had an impact on the domestic courts' decision making in relation to sex-specific criminal offences as in *R v Tan*,[20] in relation to financial provision on separation as in *J v ST*,[21] contact with one's children following parental separation as in *Re F (Minors) (Contact)*,[22] *L (Contact: Transsexual Applicant)*[23] and *H (Minors) (Public Interest: Protection of Identity)*.[24] The *Corbett* decision was upheld by the Court of Appeal in *Bellinger v Bellinger*[25] which concerned whether a marriage between a male-to-female transsexual and a male was a valid marriage: the Court of Appeal held that it was not as it was a marriage between two males as per the *Corbett* judgment and therefore contrary to s.11(c) of the

---

13 [1971] P 83 at 100.
14 (1987) 9 EHRR 56.
15 (1991) 13 EHRR 622.
16 (1999) 27 EHRR 163.
17 Although no challenge was made in relation to the equivalent Scottish provisions regarding marriage i.e. s.5(4)(e) of the Marriage (Scotland) Act 1977 if such a challenge had been made it is argued that the Scottish courts would have taken the same approach as the English courts at the time and restricted marriage to opposite sex couples: sex being determined by that registered at birth.
18 (1997) 24 EHRR 143.
19 Artificial Insemination by Donor.
20 [1983] QB 1053.
21 [1996] 2 FCR 665.
22 [1993] 2 FLR 677.
23 [1995] 2 FLR 438.
24 [1994] 1 WLR 1141.
25 [2001] EWCA Civ 1140; [2002] Fam. 150.

Matrimonial Causes Act 1973. The decision was upheld by the House of Lords as discussed below.

Therefore medical science had enabled transsexuals to alter their bodies in a way which would reduce the incongruence between physical presentation and internal psychological gender identity. However, the law throughout the UK continued to refuse to recognise this change thus leaving post-operative transsexuals in a legal limbo which was to continue until the case of *Goodwin v United Kingdom*.[26] In *Goodwin* the ECtHR held that to not recognise post-operative transsexuals for the purpose of marriage was a breach of the applicant's Article 12 rights and not providing any legal recognition of a change of sex amounted to a breach of Article 8 ECHR. This decision enabled the House of Lords in the *Bellinger* appeal to issue a declaration of incompatibility under s.3 of the Human Rights Act 1998 which provided that s.11(c) of the Matrimonial Causes Act 1973 was incompatible with the rights contained in the Convention. As a result of the *Goodwin* decision and subsequent House of Lords decision in *Bellinger* the GRA 2004 was eventually passed which enables those who are diagnosed with gender dysphoria,[27] are over the age of 18,[28] who intend to live in the opposite sex until death,[29] and who have lived as a member of the opposite sex for two years[30] to obtain a Gender Recognition Certificate (GRC) which will 'change' that person's legal sex.[31] The purpose of s.9 of the GRA 2004 is to provide a mechanism whereby transsexual individuals can change their legal sex for all purposes save the exceptions listed in the Act.[32]

In relation to the protective intention behind s.7 of the EA 2010 the explanatory notes accompanying the draft Equality Bill during the legislative process provided two examples which were intended to clarify the scope of the protective measures contained in s.7 of the EA 2010:

> A person who was born physically male decides to spend the rest of his life living as a woman. He declares his intention to his manager at work, who makes appropriate arrangements, and she then starts life at work and home as a woman. After discussion with her doctor and a Gender Identity Clinic, she starts hormone treatment and after several years she

---

26 (2002) 35 EHRR 18.
27 Gender Recognition Act 2004 s.2(1)(a).
28 Ibid. s.1.
29 Ibid. s.2(1)(c).
30 Ibid. s.2(1)(b).
31 Ibid. s.9.
32 Exceptions are contained in sections 12 (parenthood of children born before the parent acquires a Gender Recognition Certificate), 15 (succession), 16 (peerages) and 20 (gender-specific offences).

goes through gender reassignment surgery. She would be undergoing gender reassignment for the purposes of the Bill.[33]

An unemployed person who was born physically female decides to spend the rest of her life as a man. He starts and continues to live as a man. He decides not to seek medical advice as he successfully 'passes' as a man without the need for any medical intervention. He would be undergoing gender reassignment for the purposes of the Bill.[34]

The second example goes some way towards protecting those who identify as genderqueer. The individual in that scenario, although presumably not changing legal sex by means of a GRC (as he does not seek medical advice) has determined to live as a member of the sex opposite to his birth sex. This implies some degree of self-determination within the EA 2010; that one can choose one's own sex. However the protection given by this section is in fact very limited. The individual can be male or female but presumably not both; the questions therefore remain 'to what extent can the individual in scenario two fluctuate between male and female or choose an alternative path?' In addition to that another question might also be 'to what extent can the GRA 2004 conceive of those who identify as both male and female or as other than male or female?'

The problem which this chapter seeks to address is the limited potential of these outlined reforms. As noted above there is no intention to decry the benefit of these pieces of legislation as there is no doubt that their existence will have had a positive impact on the lives of many individuals whose gender identity is different from the gender assigned to them at birth. However it is arguable that these reforms do not go far enough; are not as progressive and as inclusive as they could have been. Although, as will be seen in the discussion below, there are concerns that law is not necessarily the most appropriate mechanism by which to achieve such inclusion and recognition because of the law's traditional approach to trans* individuals but also because of the role law plays in constituting the trans* legal subject.[35]

Using Butler's work to critique UK law

Butler's work is paradoxically crucial for those of us who seek to critique the current law but also to utilise law to ensure that marginalised individuals

---

33 Available at www.legislation.gov.uk/ukpga/2010/15/notes/data.pdf, 10 (accessed 26 August 2016).
34 Available at www.legislation.gov.uk/ukpga/2010/15/notes/data.pdf, 10–11 (accessed 26 August 2016).
35 For more on this argument see the following: Dean Spade, *Normal Life: Administrative Violence, Critical Trans Politics and the Limits of Law* (Brooklyn, NY: South End Press, 2011); Moya Lloyd, 'Heteronormativity and/as Violence: The "Sexing" of Gwen Araujo,' *Hypatia* 28:4 (2013), 818–34; Elena Loizidou, *Judith Butler: Ethics, Law, Politics* (London: Routledge, 2007).

are recognised by law. This is because Butler seeks to challenge the very concept of a subject who stands before the law seeking recognition and protection from the law: the very foundation of much liberal legal thought, in particular work on trans* rights which is predicated on such a pre-existing subject. As such Butler's work poses difficulties for those of us who seek to use the law as a means of ensuring that individuals obtain rights and protections because, although law may be problematic in terms of poststructural theory, it is the means by which rights and protections are given to individuals and is, therefore, the system within which we must work; the challenge is to find a way to strategically use the law to achieve our goals while being mindful of the problems that law itself causes for marginalised individuals.

The 'legal subject'

So the starting point for a critique of the law based on the work of Butler is to understand how she approaches the idea of a 'legal subject'. She notes in *Gender Trouble* that:

> [t]he domains of political and linguistic 'representation' set out in advance the criterion by which subjects themselves are formed, with the result that representation is extended only to what can be acknowledged as a subject.[36]

She continues that the 'subject turns out to be discursively constituted by the very political system that is supposed to facilitate its emancipation'.[37] Therefore in seeking recognition before, and protection within, the law creates the trans* subject and places limits on the possibility of recognition. If law creates the subject before it rather than recognises a pre-existing subject then as Butler claims the challenge is to understand how the subject 'is produced and restrained by the very structures of power through which emancipation is sought'.[38] Therefore for Butler law is not the emancipatory regime that legal theorists and campaigners believe; it is part of the system of power which creates those before it and as such places limits on which bodies are deemed capable of being recognised, of being intelligible. Crucial to Butler's analysis of the subject is that there is no position outwith the field of power constituted by '[t]he juridical structures of language and politics' but rather 'only a critical genealogy of its own legitimating practices'.[39] So the question is how does law, in providing

---

36 Judith Butler, *Gender Trouble: Feminism and the Subversion of Identity* (New York: Routledge, 1999), 4.
37 Ibid.
38 Butler, *Gender Trouble*, 5.
39 Ibid. 8.

recognition to those who supposedly, as per the perspective of traditional jurisprudence, approach it seeking recognition and rights, actually construe that very subject? The answer lies in how Butler analyses the construction of the subject through discourse and the gaps that are produced in construing a viable subject which enable marginalised ways of being to emerge. For a lawyer seeking trans* rights it is problematic to approach the issue from the perspective that law does not have all of the answers and it cannot represent us all. However, if we take the premise that law constructs the subject then it is possible to offer possibilities for reconstruction in a more inclusive manner. That is not to say that the law is moving closer to an ideal whereby all are recognised because there is no subject which precedes the law upon which recognition will be conferred but, rather, such an approach is an acknowledgement of the constructedness of the legal subject which offers the possibility of a reconstructed legal subject; a legal subject, whereby the boundaries of acceptability have been moved. Such a reconstruction renders more ways of being human intelligible. Such an approach acknowledges the role that discourse plays in constituting normality and abnormality.

Once Butler raises doubt about a pre-discursive subject she then considers how subjects emerge and one of the ways through which this occurs is via the forced reinforcement of norms such as sex and gender. In her considerable body of work she challenges the assumption that both sex and gender are natural categories which neatly separate individuals as male or female. Butler's aim is to challenge the theorising of the physical body as having a pre-discursive reality. Butler's thesis is that sex and gender are 'given' to bodies by means of regulatory norms and practices[40] and such an approach is crucial for this chapter, and indeed crucial for an examination of how systems such as law, for example, participate in the construction of the subject. Butler asks the following:

> [t]o what extent do *regulatory practices* of gender formation and division constitute identity, the internal coherence of the subject, indeed, the self-identical status of the person? To what extent is 'identity' a normative ideal rather than a descriptive feature of experience? And how do the regulatory practices that govern gender also govern culturally intelligible notions of identity?[41]

The idea of identity here is crucial; what does it mean for one to claim a sexual or gender identity and seek recognition of that? In the case law discussed above, and indeed in the legislation which forms the heart of this

---

40 Ibid. 23.
41 Ibid.

chapter, the individual before the law is pre-formed before approaching the law; the individual has a strong sense of self as male or female and merely asks that the law adapt to recognise this identity. However, Butler's work suggests that the identity of the subject is not something which exists on its own; it is not a 'descriptive feature of experience' but rather a normative ideal and as such operates in such a way as to maintain the viability, or not, of subjects. It is only when the naturalness of such identities is challenged by the emergence of practices such as non-normative sexual or gender practices that problems arise. Those whose gender and sexual practices are non-normative are not recognisable within the established system as they are disruptive to the norm *but the norm is a socially produced fact not the ahistorical, natural fact as presented*; it is a carefully constructed, and very fragile, fantasy which relies upon the silence of the discontinuous incoherent identities to maintain its 'truth'. In this sense then norms of sex and gender are used as means of causing psychic damage to non-normative and marginalised individuals; a form of normative violence which, according to Chambers 'points not to a type of violence that is somehow "normative," but to the violence of norms'.[42] Butler spends considerable time on the violence that can be done by sex and gender norms to marginalised bodies; those 'bodies that would (necessarily) violate such norms'.[43]

She asks '[d]oes sex have a history?'[44] The clear answer is yes, of course it does. It is possible to trace via various discourses the history of sex. For the purpose of this chapter, however, it is the history of legal sex which is important; the means by which law as a system of power sexed those who appeared before it. The examination of how law sexed bodies is important because it will show that law, in making pronouncements in relation to the sex of applicants placed boundaries around what expressions of sex, and indeed gender, were possible and thus intelligible within the legal system. In considering how sex, that supposedly immutable characteristic of all human beings, exists as an effect of power Butler opens the possibility that there can be a more inclusive approach to sex within law. To become male or female is not really a choice but it is not natural either. It is forced/compelled upon a body by means of regulatory norms.[45] As Butler states there is a cultural compulsion to become a woman…or become a man[46] and therefore there is no individual choice or agency involved because ' "sex"

---

42 Samuel A Chambers, 'Normative Violence after 9/11: Rereading the Politics of Gender Trouble', *New Political Science* 29:1 (2007), 44.
43 Ibid.
44 Butler, *Gender Trouble*, 10.
45 Judith Butler, *Bodies that Matter: On the Discursive Limits of 'Sex'*. (New York: Routledge, 1993), 1.
46 Butler, *Gender Trouble*, 12.

is an ideal construct which is forcibly materialized through time'.[47] Crucial to how sex is forcibly materialized is the reiteration of the norms of sex.[48] Butler points out that the reiteration process is hugely important because it is in the reiteration of the norms that their identity is shown. If sex was natural then there would be no need for reiteration of norms. She notes '[t]hat this reiteration is necessary is a sign that materialization is never quite complete, that bodies never quite comply with the norms by which their materialization is impelled'.[49]

Law is an excellent example of how sex and gender are regulated. The power of Butler is in seeing that law does not act upon a pre-existing body but 'creates' that body – gives it meaning and renders it intelligible, or not. So the question then, for those of us seeking to change the law and have a more inclusive legislative framework, is why turn to law to give rights if there is no person there to give rights to? Does the genderqueer person live in the margins, where the regulatory framework surrounding sex and gender have failed and thus exists as an example of the materialising aspect of sex as a regulatory ideal…which is getting perilously close to saying there is an 'I' before these discourses? Or, in the 'creation' of male and female legal subjects has law 'created' those who identify as neither/both/something alternative? Genderqueer is a challenge to the idea that sex and gender are naturally binary. If the sex and gender link is destabilised and indeed the sex and gender binaries are exposed as nothing more than regulatory ideals then genderqueer ceases to be a challenge, a site of resistance, and becomes merely an alternative way of being human. Saltzburg and Davis[50] claim, in their work with genderqueer youth, that:

> [i]f we long for change, we must also confront the challenge of generating new meanings [...] New patterns of social life are not secured simply by refusing or rejecting the meaning as given – for example, avoiding sexist or racist language. Rather, the strong invitation is for the emergence of new forms of language, ways of interpreting the world, patterns of representation.[51]

The quest for better laws has to continue because to seek to operate outwith the legal framework because of the problems inherent within that framework as a site of power which constitutes the sexed and gendered

---

47 Butler, *Bodies that Matter*, 1.
48 Ibid.
49 Ibid. 2.
50 Susan Saltzburg and Tamara S Davis, 'Co-authoring gender-queer youth identities: Discursive tellings and retellings,' *Journal of Ethnic and Cultural Diversity in Social Work* 19:2, (2010), 87–108.
51 Ibid. 87.

individuals in particular ways would be to abandon any real hope for developments which improve the lives of many individuals; it would leave many vulnerable individuals open to further discrimination and render them less than valid legal subjects. It is important to further consider Butler's idea of intelligibility here because it is in becoming intelligible to a particular system of power that bodies are seen as valid or not within that system. Saltzburg and Davis write that:

> [t]he polarized division of gender that culturally envelops the lives of young people identifying as gender-different, gender-queer, or transgender places them outside the sphere of what Western society judges to be normal and natural dispositions of gender-being.[52]

In making this claim they touch on the concept of intelligibility; those who fit within the norms of sex and gender are intelligible, those who do not are not and are therefore thought of as abnormal and, in the West, often pathologised and marginalised.[53] For Butler the development of subjectivity within individuals has a consequence for others. She states that the formation of subjects via exclusionary practices 'requires the simultaneous production of a domain of abject beings, those who are not yet "subjects", but who form the constitutive outside to the domain of the subject'.[54] This is crucial because Butler furthers her point thus:

> [t]he abject designates here precisely those 'unlivable' and 'uninhabitable' zones of social life which are nevertheless densely populated by those who do not enjoy the status of the subject, but whose living under the sign of the 'unlivable' is required to circumscribe the domain of the subject.[55]

The formation of subjectivity cannot take place without the possibility of 'abjection and its status for the subject as a threatening spectre'.[56] However, the concept of abjection may offer some hope for trans* individuals. Phillips notes that '[a]bjection refers to the vague sense of horror that permeates the boundary between the self and the other'.[57] but more than that it 'refers to the process by which identificatory regimes exclude subjects that they render unintelligible or beyond classification'.[58] This is important; it

---

52 Saltzburg and Davis, 'Co-authoring Gender-queer Youth Identities,' 88.
53 Ibid.
54 Butler, *Bodies that Matter*, 3.
55 Ibid.
56 Ibid.
57 Robert Phillips, 'Abjection,' *TSQ: Transgender Studies Quarterly* 1: 1–2 (2014), 19.
58 Ibid.

suggests that abjection as a process serves a crucial function in relation to developing subjectivity through the exclusion of the Other which 'serves to maintain or reinforce the boundaries that are threatened'.[59]

The question then is can abjection as a position be taken up, reclaimed, in order to push forward different ways of thinking about sexed and gendered individuals? The use of the term genderqueer is actually hugely important and symbolic. It is an act of reclamation. Butler, considering the term *queer* in *Bodies that Matter*, questions 'how is it that a term that signalled degradation has been turned [...] to signify a new and affirmative set of meanings?'[60] She argues that 'queer' is a form of speech act and as such is a performative.[61]

Queer, historically, was used to put boundaries around who were considered legitimate and who were not. The creation of a group of people as 'less-than' sought to maintain the legitimacy of the heteronormative society. It was used to abject those whose resistance and recognition challenged the supposed naturality of the heterosexual matrix. Therefore *queer* was used as a means of ensuring that the possibility of *queer* would be repudiated as to identify as queer was to take up a position as 'less-than', to be abject. Butler, in *Bodies that Matter*, notes the importance of using certain terms for political purposes rather than trying to forge new terms (as 'new' terms are never new). She notes:

> it remains politically necessary to lay claim to 'women,' 'queer,' 'gay,' and 'lesbian,' precisely because of the way these terms, as it were, lay their claim on us prior to our full knowing.[62]

We should not abandon the quest for queer recognition just because the term itself is problematic. Rather, as Butler states:

> [t]he political deconstruction of 'queer' ought not to paralyze the use of such terms, but ideally, to extend its range, to make us consider at what expense and for what purpose the terms are used, and through what relations of power such categories have been wrought.[63]

This is important because reclaiming queerness opens the possibility of changing how different subjectivities become possible. If there is no position outwith discourse from which the 'I' speaks then surely there are

---

59 Ibid.
60 Butler, *Bodies that Matter*, 223.
61 Ibid.
62 Ibid, 229.
63 Ibid.

multiple ways of taking up the 'I' position within discourse? This is not obviously true as not all identities are available as means of obtaining subjectivity. Butler notes that:

> [t]he terms by which we are recognized as human are socially articulated and changeable. And sometimes the very terms that confer 'humanness' on some individuals are those that deprive certain other individuals of the possibility of achieving that status producing a differential between the human and the less-than-human.[64]

Therefore to begin to reclaim queerness and to seek to transform it into a valid subjectivity one must first navigate taking up the 'less-than-human' position. This links to the idea of intelligibility. If one is not given recognition then one is less than fully intelligible – or not intelligible at all. Butler notes however that there can be positive aspects of being less than intelligible. She notes 'if intelligibility is understood as that which is produced as a consequence of recognition according to prevailing social norms'[65] then being less-than-intelligible allows for some degree of resistance to social norms which may, should one appropriate them for the purpose of obtaining recognition, have the potential for psychic harm. One is placed in a position of obtaining recognition at the expense of one's identity…if it is possible to say that 'identity' exists. Butler argues that:

> the 'I' that I am finds itself at once constituted by norms and dependent on them but also endeavours to live in ways that maintain a critical and transformative relation to them. This is not easy, because the 'I' becomes, to a certain extent unknowable, threatened with unviability, with becoming undone altogether, when it no longer incorporates the norm in such a way that makes this 'I' fully recognizable.[66]

Homosexuals were once discontinuous and incoherent within this sex, gender, sexuality matrix. Homosexuals' very existence challenged the coherence of the heterosexual subject; threatened to break down the fragile foundation upon which 'normal' sexuality was built. Homosexuality, however, has become a culturally coherent identity partly via legal reforms. The process of the law enforcing the intelligibility of sexed and gendered citizens can be seen by considering the case law presented above: in *Corbett*[67] the law initially placed boundaries on intelligible sexed and gendered beings

---

64 Judith Butler, *Undoing Gender* (New York: Routledge, 2004) 2.
65 Ibid. 3.
66 Ibid. 3.
67 [1971] P 83.

which continued throughout the latter half of the twentieth century into the twenty-first century when the boundaries were somewhat re-negotiated (once again by law). This relationship between social norms and law can be seen in Butler's *Undoing Gender* where she considers the role of law, among other things, in regulating gender. She does not seek to show how law regulates gender but rather starts with the question 'is there a gender that pre-exists its regulation, or is it the case that, in being subject to regulation, the gendered subject emerges, produced in and through that particular form of subjection?'[68] This sort of questioning is reflective of her earlier examinations in *Gender Trouble* and *Bodies that Matter* but in *Undoing Gender* she specifically considers the role that law plays. Adopting a Foucauldian perspective she notes that subjects are shaped and formed by regulatory power and that 'to become subject to a regulation is also to become subjectivated by it, that is, to be brought into being as a subject precisely through being regulated'.[69] Such an approach can be seen in how UK law inscribes a sex upon bodies, historically via *Corbett* as mentioned above but also in the contemporary GRA 2004; it is not so much a case of law recognising the trans* person who stands before it seeking justice and protection but rather a case of in so doing the law brings into being the trans* legal subject.

Indeed as shown above, until recently transsexuals were legally invisible but, as a result of the GRA 2004 are now intelligible so long as they meet the strict criteria within the legislation i.e. being either male or female: they are intelligible because they 'in some sense institute and maintain relations of coherence and continuity among sex, gender, sexual practice and desire'.[70] However, the wider trans* community, particularly genderqueer individuals, remains largely unintelligible.[71] Butler's thesis highlights the fragile nature of gender categories; she shows how such categories are based on systems of knowledge and power.

Gender variance and indeterminate sex destabilise the coherence of the sex, gender, sexuality matrix and, within a system which relies upon the belief that sex and gender are natural concepts, need to be 'fixed' in order to maintain the fantasy that the matrix is naturally occurring. For example, in terms of intersex children, the historical response of the medical profession was to 'correct' the variance by means of genital surgery, carried out when the person was an infant and therefore without his or her consent. The purpose of such surgery was to make the child either male or female thus reinforcing the sex binary; the position was that such variance was a

---

68 Butler, *Undoing Gender*, 41.
69 Ibid.
70 Butler, *Gender Trouble*, 23.
71 Ibid. 23–24.

developmental error, a mistake. The same can be done where there is gender variance. As Howson argues:

> [w]here there are discrepancies between the sex initially assigned to a person's body and subsequent physical or behavioural observations that call that assignation into question, the typical response of medical science is to advocate corrective interventions in order to eradicate ambiguity and ensure a fit between visible, physical characteristics and gender.[72]

Society cannot cope with individuals who are unintelligible, to borrow from Butler, in terms of their sex and gender and the relationship between them. As Weedon notes, '[d]iscourses define what it means to be a woman or man and the available range of gender-appropriate and transgressive behavior'.[73] Discourses, systems of knowledge such as law and medicine, define what it is to be a man or a woman, male or female and the extent to which one will be recognised if one transgresses these supposedly natural boundaries. Medico-legal discourses maintain the fiction that sex, gender and sexuality are natural and linked and that variant individuals are in some way wrong. However, as Butler notes, the continued existence and emergence of sexually variant or gender variant, lesbian, gay or bisexual individuals are crucially important because:

> [t]heir persistence and proliferation [...] provide critical opportunities to expose the limits and regulatory aims of that domain of intelligibility and, hence, to open up within the very terms of that matrix of intelligibility rival and subversive matrices of gender disorder.[74]

It would be tempting to argue that the law is increasing diversity of gender identity recognition and protection by means of s.9 of the Gender Recognition Act 2004 and s.7 of the Equality Act 2010 because there had been a realisation that transsexuals' Convention rights were being violated by the practice of UK non-recognition of their gender identity prior to 2004 i.e. the law is increasing intelligibility for gender variance by providing a space for such individuals within UK law. However this chapter argues that, in fact, greater intelligibility of gender variance in UK law is not the case but rather what can be seen is an increased rigidity of the binary gender system. Butler's theories on the intelligibility of gender and the role that law plays in reinforcing intelligibility can be seen when an examination of the case

---

72 Alexandra Howson, *The Body in Society: An Introduction* (Cambridge: Polity Press, 2004), 41.
73 Chris Weedon, *Feminism, Theory and the Politics of Difference* (Oxford: Blackwell, 1999), 104.
74 Butler, *Gender Trouble*, 24.

law post reform is carried out. In these cases the law very firmly placed limits on how one was to be recognised before the law paying little regard to the individual's concept of himself or herself as male or female. In so doing the law reinforced that there are very strict boundaries surrounding gender identity: one will either be male or female in UK law, not both and certainly not neither and it remains the law which will determine one's sex not the individual. For example in *J v C*[75] in 2006 the English Court of Appeal determined that a female-to-male transsexual not in possession of a GRC could not be the father of children conceived by means of assisted reproductive technology because he remained legally female at the time of the treatment. In *M v Commissioners for Her Majesty's Revenue and Customs*[76] it was held that a male-to-female transsexual remained legally male until in possession of a GRC and therefore liable to pay National Insurance Contributions until the date at which they received the GRC and in *R (on the application of B) v Secretary of State for Justice*[77] it was held that an MTF transsexual in possession of a GRC had to be treated as being legally female notwithstanding that she had, at that point, not undergone any body modification procedures. As can be seen from these three cases then the law continues to place limits on the intelligibility of gender variance albeit with slightly different boundaries than before the enactment of the GRA 2004.

Conclusion

As this analysis has shown trans* individuals in the UK are just as limited in terms of determining their own gender identity as before the reforms contained in s.9 of the GRA 2004 and s.7 of the EA 2010 were enacted. Those individuals who are considered abnormal because they do not adopt the expected sex, gender, or sexuality combination provide the space in which to challenge how the domain of intelligibility is constructed and is itself unnatural. Unfortunately, the law has to go some way yet before such individuals are legally intelligible and given recognition before the law. Indeed, as has been shown in this chapter in the very process of trans* individuals obtaining rights and protections in UK law they are yet further constituted as a particular type of subject. Perhaps this is a compromise that is necessary: that in order to ensure that individuals are able to be protected from discrimination and, as far as possible within the legal framework in which we operate, live our daily lives, it is necessary to obtain legal protection, but in so obtaining that protection the boundaries of trans* experiences that are deemed intelligible are set thus further excluding other marginalised

---

75 [2006] EWCA Civ 551.
76 [2010] UKFTT 356 (TC).
77 [2009] EWHC 2220 (Admin); [2009] HRLR 35.

identities. The GRA 2004 and the EA 2010 may be a step in the right direction but because they both limit the options to being either male or female (even though they no longer maintain the link between body and identity; between sex and gender) they ultimately reinforce that genderqueer individuals are not worthy of legal recognition and protection and, as far as possible utilising a problematic tool such as the law, the law must be further extended to include such identities as valid, intelligible identities.

The issue is that although there is some degree of legal recognition of trans* gender identity within UK law the case law would suggest that this is very much limited to those who have followed the procedures contained in the GRA 2004 and who seek to change permanently from the gender assigned at birth to the opposite gender thus ensuring that in UK law the gender binary is reinforced as the only option; there is currently no space within the GRA 2004 for those to seek a non-normative queer gender identity in law. Unfortunately the lack of case law in relation to s.7 of the Equality Act 2010 means that it is not possible to comment on how this piece of legislation will be used (or not) to protect those individuals whose gender identity is neither/both male or female. As noted above s.7 provides at least the possibility of some protection for trans* individuals; however it remains to be seen just how the courts will interpret this potentially protective and transformative section of legislation: one can only hope for an interpretation which considers the full gender spectrum as worthy of protection.

Bibliography

Butler, Judith. *Bodies that Matter: On the Discursive Limits of 'Sex'*. New York: Routledge, 1993.

Butler, Judith. *Gender Trouble: Feminism and the Subversion of Identity*. New York: Routledge, 1999.

Butler, Judith. *Undoing Gender*. New York: Routledge, 2004.

Chambers, Samuel A. 'Normative Violence after 9/11: Rereading the Politics of Gender Trouble,' *New Political Science* 29:1 (2007), 43–60.

Cowan, Sharon. 'Looking back (to)wards the body: medicalization and the GRA,' *Social and Legal Studies* 18:2 (2009), 247–52.

Howson, Alexandra. *The Body in Society: An Introduction*. Cambridge: Polity Press, 2004.

Jeffreys, Sheila. 'They Know It When They See It: The UK Gender Recognition Act 2004,' *British Journal of Politics and International Relations* 10:2 (2008), 328–45.

Lloyd, Moya. 'Heteronormativity and/as Violence: The "Sexing" of Gwen Araujo,' *Hypatia* 28:4 (2013), 818–34.

Loizidou, Elena. *Judith Butler: Ethics, Law, Politics*. London: Routledge, 2007.

Phillips, Robert. 'Abjection,' *TSQ: Transgender Studies Quarterly* 1: 1–2 (2014), 19–21.

Tompkins, Avery. 'Asterisk,' *TSQ: Transgender Studies Quarterly* 1: 1–2 (2014), 26–7.

Saltzburg, Susan and Tamara S. Davis, 'Co-authoring Gender-queer Youth Identities: Discursive Tellings and Retellings,' *Journal of Ethnic and Cultural Diversity in Social Work* 19:2, (2010), 87–108.

Sharpe, Andrew. 'A Critique of the Gender Recognition Act 2004,' *Journal of Bioethical Inquiry* 4:1 (2007), 33–42.
Spade, Dean. *Normal Life: Administrative Violence, Critical Trans Politics and the Limits of Law*. Brooklyn, NY: South End Press, 2011.
Sutherland, Elaine. *Child and Family Law*. Edinburgh: T & T Clark, 1999.
Weedon, Chris. *Feminism, Theory and the Politics of Difference*. Oxford: Blackwell, 1999.
Women and Equalities Committee, 'Transgender Equality.' HMSO 2016.

List of cases

Bellinger v Bellinger [2001] EWCA Civ 1140; [2002] Fam. 150
Corbett v Corbett [1971] P 83
Cossey v United Kingdom (1991) 13 EHRR 622
Goodwin v United Kingdom (2002) 35 EHRR 18
H (Minors) (Public Interest: Protection of Identity) [1994] 1 WLR 1141 (Civ)
J v C [2006] EWCA Civ 551; [2007] Fam. 1
J v ST [1996] 2 FCR 665 (Fam.)
L (Contact: Transsexual Applicant) [1995] 2 FLR 438 (Fam.)
M v Commissioners for Her Majesty's Revenue and Customs [2010] UKFTT 356 (TC)
R (on the application of B) v Secretary of State for Justice [2009] EWHC 2220 (Admin); [2009] HRLR 35
R v Tan [1983] QB 1053 (Crim)
Re F (Minors) (Contact) [1993] 2 FLR 677 (Civ)
Rees v United Kingdom (1987) 9 EHRR 56
Sheffield and Horsham v United Kingdom (1999) 27 EHRR 163
X, Petitioner 1957 SLT (Sh. Ct.) 61
X, Y & Z v United Kingdom (1997) 24 EHRR 143

Chapter 7

Best interests of the child in family reunification – a citizenship test disguised?

Sanna Mustasaari

Introduction: Citizenship and intersectionality[1]

Ever since *The Origins of Totalitarianism*, it has been commonplace to note that rights are dependent on the existence of a political community, a nation state, and that belonging to such a community may be identified with possession of citizenship.[2] *Jacqueline Bhabha*, a distinguished human rights scholar and children's rights advocate, coined the term 'Arendt's children' to describe and draw attention to the situation shared by a large number of children in today's world who are or risk being separated from their parents or carers and whose ties to any state are so weak that they do not, in practice, have 'a country to call their own'.[3] This chapter turns to one specific issue relating to 'Arendt's children', that of their transnational family ties and rights to family life.[4] More precisely, the issue under scrutiny is the assessment of the best interests of the child in the particular context of EU citizenship and immigrant family reunification.

The idea I wish to discuss in this chapter is that citizenship, even in its purely legal dimension as the 'right to have rights', is better conceived as a matter of extent than a fixed or static status. Its formal dimensions are intertwined with informal ones, which is why it makes sense to discuss citizenship

---

1 I want to thank Saara Pellander and Linda Hart for their invaluable support and critical comments on the ideas and analysis presented in this chapter. Any remaining errors are of course my own.
2 Hannah Arendt, *The Origins of Totalitarianism* (New York: Harcourt, 1951).
3 Jacqueline Bhabha 'Arendt's Children: Do Today's Migrant Children Have a Right to Have Rights?' *Human Rights Quarterly* 31:2 (2009), 413.
4 For the past 20 years, family related migration has been the dominant legal mode of entry to Europe. For instance in 2014, 2.3 million first residence permits were issued in the European Union (EU) to non-EU citizens. Almost a third (29.5%) of first residence permits were issued in the EU for family reasons. See Eurostat publication 20 October 2015: *EU Member States issued 2.3 million first residence permits in 2014*, available at http://ec.europa.eu/eurostat/documents/2995521/7038745/3-20102015-BP-EN.pdf/70063124-c3f2-4dfa-96d5-aa5044b927a6 (accessed 4 July 2016).

as a gradual and shifting relationship of belonging. This is because citizenship is located in a web of relations and is comprised of hierarchically organised and mutually enforcing identity markers that signal belonging. By the same token, the chapter addresses some of the complex issues relating to second generation childhood and the disadvantageous position of migrants in receiving societies.

These themes are here discussed through a close reading of one case. This case was decided by the Finnish Supreme Administrative Court in 2013 and it concerned the attempt of a transnational family[5] to enjoy family life together, despite the members of the family having both informal and legally recognised ties to two countries, Finland and Algeria.[6] Even though the selected case is merely one local example of how the citizenship position of a second generation child[7] might materialise, the argumentation present in the case is representative of immigration policies of most European countries.[8] Furthermore, the case involved an additional strand of EU law; it resulted in a preliminary ruling of the Court of Justice of the European Union (CJEU) in the case of *the Finnish Immigration Office v L.* (C-357).[9] Since EU citizenship rights are a matter of primary EU law, the case is relevant also to those Member States of the European Union that do not follow EU-wide rules on immigration. While the legal dispute in this case concerned the right of residency of *M.*, an Algerian national and a husband, father and a step father in the family, the decisive aspect of the case had to do with the rights of children and the scope of genuine enjoyment of rights granted to EU citizens by the virtue of possessing EU citizenship.

---

5 By transnational families I mean families that actively maintain a sense of familyhood and invest in their transnational family networks through shared resources, communication and caring practices, despite being located in different countries. About the concept, see for instance Harry Gouldbourne *et al., Transnational Families: Ethnicities, Identities and Social Capital* (London: Routledge, 2009).
6 KHO:2013:97, 22 May 2013, Supreme Administrative Court of Finland.
7 The term 'second generation child' refers to a child who was born in a country and whose parents are immigrants.
8 See the discussion in Karina Horsti and Saara Pellander, 'Conditions of Cultural Citizenship: Intersections of Gender, Race and Age in Public Debates on Family Migration,' *Citizenship Studies* 19:6–7 (2015), 753.
9 The joined cases of *O. and S. v Maahanmuuttovirasto* (C-356/11) and *Maahanmuuttovirasto v L.* (C-357/11), 6 December 2012. The preliminary ruling of the CJEU is part of the judgment in KHO:2013:97. In both of these cases the family in question was a reconstituted family, with the EU citizen member of the family members being the child born from the mother's earlier marriage. During the proceedings at the Finnish Supreme Administrative Court, S., the sponsor in the first case acquired Finnish nationality. Since the requirement of secure means of subsistence does not concern the family members of a Finnish national, her case was remitted back to the Finnish Migration Office as the first instance. Accordingly, her case is left outside the scope of scrutiny here and the focus will be on L.'s case.

In looking at this case, my interest lies in the ways in which the decision of the court is underpinned by various narratives of belonging and integration. In addition to a legal doctrinal reading of the case, the chapter utilises the analytical framework of feminist intersectional theory for the purpose of understanding the dynamics of the case. As such, intersectionality is a broad term that covers a variety of approaches, but here it is taken to mean a form of analysis that focuses on the interplay of social structures and hierarchically organised categories, such as those created by the legal practice.[10] On the one hand, intersectional inquiries approach identities as relational subject positions that, instead of being reducible to independent categories, create specific hierarchies where inequality becomes reproduced in novel ways.[11] Due to the dialogical nature of their operations, categories of social difference produce unique forms of advantage and disadvantage.[12] On the other hand, intersectional approaches seek to address the anti-essentialist critique that for any form of social life to meet a category means that this order of categories is first imposed on social agents.[13] In this process, the experiences of people who are situated at the intersections of various hierarchies are excluded and rendered invisible. The identity categories result from 'dynamic interaction between the individual and institutional factors',[14] and are variously situated in different legal fields, in this case family law, children's rights and migration law.[15] Legal practice constructs its subjects according to the identities that are embedded in these fields, and the individual circumstances of a case are made to match these pre-existing 'disciplinary identity constructions'.[16]

---

10 Johanna Kantola and Kevät Nousiainen, 'Institutionalising Intersectionality in Europe: Introducing the theme,' *International Feminist Journal of Politics* 11:4 (2009), 462.
11 Intersectional theory originates in feminist theory and political thought and the term was first coined by Kimberlé Crenshaw in 'Demarginalizing the Intersection of Race and Sex: A Black Feminist Critique of Antidiscrimination Doctrine, Feminist Theory and Antiracist Politics,' *The University of Chicago Legal Forum* (1989) 139–67. See also Emily Grabham et al., 'Introduction,' in *Intersectionality and Beyond: Law, Power and the Politics of Location* (New York: Routledge-Cavendish, 2009).
12 Heidi Safia Mirza, '"A second skin": Embodied Intersectionality, Transnationalism and Narratives of Identity and Belonging among Muslim Women in Britain,' *Women's Studies International Forum*, 36:5 (2013), 5–15.
13 Leslie McCall, 'The Complexity of Intersectionality,' in *Intersectionality and Beyond: Law, Power and the Politics of Location* (New York: Routledge-Cavendish, 2009), 53.
14 Kantola and Nousiainen, 'Institutionalising Intersectionality in Europe,' 469.
15 Ibid. 468.
16 Grabham uses the term to discuss the disciplining aspects of intersectionality discourse, which risks becoming the 'product of the regime in which it operates and which it was conceived to contest'. Emily Grabham, 'Intersectionality: Traumatic impressions,' in *Intersectionality and Beyond: Law Power and the Politics of Location* (New York: Routledge-Cavendish, 2009), 199.

One response to the need to recognise these disadvantageous and intersectionalised identities as well as the variability of human experience has been the creation of more open and situation-sensitive norms.[17] I suggest that the right of the child to have her best interests considered as a primary concern in all legal decision-making is an example of a legal instrument aimed at incorporating knowledge of the intersectionalised subject into the legal decision-making. In practice, however, the 'intersectionality construct' of the best interests of the child meets the 'disciplinary identity construction' inherent in immigration law, with the result that the former is made to serve the latter.[18] The analysis presented here does not apply intersectionality as a method but uses its theoretical framework to interrogate this interplay between the disciplinary identity construction and the knowledge produced about the intersectional subject, the child at the centre of the case.[19]

The argument unfolds as follows. The next section discusses three interrelated issues. First the focus is on the complexities recognised and identified in previous research on migrants' and children's citizenship. Second, the idea of the rights of the child as a remedy to those complexities is discussed and the child's right to have her best interests considered is introduced as a legal tool to recognise the intersectional identity and vulnerability of the child. Third, a point is made about the function and problems of the best interests of the child in the specific context of immigration law; the chapter confirms what several studies have previously indicated – that courts have difficulties in applying children's rights in practice. The two following sections, which discuss the case, show, however, that the rights of the child and the case-by-case approach of the best interests doctrine remain insufficient in safeguarding an equal citizenship for children. In the first one of these two sections, the scope of EU citizenship is discussed through an

---

17 For example, Williams discusses the intersectionality construct in Canadian sentencing law, which aims to address over-representation of Aboriginal people in Canadian prisons. Williams notes that with law's gaze intently fixed on family and community, broader dimensions of discrimination become invisible. Toni Williams, 'Intersectionality analysis in the Sentencing of Aboriginal Women in Canada,' in *Intersectionality and Beyond: Law, Power and the Politics of Location* (New York: Routledge-Cavendish, 2009), 95. Intersectional approach to legal research is frequently utilised in discrimination research, see for example Kantola and Nousiainen, 'Institutionalising Intersectionality in Europe'.
18 The analysis provided in this chapter is indebted to the work done by *Samuli Hurri* in *Birth of the European Individual: Law, Security, Economy* (Abingdon: Routledge, 2014), especially regarding his analysis on the role of knowledge on the individual in producing the particular kind of subject in immigration law.
19 Intersectional methodology has been successfully applied for example to analyse how privilege is constructed by courts in contact cases. See Linnéa Bruno, 'Contact and Evaluations of Violence: An Intersectional Analysis of Swedish Court Orders,' *International Journal of Law, Policy and the Family* 29:2 (2015).

examination of its underlying premises regarding family relationships and interdependencies within a family. The second one focuses on the proportionality assessment, with the evaluation of the best interests of the child at its core.

Citizenship, childhood, and the best interests doctrine

To begin with, particular forms of belonging come to underpin our conceptions of citizenship in specific legal contexts not because of their naturalness or inevitability but as a result of political processes. According to sociologist *Nira Yuval-Davis*, belonging is better conceived of as a dynamic process than a reified fixity, although it often appears as a naturalised construction of a particular hegemonic form of power relations.[20] Already in 1950, in his essay on citizenship and social class, sociologist *T.H. Marshall* discussed the shifts between the system of status and the system of contract and noted that while the modern contract is essentially a contract between men who are free and equal in status, status was never eliminated from the social system. Rather, 'differential status, associated with class, function and family, was replaced by the single uniform status of citizenship, which provided the foundation of equality on which the structure of inequality could be built'.[21]

Marshall specifically excluded children from the definition of citizen and viewed citizenship as membership of the nation state.[22] In addition, he distinguished between two meanings of social class as a system of stratification; social class could either be based on a hierarchy of status, as was the case in feudal society, or the hierarchy of positions produced by other institutions. When the hierarchy of status was eliminated through the creation of citizenship based on the principle of equality of men, the legitimate distinctions had to be grounded in other categories. This explains some of the difficulties that 'Arendt's children' face. The position of the second generation children as holders of citizenship status is challenged both by the fact that their capacity as children seems to undermine the status of citizen and by the fact that citizen by definition refers to the political community of the nation state. In line with this observation, a considerable number of

---

20 Nira Yuval-Davis, *The Politics of Belonging: Intersectional Contestations* (London: Sage Publications, 2011), 12.
21 T.H. Marshall, *Citizenship and Social Class and Other Essays* (Cambridge: Cambridge University Press, 1950), 34.
22 Ibid. 12 and 25. Marshall did argue for the importance of educating children as a genuine social right of citizenship. For him, the right to education was essentially about the right of the adult citizen that the child will become.

studies testify to the problems concerning children's citizenship,[23] as well as to the fact that migrants' access to rights is narrowed or blocked by exclusionary powers of citizenship.[24] On top of this, however, second generation children are also subject to the hierarchies produced by the subtler ways of differentiation and various 'politics of belonging'.[25]

Indeed, the construction of citizenship is in many respects notoriously racialised, gendered and in general dependent on identity factors; it excludes or disadvantages individuals and groups who do not meet the standards of normalcy underpinning the concept of citizenship.[26] Furthermore, studies have noted how the belonging of second generation children becomes contested on various sites of social life. In the Finnish context,[27] for instance, sociologist *Anna Rastas* has studied second generation youth and the ways in which racialising categorisation occurs in young people's everyday life and reproduces racialised social relations.[28] She notes how difference becomes communicated in the everyday interaction, as these young people are perceived as belonging to somewhere else and their relation to Finland and Finnishness becomes contested.[29] From a different perspective, studying how debates on family migration in Finland construct and condition citizenship and belonging, political theorists *Karina Horsti* and *Saara Pellander* note that national identity, which conditions how belonging is perceived, is heavily impacted by understandings of a culturally acceptable family. According to the authors, cultural citizenship in a Nordic welfare state is an exclusive construction based on some being considered 'culturally and morally incapable of citizenship . . . while others are included as

---

23 See, by way of example, the collection edited by Antonella Invernezzi and Jane Williams: *Children and Citizenship* (Los Angeles: Sage Publications, 2008).
24 Marie-Benedicte Dembour and Tobias Kelly (eds.), *Are Human Rights for Migrants? Critical Reflections on the Status of Irregular Migrants in Europe and the United States* (Abingdon: Routledge, 2011); Jorge A. Bustamante, 'Immigrants' Vulnerability as Subjects of Human Rights,' *International Migration Review* 36:2 (2002), 333–54; Eleanor Drywood, 'Challenging Concepts of the 'Child' in Asylum and Immigration Law: the example of EU,' *Journal of Social Welfare and Family Law* 32:3 (2010), 309–23.
25 Yuval-Davis, *Politics of Belonging*.
26 The point stressed by a plethora of studies. For discussion, see for example: Stephen Castles and Alastair Davidson, *Citizenship and Migration: Globalization and the Politics of Belonging* (Basingstoke and New York: Palgrave, 2000); Ruth Lister, *Citizenship: Feminist Perspectives* (Basingstoke: Palgrave Macmillan, 2003); Margaret Franz, 'Will to Love, Will to Fear: The Emotional Politics of Illegality and Citizenship in the Campaign against Birthright Citizenship in the US,' *Social Identities* 21:2 (2015), 184–98.
27 Finland still has a low number of immigrants, approximately 5% of the total population of 5.5 million.
28 Anna Rastas, 'Racializing Categorization among Young People in Finland,' *Young* 13:2 (2005).
29 Ibid. 152.

worthy of belonging'.[30] They point out that migrant children are framed in public discussions in ways that support these constructions.

The legal response to the problems associated with children's citizenship has been to strengthen the position of children as rights-holders.[31] The 1989 UN Convention on the Rights of the Child was generally hailed as a solution to the problems of children's limited citizenship and access to rights. Today, the doctrine of the best interests of the child and the 'due process' approach occupy a central place in the interpretation and realisation of the rights of the child, and thus form an essential backbone for the jurisprudence of the rights of the child. The transformative idea behind the right of the child to have her best interests considered as a primary concern in all actions affecting children (Article 3 of the 1989 Convention) is to ensure that the circumstances of the individual child are paid due respect in decision-making. Hence, the norm is an example of an 'intersectionality construct' *par excellence*; it aims to make use of intersectional knowledge on a case-by-case basis in order to change how law affects marginalised groups, in this case children.[32] The idea is that the judges may balance the prevailing social injustice brought about by the vulnerability of children by using the best interests test, as far as it is possible within the parameters of the law. However, this means that the legal context in which the assessment is conducted is decisive to how this 'intersectionality construct' plays out.

The Committee on the Rights of the Child has provided detailed guidelines on how the best interests norm should be applied. According to General Comment No 14 (2013),[33] the concept of the best interests is a tripartite notion.[34] It is, first, a substantive right of the child to have her best interests assessed and taken as a primary consideration when different interests are being evaluated. Second, it is a fundamental, interpretative legal principle: If a legal provision is open to more than one interpretation, the interpretation which most effectively serves the child's best interests should be chosen. And third, it is a rule of procedure. Whenever a decision is to be made that will affect a specific child, an identified group of children

---

30 Horsti and Pellander, 'Conditions of Cultural Citizenship,' 752.
31 The historical background of the children's rights movement has been traced to the changing image of childhood in Western societies as well as to the triumph of the human rights project. See the discussion in Didier Reynaert, Maria Bouverne-De Bie and Stijn Vandevelde, 'Between "Believers" and "Opponents": Critical Discussions on Children's Rights,' *The International Journal of Children's Rights* 20:1 (2012), 155–68.
32 For a similar discussion in a very different context, see Williams, 'Intersectionality Analysis in the Sentencing of Aboriginal Women in Canada,' 81.
33 Committee on the Rights of the Children General comment No. 14 (2013) on the right of the child to have his or her best interests taken as a primary consideration (art. 3, para. 1). Available at www2.ohchr.org/English/bodies/crc/docs/GC/CRC_C_GC_14_ENG.pdf (accessed 15 April 2016). Paragraphs 52–79.
34 General Comment No. 14 (2013), para. 6.

or children in general, the decision-making process must include an evaluation of the possible impact (positive or negative) of the decision on the child or children concerned. The best-interests assessment should consist of 'evaluating and balancing all the elements necessary to make a decision in a specific situation for a specific individual child or group of children' and it requires that the child's right to participate in decision-making be respected.[35]

In principle, the guidelines concerning the best interests evaluation apply also in immigrant family reunification. Courts, however, seem to have difficulties in balancing between the national norms and international obligations. First, the normative guidelines, on which they draw in interpreting rights of the child in the context of immigration control, tend to be peculiarly selected, which perhaps indicates a missing awareness regarding for example the work done by the Committee on the Rights of the Child.[36] Second, and this is a far harder issue to solve, the internal structure of immigration law often distorts the best interests of the child test. In these cases, rather than being about defining what would be in the best interests of the child, the best interests assessment becomes a tool for identifying the threshold to which the State may freely interfere with the rights and well-being of the child by means of immigration control.

As a condition of aliens' entry, the Member States of the European Union are entitled to require the sponsor to have secure means to maintain the family, so that granting a residence permit to the alien family member would not become a financial burden for the state. As these standards are usually set unattainably high, the questions of children's family rights and

---

[35] General Comment No 14 provides a detailed description of the formal process of determining the best interests, including strict procedural safeguards The elements of the evaluation include the child's view; the child's identity; preservation of the family environment and maintaining relations; care, protection and safety of the child; situation of vulnerability; the child's right to health; and the child's right to education. Moreover, preservation of the family unit should be taken into account when assessing the best interests of the child in decisions on family reunification. These ties include the extended family, friends, school and the wider environment and are particularly relevant in cases where parents are separated and live in different places. The purpose of the detailed guidelines is to guarantee that the best interests evaluation is carried out properly, so that all relevant information concerning the circumstances of the child are taken into account in decision-making. General Comment No. 14 (2013), para. 47.

[36] For example, in its landmark cases KHO:2014:50 and KHO:2014:51, 19 March 2014, the Finnish Supreme Administrative Court makes no reference to General Comment No 14, although the document was adopted nearly a year prior to the decisions. In the case law of the European Court of Human Rights, the document makes its first appearance in May 2015 in the case of *S.L. and J.L. v Croatia*, app. No. 13712/11 (7 May 2015), which concerned the property rights and the supervision of the children's interests in the selling of the children's property. In the specific context of family reunification, however, General Comment No 14 is yet to appear in the argumentation of the ECtHR.

whether their rights require exemptions to maintenance requirements are becoming more and more frequent. This presses courts to balance between the goals of immigration law and international human rights. For instance in Finland, the scope of the best interests of the child assessment in relation to family reunification and maintenance requirement has been set quite narrow; only severe individual reasons, such as a life-threatening medical condition, may result in an exemption to the maintenance requirement.[37]

Restricting the scope of the best interests assessment this radically, in fact, amounts to an infringement on the rights of the child. For instance, in the light of the case law of the European Court of Human Rights (ECtHR), the approach adopted by the Finnish court seems questionable. In *Jeunesse v The Netherlands (2014)*,[38] the ECtHR stressed that 'national decision-making bodies should, in principle, advert to and assess evidence in respect of the practicality, feasibility and proportionality of any removal of a non-parent in order to give effective protection and sufficient weight to the best interests of the children directly affected by it'.[39] Our analysis now turns to the question of whether a due best interests evaluation would be able to protect the rights of the child in the immigration context. In order to examine this, the next sections to follow will dwell on the argumentation of the CJEU and the Finnish Supreme Administrative Court in KHO:2013:97.

Transnational families and borders of belonging: the concept of family and the question of dependency

The core issue in KHO:2013:97 was whether the family had any realistic chances to live together and in which country, Finland or Algeria, their

---

37 In the two landmark cases, KHO:2014:50 and KHO:2014:51, 19 March 2014, the Finnish Supreme Administrative Court emphasised that in situations where the spouses have founded a family knowing that their residence status is uncertain, granting an exception to the maintenance requirement solely on the basis of the best interests of the child would lead to an unacceptable outcome, as the main rule of sufficient subsistence would *de facto* become overruled. The court thus stated that the possibility of disturbing the family life between the child and the alien parent is not a sufficient reason to make an exemption from the maintenance requirement. This approach to the best interests of the child in the context of immigration control is adopted by several countries, see for example Bhabha, 'Arendt's Children,' 447; Johanna Schiratzki, 'The Best Interests of the Child in the Swedish Aliens Act,' *International Journal of Law, Policy and the Family* 14:3 (2006); and Anna Lundberg, 'The Best Interests of the Child Principle in Swedish Asylum Cases: The Marginalization of Children's Rights,' *Journal of Human Rights Practice* 3:1 (2011).
38 *Jeunesse v The Netherlands [GC]*, app. no. 12738/10, 60 EHRR 789 (3 October 2014).
39 ECtHR, *Jeunesse (2014)*, para. 120. In this case the ECtHR specifically refers to the relevant articles of the Convention on the Rights of the Child. However, instead of General Comment No 14, the ECtHR refers to the Committee's statements regarding the best interests of the child as expressed in General Comment No. 7 (2005). Paragraph 74.

family life was to take place. The mother *L.*, the sponsor, was an Algerian national who had arrived in Finland in 2003 and obtained a permanent residence permit on the grounds of marriage to a Finnish citizen. Her first child was born in this marriage in early 2004. The child obtained Finnish nationality and, consequently, the citizenship of the EU, which is a legal status enjoyed by all EU citizens simply by the virtue of being nationals of some Member State of the European Union.[40] Initially introduced in the Maastricht Treaty in 1992 and now provided for in Article 20 of the Treaty on the Functioning of the European Union, EU citizenship has been subject to debate,[41] but is nevertheless rather firmly established in the case law of the CJEU.[42] It is constituted by citizenship rights, especially the four fundamental freedoms, one of which is the right to move and reside freely within the EU.[43]

Soon after the birth of the first child, *L.*'s marriage broke down, and as of 2005 she was the sole guardian of the child. In October 2006, *L.* married *M.*, an Algerian who at the time was seeking asylum in Finland. *M.*'s asylum application was rejected and he was ordered to return to Algeria. After his return, in early 2007, *L.* gave birth to the couple's child, who acquired Algerian nationality. *L.* and *M.* then applied for family reunification, but their application was rejected, as the family failed to present evidence of secure

---

40 For a discussion in the context of family law, see Katharina Kaesling, 'Family Life and EU Citizenship: The Discovery of the Substance of the EU Citizen's Rights and its Genuine Enjoyment,' in *Family Law and Culture in Europe: Developments, Challenges and Opportunities*, ed. Katharina Boele-Woelki, Nina Dethloff and Werner Gephart (Cambridge: Intersentia, 2014), 293–304.

41 The case law of the CJEU is copiously commented on in the specific context of EU citizenship law, see for example Dimitry Kochenov, 'The Essence of European Citizenship Emerging from the Last Ten Years of Academic Debate: Beyond the Cherry Blossoms and the Moon?' *International and Comparative Law Quarterly* 62:1 2013, 97; Dora Kostakopoulou, 'Ideas, Norms and European Citizenship: Explaining Institutional Change,' *Modern Law Review*, 68:2 (2005), 233. In the context of family reunification rules the issue of reverse discrimination has attracted more scholarly attention. See for instance Anne Staver, 'Free Movement and the Fragmentation of Family Reunification Rights,' *European Journal of Migration and Law* 15:1 (2013), 69–89; Chiara Berneri, 'Protection of Families Composed by EU Citizens and Third-Country Nationals: Some Suggestions to Tackle Reverse Discrimination,' *European Journal of Migration and Law* 16:2 (2014), 249–76.

42 It was announced by the CJEU for the first time in Case C-184/99 *Rudy Grzelczyk v Centre public d'aide sociale d'Ottignies-Louvain-la-Neuve*, [2001] ECR I-6193 (20 September 2001). For a thorough analysis of EU citizenship and the right to move and reside freely, see Suvi Sankari, *Legal Reasoning in Context: The Court of Justice on Articles 17 and 18EC (20 and 21 TFEU) 2000–2008*, Helsinki: Helsinki University Printing House, 2011. For versatile analyses on European citizenship, see the work of Jo Shaw and the European Union Democracy Observatory on Citizenship.

43 On discussion on what rights actually constitute the status, see Dimitry Kochenov, 'The Right to Have What Rights? EU Citizenship in Need of Clarification,' *European Law Journal*, Vol 19, 2013, 502–16.

means of subsistence. The refusal of *M.*'s entry would mean that the family would either remain separated or that *L.* and the children would move to Algeria. Hence, this decision might have the impact of forcing *L.* and the children, including the EU citizen child, to leave the territory of the European Union in order to be able to live as a family. This potential outcome of refusal of entry, then, raised the question of whether such an outcome would breach the rights of the EU citizen child, especially in the light of the principles laid down in the landmark case of *Ruiz Zambrano*,[44] and prompted the Finnish court to refer the case to the CJEU for a preliminary ruling.

The assessment of the case thus begun with what is known as the 'genuine enjoyment test'. The purpose of this legal test is to determine the scope of EU citizenship rights, in this case whether the situation and rights of the children required that an exemption be made to the maintenance requirement. The highest rank of rights, in this respect, are those attached to the status of EU citizenship. The competence to authoritative interpretation of EU primary law is located beyond the level of national courts, in the CJEU. In its preliminary ruling, the CJEU found that in the circumstances present in this case, the refusal of a residence permit of a third country national does not, *per se*, necessarily mean a denial of genuine enjoyment of substance of the rights of the EU citizen child. Thus, Article 20 TFEU does not categorically preclude a state from refusing to grant a third country national a residence permit in a situation similar to this one at hand. Importantly, though, the CJEU stated that it was for the national court to evaluate whether the particular circumstances of the case would amount to a breach of citizenship rights.[45]

As to which factors are relevant for the genuine enjoyment of citizenship rights, the first task of the national court is to consider whether there is a *direct obligation* to leave the EU territory. Since *L.* as the mother of the EU citizen child held a permanent residence permit, there was no direct

---

44 Case C-34/09 *Gerardo Ruiz Zambrano v Office national de l'emploi (ONEm)* [2011] ECR I-1177 (8 March 2011) concerned the right of two Colombian nationals to reside in Belgium on account of the EU citizenship of their minor children. This landmark ruling extended the scope of EU legal rules to apply in certain situations to 'static EU citizens', which means that a cross-border situation is no longer an absolute necessity in order for the EU law to actualise in a case. See also Case C-256/11 *Dereci and Others v Bundesministerium für Inneres* [2011] ECR I-11315 (15 November 2011).

45 Operative part of the judgment, first paragraph: 'Article 20 TFEU must be interpreted as not precluding a Member State from refusing to grant a third country national a residence permit on the basis of family reunification where that national seeks to reside with his spouse, who is also a third country national and resides lawfully in that Member State and is the mother of a child from a previous marriage who is a Union citizen, and with the child of their own marriage, who is also a third country national, *provided that such a refusal does not entail, for the Union citizen concerned, the denial of the genuine enjoyment of the substance of the rights conferred by the status of citizen of the Union, that being for the referring court to ascertain.*' (Italics SM). For similar phrasing, see Case C-256/11, *Dereci* [2011], para. 74.

obligation for her and children in her custody to leave EU territory. Second, the custody of the EU citizen child as well as the fact that the child was part of a reconstituted family were relevant.[46] The EU citizen child was not M.'s biological child nor in his custody. While the absence of the blood relationship between the M. and the EU citizen child was not decisive, it was, nevertheless, significant that the child was not legally, financially or emotionally dependent on him. But how are we to evaluate how the individual relationships of dependency are organised within a family?

According to the CJEU, a primary cause and effect relationship needs to be identified between the acts of the state and consequence of those acts. In this case the primary cause and effect relationship is the *relationship of dependency* between the Union citizen who is a minor and the third country national who is being refused a right of residence. To count for an interference with the rights of the EU citizen, the consequence of leaving the territory must be a direct result of the refusal to grant a residence permit to the third country national.[47] Following the benchmarks set by the CJEU, the Finnish Supreme Administrative Court concluded that refusing M.'s entry did not directly influence the possibilities of the child to enjoy her rights as an EU citizen.

Refusing the entry of M. placed L. in a situation where she had to choose which one of her children would have the possibility to stay in close contact with her biological father. This outcome, however, was not considered a denial of genuine enjoyment of the EU citizen's rights. While the ruling of the CJEU may be sound in that it seems to recognise the variability within families regarding the extent to which different family relations foster dependency, the formal requirement that a relationship of direct cause and effect be identified seems artificial in that the child becomes conceptualised as a 'liberal individual' – that is, isolated from the network of relations and interdependencies that in reality constitute her position as an agent.[48] Furthermore, to assume that relationships of dependency should be stable and follow a prescribed pattern and thus be easily identifiable is an example of how a 'truth' is constructed in legal reasoning by standardised assumptions.[49]

The requirement of direct dependence between the child and the third country resident parent may be criticised for reflecting a rigid and

---

46 Case C-357/11, paras 50 and 51.
47 Case C-357/11, para. 52.
48 See discussion in Fiona Kelly, 'Conceptualizing the Child through an "Ethic of Care": Lessons for Family Law,' *International Journal of Law in Context* 1:4 (2005), 375–96.
49 For an interesting discussion on how different conceptions of dependency may play out in the context of family reunification, see Saara Pellander, 'Traces of Dependency: Manifestations of Elderly Family Migration across Policy Arenas'. Paper presented at The Problematisation of Family Migration – workshop, 4–5 June 2015, University of Amsterdam, Netherlands.

atomistic understanding of family relations. While welfare dependency is being rejected through the sufficient means of subsistence requirement, the notion of dependency within a family seems to be underpinned by a view that dependency operates isolated from other relationships and independent from the totality of relations within a family. It could well be argued that family relationships, kinship formations and relations of care, affect and dependency are too manifold and fluctuating to be captured in legal prerequisites. For instance, configurational approaches to family research emphasise that individuals and relationships belonging to configurations are profoundly influenced by the configuration as a whole, which impacts the ways in which interdependencies within families organise.[50] Moreover, as political theorists *Nancy Fraser* and *Lisa Gordon* note, the use of the term 'dependency' conceals ideologies that constitute specific kinds of moral subjects.[51] Perceiving dependency as something that is inevitably part of some relationships within a family but not others actually comes close to treating social relations of dependency as personality traits, as something that exists as pre-fixed and similar in all children.

The formal categories and forms of atomistic reasoning, however, are not the only aspects open to criticism in the genuine enjoyment test. Rather, the more fundamental issues have to do with how the different categories are mobilised within the argumentation of the court in ways that reproduce the hegemonic forms of belonging, without materially investigating them. For instance, the gendered practices of parenting may be seen to intersect with class position as well as the family's deviance from the nuclear family norm. On the one hand, L. who had two children but no partner to help her care and provide for the family had no realistic opportunities to meet the stringent income requirement, as the threshold of 'sufficient mean of subsistence' is set unattainably high.[52] On the other hand, in the situation where the fathers of L.'s two children lived in different countries, it was seen as unproblematic that the children would follow L. whatever she should decide, which seems to reflect a gendered norm of parenting where children are seen to belong to their mother more than they belong

---

50 See for instance Eric D. Widmer *et al.*, 'Introduction', in *Beyond the Nuclear Family: Families in a Configurational Perspective*, ed. Eric D. Widmer and Riitta Jallinoja (Bern: Lang, 2008), 2.
51 Nancy Fraser and Lisa Gordon, 'A Genealogy of Dependency: Tracing a Keyword of the U.S. Welfare State,' *Signs* 19:2 (Winter, 1994), 323.
52 For discussion on the maintenance requirement in the context of family reunification in Finland see Saara Pellander, 'Collective Threats and Individual Rights: Political Debates on Marriage Migration to Finland,' in *Race, Ethnicity and Welfare States. An American Dilemma?* ed. Pauli Kettunen, Sonya Michel and Claus Petersen (Cheltenham: Edward Elgar Publishing, 2015), 107–27. The government is currently planning to tighten the conditions of family reunification by extending the maintenance requirement to cover family members of sponsors who obtained residence permits on the grounds of subsidiary or humanitarian protection. See government proposal 43/2016.

to their father. Furthermore, the norm of respectability, which in family studies refers to the normative ideal of what families should be like,[53] may be seen as eroding the notion of belonging of the family together. While the applicant was *L.*'s husband and the father of the younger child, the family was nevertheless a reconstituted family, in which the family bonds are seen as weaker than those in an ideal type of family.

After solving the question of the applicability of primary EU law, the second step of the evaluation was the interpretation of secondary EU law, in this case the Family Reunification Directive EC/2003/86. The CJEU pointed out that since authorisation of family reunification is the general rule, any maintenance requirement must be interpreted restrictively and in compliance with the Charter of Fundamental Rights of the European Union, with regard to the best interests of the children involved and with a view of promoting family life. Again, the CJEU stated that it is for the national authorities, when implementing the Directive and examining applications for family reunification, to make a balanced and reasonable assessment of all the interests at play, accounting particularly for the interests of the children concerned.[54]

Best interests of the child and politics of belonging

The point of departure for assessments of proportionality in family reunification cases is founded on the legitimate interest of the State to control immigration. Referring explicitly to the principles established by the European Court of Human Rights (ECtHR) in *Rodrigues da Silva and Hoogkamer v The Netherlands*; *Konstantinov v The Netherlands* and *Darren Omoregia and Others v Norway*, the Finnish Supreme Administrative Court emphasised that states are not obliged to respect immigrants' choice of the country where they wish their family life to take place.[55] This starting point is significant, as it means that interests of the family members are considered from the perspective of whether they amount to *obstacles to enjoying family life elsewhere*. In order to define whether the interests of the children required granting

---

53 The term respectability was coined by Beverley Skeggs and has recently been used in family and migration studies (see for example, Marja Peltola, *Kunnollisia perheitä: Maahanmuutto, sukupolvet ja yhteiskunnallinen asema*, in English: Respectable families – Immigration, generations and social position). The idea behind 'respectability' is that respectability is one attribute of good and ideal family, which materially usually links to a middle class way of life, and is an important element of the social positioning. See Beverley Skeggs. *Formations of Class and Gender: Becoming Respectable* (London: Sage Publishing, 1997).
54 Operative part of the judgment, second paragraph.
55 The case of *Rodrigues da Silva and Hoogkamer v The Netherlands*, 31 January 2006, Application No 50435/99; The case of *Konstantinov v The Netherlands*, 26 April 2007, Application No 16351/03; *Darren Omoregia and Others v Norway*, 31 July 2008, Application No. 265/07.

the residence permit to *M.*, the court focused on three issues: 1) the relationship rights of the eldest child; 2) the children's possibility to adapt to Algerian society; and 3) the stage of their integration into Finnish society.

In closer scrutiny, each of the three elements of the best interests evaluation emerges as underpinned by influential understandings of belonging and identity of the children. The power of these understandings lies in their presumed naturalness and legitimacy. For even if we might argue differently than the court at certain points of the decision, we must admit some legitimacy for many of the questions the court posed. In fact, these factors are listed in General Comment No. 14, and they feature also in the case law of the ECtHR.[56] The mechanisms giving birth to disadvantage operate in a subtler manner. Yet, cultural and symbolic factors present in the case are highly political, and deeply embedded in the struggles over belonging.

The first one of the issues considered by the court, the relationship rights of the eldest child, was scarcely addressed in the decision. While according to the mother, *L.*, the father of the child had objected to his child moving to Algeria, the court recognised no interference with the rights of the eldest child to have contact with her father nor with the parental rights of the father. Instead, the court pointed out that the mother was the sole holder of the custody of the child, which implies that the court viewed *L.*'s competence to make the decision about the habitual residence of the child alone as proving that she could move the child to Algeria, regardless of the objections of the other parent. Such a view would contradict several well-established principles of child law.[57] Accepting this line of reasoning would also create potentially harmful incentives to arrange the custody and care of the child with the sole purpose of meeting the requirements of the immigration process. This would effectively render empty some focal principles of child law, such as that decisions on custody and contact issues should be grounded in the best interests of the child.

In evaluating the second set of issues, namely the implications that moving to Algeria would have for the children, the court took into account, first, that both of the children had Arabic registered as their mother tongue. Their practical language skills, however, were not evaluated.[58] The

---

56 See for example, ECtHR, *Jeunesse (2014)*, paras 117, 120, and 121.
57 Were the child in joint custody of the parents, the decision to take the child abroad against the wishes of the other parent would amount to child abduction. In any case, custodial arrangements are not meant to restrict the rights of the non-custodian parent and the child to enjoy family life, which in the case of parents and children is a strongly protected right, extending even to potential family life. Parents may arrange the custody of the child in many ways and for a variety of reasons.
58 In fact, it is common in Finland for children to be bilingual, as there are two main official languages (Finnish and Swedish) in the country. The registration of one of the child's languages as mother tongue entitles the child to receive education in that language.

court considered, further, that were the children to move to Algeria, they would not experience the local culture and language as strange, despite having lived their lives thus far in Finland. In the event of moving to Algeria, they could rely on the support of their mother as well as the father of the younger child. Aged 6 and 9, the children were, according to the court, at an adaptive age and at such a stage of their schooling that moving would not endanger their education. All in all, the court concluded that even though moving to Algeria would mean a substantial change in the children's life, several facts indicated that together with their mother they were able to adapt to such a change. Consequently, their interests did not require granting an exemption regarding the requirement of secure means of subsistence. Interestingly, the case features no discussion of the grounds of *M.*'s previous asylum application. Even though *M.* had not been granted asylum, one might think that some attention to the reasons behind his asylum application would be required as part of the best interests assessment.

The third point the court considered concerned the stage of the integration of the children into Finnish society. While questioning the integration of someone who was born and has lived their entire life in a country seems somewhat peculiar, the court explicitly stated that *no such facts relating to circumstances outside home and the family had arisen that would indicate that integration to Finland was so advanced* that the children could not be required to move away from Finland with their mother, should she so choose.[59] The actual home and every-day environment of the children was bypassed by a brief remark that it was not shown that factors outside home would indicate the integration of the children was advanced. This brings to the fore yet another, albeit important, point of criticism, namely the question of which instance would be responsible for acquiring sufficient information on the circumstances of the child in family reunification cases. Since the national procedural norms enable the court to obtain further clarification and even expert opinions if necessary for solving the case, it seems problematic that the court apparently interprets the lack of evidence to amount to a certain outcome.[60] Again, the question of knowledge – who is

---

59 Original in Finnish, translation and italics SM: '*Asiassa ei ole ilmennyt myöskään muita kodin ulkopuolisia seikkoja, jotka osoittaisivat niin pitkälle edennyttä integraatiota Suomeen*, että lapsien ei voitaisi edellyttää muuttavan yhdessä äitinsä kanssa pois Suomesta, mikäli tämä niin valitsee.'

60 According to the procedural code applied in administrative courts (Hallintolainkäyttölaki, 33 §), the court may request further clarification and even expert opinions necessary for solving the case. According to research conducted in 2012 by *Virve-Maria de Godzinsky*, the courts use this possibility only occasionally (*Taking a Child into Care: Research of decision making in administrative courts*, National Research Institute of Legal Policy, Research Report No. 260, Helsinki 2012. The report, which includes an English summary, is available at www.optula.om.fi/material/attachments/optula/julkaisut/tutkimuksia-sarja/4xBiUQPOp/260_de_Godzinsky_2012.pdf (accessed 15 April 2016))

responsible for obtaining it as well as what kinds of knowledge is excluded – proves decisive.⁶¹

I suggested above that the best interests test as developed in General Comment No. 14 is an example of a legal instrument meant to foster the visibility of the intersectional identity of the child. The best interests test is supposed to operate as a mechanism that subsumes the knowledge of the individual child into the legal decision-making process. But this intersectionally situated, flesh-and-blood child is not a person that immigration law can deal with, and so the lived identity of the child is really not at the centre of the best interests assessment here. Rather, the child subject to the best interests evaluation and whose identity is investigated has to match the needs of the inquiry. This disciplinary constructed identity, the Alien who does not belong to the society that the nation state represents, is embedded in the legal practice of family reunification as the target of immigration control. The one who belongs, the-non alien, is a mere side effect of a futile inquiry into suspected 'alienness', the exception to the rule. So, the knowledge concerning the child is collected with this in mind, the main goal being the upholding of the legitimacy of the distinction between the alien and the citizen. The knowledge of the identity of the particular child is knowledge of a child who, by affiliation with a transnational family which by nature is prone to 'not-belong', is a potential alien, regardless of her formal citizenship status.⁶²

The fact that the law primarily aims to detect a match for the pre-existing 'disciplinary identity' of the non-belonging foreign child, I suggest, explains many of the awkward moments in the decision. At these awkward moments the structural biases, which function to maintain the rigid order of privilege on which the citizenship system is founded, become annoyingly visible. The ethnic origin of the children and their ties to Algeria, familiarity with Algerian culture and Arabic mother tongue are considered relevant for the decision, whereas the opposite holds for their ties to Finland and cultural identity factors emphasising belonging to Finland (presumably good skills in Finnish, identification with Finnish culture), social environment, school records or other circumstances of the children. The integration into Finnish society of these children who were born and raised in Finland is challenged on the basis of their identities marked by

---

61 In the Finnish context, studies have documented how expert knowledge on the best interests and well-being of the child has utterly different weight in family reunification in the context of child welfare and out-of-home placement of a child than in family reunification in the context of immigration law. Reija Knuutila and Heta Heiskanen, 'Lapsen etu viranomaistoiminnassa: katsaus eräisiin Maahanmuuttoviraston viimeaikaisiin kielteisiin päätöksiin,' *Oikeus* 43:3 (2014), 314–21. This is the example of how the 'truth' is a product of politics and power.
62 Bahbha, 'Arendt's Children,' 448.

ethnicity, language and position as a second generation migrant, but this integration is never evaluated in material terms, for instance by hearing from the children about their circumstances[63] or other people significant to the children, e.g. staff of their schools or nurseries. Couplings of belonging and identity through the vague use of the term 'integration' assume a relevant difference, thus necessarily involving processes of erecting boundaries, constructing hierarchies and reifying identities. Such dynamics highlight the urgency of asking 'who exactly is the figure that needs to be integrated'[64] – and, moreover, what exactly is meant by integration of second generation children, who by definition were born in the country and often have lived there their whole life?

In conceptualising what she calls the politics of belonging, Yuval-Davis distinguishes between three analytically separate realms where belonging is constructed: the realm of social locations, such as race, ethnicity, age, gender, class and nation, which operate as 'hierarchically organised positions in grids of power relations'; the realm of identifications and emotional attachments to collectivities; and the realm of ethical and political value systems used for judging belonging.[65] These distinctions serve analytical purposes; in reality they refer to complex, overlapping, and at times contradictory social processes. This complexity, however, offers the site for contestation and resistance. For in each realm, the complex symbolic order is reproduced by an array of technologies and within a range of practices.[66] Simultaneously as these various technologies take part in producing class and subjectivity, they give rise also to specific projects of belonging. Viewed in this theoretical framework, then, the exercise of evaluating the best interests of the child may function as a site of normalisation – but of struggle and resistance too. For it is within the scope of this evaluation that identities and social locations become the 'individual circumstances' of the case.

---

63 This complete muteness of children in immigration cases seems to signal a profound perception of relevant knowledge. The child may be heard if it is to evaluate the reliability of the narratives of the family members but not in order to give her opinion weight.
64 Floya Anthias, 'Moving beyond the Janus Face of Integration and Diversity Discourses: Towards an Intersectional Framing,' *The Sociological Review* 61:2 (2013), 323–43.
65 Yuval-Davis, *Politics of Belonging*, 12.
66 For instance *Magdalena Kmak* examines the moral subject of mobility laws. According to her analysis, in the context of mobility, a moral subject may only be the active and economically robust EU citizen or the passive and victimised refugee. Others, specifically irregular immigrants, are considered immoral and suspectable. Kmak, 'Between Citizen and Bogus Asylum Seeker: Management of Migration in the EU through Technology of Morality,' *Social Identities* 21:4 (2015), 395–409. In an altogether different context, feminist scholars like *Beverley Skeggs* have pointed out that affect operates as the key technology of reproducing class hierarchies. For a comprehensive introduction to the 'turn to affect', see Margareta Wetherell, *Affect and Emotion: A New Social Science Understanding* (London: Sage Publishing, 2012).

The belongings of the second-generation child constructed in the realm of social locations through various mundane practices become mobilised in the ethico-political system of immigration law, where these belongings meet the 'disciplinary identities' embedded in the legal system. By the same token, it is here where these identities and social locations may contribute to the politics of belonging in a manner that either reproduces discrimination or offers means to resist it.

Conclusion: towards an intersectional analysis of the best interests of the child?

More than 65 years ago Marshall wrote that 'social rights in their modern form imply an invasion of contract by status, the subordination of market price to social justice, the replacement of the free bargain by the declaration of rights',[67] and suggested that these principles were entrenched with the contract system itself, making it dependent on a particular system of status. Since the two systems, the one rooted in status differentiation and the other in contract, bore with them a different sphere of rights and duties, Marshall argued that the shifts between these systems lead to the expansion of rights – that is, to situations where people may invoke both systems to claim rights while escaping the corresponding responsibilities. However, in the case of second generation children, the case may be reverse. These two systems may also be invoked in a manner that allocates risks and liabilities without any corresponding rights to some individuals or groups of people, as the identity narratives that make up the informal citizenship and define belonging feed back into the formal logics of citizenship.

The review provided in this chapter suggests that citizenship, specifically the citizenship of a child, is a discontinuous legal construction, determined not solely by citizenship as a formal status derived from nationality but by a plethora of identity factors marking the belonging of a person both in the family and in the jurisdiction of a nation state. In these accounts of belonging, weight is given both to considerations regarding family configurations and to individual characteristics associated with belonging to a nation state, such as language or ethnic origin. These identity narratives are conveyed into the legal reasoning as facts to be taken into account in those phases of the decision-making that require discretion and balancing by the merits of the particular case. This balancing, including the choice of which facts are to be taken into account, is ultimately always determined at the national level – in both stages of the ruling, the interpretation of citizenship rights and the interpretation of the Directive, the CJEU referred the decision back to the national court.

---

67 Marshall, *Citizenship and Social Class*, 68.

It remains an important and morally urgent call to resist the othering processes prevailing in immigration law and to promote the best interests of the child and to demand procedural guarantees for the realisation of these interests.[68] This, however, is not sufficient and may even end up derogating the inequalities embedded in immigration laws. For it might well be that the inherent limitations of immigration control – that is, the goal of keeping outsiders out – renders immigration law eventually a mismatch with the promise of contextual justice delivered by the rights of the child. This is the case simply because the legitimacy of the state's interest to control immigration allows the state to set the threshold so high that the best interests of the child would be relevant only in extremely exceptional cases. The purpose of the intersectional reading in this chapter has been to offer another perspective into what discursively happens in the decision – that through the best interests evaluation the court in fact participates in a vigorous construction of identities that undermine the belonging of second generation children in Finnish society.

This preliminary discussion on an intersectional approach to citizenship, belonging and legal constructions of identity points, in my view, towards a significant observation. The point it highlights is that what really is at stake in immigrant family reunification cases, is not (only) that in this field, argumentation of the courts falls short of the standard defined by international law regarding the right of the child to have her best interests evaluated properly and as a primary concern in all judicial proceedings concerning her, as recommended by the UN Committee on the Rights of the Child in its General Comment No. 14. Rather, what is at stake is that the logic of this field is exclusionary to such an extent that the impact of these stringent immigration policies cannot be fixed by a case-by-case approach offered by the rights of the child and the doctrine of the best interests. There are good reasons to suggest that very basic requirements of social justice stress the need to rethink the conditions of family reunification and social positioning of second generation children and their families in receiving societies.

Bibliography

Anthias, Floya. 'Moving Beyond the Janus Face of Integration and Diversity Discourses: Towards an Intersectional Framing,' *The Sociological Review* 61:2 (2013), 323–43.

Arendt, Hannah. *The Origins of Totalitarianism*. New York: Harcourt, 1951.

Berneri, Chiara. 'Protection of Families Composed by EU Citizens and Third-Country Nationals: Some Suggestions to Tackle Reverse Discrimination,' *European Journal of Migration and Law*, 16:2 (2014), 249–76.

---

68 Bhabha, 'Arendt's Children,' 450.

Bhabha, Jacqueline. 'Arendt's Children: Do Today's Migrant Children Have a Right to Have Rights?' *Human Rights Quarterly* 31:2 (2009), 410–51.

Bruno, Linnéa. 'Contact and Evaluations of Violence: An Intersectional Analysis of Swedish Court Orders,' *International Journal of Law, Policy and the Family* 29:2 (2015), 167–82.

Bustamante, Jorge A. 'Immigrants' Vulnerability as Subjects of Human Rights,' *International Migration Review* 36:2 (2002), 333–54.

Castles, Stephen and Alastair Davidson. *Citizenship and Migration: Globalization and the Politics of Belonging*. New York: Palgrave, 2000.

Crenshaw, Kimberlé. 'Demarginalizing the Intersection of Race and Sex: A Black Feminist Critique of Antidiscrimination Doctrine, Feminist Theory and Antiracist Politics,' *The University of Chicago Legal Forum* (1989), 139–67.

Dembour, Marie-Benedicte and Tobias Kelly (eds.). *Are Human Rights for Migrants? Critical Reflections on the Status of Irregular Migrants in Europe and the United States*. Abingdon: Routledge, 2011.

Drywood, Eleanor. 'Challenging Concepts of the "Child" in Asylum and Immigration Law: The Example of EU,' *Journal of Social Welfare and Family Law* 32:3 (2010), 309–23.

Eurostat 20 October 2015: *EU Member States issued 2.3 million first residence permits in 2014*, available at http://ec.europa.eu/eurostat/en/web/products-press-releases/-/3-20102015-BP (accessed 5 March 2016).

Franz, Margaret. 'Will to Love, Will to Fear: The Emotional Politics of Illegality and Citizenship in the Campaign against Birthright Citizenship in the US,' *Social Identities* 21:2 (2015), 184–98.

Fraser, Nancy and Lisa Gordon. 'A Genealogy of Dependency: Tracing a Keyword of the U.S. Welfare State,' *Signs* 19:2 (Winter, 1994), 309–36.

Godzinsky, Virve-Maria de. *Taking a Child into Care: Research of decision making in administrative courts*. National Research Institute of Legal Policy, Research Report No. 260, Helsinki 2012. The report, which includes an English summary, is available at www.optula.om.fi/material/attachments/optula/julkaisut/tutkimuksia-sarja/4xBiUQPOp/260_de_Godzinsky_2012.pdf (accessed 15 April 2016).

Gouldbourne, Harry, Tracey Reynolds, John Solomos and Elisabeth Zontini. *Transnational Families: Ethnicities, Identities and Social Capital*. London: Routledge, 2009.

Grabham, Emily. 'Intersectionality: Traumatic impressions.' In *Intersectionality and Beyond: Law, Power and the Politics of Location*, edited by Emily Grabham, Davina Cooper, Jane Krishnadas and Didi Herman, 183–201. New York: Routledge-Cavendish, 2009.

Grabham, Emily with Didi Herman, Davia Cooper and Jane Krishnadas. 'Introduction.' In *Intersectionality and Beyond: Law, Power and the Politics of Location*, edited by Emily Grabham, Davina Cooper, Jane Krishnadas and Didi Herman, 1–17. New York: Routledge-Cavendish, 2009.

Horsti, Karina and Saara Pellander. 'Conditions of Cultural Citizenship: Intersections of Gender, Race and Age in Public Debates on Family Migration,' *Citizenship Studies* 19:6–7 (2015), 751–67.

Hurri, Samuli. *Birth of the European Individual: Law, Security, Economy*. Abingdon: Routledge, 2014.

Invernezzi, Antonella and Jane Williams. *Children and Citizenship*. Los Angeles: Sage Publications, 2008.

Kaesling, Katharina. 'Family Life and EU Citizenship: The Discovery of the Substance of the EU Citizen's Rights and its Genuine Enjoyment.' In *Family Law and Culture in Europe: Developments, Challenges and Opportunities*, edited by Katharina Boele-Woelki, Nina Dethloff and Werner Gephart, 293–304. Cambridge: Intersentia, 2014.

Kantola, Johanna and Kevät Nousiainen. 'Institutionalising Intersectionality in Europe: Introducing the theme,' *International Feminist Journal of Politics* 11:4 (2009), 459–77.

Kelly, Fiona. 'Conceptualizing the Child through an "Ethic of Care": Lessons for Family Law,' *International Journal of Law in Context* 1:4 (2005), 375–96.

Kmak, Magdalena. 'Between Citizen and Bogus Asylum Seeker: Management of Migration in the EU through Technology of Morality,' *Social Identities* 21:4 (2015), 395–409.

Knuutila, Reija and Heta Heiskanen. 'Lapsen etu viranomaistoiminnassa: katsaus eräisiin Maahanmuuttoviraston viimeaikaisiin kielteisiin päätöksiin,' *Oikeus* 43:3 (2014), 314–21.

Kochenov, Dimitry. 'The Essence of European Citizenship Emerging from the Last Ten Years of Academic Debate: Beyond the Cherry Blossoms and the Moon?' *International and Comparative Law Quarterly* 62:1 (2013), 97–136.

Kochenov, Dimitry. 'The Right to Have What Rights? EU Citizenship in Need of Clarification,' *European Law Journal* 19:4 (2013), 502–16.

Kostakopoulou, Dora. 'Ideas, Norms and European Citizenship: Explaining Institutional Change,' *Modern Law Review* 68:2 (2005), 233–67.

Lister, Ruth. *Citizenship: Feminist Perspectives*. Basingstoke: Palgrave Macmillan, 2003.

Lundberg, Anna. 'The Best Interests of the Child Principle in Swedish Asylum Cases: The Marginalization of Children's Rights,' *Journal of Human Rights Practice* 3:1 (2011), 49–70.

Marshall, Thomas Humphrey. *Citizenship and Social Class and Other Essays*. Cambridge: Cambridge University Press, 1950.

McCall, Leslie. 'The Complexity of Intersectionality.' In *Intersectionality and Beyond: Law, Power and the Politics of Location*, edited by Emily Grabham, Davina Cooper, Jane Krishnadas and Didi Herman, 49–76. New York: Routledge-Cavendish, 2009.

Mirza, Heidi Safia. '"A Second Skin": Embodied Intersectionality, Transnationalism and Narratives of Identity and Belonging among Muslim Women in Britain,' *Women's Studies International Forum* 36:5 (2013), 5–15.

Pellander, Saara. 'Traces of Dependency: Manifestations of Elderly Family Migration across Policy Arenas'. Paper presented at The Problematisation of Family Migration – workshop, 4–5 June 2015, University of Amsterdam, Netherlands.

Pellander, Saara. 'Collective Threats and Individual Rights: Political Debates on Marriage Migration to Finland.' In *Race, Ethnicity and Welfare States. An American Dilemma?* edited by Pauli Kettunen, Sonya Michel and Claus Petersen, 107–27. Cheltenham: Edward Elgar Publishing, 2015.

Peltola, Marja. *Kunnollisia perheitä: Maahanmuutto, sukupolvet ja yhteiskunnallinen asema*. University of Helsinki: Faculty of Social Sciences, Doctoral dissertation, 2014.

Rastas, Anna. 'Racializing Categorization among Young People in Finland,' *Young* 13:2 (2005), 147–66.

Reynaert, Didier, Maria Bouverne-De Bie and Stijn Vandevelde. 'Between "Believers" and "Opponents": Critical Discussions on Children's Rights,' *The International Journal of Children's Rights* 20:1 (2012), 155–68.
Sankari, Suvi. *Legal Reasoning in Context: The Court of Justice on Articles 17 and 18 EC (20 and 21 TFEU) 2000–2008*. Helsinki: Helsinki University Printing House, 2011.
Schiratzki, Johanna. 'The Best Interests of the Child in the Swedish Aliens Act,' *International Journal of Law, Policy and the Family* 14:3 (2006), 206–25.
Skeggs, Beverley. *Formations of Class and Gender: Becoming Respectable*. London: Sage Publishing, 1997.
Staver, Anne. 'Free Movement and the Fragmentation of Family Reunification Rights,' *European Journal of Migration and Law* 15:1 (2013), 69–89.
Wetherell, Margareta. *Affect and Emotion: A New Social Science Understanding*. London: Sage Publishing, 2012.
Widmer, Eric D., Anna-Maija Castrén, Riitta Jallinoja and Kaisa Ketokivi. 'Introduction.' In *Beyond the Nuclear Family: Families in a Configurational Perspective*, edited by Eric D. Widmer and Riitta Jallinoja, 1–10. Bern: Lang, 2008.
Williams, Toni. 'Intersectionality Analysis in the Sentencing of Aboriginal Women in Canada.' In *Intersectionality and Beyond: Law, Power and the Politics of Location*, edited by Emily Grabham, Davina Cooper, Jane Krishnadas and Didi Herman, 79–104. New York: Routledge-Cavendish, 2009.
Yuval-Davis, Nira. *The Politics of Belonging: Intersectional Contestations*. London: Sage Publishing, 2011.

List of cases

The Supreme Administrative Court of Finland
    KHO:2013:97 (22 May 2013)
    KHO:2014:50 (19 March 2014)
    KHO:2014:51 (19 March 2014)
The European Court of Human Rights
    Darren Omoregia and Others v Norway, app. no. 265/07 (31 July 2008)
    Jeunesse v The Netherlands [GC], app. no .12738/10, 60 EHRR 789 (3 October 2014)
    Konstantinov v The Netherlands, app. no. 16351/03 (26 April 2007)
    Rodrigues da Silva and Hoogkamer v The Netherlands, app. no. 50435/99 (31 January 2006)
    S.L. and J.L. v Croatia, app. no. 13712/11 (7 May 2015)
EU Court of Justice
    C-184/99 *Rudy Grzelczyk v Centre public d'aide sociale d'Ottignies-Louvain-la-Neuve*, [2001] ECR I-6193 (20 September 2001).
    C-34/09 *Gerardo Ruiz Zambrano v Office national de l'emploi (ONEm)* [2011] ECR I-1177 (8 March 2011)
    C-256/11 *Dereci and Others v Bundesministerium für Inneres* [2011] ECR I-11315 (15 November 2011).
    C-357/11, the joined cases *O. and S. v Maahanmuuttovirasto* (C-356/11) and *Maahanmuuttovirasto v L.* (6 December 2012)

Chapter 8

Protecting a person with dementia through restrictions of freedom? Notions of autonomy in the theory and practice of elder care

Anna Mäki-Petäjä-Leinonen[1]

Introduction

Ageing is one of the most significant changes affecting contemporary societies everywhere, imposing certain burdens, such as the increasing number of people with dementia.[2] This change in the citizenry means new challenges also for legal systems across the globe. Elder law[3] has in many different ways tried to provide safeguards for the rights of such people. Special attention has been paid to the significance of the need for protection and the right to autonomy as judicial decision-making principles. This chapter analyses the autonomy of a person with dementia and how the law operates in situations where it is necessary to restrict such a person's freedom.

I will concentrate mainly on the thought expressed by *Rosie Harding*,[4] and *Jonathan Herring*[5] in their work analysing the autonomy of people with

---

1 I am most grateful to Doctor of Philosophy *Fabrice Gzil*, Doctor of Social Sciences *Hanna-Kaisa Hoppania* and doctoral candidate in Social Sciences *Henna Nikumaa* for the fruitful discussions on autonomy and relationality and also for their critical comments on the manuscript. Notwithstanding, they are not responsible for any mistakes or interpretations made in this chapter.
2 Globally there are 38 million people with dementia. It is expected that this number will double by the year 2030 and more than triple by 2050, bringing the estimated total to some 115 million worldwide. Alzheimer's Disease International and World Health Organization, *Dementia. A Public Health Priority* (United Kingdom: World Health Organization, 2012), 12–13.
3 Elder law is defined to be: 'A specialized area of law focused on counseling and representing older persons or their representatives in later-in-life planning and other legal issues of particular importance to older adults. Unlike many other areas of the law, elder law is defined primarily by the client population to be served, not by a distinct set of legal doctrines.' See Nina A. Kohn and Edward D. Spurgeon, 'Elder Law Teaching and Scholarship: An Empirical Analysis of an Evolving Field', *Journal of Legal Education* 59:3 (2010), 414–31.
4 See Rosie Harding, 'Legal Constructions of Dementia: Discourses of Autonomy at the Margins of Capacity', *Journal of Social Welfare & Family Law* 34:4 (2012), 425–42.
5 See especially Jonathan Herring's article, 'Losing it? Losing what? The Law and Dementia', *Child and Family Law Quarterly* 21:1 (2009), 3–29.

dementia. I start by presenting the individual and relational approaches to autonomy, arguing that although these two approaches are often contradictory, both are needed to support the autonomy of people with dementia. In this chapter autonomy is scrutinised throughout the progression of dementia and over the three levels of capacity: A person with dementia may make a decision with full capacity; a person with dementia with borderline capacity may make a decision with support or participate in a decision-making process; and finally, the decisions of a person with incapacity may be made by either respecting the person's prior instructions or by a substituted decision-maker. Finally in this chapter, I shall consider whether a genuine respect for autonomy at all levels of capacity will reduce the need to use restrictive measures when caring for people with dementia. To this end I will scrutinise the forthcoming Finnish Autonomy Act and its outcomes.

Individual and relational accounts of autonomy

Respect for the autonomy of the individual is the core principle underpinning human and fundamental rights discourses. Liberalism views autonomy as a sphere of personal freedom whereby the individual may shape their life according to their own distinctive personality.[6] In addition to questions regarding the ontology of the 'self', autonomy relates to the *question of capacity*. The law assumes that after having reached certain milestones of capability, mainly maturity, we are equally capable. In law, this capacity is usually understood as an ability to understand and assess information relevant to the decision and to communicate the decision arrived at.[7] This account of autonomy presumes that for a person to be recognised as autonomous, they have to be capable of making rational decisions. The rational legal subject thus has the capacity to understand the difference between right and wrong and to bear the consequences of unwise decisions as well.[8]

The capacity to make rational decisions is not the sole conundrum in debates on autonomy. Individuals change. Take for example changes due to a dementing illness. Such changes during the life course pose interesting challenges for our understandings of autonomy and personhood. *Ronald Dworkin* suggested we distinguish between critical interests, such as those relating to the development of life goals, and experiential interests, such as the capacity to experience enjoyment and pleasure. According to him, the

---

6 See, for example, Joseph Raz's account of autonomy in *The Morality of Freedom* (Oxford: Clarendon Press, 1986), 369.
7 See, for instance, Lesley King and Hugh Series, 'Assessing Capacity' in *The Law and Ethics of Dementia*, ed. Charles Foster, Jonathan Herring and Israel Doron (Oxford and Portland: Hart Publishing, 2014), 283–7.
8 Ronald Dworkin, *Life's Dominion: An Argument about Abortion and Euthanasia* (London: HarperCollins, 1993), 224.

critical interests are more important to the autonomy and should, consequently, be taken to survive incapacity. Thereby critical interests expressed for example in an advance directive should overtake any experiential interests a person may express while incapable.[9] Others have levelled criticism against such distinction. Jonathan Herring, for one, would follow the current wishes of the person with incapacity unless they were to cause the person serious harm.[10] The way we approach changes in capacity is thus revealing of our understanding of personhood as it forces us to pose the question of whether the person remains the same or becomes different.[11]

This approach can be defined by entertaining the so-called individual (or traditional) ideal of autonomy. Beside it, relational theorists have developed *relational autonomy*, which rejects the liberalism of individual autonomy. For example, *Jennifer Nedelsky* has argued that rather than considering adults with capacity as atomistic individuals, we should consider autonomy through relationships with other people.[12] According to Herring, people in close relationships seek a compromise in their decision-making by trying to make a decision according to what is good for 'us' rather than what is best for 'me'. Hence to talk about 'my decision' is, in many respects, simply misleading. The goal of relational autonomy is thus to build up relationships that enhance our lives rather than seeking to maximise freedom.[13]

Relational autonomy thus assumes the person's ability to share their thoughts and beliefs in conversation with others. According to Harding, a key limitation of the concept 'relational autonomy', however, is the lack of any definitional interrogation of what 'relational' actually means in the everyday lives of individuals and what it means for individual decision-making to be placed in a relational context. It might even require greater capacity for self-awareness and rationality than approaches to individual autonomy.[14] The relational approach towards autonomy, therefore, can be seen as problematic in some contexts.

Relational autonomy often highlights the importance of supporting people's relationships in order to support their autonomy. But as Herring

---

9 Dworkin, *Life's Dominion*, 201–2 and 226–9.
10 Herring, 'Losing it? Losing what?', 16.
11 See, for instance, Rebecca Dresser, 'Life, Death, and Incompetent Patients: Conceptual Infirmities and Hidden Values in the Law', *Arizona Law Review* 28:3 (1986), 379–81 and 393–5 and Agnieszka Jaworska, 'Respecting the Margins of Agency: Alzheimer's Patients and the Capacity to Value', *Philosophy and Public Affairs* 28:2 (1998), 108–10.
12 Jennifer Nedelsky, 'Reconceiving Autonomy: Sources, Thoughts, Possibilities', *Yale Journal of Law & Feminism* 1:1 (1989), 21. On the four approaches to relationality in the contemporary academic literature, see Rosie Harding, 'Dementia and Carers: Relationality and Informal Carers' Experiences' in *The Law and Ethics of Dementia*, ed. Charles Foster, Jonathan Herring and Israel Doron (Oxford and Portland: Hart Publishing, 2014), 380–2.
13 Jonathan Herring, *Caring and the Law* (Oxford and Portland: Hart Publishing, 2013), 72–3.
14 Harding, 'Legal Constructions of Dementia', 430–1.

argues, although beneficial relationships are an important part of people's lives, relationships and social structures can also be oppressive and destructive of autonomy. Therefore, if a person with diminishing capacity lives within a relational context where their carers *de facto* restrict their liberty, it is hard to see relationality as beneficial to their autonomy. As Harding argues, if autonomy is predicated on the ability to share, converse and communicate with others, there is a great risk that a person with communication problems would be in danger of losing their right to autonomy. Moreover, if interpersonal relationships are emphasised, it is possible that a person with dementia could even find their social relationships oppressive.[15]

> Also *care theory* emphasizes that focusing on care relations requires paying more attention to interactions among unequals; relations which actually dominate our social life. When it comes to people with dementia, such relations of dependency are precisely at stake. Ideally these relations are good care relations, but they can also be abusive and exploitative. Hence the role of power in care relations should be acknowledged, so that measures against possibility for exploitation and neglect can also be developed.[16]

In the next section I shall scrutinise the autonomy of a person with dementia within different levels of capacity. I shall demonstrate how the approach of relational autonomy can be combined with the approach of traditional liberal autonomy and in that way grant more possibilities to respect the autonomy of a person with dementia.

Respecting the autonomy of a person with dementia

'Dementia' is defined as a condition presenting problems with memory and at least one other cognitive domain, such as verbal functions, executive functions, the perceiving or performance of learned motor skills.

---

15 Ibid, 431–2.
16 See for instance Annemieke van Drenth and Francisca de Haan, *The Rise of Caring Power. Elizabeth Fry and Josephine Butler in Britain and the Netherlands* (Amsterdam: Amsterdam University Press, 1999) and Kerstin Svensson, 'Caring Power – Coercion as Care', *Critical Practice Studies*, 4:2 (2002), 71–8 who have developed and used the concept of caring power and studied coercive care, and Eva Feder Kittay and Ellen K Feder, 'Introduction' in *The Subject of Care: Feminist Perspectives on Dependency*, ed. Eva Feder Kittay and Ellen K Feder (Lanham: Rowan & Littlefield, 2002), 2 on care and dependency. About these care theories see also Hanna-Kaisa Hoppania, *Care as a Site of a Political Struggle* (University of Helsinki: Academic dissertation, 2015, https://helda.helsinki.fi/handle/10138/157561), 41–5. Indeed, similarities between care theory and legal thought on autonomy and restrictions of freedom exist, and they could be explored more thoroughly in future research.

Dementing illnesses are progressive neurodegenerative illnesses and can be divided into three stages: mild, moderate and severe.[17] In cases of mild dementia people are usually capable of understanding and making decisions while they become legally incapable at the latest, severe stage of the dementia. There may be difficulties in assessing capacity at the moderate stage as a person might be borderline capable. In what follows I will scrutinise what the autonomy of a person with dementia means at different levels of capacity.

A person with dementia and full legal capacity: the right to make decisions

It is obvious that the mere diagnosis of dementing illness as such does not automatically remove a person's right to autonomy. However, as the disease progresses, capacity can deteriorate and it is likely that the person will, at some stage of the disease, lose their legal capacity. Nevertheless, the issue of legal capacity is time specific. A person may have the capacity to make one decision but lack the capacity to make another.[18] Stock trading and risk investment, for example, require an altogether different level of decision-making capacity than drafting a simple will or choosing a nursing home.[19] Whenever a person with dementia retains the cognitive capacity to make a particular decision, respecting their right to autonomy requires us to allow them to make that decision.

It is not always, though, an easy way to assess the capacity of a person with dementia as they can be on the verge of capacity. Herring, for one, has scrutinised the autonomy of a 'just competent' person with dementia. He argues that where the decision of a person with dementia is one that '[...] contradicts values that underlie the individual's life, it may also be regarded as not autonomous or only weakly protected under the principle of autonomy, unless it can be shown that the individual has made a conscious decision to depart from the values that previously underpinned their life.' Herring gives a hypothetical case of Andrew (a devout religious man of conservative moral views) with early stages of Alzheimer's disease spending substantial sums of money viewing internet pornography. Herring further argues that '[...] we must ask whether his recent internet behaviour is the result of a reasoned decision to reject his previous value system, or

---

17 American Psychiatric Association, *Diagnostic and Statistical Manual of Mental Disorders* (4th Edition, Text Revision, dsm-iv-tr, 2000).
18 British Medical Association and the Law Society, *Assessment of Mental Capacity: Guidance for Doctors and Lawyers* (London: BMJ Books, British Medical Association, 2004) 3–5 and 13–14.
19 Anna Mäki-Petäjä-Leinonen and Kati Juva, 'Of Sound Mind? Dementia and Aspects of Assessing Legal Capacity', *European Journal of Health Law* 22:1 (2015), 14.

whether it is a result of fleeting ill-considered decisions which are entitled to only limited respect under the principle of autonomy. If they are the latter, there is a case for saying that his family or carers are entitled to take some steps to prevent him acting in the way he is.'[20]

In my view, Herring's position is justifiable from the point of view of a *principle of protection* of a person with decreasing capacity. The basic idea of individual protection is to protect the weak from making harmful choices and from violations by third parties, the object of protection being financial as well as physical or moral integrity. It is thus clear that a person with weakening capacity is in special need of protection and that need increases together with the disease. However, this principle should become determinate only after it has been proven that a person is in real need of protection.[21]

In Herring's example, it might thus be asked that as Andrew is seen as competent – only just, but still – does he really have to make a 'reasoned decision to reject his previous value system'? Is Andrew actually expected to have a greater capacity to understand than what is expected of a 'healthy' person? Harding is right to point out that we do not generally require people without dementia to demonstrate religious, political or other entrenched worldviews in order to respect their decisions. However, it is probable that people with dementia are given less scope to make unwise decisions than others, simply because of their condition.[22]

A question worth considering in general is, how much rationality is to be expected in decision-making of a person with dementia (competent or not) when it is well known that even decisions made by healthy people are not always based on rational reasoning but merely on emotions. Even competent people make foolish decisions.[23] This is acknowledged also in the UK's Mental Capacity Act 2005, which states that a person is not to be treated as unable to make a decision merely because they make an unwise decision (s 1(4)). I have previously argued that it is justifiable in certain cases to give importance to a will expressed by a person with dementia, even though they have not been able to understand the significance of the legal act in all its

---

20 Herring, 'Losing it? Losing what?', 7–12.
21 Anna Mäki-Petäjä-Leinonen, 'Legal Status of a Person with Dementia, English summary' in *Dementoituvan henkilön oikeudellinen asema* ('The Legal Status of a Person with Dementia', Helsinki: Suomalainen lakimiesyhdistys, Academic dissertation, 2003) 368–70. See also Mol on the logic of care according to which care starts from what people need, not what they know or want. Annemarie Mol, *The Logic of Care: Health and the Problem of Patient Choice* (London: Routledge, 2008), 22.
22 Harding, 'Legal Constructions of Dementia', 429. Another reason might be the fact that they are in care relations in care homes where also the safety of the other residents or carers must be taken into consideration. This might lead to a situation where the right to consume alcohol, for instance, might be limited.
23 Herring, 'Losing it? Losing what?', 6.

aspects. If the person with dementia derives well-being from a purchase and the transaction does not affect their economic situation in any decisive way, it might not necessarily be in this person's interest that the transaction be declared void. Thus, certain leeway should be given for some irrationality in the case of a person without full legal capacity.[24] This issue is not without its difficulties because, on the other hand, an overly zealous consideration of autonomy may lead to a situation that works against the person's best interests. In some cases we might even speak of neglect or abandonment.

In the above I have introduced the individual and relational approaches to autonomy. Let us now examine how these two approaches match the ideal where a person with dementia makes their decisions as a fully competent individual. Harding has argued that by using the individual approach to autonomy and by focusing on the decision-making capabilities of the individual, 'the importance of relationality to our everyday experience of life can be erased'.[25] The Nuffield Council on Bioethics has argued the same by emphasising the fact that people are not isolated individuals, but are people whose identity is embedded in a network of relationships. According to the Council, '[T]he interests of the person with dementia are closely linked to the interests of their family and friends who are caring for them. This is an important reason why carers should receive advice and support, and this in itself can be helpful to the person with dementia as a way to enhance their autonomy.'[26]

The above-mentioned arguments are of course well justified. However, I would like to argue that it is important also to focus on the precise level of capacity of a person with dementia. Otherwise such person's opinions and will might be erased. It is true that usually a person with dementia lives with relations and may also need the advice and support of their carers in their decision-making. However, as this first constituent of autonomy suggests that a person with dementia makes a decision with full capacity, we should also beware that such a person's relations can be potentially harmful for their decision-making.[27] People with dementia are usually in relations of dependency which make them vulnerable and at risk of undue influence and abuse. Relational autonomy can however be seen as potentially more

---

24 Mäki-Petäjä-Leinonen and Juva, 'Of Sound Mind?' 34–5.
25 Harding, 'Dementia and Carers', 389. See also Sherwin and Winsby according to whom the traditional approach of autonomy focuses too heavily on evaluating the competency of the patient and not nearly enough on examining the range and nature of the options from which each patient must choose. Susan Sherwin and Meghan Winsby, 'A Relational Perspective on Autonomy for Older Adults Residing in Nursing Homes', *Health Expectations* 14:2 (2011), 184.
26 Nuffield Council on Bioethics, *Dementia: Ethical Issues* (London: Cambridge Publishers, 2009), 27.
27 Harding, 'Legal Constructions of Dementia', 431–2.

important to a person with borderline capacity as will be pointed out in the next section.

A person with dementia and borderline capacity: supported decision-making and the right to participate

As pointed out in the previous section, it is not always easy to assess the capacity of a person with dementia as they might be on the borderline of capacity. Herring has presented two examples – a just competent and just incompetent person with dementia – and demonstrated how much weight to a will of such a person should be given in their decision-making process.[28] I argue that when a person with dementia 'falls' into this category from the above mentioned, they are not fully competent at that point in their life but may have opinions and views of decisions to be made. If, on the other hand, they were fully competent, they could easily make decisions by themselves (with or without support from their family). In this section then, I will focus on situations where a person with decreased capacity makes decisions which are supported[29] or at least takes part in a decision-making process.

Herring has argued that even though a person is judged to be lacking capacity and their views are thus no longer protected by the right of autonomy, their preferences do still count for something. According to Herring, there are several other legal principles and values which can be used to give weight to their views. These principles, such as dignity and liberty, are reflected in the practice of *person-centred care*, whose key principles are: valuing people with dementia and those who care for them, treating people as individuals, looking at the world from the perspective of the person with dementia and creating a positive social environment.[30] Harding has pointed out that neither version of autonomy (individual or relational) includes a right to having one's wishes carried out, simply the right to make the relevant decision.[31] She further argues that legal understandings of autonomy for people with dementia would do well to engage with the social psychological literature and social care practice that seek to promote respect for the continued personhood of people with dementia: 'In social care practice, one way that autonomy and self-worth are maintained for

---

28 Herring, 'Losing it? Losing what?', 7–16.
29 Supported decision-making for people with mental disabilities is developed especially in Canada and Australia. In the legal sense, the Province of British Columbia in Canada is one of the leading jurisdictions in incorporating supported decision-making into law, policy and practice. On supported decision-making, see UN, OHCHR and IPU, *From Exclusion to Equality – Realizing the rights of persons with disabilities. Handbook for Parliamentarians on the Convention on the Rights of Persons with Disabilities* (Geneva: United Nations, 2007), 90.
30 Herring, 'Losing it? Losing what?' 16.
31 Harding, 'Legal Constructions of Dementia', 427.

people with dementia is through care practices which draw on the concept of person-centred care.'[32]

I would on the other hand argue that giving weight to the views of a person with decreased capacity and giving them the right to participate is actually a constituent of autonomy. That is, if we give worth to such a person's views and take seriously the ideal of continued personhood. The same applies in child law, where the justification for children's right to participate can be derived from the concept of the child's right to autonomy.[33] I agree furthermore with Herring and Harding that principles of person-centred care are well suited to this debate. As Harding has pointed out, the question is also whether the regulatory frameworks surrounding dementia care can engage with the person-centred approach to empower and support people with dementia.[34] As I shall later demonstrate, the forthcoming Finnish Autonomy Act has gone some way to adopt the ideal of person-centred care, at least at the level of principle.

I shall now demonstrate in more detail how a decision-making process might proceed for a person with borderline capacity. First of all, in some cases they might be capable of making *independent decisions supported*.[35] This objective is expressed in the Nuffield Council on Bioethics report *Dementia: Ethical Issues* where they seem to perceive the supported decision-making as a part of autonomy. Their report states that '[…] if someone has limited capability to live independently or to realise their own choices, then respect for autonomy must involve others taking active steps to act as advocates and try to promote their autonomy […] promoting autonomy will often require the provision of active support.'[36] According to Herring, when decisions need to be made for a person of doubtful capacity, decisions should be made within the person's relational context. In some cases, involving family members and carers in decision-making will enable an individual to have the capacity to make a decision they otherwise would not have.[37] In my opinion, this argument is a good one. If we argue that giving weight to the views of a person with dementia is a constituent of autonomy, then giving effect to a person's relationality and involving family members in

---

32 Ibid. 432.
33 Henna Pajulammi, 'Summary' in *Lapsi, oikeus ja osallisuus* ('Children, Rights and Participation', Helsinki: Talentum, Academic dissertation, 2014), 456.
34 Harding, 'Legal Constructions of Dementia', 433.
35 This approach may also be called as *'shared decision making'* which aims to confer agency by 1) providing information and 2) supporting the decision-making process. See for instance, Glyn Elwyn *et al.*, 'Shared Decision Making: A Model for Clinical Practice', *Journal of General Internal Medicine* 27:10 (2012), 1361–7.
36 Nuffield Council on Bioethics, *Dementia: Ethical Issues*, 27. Furthermore the UK's Mental Capacity Act 2005 highlights the importance of exploring the possibilities for supporting individual decisions before a person is declared incompetent.
37 Herring, *Caring and the Law*, 156–60.

decision-making could enable a person with dementia to make a supported decision. Alternatively they might be given a right to participate.

When a person *participates in a decision-making process*, they do not necessarily make a decision by themselves but they are involved, are listened to and their views are taken into consideration. As Harding has argued, respecting autonomy in a person-centred and relational sense does not require that any decision made by a person with limited capacity is necessarily carried out, particularly if it requires significant input from others. Rather, respecting this version of autonomy means that a person's wishes and feelings are not excluded or overridden unnecessarily, even if the outcome is the same.[38] In other words, the aim is to give some weight to a person's own views and values. This is seen as particularly important in situations where a person has lost the capacity to make independent decisions.

One might thus say that when granted a right to participate, a person is not granted a right to master the question at hand but rather to be a member of a team making decisions that concern them.[39] In this sense the right to participate can be seen as part of a weaker right than the right to 'complete' autonomy or self-determination. In the end, much depends on the decision-maker, as to how much weight is to be given to the views and values of a person with dementia. Recently the regulatory framework has laid emphasis on the participation rights of the elderly. For example, the Finnish Act on Supporting the Functional Capacity of the Older Population and on Social and Health Services for Older Persons (980/2012, later 'Elder Act') contains a section on general principles for responding to service needs (Elder Act 13 §). According to a paragraph, the services must be provided so as to support the well-being, health, functional capacity, independent living and *inclusion* of older persons. The right to participate can of course be seen as an important constituent of autonomy, but one should nevertheless keep in mind that a competent person with dementia has the right to make independent decisions. For example, the Finnish Elder Act does not even mention an older person's right to autonomy, which arguably is a serious shortcoming.

Andrew McGee points out that recently the emphasis has begun to shift away from autonomy altogether and towards respect for wishes, values and beliefs that may not stem from autonomy or which may stem from *attenuated autonomy* – an autonomy falling short of that which applies when the patient has capacity to make decisions in the legal sense. According to

---

38 Harding, 'Legal Constructions of Dementia', 439.
39 See also the UK Mental Capacity Act (s 4(4)): 'The person making the determination of a best interest of a person with incapacity must, so far as is reasonably practicable, permit and encourage the person to participate, or to improve his ability to participate, as fully as possible in any act done for him and any decision affecting him.'

McGee, these developments are extremely important because they confirm our recognition that people with dementia are persons and worthy of the utmost respect notwithstanding the loss of capacity in the legal sense.[40]

A person with dementia with clear incapacity: giving effect to advance care planning and substituted decision-making

Deterioration of cognitive capacity will eventually lead to a situation where a person with dementia will no longer be able to make independent or supported decisions nor participate in a decision-making process. In such situations a person's decisions are being made by either respecting a person's prior, clear instructions or a person's decisions are being made by a substituted decision maker. In an ideal situation, a person with incapacity has expressed their will about the given issue while still capable of doing so. With later life legal planning a person can ensure that their 'healthy' will is respected at the stage of life when they have lost the capacity to make valid decisions.[41] For instance, the Finnish legal system makes it possible to perform such legal planning by seeking a guardianship order from the local registry office, giving powers of attorney or continuing powers of attorney or drawing up an advance directive.

Advance directives and advance care plans are intertwined tools to support the autonomy of the people with dementia and to clarify their wishes and will concerning the future. Aspects of *advance care planning* are: opening the conversation, exploring options, identifying wishes and preferences, deciding about specific treatment, asking someone to speak on behalf of a person or appointing someone to be a substituted decision-maker and letting people know the views, preferences and wishes of an advance care planner. An advance care plan can also be part of an advance directive.[42] Such is the case in the Alzheimer Society of Finland's Advance Directive form. The form consists of two main sections: the legally binding expressions concerning care and the section for advance care planning. The first

---

40 Andrew McGee, 'Best Interest Determinations and Substituted Judgement: Personhood and Precedent Autonomy', in *The Law and Ethics of Dementia*, ed. Charles Foster, Jonathan Herring and Israel Doron (Oxford and Portland: Hart Publishing, 2014), 144.
41 European countries have laws with provisions whereby a competent person can explicitly appoint another to carry out certain transactions on their behalf in a case of incapacity. See Alzheimer Europe, *Dementia in Europe Yearbook 2010 with a focus on legal capacity and proxy decision making in dementia* (Luxembourg: Alzheimer Europe, 2010).
42 Alzheimer Cooperative Valuation in Europe (Alcove), *The European Joint Action on Dementia – Synthesis Report 2013*, 81. On advance care planning, see also Marike de Boer, *Advance Directives in Dementia Care. Perspectives of People with Alzheimer's Disease, Elderly Care Physicians and Relatives* (Vrije Universiteit: Academic dissertation, 2011), 65–77. See also Tom Goffin, 'Advance Directives as an Instrument in an Ageing Europe', *European Journal of Health Law* 19:2 (2012), 124–9.

part consists of the end-of-life decisions and the possibility to appoint a healthcare proxy to make treatment decisions. For medical staff this part is legally binding. The second part should be considered as the patient's wishes for treatment and care. It should be respected as much as possible, emphasising the patient's right to individual autonomy.[43]

Expressions in an advance directive tend to be either consent or refusal of possible future treatment. Traditionally, an advance directive is thus understood as mainly the expression of a person's will for end-of-life care. However, life with cognitive disabilities may last several years and involve different kinds of care decisions. In this way the wider advance care planning could actually be more important to a person with dementia than a 'traditional' advance directive. It has thus been seen as essential that various views and wishes about care could exist in an advance directive containing any wishes about specific life-values to be respected throughout the care, wishes about the future care unit, the content of the care to be given, the use of security-related technology and the views of the use of finances to obtain the best possible care and treatment.

However, later life legal planning by drawing up an advance directive is still not very common.[44] In situations where decisions have to be made for a person with incapacity without an advance directive, a person's decisions are being made by a *substituted decision-maker* ideally guided by appreciation of the person's values and life history. The substituted decision-maker, who is usually a family member, should thus try to construe the will of a person with incapacity by looking at their personal values and life history. When making choices between different procedures, the following question should be asked: 'What would a person with incapacity decide in this particular case – what would be the person's presumed healthy will?'[45] For example, both the UK Mental Capacity Act (s 6(b)) and the Finnish Patient Act (s 6.3) highlight the importance of respecting such wishes. Respecting the presumed healthy will of a person with dementia can therefore also be seen as an aspect of their right to autonomy.

The issue of whether to respect the instructions given in an advance directive, or to follow the previous values of a person, can be an easy one if a person with dementia does not have present wishes and interests of the given

---

43 See Alzheimer Society of Finland, 'Advance Directive', last modified 17 December, 2015, www.muistiliitto.fi/files/3613/7604/6221/advance_directive_2013.pdf (accessed 15 April 2016).
44 Gary Sinoff and Natalia Blaja-Lisnic, 'Advance Decisions and Proxy Decision-Making in the Elderly: A Medical Perspective', in *The Law and Ethics of Dementia*, ed. Charles Foster, Jonathan Herring and Israel Doron (Oxford and Portland: Hart Publishing, 2014), 97–9. See also Karen Harrison Dening, Louise Jones and Elizabeth L Sampson, 'Advance Care Planning for People with Dementia: A Review', *International Psychogeriatrics* 23:10 (2011), 1535–51.
45 Mäki-Petäjä-Leinonen, 'Legal Status of a Person with Dementia', 373.

issue. The problem might occur, however, if a person with dementia now has wishes and desires that stand in contravention of the previous directions or previous personal values. As we saw earlier, much philosophical discussion exists about the relationship between the 'then' self that existed prior to dementia and the 'now' self that lives in the present and may have lost all connection to the past. Proponents of the *critical interest approach* underline the importance of basing post-dementia decisions on historical lifetime values and beliefs.[46] Proponents of the *experiential interest approach*, on the other hand, argue that there can be major changes in values between the time when people complete their advance directive and when it comes into effect. According to the experiential interest approach, contemporary preferences and values, together with the present well-being of the person with dementia should be the main area for substituted decision-making.[47] According to this approach, it might be concluded that an advance directive has no claim to be strictly binding in all cases of dementia.[48]

> There are plenty of good examples in the literature of the kind of situations in which a collision between previously-given directions or life values and current wishes might occur. Often these examples refer to the religious views of a person with incapacity. For example, Herring's example of a vehement atheist Bertha, who now, having developed dementia, enjoys going to the mosque[49] or Hope & McMillan's example of Mr A, who is Jewish and has moderate dementia. Before his dementia progressed he clearly expressed the wish to avoid eating pork. Recently, he ate some bacon and pork sausages from another resident's plate and is now demanding that he too be given this food for breakfast.[50]

McGee argues that when considering the weight one should give to the current wishes of a person with severe dementia, a balance should be struck between past wishes as recorded in an advance directive or expressed to relatives or proxies, and the person's current wishes, values and needs. I would agree with McGee that ultimately each case must be decided on its own merits, taking into account the impact on the person with dementia if their current wishes are not granted.[51] According to Hope and McMillan,

---

46 Dworkin, *Life's Dominion*, 201–2 and 226–9.
47 Herring, 'Losing it? Losing what?' 21–2. See also, for instance, Jaworska, 'Respecting the Margins of Agency', 109.
48 Alcove, *The European Joint Action on Dementia*, 80.
49 See Herring, 'Losing it? Losing what?' 7.
50 Tony Hope and John McMillan, 'The Art of Medicine – Advance Decisions, Chronic Mental Illness, and Everyday Care', *The Lancet* 377 (2011), 2076.
51 McGee, 'Best Interest Determinations and Substituted Judgement', 145. See also Mäki-Petäjä-Leinonen and Juva, 'Of Sound Mind?' 34–5.

'Careful thought, compassion, and wise judgement may in the end be all we have. No algorithm resolves the enigma of the carer's art.'[52]

A final point of scrutiny concerns how the two different approaches to autonomy – the traditional, individual approach and the relational approach – match the situation where a person with dementia clearly lacks capacity to make decisions or to participate in a decision-making process. In situations where a person's decisions are being made by respecting their prior, clear instructions it can be observed that a person's autonomy is followed by taking account of the traditional approach. However, where a substituted decision-maker is involved the approach is different. In such cases the individual's relations are clearly important as the decision-maker is usually a family member who can construe the presumed will of a person with incapacity by considering that individual's values and life history. All in all, I would argue that the individual and relational approach of autonomy are equally important. They should not be seen as in conflict but rather combined in order to improve the likelihood that the autonomy of the person with dementia will be respected.

The legal system is relatively flexible and overall it facilitates beneficial decisions in respect of persons with dementia. Consciousness of the rights of persons with dementia helps morally responsible parties who are behind the decisions to make good choices. As *Thomas Wilhelmsson* has pointed out, a morally responsible decision-maker can, in their decision-making, take into consideration the possibilities for rightful choices as provided under the law.[53] In the case of a person with dementia the issue is about treatment with humanity and both protecting and respecting their right to autonomy. In what follows I shall consider how the autonomy of a person with dementia can be promoted when using restrictive measures in dementia care.

Autonomy and restrictions on freedom

Definition of restriction on freedom

Opinions about what constitutes a restriction on freedom depend on how the term is defined. Broad, everyday definitions might emphasise the prevention of a person from doing what they appear to want to do. This might,

---

52 Hope and McMillan, 'The Art of Medicine', 2077. Quite similarly Mol has argued, while writing in *Logic of Care*, that care starts from what people need, not from what they know or want. This does not imply passivity of the care receivers, nor control by the carer. Both are active participants and the art of care 'is to act without seeking to control. To persist while letting go'. See Mol, *The Logic of Care*, 28. See also Hoppania, *Care as a Site of a Political Struggle*, 44.
53 See Raimo Siltala on Wilhelmsson's thought in *Law, Truth, and Reason: A Treatise on Legal Argumentation* (Dordrecht, Heidelberg, London, New York: Springer Publishing, 2011), 231.

for example, cover preventing a person from entering or leaving a room, defined space or building, forbidding certain actions, forcing or putting pressure on someone to do something that they do not want to do or denying them the right to make certain decisions. The ways in which freedom is restricted may be broadly defined as measures or means of restraint. Examples include physical and psychological restraint as well as the use of mechanical, chemical, environmental, electronic and other means or devices.[54]

The principle of protection is always crucial when a person's physical freedom has to be restricted by using restrictive measures or other means. The only grounds for the use of restrictive measures should be that they are in accordance with the best interests and safety of a person. A conflict between the principles of autonomy and protection usually emerges in cases where a person's freedom has to be restricted. One can also scrutinise this question from the judicial point of view i.e. is the use of restrictive measures lawful? In the following sections I shall focus on what Finnish legislation determines.

Lawfulness of restrictions

Institutional care comes within the sphere of fundamental rights, especially in questions related to personal liberty. According to section 6 of the Finnish Constitution (731/1999), everyone has the right to life and personal liberty, physical integrity and security of person and no-one should be tortured or otherwise treated in a degrading manner.[55] Furthermore, it is stated that there shall be no interference in personal integrity or deprivation of liberty without legitimate grounds prescribed by an Act of Parliament. Such legislation should be precise, definite, acceptable and proportional.

The Finnish Mental Health Act (1116/1990) and the Act on Special Care for People with Intellectual Disabilities (519/1977) contain several paragraphs which address the issues of coercive measures and deprivation of freedom. However, normally these Acts do not apply to people with dementia, as they are usually treated in nursing homes for the elderly and not in the type of institutions that these Acts are targeting. Nevertheless, coercive measures are regularly used in dementia care, and it may well be the case that procedures used in nursing homes and ordinary hospitals fall foul of fundamental rights. The situation clearly breaches both the Finnish

---

54 Alzheimer Europe, *The Ethical Issues Linked to Restrictions of Freedom of People with Dementia* (Luxembourg: Alzheimer Europe, 2012), 18–21.
55 The importance of respecting the liberty of human beings is also acknowledged in Article 5 of the European Convention for the Protection of Human Rights and Fundamental Freedoms (1950) and in Article 14 of the UN Convention on the Rights of Persons with Disabilities (2006).

Constitution and UN Convention on the Rights of Persons with Disabilities (13 December 2006, later UN Disability Convention) which Finland ratified in June 2016.[56] This is the case even if the use of restrictive measures can be justified by arguing that it is in accordance with the patient's best interests.[57]

The lack of adequate legislation catering for conditions and means of restriction of freedom had been long recognised by the Ministry of Social Affairs and Health, which finally established a working group in 2010 to assemble the provisions relating to the deprivation of liberty and self-determination of all patients and clients in social care and welfare. The draft of the Act on strengthening the autonomy of such patients and clients and the conditions regulating usage of restrictive measures (the so-called 'Autonomy Act') was published in April 2014 and the new Act was meant to come into force at the end of 2014.[58] However, there were problems with the legislative process and the previous government was not able to bring the Act into force. The legislative process will continue in autumn 2016. Although at the time of writing this chapter the Act is still not in force, it seems unlikely that there will be any fundamental changes to the forthcoming legislation. It is reasonable therefore to scrutinise the proposed legislation herein, from the point of view of autonomy and restrictions on freedom.

The purpose of the draft legislation is to strengthen the autonomy of a patient/client and to allow the restrictions on freedom to be used only when necessary to ensure a person's safety or the safety of others. The objective of the legislation can thus be seen as acceptable: to strengthen the autonomy of a person with incapacity and to prevent the unjustified use of restrictive measures. The legislation specifically pertains to the care of people with mental disabilities and dementia. It is estimated that it will apply to 23,000 persons with dementia and some 1000–2000 people with mental disabilities.[59]

According to the proposed Act, the client/patient with incapacity should have their own self-determination plan. This plan could be drawn up after the capacity of a client/patient would have been judged to have deteriorated permanently in a way that they would be unable to make decisions in

---

56 Finland had already signed the UN Disability Convention in 2007. The ratification was transferred, as the Finnish legislation did not adequately reflect the articles of the Convention. Reforms were needed, for instance, to update the legislation concerning people with intellectual disabilities. Unfortunately, the reforms failed to address the issues concerning the rights of people with dementia.
57 The situation is the same in most European Countries. For more about legislation in Europe on the use of restrictive measures see Alzheimer Europe, *Dementia in Europe. Yearbook 2011 with a focus on restrictions of freedom* (Luxembourg: Alzheimer Europe, 2011).
58 Sosiaali- ja terveysministeriön raportteja ja muistioita 2014:14, *Sosiaali- ja terveydenhuollon asiakkaan itsemääräämisoikeus. Työryhmän loppuraportti* ('The right of self-determination of patients in social and healthcare', Helsinki: Sosiaali- ja terveysministeriö, 2014).
59 Ibid. 107.

social and healthcare and to understand the consequences of their actions. Furthermore it should be evident that a person, because of the deterioration of capacity, would be most likely to harm their health or safety, the health or safety of others or would do extensive damage to property. The self-determination plan should include measures on how the self-determination would be supported. Furthermore it should include the list of restrictive measures that are planned to be used in a person's care when necessary. Remarkably the draft legislation recognises the importance of an advance directive. It states that when drawing up a self-determination plan for a client/patient, the possible advance directive should be taken into account. It could well be seen that if an advance directive includes a person's thoughts about the use of restrictive measures, this could reduce the likelihood of their excessive use.

However, as the forthcoming legislation is called the 'Autonomy Act', the question arises: where are the positive, concrete regulations to support the self-determination of a client/patient? The proposal contains as many as 40 regulations, and only a few of them (and mainly in passing) mention the supporting of self-determination but without suggesting anything concrete. It seems that where strengthening and supporting autonomy is concerned, the draft legislation leans heavily on changing attitudes and care cultures. For example, it is proposed that care providers should give instructions to personnel about the means to support the autonomy of a client/patient and how to avoid the use of restrictive measures. Furthermore care providers should strengthen the autonomy of a client/patient with appropriate solutions in their immediate environment, such as furniture and devices. It is a matter of adopting a new kind of care culture which has been emphasised in research and teaching of elderly care for years.[60] It is clear that this legislation has adopted the ideal of person-centred care. And it is true that, in the matter of caring for people with dementia, many situations can be solved by highly qualified professionals without compromising individuals' fundamental rights. The following example from a Norwegian study is a good example of person-centred care:

> One patient diagnosed with senile dementia refused to take the medication given to him. The nurse accepted the patient's refusal [...] The nurse said, 'It was unnecessary to force this patient; he soon forgot

---

60 See, for example, Chris Gastmans and Koen Milisen, 'Use of Physical Restraint in Nursing Homes: Clinical-ethical Considerations', *Journal of Medical Ethics* 32:3 (2006), 148–52 and Raija Kontio *et al.*, 'Patient Restrictions: Are there Ethical Alternatives to Seclusion and Restraint?' *Nursing Ethics* 17:1 (2010), 65–76.

what he had refused, and took the medicine later.' And the patient did indeed voluntarily take his medication later that day.[61]

On the other hand, it can often be seen what the consequences are when regulations are written in the form of principles, having little to do with specific, binding orders. For instance, if the regulations rely on changing care cultures and attitudes, there is a risk that such regulations remain a dead letter. The success or otherwise of this kind of regulation will pretty much depend on a care unit and its care culture, structure and management. This kind of statute law is not necessarily suited to securing the equal treatment in supporting the autonomy of people with incapacity: the risk is that when legislation lacks specific regulations, such legislation will be totally ineffectual.

When, on the other hand, scrutinising more closely the proposed legislation from the point of view of restrictions, one can see that there are as many as 20 regulations concerning restrictions on freedom. These might include physical restraint using restrictive measures, segregation, preventing a patient from leaving the care facility, taking measures to protect the patient's/client's hygiene (basic care), taking over responsibility for the patient's/client's assets and technological surveillance.

At the time of writing, this coming new legislation has spawned a lot of debate in Finland. Even though the usage of restrictive measures is likely to involve a great deal of bureaucracy, there is a fear that the legislation will not lessen the use of such measures, but do rather the opposite. One might also ask where the dividing line between the need for precision and the acceptability of the legislation runs, if almost every conceivable measure of restriction, even using force to administer basic care, is enabled through legislation. As Alzheimer Europe has stated, one should not see the restriction on freedom through the use of restraint as a possibility; it is always a failure of good care.[62]

A person with dementia and restrictions of freedom: two examples

As mentioned earlier, the principle of protection is always crucial when a person's physical freedom has to be restricted by using restrictive measures or other means. Furthermore in such cases, a conflict between the principles of autonomy and protection usually emerges. The question then is whether to allow a person with diminishing capacity to make irrational

---

61 Åshild Slettebø and Eli Haugen Bunch, 'Solving Ethically Difficult Care Situations in Nursing Homes', *Nursing Ethics* 11:6 (2004), 548.
62 Alzheimer Europe, *The Ethical Issues Linked to Restrictions of Freedom*, 76.

decisions and take risks or whether to protect them from making harmful choices.

Let's take the example of a person with dementia who wants to walk about freely in a long-term care facility. If a member of the care personnel sees that there is a great risk of that person falling and harming themselves, one has to consider whether a person with dementia can be allowed their liberty or whether it is necessary to restrict their freedom (e.g. by using a geriatric chair) in order to protect them. The question of risk-taking is often very difficult especially if the person with dementia has family members who have strong opinions about the matter. Some family members might want every possible restrictive measure to be used in order to protect the safety of a person with dementia while others might insist that it is absolutely forbidden in the name of autonomy to use any kind of restraint.

We can thus perceive that there might be a problem of relationality, if family members have views that differ from those of a person with dementia on their right to take risks. As Harding has pointed out, if a person with dementia lives within a relational context where their carers do not allow them to leave home alone for fear of getting lost, then it is hard to consider relationality as beneficial to their autonomy.[63] It is also possible that a principle of protection is more readily selected in care settings if a person with dementia is surrounded by a family with strong views to protect such person. While it is argued that this is for reasons of safety, equally it might undermine the autonomy of a person with dementia and their right to take risks.

In what follows I shall examine the use of restrictive measures by means of two examples: home intervention and the use of a geriatric chair. The forthcoming Finnish Autonomy Act will also have regulations addressing these issues, which can be seen as a good outcome.

A person with dementia living alone and home intervention

The fact is that not all persons with dementia are necessarily in a relationship or have close relations. It has been estimated that some 32,000 people with dementia are living alone in Finland, some of whom are truly lonely with no safety net to protect them.[64] If one assumes that their relations consist of home service, this is not always the case either. Some of them

---

63 Harding, 'Legal Constructions of Dementia', 431. However, if this worry about getting lost is a very realistic scenario, then it could be justified to restrict autonomy in the name of protection and good care. In that case relationality can be seen as beneficial because it protects from harm, regardless of the fact that at the same time it reduces autonomy.
64 Kati Juva et al., 'Pitkäaikaishoitoon joutumisen vaaratekijät ja hyvä ympärivuorokautinen hoito', in *Muistisairaudet*, ed. Timo Erkinjuntti, Juha Rinne and Hilkka Soininen (Helsinki: Duodecim 2010), 514.

refuse to get help for example because of lack of insight or a determination to cope by themselves. The problem occurs when a single-dwelling person with dementia, clearly in need of help, refuses home service or to move to more suitable accommodation.

In such a situation the social and health care professionals are often faced with a dilemma – intervene or respect the right to autonomy. The problem has been that the Finnish legal system has not had clear instructions for this kind of situation. Furthermore, the autonomy of a person with dementia is sometimes respected just because the professionals want to avoid intervening in a difficult situation or refrain from offering services in a situation where the resources are limited. An exaggerated respect for autonomy may however lead to a situation that works against the person's best interests. In some cases it can even amount to neglect or abandonment. As a dementia work professional described the situation (quoted in my previous study):

> The person is heard but mostly so that services are declined if the person is difficult. For example, a person living alone does not want home help so the home help ignores the client citing the right to autonomy. The client is unable to wash, change clothes, prepare meals, clean, administer drugs etc. The client may have inflammations, high/low blood sugar, anaemia, food poisoning, anxieties, worms in the fridge, dirty clothes behind the couch, unpaid bills, conflicts with neighbours -> wanders and falls -> hip fracture -> emergency unit -> hospital ward -> long-term unit. If the basic care had been in order, the client's functional capacity would have allowed many good years at home. Autonomy <-> abandonment?[65]

The Nuffield Council on Bioethics has pointed out that these kinds of problems might occur because the concept of autonomy is often understood in the sense of 'having no interference' and enjoying the 'right to be left alone'. However, in the setting of dementia, this kind of interpretation can be dangerous and quickly degenerates into neglect. Legal norms apparently aimed at promoting autonomy can sometimes affect the relationships between professionals and the patient, leading practitioners to adopt defensive attitudes and limit their services to care.[66] The forthcoming Finnish Autonomy Act would however bring a solution to this problem. It is suggested that it would be possible for social and welfare personnel to enter a person's home to check the occupant's safety if there is reason to believe

---

65 Anna Mäki-Petäjä-Leinonen, *Ajoissa apua avohuollosta – Selvitys yksin asuvan muistisairaan oikeusturvan toteutumisesta* ('Care in the community – getting help in time. An investigation into legal safeguards of persons with dementia who live alone', Helsinki: Muistiliiton julkaisusarja, Raportti 2/2010) 26–7.
66 Nuffield Council on Bioethics, *Dementia: Ethical Issues*, 26.

that their life or health is in serious danger. It would also be possible to transfer such a person from home to a care facility to be checked or cared for, if it is necessary in order to protect their life or health and if they do not understand the consequences of a refusal of treatment. This regulation would spell an essential change in a situation where care personnel have had inadequate legal means at their disposal.

The geriatric chair and its justification

Tying a person in place has been one of the first measures to use technology in dementia care.[67] The use of geriatric chairs is common in care facilities for people with dementia but from time to time there has been doubt whether the use of such chairs can be justified. The following example, which describes this problem, is from a Finnish observation study whose objective was to investigate inappropriate treatment and its context in the care of people with dementia:

> Helmi, an elderly woman living in a nursing home, has been left alone sitting in a geriatric chair. The nursing staff pays no attention to her, which causes the deterioration of her well-being. The primary reason for tying her up is her poor balance.
> 14:22 Helmi sits in geriatric chair, she has been tied to the chair using a simple bow. She sits calmly and eats a bun.
> 15:10 Helmi tries to turn to the window in her chair. She has a napkin on her table. She starts to fold it.
> 16:32 Helmi drops her napkin on the floor.
> 16:35 She shifts position in her chair, with her feet by the side, and tries to push the chair. Tries to pick up the napkin with her feet.
> 17:12–45 Helmi really tries to get out of the chair. Furthermore she wipes the table with her apron.
> 17:48 Helmi continuously tries to get out of the chair.
> 18:10 Helmi has put her apron on her head, puts her fingers to her mouth and calms down.
> 18:48 Helmi sleeps. Nurses come and start to take her to her room saying: Now it's too late to walk her.[68]

Even though restriction of freedom in this case is argued for health reasons, it illustrates how this kind of care is clearly against fundamental rights; it

---

67 Päivi Topo, 'Dementia, teknologia ja etiikka', *Gerontologia* 21:3 (2007), 224.
68 Topo, 'Dementia, teknologia ja etiikka', 224. About this observation study see also Saila Sormunen *et al.*, 'Inappropriate Treatment of People with Dementia in Residential and Day Care', *Aging & Mental Health* 11:3 (2007), 246–55.

violates personal liberty and physical integrity. It is also a sad example of dementia care, where the quality of care fails to meet good standards. No one should be left alone, sitting for hours in a geriatric chair. However, it seems that in some care units this is an everyday routine, the reason being limited resources, care culture and attitudes.[69] It should also be borne in mind that eventually the excessive use of restrictive measures can be a matter of abuse or negligence.

The forthcoming Autonomy Act after all strives to solve this problem. Within the Act it would be forbidden to leave a person in a geriatric chair. According to the proposal, care personnel could make a decision to restrict clients/patients' freedom to move from a bed or a chair by using restrictive measures when they are resting or eating. The explanatory part of the proposal states that this regulation would not allow the incompetent elderly patient to be left unattended, a patient who wishes to walk about freely, in a geriatric chair in a way that they cannot leave the chair by themselves. This is not a situation where using restrictive measures is necessary to enable a person to rest or eat.[70]

Conclusions

In this chapter I have scrutinised the autonomy of a person with dementia according to three levels of capacity: a person with dementia makes a decision with full capacity; a person with dementia with borderline capacity makes a decision with support or takes part in a decision-making process; and finally, the decisions of a person with incapacity are being made by either respecting a person's prior instructions or by a substituted decision-maker ideally guided by appreciation of the person's values and life history.

In certain of these levels of capacity, a relational approach of autonomy can play an essential role. Some others, however, are better suited to the traditional approach. I have therefore argued that both the individual and the relational approach of autonomy can be seen as important when promoting the autonomy of a person with dementia. They should not be seen as in conflict but rather be combined in order to enhance respect for the autonomy of a person with dementia.

I have also considered the forthcoming Finnish Autonomy Act and addressed how the legislation has adopted the principles of person-centred care in order to support the autonomy of a patient/client with incapacity.

---

69 Sabine Goethals, Bernadette Dierckx de Casterlé and Chris Gastmans, 'Nurses' Decision-making in Cases of Physical Restraint: A Synthesis of Qualitative Evidence', *Journal of Advanced Nursing* 68:6 (2012), 1206–7. See also Hoppania, *Care as a Site of a Political Struggle*, 92–3.
70 Sosiaali- ja terveysministeriön raportteja ja muistioita 2014:14, *Sosiaali- ja terveydenhuollon asiakkaan itsemääräämisoikeus* ('Self-determination of social and health care patients'), 141.

I have however expressed some concerns about legislation which relies so heavily on changing attitudes and care cultures. The main focus of the forthcoming legislation however is to prescribe for the use of restrictive measures for a patient/client with incapacity. Even though there have been some concerns about this kind of regulatory framework, I have in this chapter focused on two welcome outcomes: home intervention and prohibition to leave a patient/client in a geriatric chair.

Bibliography

Alzheimer Cooperative Valuation in Europe (Alcove). *The European Joint Action on Dementia – Synthesis Report 2013*.
Alzheimer's Disease International and World Health Organization. *Dementia. A Public Health Priority*. United Kingdom: World Health Organization, 2012.
Alzheimer Europe. *Dementia in Europe Yearbook 2010 with a focus on legal capacity and proxy decision making in dementia*. Luxembourg: Alzheimer Europe, 2010.
Alzheimer Europe. *Dementia in Europe. Yearbook 2011 with a focus on restrictions of freedom*. Luxembourg: Alzheimer Europe, 2011.
Alzheimer Europe. *The Ethical Issues Linked to Restrictions of Freedom of People with Dementia*. Luxembourg: Alzheimer Europe, 2012.
Alzheimer Society of Finland. 'Advance Directive'. Last modified 17 December, 2015. Available at www.muistiliitto.fi/files/3613/7604/6221/advance_directive_2013.pdf (accessed 15 April 2016).
American Psychiatric Association. *Diagnostic and Statistical Manual of Mental Disorders*. 4th Edition, Text Revision, dsm-iv-tr, 2000.
British Medical Association and the Law Society. *Assessment of Mental Capacity: Guidance for Doctors and Lawyers*. London: BMJ Books, British Medical Association, 2004.
de Boer, Marike. *Advance Directives in Dementia Care. Perspectives of People with Alzheimer's Disease, Elderly Care Physicians and Relatives*. Vrije Universiteit: Academic dissertation, 2011.
Dresser, Rebecca. 'Life, Death, and Incompetent Patients: Conceptual Infirmities and Hidden Values in the Law,' *Arizona Law Review* 28:3 (1986), 373–405.
Dworkin, Ronald. *Life's Dominion: An Argument about Abortion and Euthanasia*. London: HarperCollins, 1993.
Elwyn, Glyn, Dominick Frosch, Richard Thomson, Natalie Joseph-Williams, Amy Lloyd, Paul Kinnersley, Emma Cording, Dave Tomson, Carole Dodd, Stephen Rollnick, Adrian Edwards and Michael Barry. 'Shared Decision Making: A Model for Clinical Practice,' *Journal of General Internal Medicine* 27:10 (2012), 1361–7.
Feder Kittay, Eva and Ellen K. Feder. 'Introduction'. In *The Subject of Care: Feminist Perspectives on Dependency*, edited by Eva Feder Kittay and Ellen K. Feder, 1–13. Lanham: Rowan & Littlefield, 2002.
Gastmans, Chris and Koen Milisen. 'Use of Physical Restraint in Nursing Homes: Clinical-ethical Considerations,' *Journal of Medical Ethics* 32:3 (2006), 148–52.
Goethals, Sabine, Bernadette Dierckx de Casterlé and Chris Gastmans. 'Nurses' Decision-making in Cases of Physical Restraint: A Synthesis of Qualitative Evidence,' *Journal of Advanced Nursing* 68:6 (2012), 1198–209.

Goffin, Tom. 'Advance Directives as an Instrument in an Ageing Europe,' *European Journal of Health Law* 19:2 (2012), 121–40.

Harding, Rosie. 'Legal Constructions of Dementia: Discourses of Autonomy at the Margins of Capacity,' *Journal of Social Welfare & Family Law* 34:4 (2012), 425–42.

Harding, Rosie. 'Dementia and Carers: Relationality and Informal Carers' Experiences'. In *The Law and Ethics of Dementia*, edited by Charles Foster, Jonathan Herring and Israel Doron, 379–91. Oxford and Portland: Hart Publishing, 2014.

Harrison Dening, Karen, Louise Jones and Elizabeth L. Sampson. 'Advance Care Planning for People with Dementia: A Review,' *International Psychogeriatrics* 23:10 (2011), 1535–51.

Herring, Jonathan. 'Losing it? Losing what? The Law and Dementia,' *Child and Family Law Quarterly* 21:1 (2009), 3–29.

Herring, Jonathan. *Caring and the Law*. Oxford and Portland: Hart Publishing, 2013.

Hope, Tony and John McMillan. 'The Art of Medicine – Advance Decisions, Chronic Mental Illness, and Everyday Care,' *The Lancet* 377 (2011), 2076–7.

Hoppania, Hanna-Kaisa. *Care as a Site of a Political Struggle*. University of Helsinki: Academic dissertation, 2015. Available at https://helda.helsinki.fi/handle/10138/157561 (accessed 15 April 2016).

Jaworska, Agnieszka. 'Respecting the Margins of Agency: Alzheimer's Patients and the Capacity to Value,' *Philosophy and Public Affairs* 28:2 (1998), 105–38.

Juva, Kati, Päivi Voutilainen, Tiina Huusko and Ulla Eloniemi-Sulkava. 'Pitkäaikaishoitoon joutumisen vaaratekijät ja hyvä ympärivuorokautinen hoito'. In *Muistisairaudet*, edited by Timo Erkinjuntti, Juha Rinne and Hilkka Soininen, 514–28. Helsinki: Duodecim 2010.

King, Lesley and Hugh Series. 'Assessing Capacity'. In *The Law and Ethics of Dementia*, edited by Charles Foster, Jonathan Herring and Israel Doron, 283–300. Oxford and Portland: Hart Publishing, 2014.

Kohn, Nina A. and Edward D. Spurgeon. 'Elder Law Teaching and Scholarship: An Empirical Analysis of an Evolving Field,' *Journal of Legal Education* 59:3 (2010), 414–31.

Kontio, Raija, Maritta Välimäki, Hanna Putkonen, Lauri Kuosmanen, Anne Scott and Grigori Joffe. 'Patient Restrictions: Are there Ethical Alternatives to Seclusion and Restraint?' *Nursing Ethics* 17:1 (2010), 65–76.

McGee, Andrew. 'Best Interest Determinations and Substituted Judgement: Personhood and Precedent Autonomy'. In *The Law and Ethics of Dementia*, edited by Charles Foster, Jonathan Herring and Israel Doron, 135–47. Oxford and Portland: Hart Publishing, 2014.

Mäki-Petäjä-Leinonen, Anna. 'Legal Status of a Person with Dementia, English summary'. In *Dementoituvan henkilön oikeudellinen asema* ('The Legal Status of a Person with Dementia'). Helsinki: Suomalainen lakimiesyhdistys, Academic dissertation, 2003.

Mäki-Petäjä-Leinonen, Anna. *Ajoissa apua avohuollosta – Selvitys yksin asuvan muistisairaan oikeusturvan toteutumisesta* ('Care in the community – getting help in time. An investigation into legal safeguards of persons with dementia who live alone'). Helsinki: Muistiliiton julkaisusarja, Raportti 2/2010.

Mäki-Petäjä-Leinonen, Anna and Kati Juva. 'Of Sound Mind? Dementia and Aspects of Assessing Legal Capacity,' *European Journal of Health Law* 22:1 (2015), 13–37.

Mol, Annemarie. *The Logic of Care: Health and the Problem of Patient Choice*. London: Routledge, 2008.

Nedelsky, Jennifer. 'Reconceiving Autonomy: Sources, Thoughts, Possibilities', *Yale Journal of Law & Feminism* 1:1 (1989), 7–36.
Nuffield Council on Bioethics. *Dementia: Ethical Issues*. London: Cambridge Publishers, 2009.
Pajulammi, Henna. 'Summary'. In *Lapsi, oikeus ja osallisuus* ('Children, Rights and Participation') Helsinki: Talentum, Academic dissertation, 2014.
Raz, Joseph. *The Morality of Freedom*. Oxford: Clarendon Press, 1986.
Sherwin, Susan and Meghan Winsby. 'A Relational Perspective on Autonomy for Older Adults Residing in Nursing Homes'. *Health Expectations* 14:2 (2011), 182–90.
Siltala, Raimo. *Law, Truth, and Reason: A Treatise on Legal Argumentation*. Dordrecht, Heidelberg, London, New York: Springer Publishing, 2011.
Sinoff, Gary and Natalia Blaja-Lisnic. 'Advance Decisions and Proxy Decision-Making in the Elderly: A Medical Perspective'. In *The Law and Ethics of Dementia*, edited by Charles Foster, Jonathan Herring and Israel Doron, 97–103. Oxford and Portland: Hart Publishing, 2014.
Slettebø Åshild and Eli Haugen Bunch. 'Solving Ethically Difficult Care Situations in Nursing Homes', *Nursing Ethics* 11:6 (2004), 543–52.
Sormunen, Saila, Päivi Topo, Ulla Eloniemi-Sulkava, Outi Räikkönen and Anneli Sarvimäki. 'Inappropriate Treatment of People with Dementia in Residential and Day Care,' *Aging & Mental Health* 11:3 (2007), 246–55.
Sosiaali- ja terveysministeriön raportteja ja muistioita 2014:14. *Sosiaali- ja terveydenhuollon asiakkaan itsemääräämisoikeus. Työryhmän loppuraportti* (Ministry of Social Affairs and Health. 'The right of self-determination of patients in social and healthcare') Helsinki: Sosiaali- ja terveysministeriö, 2014.
Svensson, Kerstin. 'Caring Power – Coercion as Care,' *Critical Practice Studies*, 4:2 (2002), 71–8.
Topo, Päivi. 'Dementia, teknologia ja etiikka,' *Gerontologia* 21:3 (2007), 221–20.
UN, OHCHR and IPU. *From Exclusion to Equality – Realizing the rights of persons with disabilities. Handbook for Parliamentarians on the Convention on the Rights of Persons with Disabilities*. Geneva: United Nations, 2007.
van Drenth, Annemieke and Francisca de Haan. *The Rise of Caring Power. Elizabeth Fry and Josephine Butler in Britain and the Netherlands*. Amsterdam: Amsterdam University Press, 1999.

Chapter 9

What to do with the other in human rights law? Ethics of alterity versus ethics of care

Dorota Gozdecka and Sanna Koulu

Introduction

Traditionally, law is well suited for resolving certain kinds of conflicts: for instance, conflicts between the parties to a market transaction or criminal acts where the perpetrator and victim do not know each other. What these conflicts have in common is their reasonably clear-cut nature. It is often clear who is at fault, and only in special cases will the personal traits or circumstances of the parties be taken into account. It is considered both legally correct and ethically reasonable that the party at fault will be liable to pay compensation for breach of contract or that the person intentionally committing a crime will be held responsible.

However, the role of ethics in human rights law is more nuanced, especially in the area of care where interpersonal and ethical issues are less clear-cut. Law in general and human rights law in particular often have a hard time dealing with thorny issues between persons in close relationships with each other, matters involving persons considered to be unfit to be parents, issues of conception or adoption. Part of the difficulty in these situations stems from, on the one hand, the role of ethics in human rights law and, on the other hand, the subject to whom ethical duties are owed.

Law has frequently been criticised for its one-dimensional, too-abstract rules and its inability to consider nuances of interpersonal relations.[1] Human rights law is not immune and suffers from many symptoms of the same legal illness. In this chapter we hope to illustrate how the poverty of legal ethics in human rights law dealing with relationships of care can be relieved. Mindful that human rights are only a partial answer, we acknowledge that their universality and their focus on the equality of right-holders

---

1 Drucilla Cornell, 'Post-structuralism, the Ethical Relation, and the Law,' *Cardozo L. Rev.* 9 (1987), 1587; Desmond Manderson, *Proximity, Levinas, and the Soul of Law.* (Montreal, London: McGill-Queen's University Press, 2006); Costas Douzinas and Ronnie Warrington. '"A Well-founded Fear of Justice": Law and Ethics in Postmodernity,' *Law and Critique* 2.2 (1991), 115.

typically reproduce the problems of accounting for the other. In other words the jurisprudence of human rights has its own difficulties in perceiving the duties towards the subject of rights and in particular the subject who is 'relational' instead of an island of their own. While this difficulty appears daunting, we believe inroads can be made via an examination of ethics in law. We focus primarily on the role ethics fulfils for recognition of particular types of subjects, namely those in relationships of care.

We begin by briefly examining the necessity of ethics in law before moving on to look at the role of ethics in human rights law, and at two alternative accounts of legal ethics that have been offered to relieve the poverty of ethical response of law in the realm of rights. We distinguish two concurring accounts of ethics that can be used when approaching rights in relationships of care and duty: first the *ethics of alterity* in the vein of Emmanuel Levinas, and second *ethics of care* as originally defined by Carol Gilligan. While much has been written on both accounts of ethics and their potential conflict, in this chapter we wish to continue the discussion on the differences between them.[2] We argue that there is a crucial difference in how these two accounts see the subject of ethical response of law, and that their juxtaposition is fruitful for a legal response of human rights law. In the next to last section we flesh out these ideas in the context of the case law from the European Court of Human Rights. In this section we have chosen to focus on three cases dealing in particular with relationships of care and duty. We conclude with a brief discussion on the usefulness of these ethical accounts for legal reasoning in the area of rights, and assert that they play a symbiotic role that can help in recognising different types of the Other in legal contexts.

Ethics in law and their relevance for human rights

The distinction between law and ethics is as old as the interplay between the two. Beginning with Aristotle's *Ethics*, justice and ethics appear to be closely interlinked. In Miller's words, for Aristotle:

> [u]niversal justice and ethical virtue are the same state, but they differ in being or essence, in that justice has the qualification, in relation to another. A person may exercise ethical virtue in his personal affairs but be unable to do so towards others. The worst person acts wickedly towards both himself and others, whereas the best person acts virtuously not only towards himself but also towards others.[3]

---

2 E.g. Seyla Benhabib, 'The Generalized and the Concrete Other: The Kohlberg-Gilligan Controversy and Feminist Theory,' *Praxis international* 4 (1985), 402; Annette C. Baier, 'What do women want in a moral theory?,' *Nous* (1985): 53; Annette C. Baier, 'Trust and Antitrust,' *Ethics* 96 (1986), 231.
3 Fred Dycus Miller, *Nature, Justice, and Rights in Aristotle's Politics* (Oxford: OUP, 1995), 69.

For Aristotle, in other words, to act justly was also to act ethically. But the perception of justice as an ethical affair was fundamentally shaken by the separation of law and morality brought about by relinquishing natural law.[4] With the separation of the two came the necessity of answering whether law can constitute ethics or whether it can contain ethics within itself. The much-discussed estrangement of law and ethics gave rise to the fundamental question of what *sort* of ethics law ought to have or not have. Relying on Kantian notions of ethics, the perception of ethical duties became affixed on a precarious rift between legal duties and ethical duties.[5] Typical accounts of legal ethics (further: ethics of justice) that relied on Kantian rift focused on generalised notions of the other.

Contesting the accounts of ethics builds on the Kantian distinctions as insufficient critical accounts of justice have examined not only whether law as such is an ethical affair but also whether human rights in particular ought to be based on ethical approaches.[6] In compelling subjects to fulfil legal duties law may generate unethical outcomes and the pursuit of justice may in fact become injustice. The classic example of Antigone's ethical dilemma and its utilisation for legal philosophical considerations[7] focuses on the question 'what if law sanctions unethical conduct and results in injustice'? It is unsurprising that positivised human rights law has been at risk of generating analogous injustices. The primary focus of rights on safeguarding individual interests, and on preventing other persons from trespassing upon them, may contribute to an ever on-going expansion of individual interests and thus perpetuate existing injustices under the banner of human rights law. When this happens, human rights law just like any other area of law might strengthen the position of already privileged subjects against marginalised ones.[8]

Therefore if we want to take human rights seriously, we need to look into the ethics involved and also acknowledge that more than one understanding of legal ethics exists.[9] The task of integrating ethical concerns in

---

4 Beginning from Kant many legal thinkers have touched upon the issue. In the 20th century H.L.A. Hart famously proposed a minimum content for law: a base set of norms that law was a priori expected to have (H.L.A. Hart, *The Concept of Law* (Oxford: OUP, 1994), 193 –). These theories remain somewhat uneasy about the connections between law and ethics.
5 Benhabib, 'The Generalized and the Concrete Other'.
6 Costas Douzinas, *The End of Human Rights* (Oxford and Portland: Hart Publishing, 2000); William Paul Simmons, *Human Rights and the Marginalised Other* (Cambridge: Cambridge University Press, 2014); Emmanuel Levinas, 'The Rights of Man and the Rights of the Other', in Emmanuel Levinas, *Outside the Subject* (London: Continuum, 2008), 91–8.
7 Ari Hirvonen, *Oikeuden käynti: Antigonen laki ja oikea oikeus.* (Helsinki: Loki-kirjat, 2000); Julen Etxabe, *The Experience of Tragic Judgment* (New York: Routledge, 2013).
8 E.g. Levinas, 'The Rights of Man and the Rights of the Other,' 95.
9 E.g. Benhabib, 'The Generalized and the Concrete Other', Joy Kroeger-Mappes, 'The Ethic of Care vis-à-vis the Ethic of Rights: A Problem for Contemporary Moral Theory,' *Hypatia* 9:3 (1994): 108.

law, including human rights law, is daunting and frequently calls law to do the impossible.[10] A fundamental difficulty in bridging the divide between legal rules and ethics lies in identifying, recognising and responding to the voice of the other[11] or in other words, asking to whom the relevant duty is owned. And it is already here that at least two alternative accounts to the traditionally understood ethics of justice appear – namely the ethics of alterity and the ethics of care.[12] These accounts of ethics are related when it comes to challenging the abstract nature of legal rules and distinguishing *the particular* from *the universal*, but differ when it comes to defining who the other is and to understanding how and in what circumstances law should respond to otherness. As Seyla Benhabib reminds us, challenging the traditional ethics of justice, law continues to rely on a universalistic presumption of an autonomous rational self and is reluctant to recognise the uniqueness of the position of a concrete other instead of generalised other.[13] By the generalised other Benhabib understands the conception of each individual as a moral and rational person endowed with equal moral rights. In contrast the concrete other is a unique individual with a certain life history, disposition, endowment, needs and limitations.[14] Crucially, Benhabib proposes that law can indeed be capable of responding to the standpoint of concrete otherness.[15] But in its response to concrete otherness and its history, dispositions, and needs, human rights law – just like other legal efforts – risks excluding rather than including otherness.[16] The generalised other is rarely a person endowed with her own particularities but a sum total of all that remains outside the boundary of oneself.[17] To prevent law, in particular human rights law, from generalising the other both the ethics of alterity and the ethics of care have attempted to resolve

---

10 Costas Douzinas, 'Human Rights and Postmodern Utopia,' *Law and Critique* 11.2 (2000): 219.
11 Simmons, *Human Rights Law and the Marginalized Other*, 160.
12 The concept of ethics of care was originally coined by Carol Gilligan in her influential study *In a Different Voice. Psychological Theory and Women's Development* (Cambridge, MA: Harvard University Press, 1982).
13 Seyla Benhabib, *Situating the Self: Gender, Community, and Postmodernism in Contemporary Ethics* (Cambridge: Polity Press, 1994).
14 Seyla Benhabib, 'In Defense of Universalism. Yet Again! A Response to Critics of Situating the Self,' *New German Critique* (1994): 173, at 179.
15 Ibid.
16 *Derrida* describes the ontological trap of defining the Other in the following way: 'Man calls himself man only by drawing limits excluding his other from the play of supplementarity: the purity of nature, of animality, primitivism, childhood, madness, divinity. The approach to these limits is at once feared as a threat of death, and desired as access to a life without differance. The history of man calling himself man is the articulation of all these limits among themselves', Jacques Derrida, *Of Grammatology* (Baltimore: JHU Press, 1998), 244.
17 It is in fact the Other's existence that allows the Self to find its own limitations, Cornell, 'Post-structuralism,' 1618.

the relationship between the universal and the particular, albeit in a different manner.

Our first port of call consists of focusing on *the ethics of alterity*, an account of ethical thinking based especially on the work of Emmanuel Levinas. Here, three issues will be addressed: first, why human rights are a site for ethical thinking, second, how human rights can respond to the other's concerns, and third, who the proposed other is.

Facing the stranger – to whom do the rights owe the ethical response?

While many deconstructive readings are driven by the desire to be faithful to otherness,[18] understanding the reason for the ethical response and the responsibility to otherness differs. Classical conceptualisations of rights as tools for protecting individual interests[19] remain viable with or without the presence of the other. If we understand the nature of rights as protected interests, the mere presence of the other does not prevent the rights from developing into tools used in a battle of interests. In the conflict of interests, the rights of the other then become subordinated to the interests of those subjects that are closer to the universal rather than the particular. As a result the interests of the other are marginalised.[20] In such an account, even if otherness is recognised as existing, it remains without an adequate ethical response.

To prevent such a conflict of interests human rights have been reconceptualised as an ethical venture based on the notion of responsibility.[21] Beginning from Levinas, thinkers following in his footsteps have attempted to rebuild the ethical potential of rights as an essentially ethical concept based on the ideas of responsibility and answerability.[22] In these accounts the idea of rights is built on the Levinasian understanding of *answerability* for the rights of the other. Standing face to face with the other, the self and its ego dissolve in the act of responsibility for the other, whose face stands in front of the self as the barrier that cannot be penetrated but at the same time as an ultimate symbol of ethical duty.[23] Rooted in responsibility, rights cease to be seen as mere interests and privileges but as ethical tools of answerability. Levinas asserts that rights ought to be seen not as a privilege but as

---

18 Simon Critchley, *The Ethics of Deconstruction: Derrida and Levinas* (Edinburgh: Edinburgh University Press, 2014), 251, Cornell, 'Post-structuralism,' 1613.
19 E.g. Joseph Raz, *The Morality of Freedom* (Oxford: OUP, 1986).
20 Levinas, 'The Rights of Man and the Rights of the Other,' 96.
21 Levinas, 'The Rights of Man and the Rights of the Other'; Douzinas, *The End of Human Rights*; Simmons, *Human Rights Law and the Marginalized Other*.
22 Levinas, 'The Rights of Man and the Rights of the Other,' 96.
23 Ibid. 98.

a 'duty to the other for which I am answerable'.[24] The Self thus becomes not merely an entity accumulating rights for personal gains, but instead an entity responsible and answerable for the rights as ethical duties. Such a formulation attempts to avoid the ontological trap by replacing the questions 'Who am I? What are my interests against my other?' with the question 'What am I answerable for?' While standing face to face with the other the self dissolves in the act of inexhaustible responsibility.[25]

Levinasian ethics of alterity have been criticised for their ethical and purely philosophical focus, however, and Levinasian theory has been accused of lacking the potential for effective translation of answerability into the realm of the legal and the political.[26] Can ethical philosophy provide the answer to the question of how to reconcile the claims of all the others?[27] If we want to translate this mode of thinking to the domain of rights, the ontological focus on the self and the other must go beyond mere abstract challenges to the philosophical premises of modernity.[28] In other words, the other of the ethics of alterity continues to be highly abstract and risks replicating the problems of the generalised and universalistic conceptions of the other. Here it is worth noting that the other of Levinas is not directly comparable to the famous conception of the generalised other coined by Seyla Benhabib in her 'The Generalized and the Concrete Other: The Kohlberg-Gilligan Controversy and Feminist Theory'.[29] Levinas like Benhabib theorised his accounts of the other in contrast to Kantian-based notions of the self and the other as rational, fully autonomous beings. Despite this focus Levinas' construction of the other may be unable to stimulate the shift of focus from the abstract to the concrete because of the fact that Levinasian responsibilities arise in the mysterious presence of the third person, which triggers the ethical response and as such remains hard to concretise.[30] And

---

24 Ibid. 98.
25 Emmanuel Levinas. *Totality and Infinity* (Pittsburgh, PA: Duquesne University Press, 1969), 245.
26 Alain Badiou, *Ethics: An Essay on the Understanding of Evil* (London, New York: Verso, 2001); Simmons, *Human Rights Law and the Marginalized Other*, 90.
27 Nick Smith, 'Questions for a Reluctant Jurisprudence of Alterity,' in *Essays on Levinas and Law: A Mosaic*, ed. Desmond Manderson (Basingstoke: Palgrave Macmillan, 2009), 68–71.
28 Ibid. 71.
29 Benhabib, 'The Generalized and the Concrete Other'. Benhabib's concept of the generalised other refers to universalistic models valorising the standpoint of the 'generalized other' at the expense of that of the 'concrete other' and the specific histories, identities and life experiences of diversely situated participants. When compared with Levinasian thought, this distinction would mirror the barrier between the self and the other that Levinas considers. Benhabib's 'generalised other' is not identical but similar to Levinasian self and 'concrete other' resembles 'the other' of Levinasian theory.
30 Levinas, *Totality and Infinity*, 212.

that very concretisation is required for the contextualisation of rights in the light of concrete difference:

> The standpoint of concrete other, [...], requires us to view each other and every rational being as an individual with a concrete history, identity and affective-emotional constitution. In assuming this standpoint, we abstract from what constitutes our commonality and focus on individuality. We seek to comprehend the needs of the other, his or her motivations, what she searches for and what s/he desires. [...] Our differences in this case complement rather than exclude one another.[31]

It is without doubt though that Levinasian ethics of alterity have helped to imagine human rights as an ethical project capable of including the voice of the marginalised. While without such a voice 'the other cannot interrogate the original violence of the system's institutions';[32] the conceptions of alterity must embrace the concrete voice of the concrete other in concrete circumstances.

In order to embrace a variety of subjects, including those that may not be independent of others to the same extent as law likes to imagine, a further-reaching account of ethics has been coined by the theorists on the *ethics of care*. While answerability is always asymmetrical, the full dimension of this asymmetry is revealed when we realise that some subjects are even closer to the self than we initially imagined.

Family relations, human rights and the ethics of care – when the other is close to the self

While we might conceive of a diversity of responsibilities owed to different others, in *ethics of care* the special focus is given to intimate or caring relations.[33] The encounter of the ethics of justice, ethics of alterity and the ethics of care has generated multiple approaches in the attempt to shift the focus from the general concerns of otherness to specific concerns of concrete others: i.e. persons to whom we owe responsibilities by virtue of our specific relationships with them. While the ethics of alterity may be able to address the poverty of legal ethics on the universal level, they still run the

---

31 Benhabib, *Situating the Self*, 159.
32 Simmons, *Human Rights Law and the Marginalized Other*, 124.
33 As *Virginia Held* notes, 'Some theorists do not like the term "care" to designate this approach to moral issues and have tried substituting "the ethic of love," or "relational ethics," but the discourse keeps returning to "care" [...]' Virginia Held, *The Ethics of Care. Personal, Political and Global* (Oxford: OUP, 2006), 9.

risk of erasing specificities of the responsibility we owe to concrete others in caring relationships.[34]

This insufficiency is particularly clear when we realise that care has turned out to be a remarkably hard concept to pin down especially in legal research.[35] Care might involve providing food, clothing, or a home, or it might mean taking care of a small baby's needs. It often involves power,[36] even if not in as straightforward a form as we might think. Care is usually not a question of one-sided, altruistic giving or providing for someone, but instead it implies participation in a mutually rewarding, affectionate or caring relationship.

Such a reciprocity of affection is often assumed to exist in family relationships, but its implications for law remain vague. The quality of affection in relationships has become a crucial question. However, it is not so clear what role affection or care should have for the legal regulation of intimate or family relationships. If the foundation of the family is in the affectionate, pure relationships between its members, should law give weight to the *quality* of the caring in the relationships?[37] Feminist jurisprudence especially has examined the tension between the independence required of the legal subject, and the networks of interdependency we all live in.[38]

This tension might be expressed as the dichotomy between an ethics of justice and an ethics of care. The distinction was originally coined in 1982 by *Carol Gilligan*, who sought to discover a particularly feminine way of

---

34 For a thorough reimagining of the role of relationships in general, see Jennifer Nedelsky, *Law's Relations. A Relational Theory of Self, Autonomy and Law* (Oxford: Oxford University Press, 2011), though Nedelsky notes several points of divergence in her work and some of the discussion on ethics of care (e.g. pp. 87–9).
35 For some of the extensive discussion on care, see e.g. Martha A. Fineman, *The Autonomy Myth. A Theory of Dependency* (New York: The New Press, 2005) and Joan Tronto, *Moral Boundaries. A Political Argument for an Ethic of Care* (New York: Routledge, 1993).
36 As Eekelaar has noted succinctly, 'to exercise care is also to exercise power'. John Eekelaar, *Family Law and Personal Life* (Oxford: Oxford University Press, 2006), 178–9. For more in-depth discussion, see e.g. Tronto, *Moral Boundaries*, 122–4.
37 It is worth noting that while this question intrudes into the realm of morality and privacy in relationships, it is structurally rather different from the earlier inspection of parties' conduct. For example, before the no-fault divorce was adopted in Finland in 1987, a spouse guilty of an extra-marital affair stood liable to lose any right to the other's assets and could be obligated to pay compensation to the innocent spouse. While these provisions were firmly linked to moral issues, they were only concerned with the parties' behaviour and conduct, not their private thoughts or feelings.
38 See for instance Nedelsky, *Law's Relations*, 27–30, where the author emphasises that dependence and interdependence are not just episodic – as legal structures might suggest – but 'a constant part of the human condition'.

understanding and resolving ethical issues.[39] Since then, the idea of ethics of care has been developed by e.g. *Virginia Held*, who notes that 'the central focus of the ethics of care is on the compelling moral salience of attending to and meeting the needs of the particular others for whom we take responsibility'.[40]

Not all have been supportive of this distinction and the discussion on ethics of justice and ethics of care became subject to heated controversy between Carol Gilligan and Lawrence Kohlberg.[41] This still-unresolved controversy attracted our particular attention when framed as the question of rights. *Joy Kroeger-Mappes*[42] has noted that Gilligan's distinction between ethic of rights and ethic of care relies on the hierarchy of rights and the conception of individuals as opponents in the contest of rights – a vision that, as explained above, we too find too simplistic and ill-suited. To relieve the tension of this distinction, Annette C. Baier[43] has suggested that ethics of rights can be bridged with the concept of 'trust' and that ethic of care can transform the ethic of rights. Kroeger-Mappes, on the other hand, insists that the two are a part of one system rather than two.[44]

In this ongoing effort of relieving the generalisations of traditional ethics of justice we believe that both ethics of care and ethics of alterity can be used as a symbiotic counterbalancing tool. Caring relationships are often considered to form the basis for responsibilities that are more deeply felt and more personal than those we have with regard to the generic other. The precise basis of such responsibilities is less clear, however. Traditionally they might be held to derive from commitments made in some sort of ceremony, where the person's vow e.g. 'to have and to hold from this day forward, for better or for worse, for richer, for poorer, in sickness and in health'. Similarly it is thought natural that parents have responsibilities towards their children, as choosing to procreate does involve an important

---

39 Carol Gilligan, *In a Different Voice. Psychological Theory and Women's Development* (Cambridge, MA: Harvard University Press, 1982).
40 Held, *The Ethics of Care*, 9–10. It may be argued that ethics of care is not a comprehensive moral account; as Seyla Benhabib notes, 'the recognition of the dignity and worthiness of the generalized other is a *necessary*, albeit not *sufficient*, condition to define the moral standpoint in modern societies. In this sense, the concrete other is a critical concept that designates the *ideological* limits of universalistic discourse.' (Benhabib, 'The Generalized and the Concrete Other,' 415–16).
41 Benhabib, 'The Generalized and the Concrete Other,' 402–24.
42 Kroeger-Mappes, 'The Ethic of Care vis-à-vis the Ethic of Rights,' 108–131.
43 Baier, 'What do Women Want in a Moral Theory?,' 53–63; Baier, 'Trust and Antitrust', 231–60.
44 Kroeger-Mappes, 'The Ethic of Care vis-à-vis the Ethic of Rights,' 108.

commitment.[45] These kinds of voluntarily adopted commitments are well suited to our understandings of what is right and just. Thus they can be addressed at least somewhat satisfactorily within the limits of the ethics of justice.[46]

The questions, however, become more complicated with regard to relationships that do not follow typical patterns. For example, do any kind of rights and responsibilities of care endure in neglectful or abusive relationships?[47] It is here that the ethics of alterity can supplement the uncertainties of ethics of care. Do different duties of responsibility apply to non-traditional families, like those conceived with the help of contemporary biotechnology or those formed by same-sex partners? While ethics of alterity help us to approach atypical relationships, ethics of care offer a potential way forward in recognising the nuances and complexity of responsibilities in such caring relationships.

A symbiosis of the ethics of alterity and the ethics of care – a difference that makes a difference?

As accounts of ethics, the ethics of alterity and ethics of care are in many ways similar. They attempt to challenge the universalising ethics of justice perpetuating the divide between the universal and the concrete. In both accounts, the responsibility at hand springs specifically from the relationship between self and the other, and the concept of answerability is characterised as inexhaustible. However, there is a fundamental difference in how the two accounts conceive of otherness. The ethics of care is not contented with just the recognition of otherness; instead it demands a recognition of the other as someone who is very particular to self. Even when rights are based on responsibility for alterity, in ethics of alterity the relationship is transcendental and conceived on a very abstract level, while in ethics of care it turns out to be not only very particular, but closely related to the self. We would argue that while the ethics of alterity have proven fruitful in considering law's response to otherness and breaking down the universalism of

---

45 See David Archard, *Children: Rights and Childhood* (New York: Routledge, 2004), 139, where the writer discusses this commitment in the context of the right to bear children.
46 See e.g. Julie A. White and Joan C. Tronto, 'Political Practices of Care: Needs and Rights'. *Ratio Juris* 17:4 (2004), 425. More concrete examples can be found e.g. in research in family law: Carol Smart and Bren Neale's research on the ways people weigh issues of child custody and care revealed interesting differences between mothers and fathers and showed potential scope for discussing family matters from the viewpoint of ethics of justice (*Family Fragments?* (Cambridge: Polity Press, 1999). Ethics of justice might also be valuable in recognising and valuing domestic contributions.
47 Abusive or neglectful relationships may pose quite complicated personal and ethical dilemmas. For some of the discussion, see Nedelsky, *Law's Relations*, 32 and 473–4, and Tronto, *Moral Boundaries*, 142–5.

law, caring relationships and specific others in those relationships require an even deeper-going ethical account that can reach beyond abstract understandings of otherness.[48]

Together ethics of alterity and ethics of care allow for the recognition of specific family situations that are not easily covered by the universal notions of a 'typical' or 'traditional' family. These notions risk being used in a universalising manner as our conceptions of responsibility are often linked to our generalised conceptions of families and normality. It may be easier for law to recognise the ethical duties and responsibilities that spring from traditionally structured relations. We might treat families and relationships that fit our conceptions of normality as more real and more valid, in that we also acknowledge the responsibilities as more real in some way.[49] Meanwhile ethics of alterity allows human rights law to face this 'other' of family law – it becomes useful in approaching the relationships that do not fit the universalistic conceptions of 'the family'. When this otherness is recognised ethics of care can shine more light on the nature of concrete responsibilities and vulnerabilities that arise within all families.

In the following section, we look into the case law of the European Court of Human Rights in order to trace out how this difference between the two accounts might be visible in practice. We have chosen three cases that illustrate first, what happens when neither account of ethics is taken into account when intimate relationships are at stake, second, how in particular situations ethics of alterity can be employed to protect relationships of care, and third, how ethics of care step in when ethics of alterity prove unable to address specificity of care.

Intersections: families, ethics of alterity and ethics of care in the European Court of Human Rights

Up to this point our analysis has reflected on a range of theoretical issues related to the place of ethics in law and to the kinds of ethics that might be pertinent. Yet, the theoretical focus of the philosophy of alterity becomes truly illuminated when considered through the prism of legal practice. Agreeing with Manderson[50] we see the space of uncertainty in legal practice as a site for the working of ethics in practice, especially in relation to sensitive family matters and the caring responsibilities within it. Jurisprudence

---

48 Joan C. Tronto also notes, intriguingly, that otherness may in fact arise out of a failure to recognise care (Tronto, *Moral Boundaries*, 123), and points out that care is often marginalised and trivialised. While this discussion is outside the scope of this chapter, we would like to emphasise the importance of care in legal contexts as well.
49 For discussions of normative ideals of families, see e.g. Catherine Donovan, 'Genetics, Fathers and Families: Exploring the Implications of Changing the Law in Favour of Identifying Sperm Donors,' *Social & Legal Studies* 15:4 (2006), 494.
50 Manderson, *Proximity*, 78.

always implies a recursive view: the concrete case offers a site for assessing the legal (and, indirectly, the moral) responsibilities of the parties towards each other, while it also constitutes a site where the ethical views embedded in legal practices are re-enacted.

Below, we analyse three cases from the European Court of Human Rights that illustrate a diversity of legal responses towards ethical dilemmas. We selected these three cases due to their nature. All of them concern ethically sensitive family situations, with atypical family relations and atypical problems of care. All of them pose the same risks: applying typical notions of the generalised other and losing the particular by reference to the universal, and disregarding the specificities of care in these atypical situations.

The first, *S.H. v Austria*, illustrates the traditional division between ethics of justice and caring relationships and does not take into consideration a greater nuance or attention to particularity and concreteness. In *S.H. v Austria* the balancing prioritised proper family over otherness and failed to respond to both responsibilities of care and responsibility to alterity. We chose this case to illustrate what happens when these responsibilities are neglected in interpretation of human rights, risking further marginalisation of already vulnerable family relations.

In the two subsequent cases dealing with ethically sensitive family issues, the relationship we wish to show between the ethics of alterity and the ethics of care is clearer. The cases of *X and Others v Austria* and *P., C. and S. v the United Kingdom* illustrate the fine balancing between the universal and the concrete, and show how the close relationship between ethics of alterity and ethics of care works in different circumstances. The decision in *X and Others v Austria* took an approach based primarily on recognition of alterity to address the ethics of care without rejection of 'the other' of family law. Meanwhile *P., C. and S. v the United Kingdom* prioritised the ethics of care to relieve the poverty of the ethics of alterity – while ethics of alterity was able to account for this atypical family as a subject of rights, it could not sufficiently address the specificities of care in this very particular family situation.

S.H. v Austria

In *S.H. v Austria* the ECtHR dealt with the ban on certain forms of artificial procreation in Austrian legislation. Certain procedures leading to the establishment of a family were banned primarily due to their controversial moral nature. In particular, the legislation banned the procedure of ovum donation for the purposes of artificial procreation. In defence of the ban the government insisted that the Member States had the right to balance rights with 'specific social and cultural needs and traditions of their countries'. The reference to tradition supported the key argument underlying the legislation, namely that of preventing the emergence of 'atypical family relationships'.⁵¹ In the first instance, the ECtHR rejected this defence and focused on the discriminatory impact of these provisions on couples suffering from these particular types of infertility. The Chamber found the provisions to be in breach of Article 8 of the European Convention securing the right to private and family life. The chamber judgment underlined that discriminatory treatment of certain types of infertility had no objective and reasonable justification and lacked proportionality between the aims sought and means employed.⁵²

In the revised judgment, however, the Court was reluctant to focus on the arguments of the applicants or to examine the ethical consequences of discriminatory provisions. Instead the revised judgment focused on the social expectations related to the paradigm of a 'proper family'. Reluctant to draw a boundary as to which family is a 'proper' one and which is 'atypical', the Grand Chamber took a defensive stance and underlined that its 'task is not to substitute itself for the competent national authorities in determining the most appropriate policy for regulating matters of artificial procreation'.⁵³ The judgment subsequently focused on the national authorities' mandate to give an opinion on the 'exact content of the requirements of morals in their country'.⁵⁴ These local morals sustaining established 'cultural needs' clearly favoured a paradigm 'normal family'. The Court held that the state is allowed to regulate 'important aspects of private life' in case of weighty competing interests, and establish rules of 'an absolute nature'.⁵⁵

Such a framing of the proper family left no room for the workings of the ethics of alterity or the ethics of care. First, the exclusion of those standing outside the narrow confines of a 'proper family' was sanctioned by reference to absolute and 'universal' nature of legal rules. Second, the 'concrete identity of the other'⁵⁶ and their relations of care became invisible and the particular circumstances of infertility were rendered irrelevant when faced with mandate of authorities to regulate aspects of privacy. In this case human rights law fell into the ontological trap of treating the concrete other as no more than an excuse for epitomising a universal standard encapsulated in the norm of a 'normal family'. The response of law did not account either for the rights of a non-typical family nor for the caring nature of the relations concerned. The potential of atypicality removed the putative family relationship from the confines of the normal. This response to the circumstances of a concrete family erased any consideration of care between these particular partners and the necessity

---

51 ECtHR, *S.H. v Austria*, app. no. 57813/00, (3 November 2011) para. 113.
52 ECtHR, *S.H. v Austria*, (1 April 2010), Chamber Judgment, para. 64
53 ECtHR, *S.H. v Austria*, 2011, para. 92
54 Ibid. para. 94
55 Ibid. para. 110.
56 Benhabib, *Situating the Self*, 158.

of recognition of their circumstances. In other words the other became invisible in the omnipresence of the universal.[57]

This erasure of the other and the other's relations of care, however, is not the only approach that human rights law can offer when it comes to accounting for particular others and their relations of care. In the two following cases concerning similarly controversial family matters the Court took a slightly different approach and fine-tuned its considerations in line with ethics of alterity and ethics of care. The Court analysed the traditional moral and cultural construct of a 'proper family' and engaged in careful balancing between the universal and the concrete.

X and Others v Austria

Our second case is as topical as matters of artificial procreation. The recent case *X and Others v Austria*[58] dealt with second parent adoption by same-sex couples in Austria, and unlike the case above was decided in favour of the applicants. In our view, the case presented a new approach to the relationship between the universal and the particular and revealed a symbiotic working of the ethics of rights and ethics of care. The case was decided in early 2013 and concerned the question whether the second *de facto* parent in a same-sex relationship with the mother could adopt her partner's child. According to Austrian legislation such adoption was possible only for heterosexual couples, and Austrian courts had refused to confirm the adoption. The domestic courts quoted the importance of the 'traditional biological family' as embedded in law as a 'matter of principle',[59] and the legal impossibility of granting the right to adoption to the same-sex partner of the biological parent. In other words, the paradigm of a 'normal family' prevented the Austrian courts from acknowledging the duty of care in the circumstances of these concrete parents.

---

57 It is noteworthy to remind that in another case dealing with a similarly sensitive issue of preimplantation diagnostics (ECtHR, *Costa and Pavan v Italy*, app. no. 54270/10, (11 February, 2011)) the Court found that allowing for abortion rather than PGD not only lacked consistency but also interfered with the right to privacy and put a disproportionate burden on the applicant. Interestingly the Court acknowledged both the otherness of the applicant, whose circumstances were given due consideration, as well as her own ethical dilemmas related to her caring responsibilities within the family unit. The Court underlined that the applicant's 'anxiety' and 'painful decisions' related to carrying a foetus with a serious genetic disease could not simply be underestimated. The paradigm of a 'proper family' and the imagined 'proper' duty of care according to a universally accepted standard were circumvented by a focus on the concrete circumstances of the Other and their assessment in terms of heaviness and proportionality.
58 ECtHR, *X and Others v Austria*, app. no. 19010/07, (19 February 2013).
59 Ibid. para. 18.

In this case, however, the ECtHR did not accept the universalist paradigm of a 'normal family' at face value. Instead the Court placed special emphasis on the identity of these concrete parents by explicitly underlining that when identity is at stake the State's margin of appreciation should be narrow.[60] Thus the Court did not simply affirm the importance of non-negotiable cultural and moral principles embedded in the paradigm of a 'traditional biological family'. Instead, the judgment underlined the specificity of the individual case. It stated that while striking a balance when it comes to 'rights of sexual minorities is in the nature of things a difficult and delicate exercise, which may require the State to reconcile conflicting views and interests perceived by the parties concerned as being in fundamental opposition' it was important to provide weighty enough reasons to justify discrimination of the same-sex parents as necessary in a democratic society.[61]

Furthermore, the Court explicitly acknowledged the importance of caring responsibilities for the very construction of the family, as it emphasised that the mother and her partner were caring for the child jointly and that such care and the nature of the relationship between all three applicants amounted to 'family life'.[62] This judgment explicitly challenged the universal paradigm by first turning to something very like the ethics of alterity in acknowledging difference against a universalist understanding of the subjects of family law. Second it complemented this consideration of alterity by referring to the responsibility for care in this particular relationship and placing it at the core of the family life. The judgment expanded both the pre-existing conceptions of a family, and the understanding of the responsibility for care. Thanks to such a symbiotic approach applying the two ethics, nuances of contemporary particularity in family law were given due attention and the traditional position of the law was challenged with the help of human rights law.

P., C. and S. v the United Kingdom

The case of *P., C. and S. v the United Kingdom*[63] revealed law's difficulties in approaching matters of alleged neglect and lack of care and showed how the symbiosis of the two accounts of ethics may require a stronger emphasis on ethics of care to solve the particular family situation. This highly complex case concerned a mother, P., who was said to suffer from MSBP,[64] and

---

60 Ibid. para. 148.
61 Ibid. para. 99.
62 Ibid. para. 96.
63 ECtHR, *P., C. and S. v the United Kingdom*, app. no. 56547/00, (16 July 2002).
64 Munchhausen Syndrome By Proxy – sufferers of this syndrome induce illness in people they care for, usually children, to seek attention from medical authorities.

the child protection measures undertaken by authorities in the United Kingdom while she was pregnant with her second child. Relying on P.'s personal history with her first-born, the UK authorities reached the conclusion that she would constitute a danger to her new baby upon its birth.

At the time that the measures were taken, there was no evidence that P. intended to cause harm to the baby. However, the authorities gave weight to P.'s history with her first-born, whom she allegedly fed laxatives to cause diarrhoea and attract the attention of medical professionals. Therefore the authorities issued an emergency protection order to be executed at the child's birth, and separated the mother from her child upon birth without giving her and her partner C. a chance to build a family unit. Eventually the child S. was freed for adoption and placed with a new family. As a result P. and C. were allowed to maintain only minimal contact with their daughter via postcards and mail at the discretion of her new parents.

In its judgment the European Court of Human Rights found that the authorities' actions were in violation of the right to private and family life (Article 8 of the Convention) as well as of the right to fair hearing in Article 6. While the Court noted that it did not wish to substitute itself for relevant domestic authorities (see *S.H. v Austria* above), it agreed that the case required a careful assessment. In this assessment the Court focused strongly on the nature of family relationships: 'As regards the extreme step of severing all parental links with a child, the Court has taken the view that such a measure would cut a child from its roots and could only be justified in exceptional circumstances'.[65]

With regard to the removal of the child at birth, the Court found that the draconian measures undertaken by the authorities were not necessary in a democratic society and constituted a breach of the parents' rights. While the Court did not discuss the parents' responsibilities for care and their potential for fulfilling them, the specificity of the caring relationship was a decisive factor in the outcome reached. With no evidence of life-threatening harm to the child, the Court decided that the parents should have been given the right to carry out their responsibilities of care.

By underlining the importance of the relation generating the responsibilities of care the Court not only acknowledged the specific circumstances of the other – a family in an atypical situation – but went further and examined the emotional links generated by specific family roots. In this assessment the judgment observed that there was an emotional disadvantage that the applicants suffered when faced with the law and legal proceedings. The Court acknowledged that the specificity of emotional bond at stake had an impact on how the applicants acted in the case and on the outcome

---

65 ECtHR, *P., C. and S. v the United Kingdom*, para. 118.

reached.[66] The Court noted that the authorities had procedural obligations and duties towards the parents, in dealing with such specific relationships of care:

> It was crucial for the parents in this case to be able to put forward their case as favourably as possible, emphasising for example whatever factors militated in favour of a further assessment of a possible rehabilitation, and for their viewpoints on the possible alternatives to adoption and the continuation of contact after adoption to be put forward at the appropriate time for consideration by the court.

The argumentation in the latter half of the case, concerning adoption proceedings, reflects this consideration clearly. The Court notes that it 'does not propose to attempt to untangle these opposed considerations, which raise difficult and sensitive issues concerning S.'s welfare', but instead focuses on the position of the parents.[67] The argumentation bridges ethics of care, in recognising the vulnerability of the parents with regard to the child, and ethics of alterity, in highlighting the procedural obligations of the authorities to specific family situations in which that vulnerability arises. While it is hard to know which material judgment in the original case would have been best for the child, or most sensitive to the relations of care being disrupted, this focus on the position of the parties involved shows the interplay of the two accounts of ethics.

Conclusion

Theories relying on the Kantian rift between ethics and law are not sufficient in a late modern world, as we accept the idea of reality being socially constructed and historically contingent. New models of ethics are relevant both for providing justification of legislation and legal decision-making and for explaining law. As we illustrated in this chapter law always embodies some understanding of ethics and justifiability. In resolving the difficulty with the position of ethics in law we followed Manderson's assertion that there is always 'a space of uncertainty within the workings of the legal system'.[68] Despite the major difficulties of bringing different accounts of ethics together with law, Manderson reminds us that they both meet in the space of legal uncertainty and result in creative antagonism, where ethics act as 'a scruple that constantly discomforts law and impels it to move'.[69] We have therefore emphasised

---

66 Ibid. para. 137.
67 Ibid. para. 136.
68 Manderson, *Proximity*, 78.
69 Ibid. 83.

that there is always an inherent ethical element in law,[70] which becomes particularly visible once law acknowledges a duty of care.[71]

Here, the important consideration is what kind of legal thinking might emerge from adopting an ethical account that focuses on otherness. In our view it is also clearly valuable for legal assessment of intimate and caring relationships to actually account for the care that is so foundational for them. However, considering relationality and responsibility for otherness might also transform our thinking on legal relationships in general, as Jennifer Nedelsky has proposed. It is not enough to require law to account for the responsibility towards the universal other; law also needs to be able to address the other in relationships of care.

Therefore we argue that in order to challenge the universalising logic of the ethics of justice, ethics of care and ethics of alterity together can be used as bridging tools. We see the coexistence of these accounts of ethics as symbiotic. As we saw in considering case law in the previous section, the poverty of ethics of justice can be answered by the ethics of care but the normative generalisations of the ethics of care can be alleviated by ethics of alterity.

The symbiotic use of the two accounts of ethics allows a response to differences between different forms of families and accounting for the particularities of care within them. In other words, ethics of care may offer a potential way forward in recognising the nuances and complexity of responsibilities in caring relationships and thus to respond to the poverty of ethics of alterity in this regard. At the same time, our understanding of care can fall prey to our conceptions of normality, if not challenged by a broader conception of responsibility towards the other. In brief, the ethics of alterity may relieve the ethics of care from being imagined too narrowly and mirrored on traditional relationships and their duties, while ethics of care are capable of accounting for nuances of care within non-typical relationships. Both accounts are important in preventing the rejection of certain particularities, such as same-sex relationships, untraditional choices of conception or identities that challenge the ideas of normality. The subtle difference between the two accounts proves valuable in accounting for the multifaceted nature of concrete otherness.

Bibliography

Archard, David. *Children: Rights and Childhood*. New York: Routledge, 2004.
Badiou, Alain. *Ethics: An Essay on the Understanding of Evil*. London, New York: Verso, 2001.
Baier, Annette C. 'What do Women want in a Moral Theory?' *Nous* (1985): 53.

---

70 Ibid. 78.
71 Ibid. 83–91.

Baier, Annette C. 'Trust and Antitrust,' *Ethics* 96 (1986): 231.
Benhabib, Seyla. 'The Generalized and the Concrete Other: The Kohlberg-Gilligan Controversy and Feminist Theory,' *Praxis international* 4 (1985): 402.
Benhabib, Seyla. 'In Defense of Universalism. Yet Again! A Response to Critics of Situating the Self,' *New German Critique* (1994).
Benhabib, Seyla. *Situating the Self: Gender, Community, and Postmodernism in Contemporary Ethics*. Cambridge: Polity Press, 1994.
Cornell, Drucilla. 'Post-structuralism, the Ethical Relation, and the Law,' *Cardozo L. Rev.* 9 (1987): 1587.
Critchley, Simon. *The Ethics of Deconstruction: Derrida and Levinas*. Edinburgh: Edinburgh University Press, 2014.
Derrida, Jacques. *Of Grammatology*. Baltimore: JHU Press, 1998.
Donovan, Catherine. 'Genetics, Fathers and Families: Exploring the Implications of Changing the Law in Favour of Identifying Sperm Donors,' *Social & Legal Studies* 15:4 (2006), 494.
Douzinas, Costas and Ronnie Warrington. '"A Well-founded Fear of Justice": Law and Ethics in Postmodernity,' *Law and Critique* 2.2 (1991): 115.
Douzinas, Costas. 'Human Rights and Postmodern Utopia,' *Law and Critique* 11.2 (2000).
Douzinas, Costas. *The End of Human Rights*. Oxford and Portland, OR: Hart Publishing, 2000.
Eekelaar, John. *Family Law and Personal Life*. Oxford: Oxford University Press, 2006.
Etxabe, Julen. *The Experience of Tragic Judgment*. New York: Routledge, 2013.
Fineman, Martha A. *The Autonomy Myth. A Theory of Dependency*. New York: The New Press, 2005.
Gilligan, Carol. *In a Different Voice. Psychological Theory and Women's Development*. Cambridge, MA: Harvard University Press, 1982.
Hart, H.L.A. *The Concept of Law*. Oxford: Oxford University Press, 1994.
Held, Virginia. *The Ethics of Care. Personal, Political and Global*. Oxford: Oxford University Press, 2006.
Hirvonen, Ari. *Oikeuden käynti: Antigonen laki ja oikea oikeus*. Helsinki: Loki-kirjat, 2000.
Kroeger-Mappes, Joy. 'The Ethic of Care vis-à-vis the Ethic of Rights: A Problem for Contemporary Moral Theory,' *Hypatia* 9:3 (1994): 108.
Levinas, Emmanuel. *Totality and Infinity*. Pittsburgh, PA: Duquesne University Press, 1969.
Levinas, Emmanuel. 'The Rights of Man and the Rights of the Other.' In Emmanuel Levinas, *Outside the Subject*. London: Continuum, 2008, 91–8.
Manderson, Desmond. *Proximity, Levinas, and the Soul of Law*. Montreal: McGill-Queen's Press, 2006.
Miller, Fred Dycus. *Nature, Justice, and Rights in Aristotle's Politics*. Oxford: Oxford University Press, 1995.
Nedelsky, Jennifer. *Law's Relations. A Relational Theory of Self, Autonomy and Law*. Oxford: Oxford University Press, 2011.
Raz, Joseph. *The Morality of Freedom*. Oxford: Oxford University Press, 1986.
Simmons, William Paul. *Human Rights and the Marginalised Other*. Cambridge: Cambridge University Press, 2014.
Smart, Karen and Bren Neale. *Family Fragments?* Cambridge: Polity Press, 1999.

Smith, Nick. 'Questions for a Reluctant Jurisprudence of Alterity,' in *Essays on Levinas and Law: A Mosaic*, edited by Desmond Manderson, 68–71. Basingstoke: Palgrave Macmillan, 2009.
Tronto, Joan. *Moral Boundaries. A Political Argument for an Ethic of Care*. New York: Routledge, 1993.
White, Julie A. and Joan C. Tronto. 'Political Practices of Care: Needs and Rights,' *Ratio Juris* 17:4 (2004), 425.

List of cases

ECtHR, *Costa and Pavan v Italy*, app. no. 54270/10, (11 February, 2011)
ECtHR, *P., C. and S. v the United Kingdom*, app. no. 56547/00, (16 July 2002)
ECtHR, *S.H. v Austria*, app. no. 57813/00, (3 November 2011)
ECtHR, *X and Others v Austria*, app. no. 19010/07, (19 February 2013)

Part III

Personhood, property and contribution

Chapter 10

Families, identity and belonging
Rethinking personhood and property in Botswana

Anne Griffiths

Introduction

In Botswana the family is at the centre of individuals' perceptions of identity and belonging. It also forms part of a network that encompasses a more extended social group of individuals, kin and households contributing to their well-being and livelihoods, especially in the south. This chapter explores these dimensions that inform notions of personhood through an examination of the shifts in the customary law of inheritance in Botswana.[1] It is based on fieldwork carried out among Bakwena[2] between 1982–1989, 2009–2010, and that is ongoing.[3] It investigates the shifting norms that have brought about changes in the way in which gender relations are perceived that reveal women having greater access to resources and property, including land. By highlighting what is taking place on the ground as an everyday part of the life course, it focuses on uncontested and general transmissions of property rather than on contested relations and disputes. By revealing what is

---

1 The legal system of Botswana comprises statutory law that is written law (based primarily on English law) and case law informed by Roman-Dutch or Cape Colonial law, as well as customary law that is unwritten and based on oral transmission. Under the Customary Law [Application and Ascertainment] Act no.51 [1969] customary law is defined under s.2 as being 'in relation to any particular tribe or tribal community, the customary law of that tribe or tribal community so far as it is not incompatible with the provisions of any written law or contrary to morality, humanity or natural justice'. In contrast, common law is defined under s.2 as 'any law, whether written or unwritten, in force in Botswana, other than customary law'.
2 In Setswana, the official language of Botswana along with English, the prefixes 'Ba' and 'Mo' are the plural and singular modifiers of nouns designating persons, so 'Bakwena' is the plural forms of Kwena (Kwena people/persons) and 'Mokwena' is the singular form (a Kwena person). Similarly 'Batswana' stands for the plural of Tswana persons or citizens and 'Motswana' stands for an individual citizen.
3 I am indebted to the Leverhulme Trust for funding the research during 2009–2010 and to the government of Botswana and all who participated in the research, especially my research assistants, Phidelia Dintwe, Phenhyo Thebe, Kawina Power and Boinelo Baakile. I would also like to thank the International Research Centre on Work and the Human Lifecycle in Global History, Humboldt University, Berlin for allowing me to analyse my data as a senior research fellow there from 2010–2011.

happening on the basis of consensual relations that often remain hidden from view, it explores the changing notions of personhood within the domain of families and households, highlighting the factors promoting change in the ways in which relations between persons and property are perceived.

Particular emphasis is placed on land that is a key component in providing for the alleviation of poverty and well-being of individuals, families and households. For as the government of Botswana notes, 'studies worldwide have shown that the impact of population growth on poverty is strongest at the micro-level, that is, at the level of households and communities acknowledging that female headed households are among the poorest in the country'[4] and that 'poverty remains one of the major development challenges for Botswana'.[5] In tackling poverty, how land – a key resource for their livelihoods – is acquired and transferred is an important consideration, especially for women and children whom it is generally recognised feature disproportionately among the poor.[6]

From this perspective, this chapter addresses 'the person of law' in the context of transmission of land through inheritance under customary law, exploring how legal subjects, in this case women family members, are conceptualised in terms of the roles they perform and how an evaluation of these roles may be transformed over time through engagement with changing notions of personhood, linked to perceptions of identity and belonging. These terms have been the subject of ongoing debate and critique within the humanities, especially among anthropologists[7] and I would like

---

4 Government of Botswana, *National Development Plan (NDP 6) 1981–1991* (Gaborone: Ministry of Finance and Development Planning), 24.
5 Ibid.
6 Thokozile Ruzvidzo and Hanna N. Tiagha, 'The African Gender Development Index' in *Gender Instruments in Africa: Critical Perspectives, Future Strategies*, ed. Christi van der Westhuizen (Pretoria: Institute for Global Dialogue, 2005), 22–47.
7 See Marcel Mauss, 'A Category of the Human Mind: The Notion of Person; the Notion of Self' (1938) translated by W.E. Halls in *The Category of the Person: Anthropology, Philosophy, History*, ed. Michael Carrithers, Steven Collins and Steven Lukes, (Cambridge: Cambridge University Press,1985); Meyer Fortes, 'The Concept of the Person' in *Religion, Morality and the Person: Essays on Tallensi Religion*, ed. Jack Goody (New York: Cambridge University Press, 1973); Clifford Geertz, 'From the Native's Point of View: On the Nature of Anthropological Understanding' in *Culture Theory: Essays on Mind, Self and Emotion*, eds. Richard A Shweder and Robert A. Levine (New York: Cambridge University Press, 1984); Susan Reynolds Whyte, 'The Widow's Dream: Sex and Death in Western Kenya' in *Personhood and Agency: The Experience of 'Self and Other' in African Cultures*, Papers presented at a Symposium of African Folk Models and Their Applications, held at Uppsala University, August 23–30, eds. Jackson Michael and Ivan Karp (Washington D.C.: Smithsonian Institution Press, 1990); Anthony P. Cohen, *Self Consciousness: An Alternative Anthropology of Identity* (London: Routledge, 1994); Katherine A. Snyder, 'Modern Cows and Exotic Trees: Identity, Personhood and Exchange among the Iraqw of Tanzania', *Ethnology* 41:2 (2002), 155–73; Sherry B. Ortner, 'Subjectivity and Cultural Critique', *Anthropological Theory* 5:1 (2005), 31–52; Joao Biehl, Byron Good and Arthur Kleinman (eds.), *Subjectivity: Ethnographic Investigations* (Berkeley: University of California Press, 2007).

to outline how I propose to use them. As Middleton observes, 'concepts surrounding the understanding of "personhood" are central to all peoples and their understandings of their own society'.[8] It has also been noted that 'today, studies of "personhood" have grown to include both the ways in which cultures studied explain their cultural markers and confer stages of "personhood", *as well as* (own italics) the ways in which individuals have been seen to perceive themselves and their place within society'.[9]

In the context of my research, these cultural markers involve women's relationships within families and households as they evolve over the course of the lifecycle, embracing their birth, development, coming of age, giving birth (and possibly marriage) and death. At the same time, my interviews and life histories of individuals and household family members also provide an awareness of how these persons perceive themselves and their relations through processes of socialisation that may change over time. Thus personhood embodies both sociocultural aspects (that include aspects of law), as well as, more subjective, experiential elements that Jacobson-Widding refers to as 'what I am supposed to be',[10] along with, 'what I feel that I am'.[11] These elements come together through agency that 'allows one to constitute a sense of "self" and "identity" which is in turn acquired as a result of the social construction of "personhood"'.[12] These mutually constitutive features, that include belonging through a sense of experience, give rise to 'identity' that according to Epstein 'represents the process by which the person seeks to integrate his various statuses and roles, as well as his diverse experiences, into a coherent image of "self"'.[13]

Research location and empirical data

My research was carried out in Kweneng district, in the village of Molepolole (population around 70,000 of the total population of 2,040,000 in the country in 2010) that is both the administrative regional centre for the district, as well as the capital of the Bakwena polity, where I did fieldwork

---

8 John Middleton 'The Concept of the Person Among the Lugbara of Uganda' in *La Notion de Personne en Afrique Noire*, Germaine Dieterlen (Paris: Edition du Centre National de la Recherche, 1973), 492.
9 Laura P. Appell-Warren, '"Personhood": An Examination of the History and Use of a Concept in the Anthropological Literature'. A Thesis Presented to the Faculty of the Graduate School of Education of Harvard University in Partial Fulfillment of the Requirements for the Degree of Doctor of Education, (2007, UMI Number: 3271672), 105.
10 Anita Jacobson-Widding, 'The Shadow as an Expression of Personhood', Jackson and Karp (eds.), *Personhood and Agency*, 31.
11 Ibid.
12 Appell-Warren, 'Personhood' Thesis, 90.
13 Arnold Leonard Epstein, *Ethos and Identity: Three Studies in Ethnicity* (London: Tavistock, 1978), 101.

between 1982 and 1989. This made it an appropriate site for developing my research on land, which I conducted in 2009–2010 and that is ongoing. Part of my earlier research involved life histories of family groups from Mosotho *kgotla*[14] covering three generations, including the Makokwe and Radipati families.[15] My later research extended these families' life histories to cover data for five generations, documenting continuities and differences in intergenerational access to land.[16] It also built on the use of archival material, court and land board records, participant observation and interviews with government departments, officials and NGOs.[17]

To obtain a sense of the extent to which the normative framework of customary law might be changing with regard to women's control over land, I examined 4041 land certificates. These dealt with transfers of both residential and arable land from 1999 to 2009. Inheritance involves the transfer of land that must be approved and certified by the Land Board through an alteration to the land certificate. It is important to note here that it was not possible to conduct a random sample of certificates for each year because of the state of Sub-Land Board records. Relevant information specifying the sex, age and marital status of both transferor and transferee and whether or not they are related was not always available given the failure to keep adequate records in the past. Inadequate record keeping has been a complaint ever since Land Boards were established and surfaces time again in appeals taken to the Land Tribunal. This meant that my research assistant, Phidelia Dintwe and I were limited to examining those records that we could actually get our hands on.

---

14 A kgotla is central to the socio-politico-administrative structure of a Tswana morafe or polity (tribe) that is formed around the physical location of households. It is the assembly centre (both the physical location and the body of members) of a group of households presided over by a male headman or ward head; in the past, but no longer, all household heads were related through the male line. A number of kgotlas grouped together, known as dikgotla, are structured through a tightly organised hierarchy of progressively more inclusive administrative groupings, beginning with households that make up a kgotla or dikgotla, and extending through wards which are the major units of political and legal organisation of the morafe as a whole. At the apex of this system, is the chief's ward, Kgosing, where the chief's kgotla is located that governs the morafe and dispenses justice through its function as a court.
15 For details see Anne Griffiths, *In the Shadow of Marriage: Gender and Justice in an African Community* (Chicago: University of Chicago Press, 1997).
16 For an update on the descendants of Makokwe and Radipati see Anne Griffiths, 'Re-envisioning the Local: Spatiality, Land and Law in Botswana', *International Journal of Law in Context* 9:2 (2013), 213–38.
17 For details see Anne Griffiths 'Engaging with the Global: Perspectives on Land from Botswana', in *Framing the Global: Entry Points for Research*, ed. Hilary Kahn (Bloomington: Indiana University Press, 2014), 112–36.

Inheritance: sociocultural dimensions

Past constraints on women's access to property and land: a gendered dimension

My earlier research established that transmission of property among families is focused on maintaining future generations with an emphasis on preserving assets for children. Given the patrilineal framework of family life in Tswana society, where power is exercised – through the man's father where the parents are married, or through the woman's father where they are not – it is not surprising that male offspring are privileged over female offspring when it comes to inheritance under customary law, where the eldest son is allocated the major share of the property in recognition of the responsibilities that he adopts as head of the family. For this reason, he not only had the role of custodian with regard to his children, but also had responsibilities for representing and maintaining extended kin (beyond his immediate nuclear family) where he was the senior male among the network of family members. Thus family groups, such as the Makokwe family group that featured in my Molepolole research, were linked into co-operative networks extending across several households that contributed to the livelihoods of individuals and kin through pooling of resources among and between generations.[18]

Among children, daughters inherited less than their brothers because it was envisaged that they would marry, going to live among their husband's relatives where their husband would establish their own residential yard. Through marriage, these women's children would be affiliated with their husband's family group where property devolves from father to son. What daughters tended to inherit was their mother's personal property such as clothes and domestic utensils. They might also inherit fields that had been allocated to and worked by their mothers. In contrast, brothers inherited ploughs, cattle, guns and other family property (including land) their father may have had. Among siblings property was not shared equally but depended on birth order, as underlined in discussions below.

Among Bakwena, as with other Tswana merafe or polities (often glossed as 'tribes'), it was common for parents to link brothers and sisters creating a special relationship between these individuals and their offspring in successive generations, forming a set of supportive relations. In the past this was particularly relevant for the circulation of property because where bogadi (bridewealth) was paid for a daughter, the cattle received for her would go towards fulfilling her linked brother's requirement when he married and so reciprocity and obligations were constituted through ongoing

---

18 Griffiths, *In the Shadow of Marriage*, 62–105.

generations. While linking is not referred to today, nonetheless sibling relationships continue to have an important role in maintaining family relationships and in handling inheritance. Ever since the 1930s out-migration by significant numbers of men has disrupted labour patterns, marriage has featured less prominently and large numbers of women have children but remain unmarried.[19] In these cases, where they are unable to acquire land and build their own households, they remain in the natal family compound sharing the space with other siblings and members of the household who reside there. This may create overcrowding often leading to disputes, but it may also result in their own sibling cohort making over control of the residence to them, which is contrary to customary norms of inheritance discussed below.

Conversations with customary officials, such as ward headmen, in Molepolole in 2010, had much in common with earlier discussions on inheritance that I had with them in the 1980s although there were marked changes. What emerged from these dialogues was that where inheritance is concerned, sex, birth order and status continue to occupy an important role. With regard to land, headmen from Dikoloing ward explained 'in our culture there were two ploughing fields, one allocated to the mother [wife] and one for the husband'. All agreed that a daughter would inherit a mother's field and that a son would inherit his father's field. They went on to note that 'usually the field allocated to the mother is allocated to the youngest daughter provided she is not married' and that 'the father's field goes to the eldest son' who 'will also be given the borehole and a gun'. However, they were careful to stress 'that even if it is done like this [according to tradition/culture] the children have to meet and agree even although they know that according to our tradition it has to go to the eldest son'. This is because there is an understanding that, notwithstanding established customary norms of inheritance, families can reach their own agreements that may displace such norms provided there is consensus among their members.

When asked what happens to the residential yard, with its front and back house, the headmen from Mokgalo stated that the 'front house is given to the eldest son and the back house goes to the eldest daughter'. Recognition of the eldest son is important because he represents the family in public matters, but headmen from other wards argued that it was the youngest son who inherited the yard. In interviews outside Molepolole, government officials, civil servants and professionals (such as lawyers), were of the view that it was the youngest son who got the residential yard, although some claimed that there was a difference between the north and the south of the

---

19 Issac Schapera, *Migrant Labour and Tribal Life: a Study of the Condition of the Bechuanaland Protectorate* (London: Oxford University Press, 1947), 173.

country, with the north giving this property to the eldest son, and the south, where Molepolole is situated, going to the youngest. Given the fact that the distribution of assets is unequal, members of Mogkalo ward observed that in terms of the general distribution of the estate (excluding the residential yard) 'young children complain a lot about most of the possessions going to the eldest son. It [property division] is a very difficult issue'.

In some cases, following traditional practices, property was earmarked for certain individuals during the parents' lifetime. This was especially the case with cattle, and sometimes daughters, as well as sons, were beneficiaries. The senior men of Dikoloing ward acknowledge that it happens 'especially with regard to livestock. Children are given cattle while their parents are still alive'. They explain, however, that while cattle may be earmarked for individuals 'that does not mean that you have complete control of that animal'. If the family is in need 'that animal can be taken and slaughtered [or sold]'. While some daughters may acquire livestock through earmarking or inheritance (particularly where a mother had beasts acquired through the sale of produce from her fields and therefore viewed as part of her estate) the general view was that 'in our society boys usually look after livestock and women do domestic activities. Boys inherit livestock and women will inherit household equipment'.

My earlier research documented how women were generally at a disadvantage in acquiring resources because of their position within the gendered hierarchy of a family network constructed around patrilineal norms that subordinated their claims to property.

Gendered identities: transformations allowing for change

What is clear from my more recent research is that while there may be continuity in upholding some customary norms others have changed. For these norms, that form part of the fabric of sociocultural life, encompassing social, political and economic relations between individuals, families and households (including legal provisions) have become subject to transformation over time. In divorce cases, for example, especially those featuring in the High Court, women now feature as custodians of the family residence for their children. This means that the customary land certificate will bear their name, instead of that of their ex-husband. It is important to note that this recognition only exists to enable them to hold the property until their children come of age. Changes in the law have also made it possible for married women to hold property in their own right. Under the Abolition of Marital Power Act 2004 women married under community of property laws are no longer subject to their husband's exercise of marital power over matrimonial property. This means that married women can now acquire land certificates in their own right as amendments have also been made to the Deeds Registry Act.[20] Similarly, the position of widows seems to have acquired a different status. This is evident from headmen in Molepolole acknowledging that today under customary law, 'when the husband dies everything is transferred to the wife including the brand of cattle' whereas in my discussion in the 1980s it was the deceased's brothers and uncles who were said to oversee the estate and determine transfers to beneficiaries.

What is clear is that norms for both written and unwritten law prove to be mutually constitutive in their shift towards a more inclusive approach to women that removes barriers underpinning their minority status. For while women like men may have status as citizens, gender has operated in the past to create a 'minority' status for women in relation to inheritance in Botswana. This is so regardless of whether they are located within the formally designated systems of 'common'[21] or 'customary'[22] law. Within this shifting milieu of institutional and legal change there is also the situation of family members reaching their own voluntary agreements about distribution of land on succession that may differ in practice from the established norms of customary law with regard to birth order, sex and status of the beneficiary. This is recognised by the headmen themselves, who stressed that what is central to the process of inheritance is the consultation and consensus reached among family members, especially the deceased's children, as to how family property should be distributed. It is these shifting considerations that this chapter explores.

Regulating the administration of land under customary tenure

To obtain a sense of the extent to which families substituted their own decisions in place of recognised customary norms with regard to beneficiaries, (especially women), I examined land certificates at Kweneng Sub-Land Board (KSLB) dealing with transfers of both residential and arable land. This is because, while there are three types of land tenure in Botswana, state land (used to develop cities, commercial urban activities), freehold (a minuscule segment, recognising 19th century grants to South Africans) and customary land tenure, the latter represents 70 percent of land tenure in the country and forms the basis of tenure in Kweneng District. Today, land

---

20 See s.18 of the Deeds Registry Act [Cap 33:02].
21 Common law is defined as 'any law, whether written or unwritten, in force in Botswana, other than customary law' s.2 of the Customary Law (Application and Ascertainment) Act (No.51 of 1969).
22 In contrast to the definition of common law, customary law is defined as being 'in relation to any particular tribe or tribal community, the customary law of that tribe or tribal community so far as it is not incompatible with the provisions of any written law or contrary to morality, humanity or natural justice' under s. 2 of the above 1969 Act.

under customary tenure is administered by Land Boards under the Tribal Land Act 1968, passed barely two years after the country (formerly the Bechuanaland Protectorate established in 1885) acquired its independence in 1966. It promoted substantial changes to the dominant Tswana tribal systems of land tenure that had been left intact during the colonial era, for the Act handed over powers previously vested under customary law in chiefs and their representatives to Land Boards. In 1973 subordinate Land Boards were created and empowered to allocate land under customary law for residential purposes, ploughing, grazing cattle and other stock and of other 'communal' uses. There are seven such Land Boards in Kweneng[23] under the jurisdiction of the main board, Kweneng Land Board (KLB).

To acquire a sense of women's access to land (beyond life histories) my research involved examining land certificates at KSLB. This involved examining records for both residential and arable land over ten years (1999 to 2009); 4041 certificates were examined. These dealt with residential plot allocations, transfers and extensions, as well as field allocations/registrations, transfers and extensions. In addition, I examined 1200 leases of which 600 were residential and 600 were commercial. The limitations of written records are well known but it was important to examine these data because there is very little empirical evidence on the extent to which women are featuring when it comes to applying for land.[24] As Ng'ong'ola, Professor of law at Botswana University, observed to me, 'Land Boards claim to follow a gender-neutral policy on allocations. But it would be interesting to apply your type of analysis to the actual situation on the ground. There is not much information on how women have been faring in their dealings with Land Boards'.[25]

Redefining formal Land Board jurisdiction: rethinking 'belonging'

Initially the Tribal Land Act 1968 sought to retain tribal affiliation as the prerequisite for occupation and use of land in tribal areas. Thus a person had to belong to a particular tribal group to fall within the jurisdiction of a Land Board. This was amended in 1993 to provide that 'all rights and title to land in each tribal area [...] vest in the Land Board [...] in trust for the benefit and advantage of citizens of Botswana and for the purpose

---

23 These are Lephephe, Thamaga, Mogoditshane, Letlhakeng, Lentsweletau, Molepolole (Sub-Land Board), and Motokwe.
24 Botswana is currently engaged in computerised mapping of land tenure throughout the country under LAPCAS, Land Administration Procedures Capacity and Systems.
25 Personal communication 2003.

of promoting the economic and social development of all the peoples of Botswana'.[26] This amendment, permitting any citizen of Botswana to apply for land to *any* Land Board in the country, decoupled 'belonging' and 'tribal affiliation' both of which inhered in the type of citizenship that was required for Land Boards to have jurisdiction. This move has generated a great deal of controversy and debate among citizens countrywide that features regularly in local and national newspapers.

The composition of Land Boards extended beyond local or tribal membership in that members were appointed through a variety of constituencies, which in 2009–2010 included the Minister of Lands and Housing, as well as the Ministries of Agriculture, Commerce and Industry, along with election by people living in Kweneng district. Originally, chiefs were initially included as ex-officio members of the Board, but were then rendered ineligible under an amendment to the 1968 Act in 1999.[27] At the time of my research KLB was operating with only nine instead of twelve members. Of these members, who were elected at the chief's kgotla or appointed by the Ministries, four were women.

The shifting parameters of customary law: land certificates

While Land Boards are responsible for the allocation and transfer of all Tribal Land, when it comes to questions of inheritance they refer the matter to the Tribal Authorities under the jurisdiction of the chief and the chief's representatives. Once these have made a determination, the matter is remitted back to the Land Board to reject or implement the transfer by amending the land certificate. In this process the norms of customary law are applied, unless there is a written will that supersedes its application, or some other factor comes into play removing it from the remit of the customary system.

The sociocultural framework within which decisions about inheritance are made is open to variation and change where families reach their own consensus on who should inherit family property. To obtain a sense of the extent to which the normative framework of customary law (as outlined earlier) is departed from or is changing with regard to women's control over land, I examined land certificates at KSLB. These dealt with transfers of both residential and arable land from 1999 to 2009. Inheritance involves the transfer of land that must be approved and certified by the Land Board through an alteration to the land certificate.

---

26 Under s. 10(1).
27 They have since been reinstated under regulations dealing with the composition of Land Boards under the Tribal Land (Amendment of Schedule Order), 18 March 2011.

Of the 4041 certificates that I studied, 629 involved residential transfers and 367 dealt with fields. In addition, 259 appointments recorded in the chief's kgotla for 2009, dealing with the administration of deceased persons' estates, were scrutinised to find out the sex of those appointed to administer the estate and the degree to which there was a family relationship between the appointee and the deceased. Given concerns over property grabbing, especially by brothers and uncles of the deceased in the past, seeing who acquires authority to administrate an estate is important with regard to who has legal control over it, although it may not prevent de facto seizing of assets.

Residential transfers to women and men

Not all transfers involve cases of inheritance. While customary land cannot be sold, money can change hands in respect of developments built on it subject to approval by the Land Board. Out of the 629 residential transfers, 327 were to women, 297 were to men and there were 5 whose gender was unclear.[28] Thus women with 52 percent of transfers slightly outnumbered men with 47 percent. However, information on the relationship between parties was unclear. This is because application forms that should have been lodged with the certificates, recording gender, relationship of transferor to transferee, marital status, etc. were often missing so that data were incomplete. This was particularly the case for the years 1999 to 2004. For the years 2005 to 2009, however, we had access to 436 transfers with more recorded data. Of these 629 residential transfers, 189 clearly took place between parties that were related (30 percent of cases) although the actual numbers may be higher (because not all the forms recorded all the required data).

Nonetheless, it is clear from these records that women are featuring as transferees along with men. While the numbers reveal fewer transfers between related parties, this is not surprising because not all the data was submitted with every form, and in any event, it is common for people to transfer residential plots for money, especially in the catchment area for the capital city Gaborone (within which Molepolole is located) where there is huge pressure on land.[29] Under these conditions, the number of transfers to women and men appear to be more or less equal, with slightly more to

---

28 In Botswana citizens have an identity card, an Omang, whose fifth number reveals the sex of the holder. If it is a 1 it is male and if it is a 2 it is female. Where this information was not available or clearly incorrect the name was used but it should be noted that there are many names in Botswana where the sex of the person is ambiguous and cannot be verified without further information that was not available in these cases.
29 For discussion see Anne Griffiths, 'Delivering Justice: The Changing Gendered Dynamics of Land Tenure in Botswana' in Special Issue on International Development Interventions, *Journal of Legal Pluralism and Unofficial Law* 63 (2011), 231–62.

women. This marks a change from the position I encountered when I first carried out research in the 1980s.[30]

Transfers between related parties: type of family relationship

Where parties were related, the majority of transfers involved direct descendants of the nuclear family, that is, daughters and sons, accounting for 57 percent of the transfers.[31] Among this group, there were more transfers to daughters than to sons.[32] These results suggest that property is being circulated and transmitted among a smaller, more nucleated family group, rather than among more extended kin. Where this is taking place, the majority of transfers are post-mortem,[33] indicating that they involve inheritance as they are backed up with written agreement made by family members and witnessed by their local headman.[34] In comparison, the majority of transfers where no recorded information on relationship is present are inter vivos transfers,[35] which is what one would expect where a sale of developments on land takes place.

Field transfers to women and men

In contrast with residential transfers, out of the 247 transfers compiled for the years 1999 to 2009, a higher proportion went to men at 60 percent[36] compared to 40 percent [37]of women. However, it must be noted that it was particularly hard to get access to data on fields as many of the records appear to have been misplaced in the move to the Sub-Land Board's new premises. Finding women less represented than men was somewhat surprising given my earlier findings from the life histories where this was one type of property that women did appear to inherit and pass on. As with the residential transfers, where field transfers were to parties who were related,[38]

---

30 For a more detailed discussion of these changes and for breakdown of status and relationship between transferor and transferee where parties are related see Anne Griffiths, 'Managing Expectations: Negotiating Succession under Plural legal Orders in Botswana', in *Managing Family Justice in Diverse Societies*, eds. Mavis Maclean and John Eekelaar (Oxford: Hart Publishing, 2012), 221–46.
31 That is in 107 cases.
32 59 were to daughters and 48 were to sons.
33 That is in 129 out of 189 cases.
34 While property may be earmarked under customary law for family members before the owner dies this is not often done today, at least not with regard to land.
35 That is in 211 out of 247 transfers.
36 That is 147 men.
37 That is 100 women.
38 That is in 104 cases.

the vast majority were to sons and daughters (70 percent of cases) with overall numbers of women and men almost equally split between 51 women and 53 men. Where parties were related it was also the case that the majority of these transfers were post-mortem.[39]

What is clear from the records is that women are inheriting residential plots and to a lesser extent fields. This is in line with more general findings, including the overall records from KSLB that were examined. Out of the 4041 certificates, over half were registered in women's names.[40] Women also feature in leases, out of 600 residential leases women featured in 292 cases; and out of 600 commercial cases, women were present in 196 cases. It should also be noted that in transfers women are not only featuring as transferees but are also engaged in transferring property as transferors. Where data is recorded, between 2005 and 2009, 386 residential transfers involved women as transferors in 191 cases, compared with 195 transfers by men. In the case of fields, 246 transfers involved 130 women as transferors compared with 86 transfers by men.

Administering the estates of deceased persons: women as appointees

The visible presence of women in these transactions is also apparent in an examination of appointments to the estates of deceased persons. Records in the chief's kgotla in Molepolole for the year 2009 revealed that out of 230 cases where the sex of the appointee was known, 71 percent of appointments involved women compared with 29 per cent of men. In the case of 111 estates belonging to deceased men, wives were appointed to administer the estate in 54 cases. This marks a new development as my past research clearly documented that wives were not viewed as persons who should be dealing with their deceased husband's estate. While women represent a larger proportion of the population demographically in Botswana[41] this does not provide an adequate explanation alone for these appointments. For in 28 cases where wives were appointed, these appointments were approved by a male relative of the deceased and of these, over half (15) involved approval by the deceased's brother. In the past, it was this person who was generally viewed as the appropriate person to administer a deceased male's estate, as the deceased's sibling and uncles of the deceased's descendants play a key role in family affairs. The remaining 26 wives' appointments were approved

---

39 That is in 62 cases.
40 That is in 2063 cases.
41 Kweneng District Development Plan (KDDB6) 2003–2009 (Kweneng District Council, Kweneng District Development Committee, Ministry of Local Government), 7.

by the daughters of the deceased (eight), the appointee's sisters-in-law (nine) and the appointee's mother-in-law (six).

After wives, the largest category of relatives to be appointed in 230 cases were daughters of the deceased, who accounted for 45 appointments, followed by sons of the deceased who were appointed in 29 cases. Overall, appointments involving children of the deceased represented 32 percent of cases. Where daughters were appointed, over half of their appointments had male approval (in 26 out of 45 cases), and over half of these involved approval by male siblings, that is brothers. Where daughters were appointed by a female relatives (in 17 out of 45 cases), they were generally appointed by sisters (six) and aunts (six). In the case of sons, just over half were appointed by siblings (in 14 out of 29 cases), followed by uncles and aunts (five) and mothers (three).

Shifts in inheritance practices: transformation and change

What has brought about these shifts in women's access to and control over land? For while some families follow the traditional customary norms with regard to inheritance, others do not. For example, in the case of Makokwe's second son, Nkgadikang, it was his youngest son, Rammutla, who inherited the residential family yard when his father died although his mother was still alive. Within the same family group, however, Nkgadikang's daughter and a son by his first marriage, were permitted to inherit the residential family yard jointly, allowing them to sell the developments on it and split the proceeds between them. In yet another case, the youngest daughter was allowed to take control of the natal household with the agreement of her older brothers. Clearly there has been a re-evaluation of familial and household relationships that has contributed to these changes in allocation of property and inheritance that is not just evident from my research in Kweneng, but has been documented for other parts of the country.[42]

In the past, women were viewed as persons who would leave the natal household and marry out, going to settle with their husband's family. This meant that property, including land, was kept within the women's family through a patrilineal system that favoured male inheritance. This fitted with the kgotla system, outlined at the beginning of this chapter, where a group of households related through a common male ancestor was governed by a senior male headman. Indeed, the founding members of Mosotho kgotla,

---

42 See Faustin Tirwirukwa Kalabamu, *Changing Gender and Institutional Roles in Self-Help Housing in Botswana: The Case of Lobatse* (Lesotho, The Institute of Southern African Studies, 2003); 'Towards Egalitarian Inheritance Rights in Botswana: The Case of Tlokweng', *Development Southern Africa* 26:2 (2009), 209–23.

where I carried out my initial research on life histories in the 1980s, were all related through men who shared a common male ancestor. Thus male control over households meshed with the socio-political structure on which Tswana polities ('tribes'), including Bakwena, were constructed, with the chief at the apex of the system governing the polity from the chief's kgotla.

This structure, predicated on women marrying out, however, was an idealised, normative construction that has long been departed from in practice. The anthropologist, Schapera, noted in the 1930s that women often remained with their husbands in or near to the woman's family household and this was borne out by my research on life histories from Mosotho kgotla where unmarried women often remained with their children within the natal household. Familial relations were becoming reconstructed due to out-migration that began in colonial times and that continued into the post-independence period, giving the country the status of a labour reserve.[43] This had an impact on marriage, creating a situation where those who married did so at a much later stage in life than in other parts of Africa.[44] It also created a situation where there were large numbers of unmarried women having children who remained in the natal household. This continues to be a feature of family life in Botswana today, with marriage representing a minority status among all those relationships in which children are born.[45]

At the same time as unmarried women with children were remaining in their natal household, there was a downsizing in co-operative labour among families that meant that the extended, supra-household forms of collaboration (organised around migrant labour and subsistence agriculture) gradually disappeared. While extended kin networks get together for major life events they no longer feature as a key element in the promotion of families' livelihoods. This is because families have become smaller and more nucleated when it comes to providing support for their members. Such support today tends to be concentrated among a smaller network of members, usually consisting of parents, children and grandchildren, rather than based on broader kin relations incorporating the families and households of siblings. The widow of Ntlogelang, one of Makokwe's sons, observed in an interview in 2010 that families do not pool their labour to act co-operatively as they did in the past. For although extended kin do come together for 'weddings and funerals' their grandchildren 'are not keen to work jointly like their parents' and that 'they are only interested in taking care of their immediate families'.[46]

---

43 Schapera, *Migrant Labour and Tribal Life*, 42.
44 Griffiths, *In the Shadow of Marriage*, 23.
45 The *Botswana Demographic Survey 2006* (Gaborone: Central Statistics Office, Government of Botswana, 2006), 26 records that 65 percent of the population has never married and that 47 percent of households in the country are headed by women.
46 Griffiths, 'Delivering Justice', 249.

While a chief remains at the head of a polity, his control over land has passed to Land Board members who now administer it for the benefit of *all* citizens of Botswana. This means that land is no longer allocated according to tribal affiliation (as was the case in the past) so that a person coming from the north of Botswana can apply for land in Kweneng District in the south without having to be a Mokwena. Thus the composition of the Kwena polity, where land and governance were once inextricably linked to political, economic and social constellations within it, is undergoing changes. For it is not only the case that kgotla members may be unrelated today, but that they may also come from another polity altogether.

Under these conditions, the perception of women and their role in family life has come to be re-evaluated. For with these changes in the constitution and practice of economic, social and political relations, notions of 'belonging' have come to be reconfigured. Within a more nuclear family unit women are more heavily depended upon for providing caregiving services for their parents, as well as for economic support. They are seen as the mainstay of this type of family, because their brothers are viewed as having commitments elsewhere, most notably with regard to their unmarried female partners and their children, that involve the expenditure of resources beyond family members in their natal household. This is especially the case where these men leave the family compound to establish their own households with dependants elsewhere. While fission has always featured in the development of families and households, due to the extended household lifecycle incorporating unmarried women and children this is now occurring at a much later stage in the lifecycle of both households and individuals.

Under these circumstances, that families can and do reach their own agreements as to the inheritance of residential yards and fields by allocating them to women, is acknowledged by Molepolole residents. When asked if families make such arrangements, the members of Dikoloing ward commented that 'due to modernisation it happens a lot'. A young woman from Lekgwapheng ward volunteered the information that her aunt had inherited the family yard because the family members agreed that this should be so and wrote letters to KLB agreeing to this. In Ntlooengwae ward, the headman explained that in his view the reason why women are appearing on land certificates today is because 'when one of the siblings looks after the other siblings or parents the plot will be transferred to the person who was looking after other family members'. This kind of caregiving was taken for granted in the past and was not generally recognised as a ground for transmission of property. However, now that reliance on caregiving and support is placed on a smaller circle of family members such activities have gained a prominence and recognition that was unacknowledged in times gone by.

Members of KLB also acknowledged caregiving as a factor that may be taken into account in allocating property, along with considerations of poor economic resources. For example, a member of the KSLB is the eldest child in a family with eight children including six girls and two boys. He explained that in his family he and his siblings 'have given our other's house in Tshosa ward to our younger sister. This is because she is still young and doesn't have a lot of money'. It turns out that this sister is not the youngest child in the family. Of the four sisters who come after him, one is a nurse, one is an engineer who trained in the UK, one is a civil engineer, and the fourth sister is working for the Land Board. They are all married. Then comes the sister who is not married and who is working in a mining town, Jwaneng, 'in a very simple job in one of the shops'. The youngest child is 'a sister, [who] is studying information technology at the University of Botswana and will be graduating this year (2010)'. In reaching their decision the family did not give the plot to their youngest sister 'because she will be able to pursue a good living' whereas the other 'poor sister is not married and not getting a lot of money'. Such reallocation of resources is in keeping with the observations made by members of Ntlooengwae ward, who observed that in reaching these decisions on inheritance, the wealth and status of siblings may play an important role so that 'the poorest sibling who may be unemployed will be given the yard because the other siblings are in work and have already acquired other plots'.

From another perspective, enhanced education, as well as an increase in informal and formal sector employment, has enabled women to gain access to resources that not only enable them to support their parents but to provide for economic investment in the household.[47] With these developments there has been a shift in attitudes towards women. As one male land board member commented in 2010:

> as the country develops more women have access to resources. Our mentality was initially that a woman belongs in the kitchen. That view has now changed. We recognise that women have contributed to the economy, not just as child minders, and that women are getting access to jobs that were predominantly male in the past.

This is recognised by local headmen on the ground. As the headman for Ntlooengwae ward commented, another reason why women are featuring on land certificates today may be due to the fact that 'the yard was developed by that particular person and having invested a lot in that plot the certificate will be transferred to the person who developed the plot'. This was the case with Radipati's daughter, Goitsemang, in the 1980s. Although no formal land certificate was involved, Mosotho kgotla members supported Goitsemang against her brother David's attempts to take control of the yard

---

47 See Griffiths, 'Delivering Justice', 243–4.

because of the financial investment she had made in it. This is possible according to the senior adjudication officer of Kweneng Land Board (a woman), because more women today are more educated and 'have the ability to hold their own money' and to 'stand on their own'. This has come about 'because of human rights'[48] and a situation where some women are less reliant on men for access to economic resources including money. This has given rise to a situation where, according to a female member of KLB, women 'go ahead in applying for land [because they have no husband to depend on]'. According to her 'Batswana women have children before marriage. Then they think of having their own place. They don't want to stay in the family home [because this may cause problems and disputes]'.

Re-evaluating personhood: the differential status of women in family networks

What emerges is a shift in the way in which domestic labour and caregiving, which was formerly taken for granted, as part of a woman's role within the family and household to which she belongs, is viewed. For it is clear that such work has been subject to re-evaluation by some families, allowing for a degree of recognition that was not present in the past. At the same time, however, there is also a growing recognition of the economic power of women, through enhanced education and formal and informal sector employment that has enabled them to accumulate resources to acquire and develop land. These are women to whom I have referred to in earlier publications as 'Can Do Women'.[49] Such women may be unmarried women acting on their own account and that of their children, or they may represent those who have made a financial investment in the expansion and refurbishment of the natal family household and yard. Such an example is provided by Radipati's eldest daughter, Goitsemang, whose financial investment in the family compound won her the support of Mosotho kgotla members who declined to support her brother David when he sought to remove her from the premises to take control of the yard.

These differing forms of access to and control over land, revealed through approaches taken to inheritance on the ground, highlight diverging family profiles and the effects of social stratification on resources. Elsewhere, I have written at length about the way in which social networks continue to

---

48 This is not just in relation to formal government policies (including legal ones) but is also evident at a more local level where attitudes expressed by residents of Molepolole and officials serving them reveal a growing recognition of women's legitimate claims to family property, including land. This has been brought about in part by the work of NGOs like Ditshwanelo (Centre for Human Rights) who have run workshops on this subject throughout the country, as well as the work of Emang Basadi (Stand Up Women).
49 Griffiths, 'Delivering Justice', 243.

play an important role in facilitating access and control over land, through an extended account of the life histories of the members of the Makokwe and Radipati family. It is not possible to replicate these histories here,[50] but they demonstrate that access to resources gives rise to 'class' dimensions, created out of a constellation of factors that contribute to the accumulation of human/social, as well as economic capital. These factors include education, employment (formal and informal) and the capacity to enhance self-development and to actively pursue opportunities. Thus agency becomes an active feature of personhood that is dependent upon individuals' and families' access to resources.

For women, as for men, their personhood is constructed out of those networks to which they are affiliated, with the limits and constraints on, or opportunities that they provide for development. My research has demonstrated how the members of Radipati's family have acquired a degree of upward social mobility derived from the accumulation of their genealogical histories that have enhanced their access to resources (including land) over generations. In contrast, the members of Makokwe's family have not been so fortunate, for their rural pursuits, engaging in subsistence agriculture and cultivation of livestock, along with insecure and intermittent employment, have consigned them to a lower position within a socially stratified society, where more nucleated family units have, in fact, given rise to more limited forms of support.

Under these circumstances, women's access to and control over land will be dependent upon how their personhood is constructed. This not only involves cultural markers that accompany their progress through the life-cycle, but also, as acknowledged at the beginning of this chapter, how they perceive themselves and are perceived in terms of their place within society. This has implications for the transmission of land including inheritance. For where families have sufficient resources they can engage in the kind of decision-making discussed earlier, allocating land to women where they are caregivers or in need of support, or where they have made financial investments in developing the natal household. Their resource base is such that they have the scope to re-evaluate the contribution of women's work in a more positive manner. However, where families find themselves under constraints and where access to resources is not so accessible, they are much less likely to act in the way. Indeed, lack of resources is much more likely to lead to conflicts and disputes, which according to the members of Lekgwa-pheng ward, result in chiefs working 'overtime to deal with these disputes'. What is apparent is the social inequality that differential access to resources, including land, gives rise. Nonetheless, this chapter has demonstrated that a shift is taking place in the construction of women's personhood, creating

---

50 See Griffiths, 'Re-envisioning the Local'.

space for women's roles to be more positively evaluated, along with greater recognition of their contributions to family life and their worth.

Bibliography

Appell-Warren, Laura P. *'Personhood': An Examination of the History and Use of a Concept in the Anthropological Literature*. A Thesis Presented to the Faculty of the Graduate School of Education of Harvard University in Partial Fulfillment of the Requirements for the Degree of Doctor of Education, (Ann Arbor, ProQuest Dissertations Publishing, UNI Number: 3271672, 2007).

Biehl, Joao, Byron Good and Arthur Kleinman (eds.). *Subjectivity: Ethnographic Investigations*. Berkeley: University of California Press, 2007.

Cohen, Anthony P. *Self Consciousness: An Alternative Anthropology of Identity*. London: Routledge, 1994.

Epstein, Arnold Leonard. *Ethos and Identity: Three Studies in Ethnicity*. London: Tavistock, 1978.

Fortes, Meyer. 'The Concept of the Person.' In *Religion, Morality and the Person: Essays on Tallensi Religion*, edited by Jack Goody, 247–86. New York: Cambridge University Press, 1987.

Geertz, Clifford. 'From the Native's Point of View: On the Nature of Anthropological Understanding.' In *Culture Theory: Essays on Mind, Self and Emotion*, edited by Richard A. Shweder and Robert A. Levine, 123–36. New York: Cambridge University Press, 1984.

Government of Botswana. *Botswana Demographic Survey 2006*. Gaborone: Central Statistics Office, Government of Botswana, 2006.

Griffiths, Anne. *In the Shadow of Marriage: Gender and Justice in an African Community*. Chicago: University of Chicago Press, 1997.

Griffiths, Anne. 'Delivering Justice: The Changing Gendered Dynamics of Land Tenure in Botswana.' In Special Issue on International Development Interventions, *Journal of Legal Pluralism and Unofficial Law* 63 (2011), 231–62.

Griffiths, Anne. 'Managing Expectations: Negotiating Succession under Plural Legal Orders in Botswana.' In *Managing Family Justice in Diverse Societies*, edited by Mavis Maclean and John Eekelaar, 221–46. Oxford: Hart Publishing, 2012.

Griffiths, Anne. 'Re-envisioning the Local: Spatiality, Land and Law in Botswana,' *International Journal of Law in Context* 9:2 (2013), 213–38.

Griffiths, Anne. 'Engaging with the Global: Perspectives on Land from Botswana'. In *Framing the Global: Entry Points for Research*, edited by Hilary Kahn, 112–36. Bloomington: Indiana University Press, 2014.

Jacobson-Widding, Anita. 'The Shadow as an Expression of Personhood.' In *Personhood and Agency: The Experience of Self and Other in African Cultures*, edited by Michael Jackson and Ivan Karp, 3–58. Washington and Stockholm: Smithsonian Institution Press and Almquist and Wiksell International, 1990.

Kalabamu, Faustin Tirwirukwa. *Changing Gender and Institutional Roles in Self-Help Housing in Botswana: The Case of Lobatse*. Lesotho: The Institute of Southern African Studies, 2003.

Kalabamu, Faustin Tirwirukwa. 'Towards Egalitarian Inheritance Rights in Botswana: The Case of Tlokweng,' *Development Southern Africa* 26:2 (2009), 209–23.

Kweneng District Development Plan (KDDB6) 2003–2009. Kweneng District Council, Kweneng District Development Committee, Ministry of Local Government, Government of Botswana, 2003.

Mauss, Marcel. 'A Category of the Human Mind: The Notion of Person; the Notion of Self,' (1938) translated by W.E. Halls. In *The Category of the Person: Anthropology, Philosophy, History,* edited by Michael Carrithers, Steven Collins and Steven Lukes, 1–25. Cambridge: Cambridge University Press, 1985.

Middleton, John. 'The Concept of the Person among the Lugbara of Uganda.' In *La Notion de Personne en Afrique Noire,* edited by Germaine Dieterlen, 492–506. Paris: Edition du Centre National de la Recherche, 1973.

Ortner, Sherry B. 'Subjectivity and Cultural Critique.' *Anthropological Theory* 5:1 (2005), 31–52.

Reynolds Whyte, Susan. 'The Widows Dream: Sex and Death in Western Kenya.' In *Personhood and Agency: The Experience of Self and Other in African Cultures,* Papers presented at a Symposium of African Folk Models and Their Applications, held at Uppsala University, August 23–30, edited by Michael Jackson and Ivan Karp, 95–114. Washington DC: Smithsonian Institution Press, 1990.

Ruzvidzo, Thokozile and Hanna N. Tiagha, 'The African Gender Development Index.' In *Gender Instruments in Africa: Critical Perspectives, Future Strategies,* edited by Christi van der Westhuizen, 22–47. Pretoria: Institute for Global Dialogue, 2005.

Schapera, Isaac. *Migrant Labour and Tribal Life: a Study of the Condition of the Bechuanaland Protectorate.* London: Oxford University Press. 1947.

Snyder, Katherine A. 'Modern Cows and Exotic Trees: Identity, Personhood and Exchange among the Iraqw of Tanzania,' *Ethnology* 41:2 (2002), 155–73.

Statutes

Deeds Registry Act [Cap 33:02]
Customary Law (Application and Ascertainment) Act (No.51 of 1969)

Statutory regulations

The Tribal Land (Amendment of Schedule Order), 18 March 2011

Chapter 11

The breadwinner, the homemaker and the worker/carer
New stereotypes for old?

Jane Mair

Outdated stereotypes

> The ideal worker, who is available to work long hours [...] is dependent on a domestic norm, that is, a full-time carer engaged in family work of household and childcare [...][1]

Once upon a time, not so long ago, the rules were clear in both the market and the family: men went to work and women stayed at home, particularly when the men became husbands and fathers and the women became wives and mothers.[2] In the 1970s[3] and before, there was a dominant model of the family built on marriage between a stereotypical breadwinner and homemaker: the former invariably male and the latter female. During marriage the wife cared for the family, in return she was financially supported by her husband and on divorce her expectation was that this support would continue in the form of ex-spousal maintenance.[4] This gendered model from family law was reflected in employment law where men were full-time workers, earning a family wage and women, if they worked at all, did so for 'pin money' and often part time. The ideal employee was full time, permanent and male and the ideal wife was committed to caring for her family.

---

1 Sara Charlesworth, 'Managing Work and Family in the "Shadow" of Anti-discrimination Law' in Jill Murray (ed.), *Work, Family and the Law, Special Edition Law in Context* 23:1 (2005), 88 at 95.
2 This is a model which is explored in detail in Jane Lewis, 'The Decline of the Male Breadwinner Model: Implications for Work and Care,' *Social Politics* 8:2 (2001), 152.
3 The 1970s can be identified as a key point for many reasons but in the context of this chapter, which focuses particularly on Scotland and more broadly the UK, the 1970s saw the introduction of sex discrimination legislation and the beginning of a period of significant change in adult family law, identified in particular with a move towards no-fault divorce.
4 The historical background of the legal obligations in Scotland is explored by the Scottish Law Commission in *Aliment and Financial Provision*, Memorandum No 22, Vol. 1 (Edinburgh, 1976). The position in England is explored in John Eekelaar and Mavis Maclean, *Maintenance after Divorce* (Oxford: Clarendon Press, 1986), chapter 1.

Recent decades have witnessed significant change in both work and family and these stereotypes and models now seem out of date and of little relevance. Over the past 30 years or so, both family law and employment law have been transformed through legislation and an extensive policy agenda, underpinned by shared objectives of challenging stereotypes, eliminating discrimination and facilitating both men and women equally in fulfilling roles in paid employment and parenting. Equality legislation outlaws different treatment and different pay for male and female workers[5] and family law favours gender-neutral language; treating husbands and wives as spouses and mothers and fathers as parents. Not only have the old-fashioned, gendered distinctions been questioned but the very split between work and family has been challenged. Men and women, fathers and mothers, are increasingly encouraged to adopt interchangeable roles as employees and parents and expected to move easily between the spheres of workplace and home.

It is not only the shape of these particular models, both familial and workplace, which has shifted but also the discourse within which these models were previously understood; from an assumption of conformity and compliance to an expectation of diversity.[6] Rather than family law made to fit one ideal type of family, family law is now presented as meeting the needs of a range of families. In employment law too, while the full time, permanent employee remains the gold standard, there are statutory moves towards inclusion in terms of more flexible workers and working relationships and intellectual attempts to construct new legal frameworks, capable of encompassing an increasingly diverse workforce.[7] Seemingly simple norms of male breadwinner and female homemaker have been swept away by multiple narratives and complex discourses around flexibility; capabilities; agency;[8] fatherhood and fathering;[9] parenting, caring and an ethic of care.[10]

---

5 Gender equality legislation in the UK stems from the Equal Pay Act 1970 and the Sex Discrimination Act 1975. The law is currently to be found in the Equality Act 2010.
6 A process made explicit in the family context in Michele Barrett and Mary McIntosh, *The Anti-social Family* (London: Verso, 1982).
7 See e.g., Mark Freedland, 'From the Contract of Employment to the Personal Work Nexus,' *Industrial Law Journal* 35:1 (2006), 1.
8 See e.g. Barbara Hobson, Ann-Zofie Duvander and Karin Hallden, 'Men and Women's Agency and Capabilities to Create a Work Life Balance in Diverse and Changing Institutional Contexts', in *Children, Changing Families and Welfare States*, ed. Jane Lewis (Cheltenham: Edward Elgar, 2006), chapter 13.
9 See in particular the work of Richard Collier, 'A Hard Time to Be a Father? Reassessing the Relationship between Law, Policy and Family (Practices),' *Journal of Law and Society* 28:4 (2001), 520.
10 Ideas associated in particular with the work of Carol Gilligan, *In a Different Voice: Psychological Theory and Women's Development* (Cambridge, MA: Harvard University Press, 1982); Joan C. Tronto, *Moral Boundaries: A Political Argument for an Ethic of Care* (New York: Routledge, 1993).

Transcending the dichotomies

> The dichotomization of market and family pervades our thinking, our language and our culture. It limits and impoverishes the ways we experience our affective and productive lives. The possibilities we can imagine for restructuring our shared existence, and the manner in which we attempt change.[11]

Much of the legal policy and reforms around the intersection of work and family, which has developed over recent decades, has its roots in feminist theory and debate and stems in particular from a familiar feminist device of the dichotomy; used to expose, explain and challenge constructed and constricting stereotypes. The public/private dichotomy in particular has been instrumental in challenging the model of male breadwinner and female homemaker in family life and family law: highlighting the split – real and ideological – between the public existence of the husband and the private sphere of the wife.[12]

A classic example of such feminist analysis was Olsen's 1983 critique of the family and the market.[13] In her model, dichotomies operated in conjunction with a series of 'complex dualisms',[14] creating not only a separation of spheres, such as the market and the family, but also associating one with men and masculine values and the other with women and femininity. For so long as our vision remained constrained by the market/family dichotomy, the potential for legal reform would be limited. According to Olsen's classification, the only options were to make the market more like the market or make the market more like the family and, on the other side of the balance, make the family more like the family or make the family more like the market. Her optimism for future transformation lay in the possibility of transcending the dichotomy and its associated dualisms. By so doing, not only could individuals, male or female, move freely between market and family but attributes associated with the feminine family would cease to be undervalued or overlooked in comparison to the higher value accorded to the characteristics of the male market.

---

11 Frances E Olsen, 'The Family and the Market: A Study of Ideology and Legal Reform,' *Harvard Law Review* 96:7 (1983), 1497.
12 See e.g. Katherine O'Donovan, *Sexual Divisions in Law* (Weidenfeld & Nicolson, 1985), chapter 1. See too Ruth Gavison, 'Feminism and the public/private distinction,' *Stanford Law Review* 45:1 (1992), 1.
13 Olsen, 'The Family and the Market: A Study of Ideology and Legal Reform'.
14 Ibid. 1575.

Olsen's vision of transcending dichotomies, a family law version of 'third way' thinking,[15] has resonance with many of the legal changes that have taken place since, both within the market – employment law – and within the family. In recent decades, employment law has developed a whole new dimension of rights, aimed at accommodating individuals who have both professional and family responsibilities and family law has been reformed to reflect the workplace equality of men and women and their shared responsibility for care. Breadwinners and homemakers have been reconstructed as 'earner-carers'[16] and the divided sectors of market and family have been reconstituted as an integrated space for work/life balance. A model has developed which is built not only on gender equality but also on integration of work and family commitments, as a consequence of which, the divisions between market and family, if not yet transcended, have at least been blurred.

Modern workplaces and modern families

Similar changes have occurred throughout Europe although at different speeds, with varying impact and to some extent grounded in cultural and social context.[17] Situated within a broad European background, the following discussion will focus on UK employment law and policy and Scots family law.[18]

Employment law and the accommodation of family

Since the 1970s, there have been significant changes in law and policy affecting the employment of women and the provision of family related

---

15 Anthony Giddens, *The Third Way* (Cambridge: Polity, 1998): for further discussion of third way thinking in this context see, Selma Sevenhuijsen, 'A Third Way? Moralities, Ethics and Families: An Approach through the Ethic of Care,' in *Analysing Families: Morality and rationality in policy and practice*, eds. Alan Carling, Simon Duncan and Rosalind Edwards (London: Routledge, 2002), 129–44.
16 Michelle Weldon-Johns, 'From Modern Workplaces to Modern Families – Re-envisioning the Work–family Conflict,' *Journal of Social Welfare and Family Law* 37:4 (2015), 397–8.
17 See e.g. European Foundation for the Improvement of Living and Working Conditions, *The Second European Quality of Life Survey: Overview* (Luxembourg: Publications Office of the European Union, 2009): www.eurofound.europa.eu/sites/default/files/ef_publication/field_ef_document/ef0902en_7.pdf; Claudia Geist, 'The Welfare State and the Home: Regime Differences in the Domestic Division of Labour,' *European Sociological Review* 21:1 (2005), 23.
18 Employment law and policy in Scotland is principally regulated by the Westminster Parliament and therefore it is consistent throughout the UK whereas family law is a matter devolved to the Scottish Parliament and it is significantly different from English law, particularly in respect of financial provision on divorce which is the main focus in this chapter.

rights. Initially the focus was on formal equality, required by the Sex Discrimination Act 1975 and the Equal Pay Act 1970. Men and women were to be treated equally in work except where the special status of pregnancy and maternity demanded accommodation of difference in order to achieve substantive equality.[19] A second phase was characterised by enhanced protection of pregnancy and maternity, led by the jurisprudence of the European Court of Justice[20] and detailed in the European Pregnant Workers' Directive.[21] While these developments strengthened legal protection for individual workers, they came at a price and were seen, at least from the UK perspective, as a burden on employers.[22] Pregnant employees were a fact of life and they had to be accommodated but such accommodation was perceived as a problem for business.[23] A third phase was marked by the coming into power of New Labour in 1997, when maternity rights were rebranded as family-friendly policies.[24] Family-friendly working and work–life balance:[25] the language itself signalled a break with the old and the move to a new message that these rights were not just for mothers. The burdens and the benefits were more evenly spread, and new policies were presented with a positive spin. Facilitating the accommodation of work and family could bring benefits for all; increased gender equality in paid work and in parenting, better motivated and more productive employees, higher rates of employment and lower welfare costs.

The work and family agenda has continued to develop through various consultations, reforms and regulations, most recently in the form of *Modern Workplaces*.[26] While gender-specific maternity and paternity rights continue to exist, they have now been overlaid by a new statutory framework for shared parental leave which emphasises individual choice, family flexibility

---

19 Sex Discrimination Act 1975, s. 2(2); Equality Act 2010, s. 13(6).
20 *Dekker v Stichting Vormingscentrum voor Jonge Volwasenen Plus* [1990] ECR I-3941; *Webb v EMO Air Cargo (UK) Ltd* [1993] 1 CMLR 259; *Tele Danmark A/S v Handels-og Kontorfunktionaerernes Forbund I Danmark* [2001] ECR I-6993.
21 Directive 92/85/EC.
22 See e.g. Nicole Busby, 'Divisions of Labour: Maternity Protection in Europe,' *The Journal of Social Welfare and Family* 22:3 (2000), 277.
23 Jane Mair, 'Maternity Leave: Improved and Simplified?' *Modern Law Review* 63 (2000), 877.
24 *Fairness at Work*, White Paper, Cm 3968, 1998, chapter 5. Available at webarchive.nationalarchives.gov.uk/+/www.berr.gov.uk/files/file24436.pdf (accessed 14 March 2016).
25 A range of measures relating to paternity leave, parental leave and flexible working were introduced over time by various statutory provisions including the Maternity and Parental Leave etc Regulations 1999; Flexible Working (Eligibility, Complaints and Remedies) Regulations 2002; Paternity and Adoption Leave Regulations 2002.
26 The various stages of the government's *Modern Workplaces Consultation* are available at www.gov.uk/government/consultations/consultation-on-modern-workplaces (accessed 14 March 2016).

and co-parenting.²⁷ This shift in UK law and policy is situated within a broader EU context. In Europe the recognition of family responsibilities was initially constructed within the context of sex equality;²⁸ it developed through special rights for pregnant workers²⁹ and provision for parental leave³⁰ and burgeoned into a key policy concern described as the reconciliation of family and professional life.³¹ The challenge is no longer restricted to the individual employer trying to arrange cover for the occasional female employee on maternity leave but it has grown to encompass the social, political and personal imperative to make 'two spheres of life [work and family] mutually compatible'.³² The benefits are no longer presented narrowly in terms of individual employees or their families but the reconciliation of work and family sits at the heart of EU policies for growth and inclusion; a strand of citizenship, central to the achievement of increased employment targets³³ and a key strategy for tackling problems of demographic change.³⁴

Family law and the expectation of work

Family-friendly policies and the work–life agenda have begun to cross the dividing line between market and family, from the side of the workplace, but what of movement in the other direction? While employment law has been changing in order to accommodate the worker/carer, to what extent have these moves been mirrored in family law?

In Scots law there is little legal regulation or judicial commentary on the marriage relationship to give insight into what is expected in terms of spousal roles and so it is to the rules relating to divorce and in particular to property sharing and financial provision that we must look for retrospective comment on marriage. The law on financial provision on divorce was

---

27 Introduced by the Children and Families Act 2014 and effective in respect of babies born on or after 5 April 2015. The detailed framework is set out by the Shared Parental Leave Regulations 2014, SI 2014/3050.
28 E.g. in *Dekker v Stichting Vormingscentrum voor Jonge Volwasenen Plus* [1990] ECR I-3941.
29 Directive 92/85/EC.
30 Parental Leave Directive 96/34/EC, replaced by Directive 2010/18/EU.
31 See e.g., Council of the European Union Conclusions, *Women and the Economy: Reconciliation of work and family life as a precondition for equal participation in the labour market*, 2 December 2011, 17816/11 SOC 1050. Available at http://ec.europa.eu/justice/gender-equality/files/concil_conlusion_pl2011_en.pdf (accessed 28 July 2016).
32 Ibid. 6.
33 Commission Communication on Europe 2020, A strategy for smart, sustainable and inclusive growth COM(2010) 2020 final, Brussels, 3.3.2010: http://eur-lex.europa.eu/LexUriServ/LexUriServ.do?uri=COM:2010:2020:FIN:EN:PDF: accessed 28 July 2016.
34 See European Commission Roadmap, *New start to address the challenges of work–life balance faced by working families*, August 2015. Available at http://ec.europa.eu/smart-regulation/roadmaps/docs/2015_just_012_new_initiative_replacing_maternity_leave_directive_en.pdf (accessed 14 March 2016).

reformed in 1985 and at that time a key objective was to address criticisms of the previous system with its over-reliance on continuing maintenance for ex-wives. The Family Law (Scotland) Act 1985 (FLSA 1985) represented a fresh approach based on a more modern model which saw marriage as an equal partnership and, in various ways, reflected the already, or anticipated, changing employment and social position of women and the expected participation of men in care.

The 1985 Act is based on five statutory principles set out in section 9: that the property of the couple accumulated during the marriage should be shared fairly on divorce;[35] that any economic advantage obtained as a result of contributions of the other spouse or any economic disadvantage suffered as a result of contributions made to the other spouse, or the family, should be balanced on divorce;[36] that the ongoing burden of childcare in respect of children under the age of 16 should be shared fairly;[37] that a spouse who has been substantially dependent on the other during marriage may be given a period of readjustment subject to a maximum of three years;[38] and that provision can be made for the relief of severe financial hardship arising from the divorce.[39]

The preferred outcome on divorce is that there should be a clean financial break between the parties, ideally secured by means of equal sharing of the matrimonial property (first principle). The second principle, while expressed in neutral terms, is intended to recognise the potential for disadvantage on divorce which might result where one spouse sacrifices paid employment in favour of providing unpaid domestic care.[40] The third principle reinforces the shared responsibilities of both parents and is intended to take account of the indirect costs of childcare which are likely to fall on the parent with future primary care of the children. The fourth principle reflects and encourages the interaction of work and family which is found in employment law: even where one spouse has been out of paid employment for a while there is an expectation that he or she will return to it as quickly as possible, and any additional support during that period of readjustment will be subject to a maximum of three years. The fifth principle is intended as a last resort, to be used only rarely, usually where there is insufficient matrimonial property to share and where readjustment to independent life is not otherwise attainable.

---

35 FLSA 1985, s. 9(1)(a): 'the first principle'.
36 Ibid. s. 9(1)(b): 'the second principle'.
37 Ibid. s. 9(1)(c): 'the third principle'.
38 Ibid. s. 9(1)(d): 'the fourth principle'.
39 Ibid. s. 9(1)(e): 'the fifth principle'.
40 Recognition of non-financial contributions is specifically provided in s. 9(2).

The range of principles reflects the diversity of relationships; it is sufficiently broad to take account of different models of married life. The starting point for fair sharing of matrimonial property[41] is that it should be shared equally unless there are special circumstances leading to some other method of division being fair.[42] Special circumstances specifically exclude earned income as the source of money used to acquire matrimonial property and to that extent any higher claim of the breadwinner is ignored.[43] The value of childcare and other domestic services, such as housework, is specifically acknowledged in terms of the second principle[44] with the express inclusion of non-financial contributions and in the third principle which makes provision for sharing the continuing economic burden of childcare,[45] as distinct from financial provision or maintenance owed direct to the children. The fourth principle, which provides for a period of readjustment for a spouse who has been substantially dependent during marriage on the other, seems to have in mind specifically the parent who has adjusted his or her paid employment during marriage in order to undertake domestic care. Any provision for readjustment under this principle is subject to a maximum of three years and in deciding what award to make, if any, the court is directed to consider a range of factors including the age and earning capacity of the claimant and any intention to undertake a course of education or training.[46]

While the five principles reflect a range of different types of marriage and a variety of spousal roles, there is an underpinning preference for a clean break type of settlement and this can be seen particularly in the orders which the court may make. Section 8 highlights flexibility and diversity in that it provides for capital sum payment, property transfer, pension sharing and periodical allowance but the use of periodical allowance is clearly limited. An order for periodical allowance may be made only where justified by the third, fourth or fifth principles and even then, only where the other orders would be insufficient or inappropriate.[47] While there is flexibility for couples to arrange their spousal roles as they wish, there is a clear expectation that, on divorce, they should be able to readjust, if necessary, to independence and economic self-sufficiency.

---

41 FLSA 1985, s. 9(1)(a).
42 Ibid. s. 10(1).
43 Ibid. s. 10(6).
44 Ibid. s. 9(1)(b) and (2).
45 Ibid. s. 9(1)(c).
46 Ibid. s. 11(4).
47 Ibid. s. 13(2).

Work/family balance and the place of care

> We need to create a new system of parental leave that works for modern lives and respects a family's right to choose how to care for their child.[48]

In challenging the split between public and private and seeking to transcend the dichotomy between market and family, there were linked objectives. One was to move beyond the gendered nature of both paid employment and family care and to facilitate greater choice and easier movement between the two so that individual men and women could be both public employees and private family members. This is an objective made explicit in much of the policy underpinning the move from maternity rights through family-friendly reforms to the vision of a modern workplace. Facilitated by a range of flexible employment rights, and supported by the domestic involvement and shared care-giving of a partner, employees should be able to combine work and family and move successfully and seamlessly between them. Belief in this framework is clearly built into the family law framework for financial provision on divorce. Equality in the market will be best achieved when equality in the family is in place and fairness on divorce relies on the market working as expected. There is, however, growing frustration with the pace of change in terms of both paid work and family care. The patterns which emerge, both from research and from experience, remain clearly gendered.[49]

A second anticipated effect of moving beyond the market/family dichotomy was the equalisation of values and commodities associated with each: in this specific context, the equal recognition of paid work and unpaid care. Work/life agenda laws and policies, however, continue to attract criticism for their narrow work-centric perspective and their undervaluation of care. This one-sided perspective is clear in EU policy and highlighted, for example, in a Resolution of the European Parliament from 2009 where, with reference to the fact that women with dependent children had only a 62 percent employment rate, it was commented that, 'it is intolerable to allow the resources in question [i.e. mothers] and their potential to go to

---

48 *Modern Workplaces Consultation – Government Response on Flexible Parental Leave, to Modern Workplaces Consultation*, November 2012, Foreword available at www.gov.uk/government/uploads/system/uploads/attachment_data/file/82969/12-1267-modern-workplaces-response-flexible-parental-leave.pdf (accessed 14 March 2016).
49 See e.g., European Foundation for the Improvement of Living and Working Conditions, *Third European Quality of Life Survey – Quality of life in Europe: Families in the economic crisis* (Luxembourg Publications Office of the European Union, 2014). Available at www.eurofound.europa.eu/sites/default/files/ef_publication/field_ef_document/ef1389en.pdf (accessed 14 March 2016).

waste'.⁵⁰ Similar concerns have been raised in the UK, sparked for example by plans of the previous Coalition government to introduce improved childcare vouchers for dual-earning couples while overlooking parents who stayed at home.⁵¹ The focus to date has been principally on the rights of parents to work but increasingly it is argued that the right to work should be accompanied by a right to care.⁵²

That the workplace should struggle to accommodate domestic responsibilities and family life is, perhaps, only to be expected. Employment and employers are being asked to respect obligations and accommodate patterns of behaviour which are, at best, only indirectly linked to their primary concern for productivity and profit. The traditional and accepted site of care is, however, within the family and it is there, in family law, that we might expect to find evidence of much greater understanding of caring roles and the value of care. As Herring has highlighted, '[c]are is at the centre of family life'.⁵³ To what extent, however, is the centrality of care and its value to family life reflected in financial provision on divorce? Or, in an attempt to move away from gendered roles in family law, has care become secondary to paid employment and the full time carer-spouse become less valued than the spouse who combines family care with paid employment? The statutory framework for financial provision on divorce reflects in several ways the expectation of gender equality in the workplace and the possibility of relatively easy movement between paid employment and family based support. As with the detailed provisions of employment law, however, the test lies in how they work in practice.

A practical challenge

The *Second European Quality of Life Survey: Family life and work*⁵⁴ found that 'Europeans are more dissatisfied with the amount of time they spend with their family than with the amount of time spent at work, family life being more adapted to employment requirements than work arrangements are to family life'. Undoubtedly there have been significant improvements in

---

50 European Parliament resolution of 3 February 2009 on non-discrimination based on sex and intergenerational solidarity (2008/2118 (INI).
51 Available at www.telegraph.co.uk/news/politics/9959640/Nick-Clegg-denies-Coalition-is-penalising-stay-at-home-mothers.html (accessed 14 March 2016).
52 An idea developed by Nicole Busby in *A Right to Care? Unpaid Work in European Employment Law* (Oxford: Oxford University Press, 2011).
53 Jonathan Herring, *Caring and the Law* (Oxford: Hart, 2013), 187.
54 European Foundation for the Improvement of Living and Working Conditions, *The Second European Quality of Life Survey: Overview* (Luxembourg: Publications Office of the European Union, 2009), ch 3. Available at www.eurofound.europa.eu/sites/default/files/ef_publication/field_ef_document/ef0902en_7.pdf (accessed 14 March 2016).

family related employment rights but the real test is not how extensive or innovative they sound but how they work in practice. No matter how reasonable and generous the rights may appear, they are only likely to be of long term benefit if they accommodate some at least of the practical challenges of real, everyday family life.

'Child-care is, of course, a longer term business than childbirth'[55] and, in practice, caring for children will continue long after the specific rights to maternity, paternity and parental leave have been exhausted. The Scottish principles for financial provision on divorce appear to accommodate the ongoing nature of childcare, particularly in the second principle which provides for recognition of career disadvantage and the third principle which requires the future sharing of the burden of childcare. In practice, however, their effectiveness may be limited. The disadvantage of a career break may not be immediately obvious but is likely to emerge and increase over time. Section 11(2) of the Family Law (Scotland) Act 1985 states that disadvantage must have been suffered either before or during the marriage but, as interpreted in *Dougan v Dougan*,[56] there are significant limitations if the court takes the view that 'future loss [...] is imponderable'.[57] The court in this case had the benefit of clear and detailed figures showing the loss of earnings likely to be suffered by the woman because of, first, a change of position to a lower grade in order to secure a change of workplace location to bring her closer to her future husband, and second, a move to part time work in order to care for her daughter. The mother in this case had suffered little disadvantage during the marriage itself but the decisions she made during that time were likely to lead to long term disadvantage. This was a very short marriage where in fact the child was born after the couple had separated and the father, although paying child support, was in no other way involved with the care or upbringing of the child. 'The issue of future loss [arose] sharply in this case because the marriage was a short one'[58] but the sheriff felt constrained by the terms of the Act and unable to take into account the future loss, although a capital sum payment was ordered in respect of her past disadvantage.

If in fact the legislation does not permit the court to take account of ongoing or future disadvantage, this is a major limitation and fails to take realistic account of the impact of an earlier career choice. This was recognised by another sheriff in a case of the same year, *Cahill v Cahill*[59] where,

---

55 Elizabeth M. Meehan, *Women's Rights at Work: Campaigns and Policy in Britain and the United States* (London: Macmillan, 1985), 187.
56 1998 SLT (Sh Ct) 27.
57 Ibid. 30.
58 Ibid.
59 1998 SLT (Sh Ct) 96.

doubting the approach in *Dougan*, he commented that the provision of the Act which defines disadvantage:[60]

> specifically refers to earning capacity and if earning capacity becomes disadvantaged in the course of marriage I have difficulty in seeing how that loss can be evaluated except by reference to an extended period of time part of which may be after the dissolution of the marriage.[61]

If disadvantage by giving up employment or moving to part time working is to be taken into account, then it has to be done in a way which realistically reflects the likely pattern of career progression. The impact of childcare on earning potential is likely to continue long after the point of childbirth or the end of parental leave entitlement.

Who cares?

For the work and family agenda to achieve its full potential, change is required not only in the workplace but also in the family: there needs to be a 'de-gendering of care'.[62] One of the apparent benefits of modern parental or family based rights as opposed to earlier focus on maternity rights is that they challenge an entrenched view that childcare is the responsibility of the mother. While there have undoubtedly been changes in family life in recent decades, they may, however, be less marked than anticipated. A recent report prepared for the European Commission into *The Role of Men in Gender Equality*[63] found evidence of 'a remarkable change in men's participation in care' but only 'in certain parts of Europe'[64] and even then, the position remained that 'men with young children continue to have higher employment rates compared to those without children, while for women the opposite holds'.[65] There are differences across Europe and the reasons and motivations are complex but the evidence is clear that family roles and family responsibilities remain gendered.

---

60 FLSA 1985, s. 9(2).
61 1998 SLT (Sh Ct) 96 at 99.
62 Ruth Rubio-Marin, 'The (Dis)establishment of Gender: Care and Gender Roles in the Family as a Constitutional Matter,' *International Journal of Constitutional Law* 13:4 (2015) 787, at 806.
63 *The Role of Men in Gender Equality – European strategies and insights*; prepared for European Commission, DG Justice – Unit D2 Gender equality Contract ref no VC/2010/0592, (Luxembourg: Publications Office of the European Union, 2013). Available at http://ec.europa.eu/justice/genderequality/files/gender_pay_gap/130424_final_report_role_of_men_en.pdf (accessed 14 March 2016).
64 Ibid. 7.
65 Ibid. 5.

A recent study in Scotland of separation agreements showed that, of those couples who made arrangements for post-separation childcare, 90 percent agreed that residence of the children would be with the mother.[66] To some extent in contradiction of the high media and policy profile of shared parenting, and despite employment policy which seeks to promote shared roles, practical responsibility in many cases appears to remain with mothers. There is a danger as employment rights expand and improve, and as policy becomes more ambitious, of assuming that work and family balance is within the reach of many employees. The effectiveness of employment law and policy must, however, be assessed realistically against the background of family life, which may not be as equal as we sometimes assume. While employment law promotes the model of shared parental leave and family law subscribes to shared parenting, it is important that each remains aware of what is happening in practice.

The value of care?

> Domestic labour is never abstracted, never quantified [...][67]

The second principle of the Family Law (Scotland) Act 1985, which enables balancing of advantage and disadvantage and which expressly 'includes indirect and non-financial contributions [...] in particular, any such contribution made by looking after the family home or caring for the family',[68] appears ideally suited to reflect the central role of domestic care within the family and to compensate for economic disadvantage which might result for those who have restricted their paid work in order to care for their family. In general, this principle has had relatively little effect, one reason being that the court is directed to take into account the extent to which any such disadvantage has already been balanced by sharing of the matrimonial property or otherwise. This 'otherwise' is often interpreted as referring to the wife's maintenance during the relationship. The courts are rarely willing to engage in a process of financial accounting but instead fall back on expectations of the standard roles of breadwinner and homemaker.

While the 1985 Act is sometimes criticised for being overly prescriptive, it is clear in many of the decisions that, within the principles, there remains considerable scope for judicial discretion and the court's impression of the

---

66 Mair, Wasoff and Mackay, *All Settled?*, 2013, www.crfr.ac.uk/assets/MinutesofAgreement 20131.pdf.
67 Bonnie Fox, 'Women's Double Work Day: Twentieth-century Changes in the Reproduction of Daily Life,' in *Hidden in the Household: Women's Domestic Labour under Capitalism*, ed. Bonnie Fox (Ontario: The Women's Press, 1980), 184.
68 FLSA 1985, s. 9(2).

parties and the extent to which they have fulfilled their expected roles can be significant. In *Adams v Adams*,[69] while the wife (pursuer) argued that her husband (defender) had been able to further his career whereas she had been prejudiced by caring for the children, it was stressed by the court that:

> in all the years during which they lived together, the defender contributed more than the pursuer to the household finances and during the periods when she was out of employment [following the births of their children] he supported the family on his own.[70]

In *Wilson v Wilson*,[71] however, the impression of the husband (defender) was that he had taken advantage of the care provided by his wife (pursuer) in order to focus on his business and that the:

> economic advantage derived by the defender through retaining or ploughing back profits in the company had not throughout the marriage been balanced by an economic advantage to the pursuer such as a better lifestyle.[72]

While Mrs Adams' caring contribution was at least matched by her husband's financial contribution and therefore no balancing payment was required, Mrs Wilson was entitled to recognition on divorce for her domestic care, which had not been adequately compensated during their relationship. While it can be misleading to look at these specific issues in isolation from the overall scheme of financial provision, it is notable that the assessment of contributions in these cases is highly impressionistic.

In a few cases, the question of the value of the wife's unpaid domestic care has been considered in relation to 'bought in' care. *Coyle v Coyle*[73] concerned a relatively wealthy couple who had been married for 20 years. Mrs Coyle gave up a successful career with British Caledonian airways and the prospect of significant further opportunities when she got married because her husband did not want her to work. While she ran the house and cared for their three children, her husband worked long and unsocial hours in the family business with the result that his share of the business rose from £44,000 when they married to £619,000 by the date of separation. She sought to argue that her husband had sustained an economic advantage (i.e. the ability to work hard free from family responsibilities) derived

---

69 1997 SLT 144 (OH).
70 Ibid. 148.
71 1999 SLT 249 (OH).
72 Ibid. 254.
73 2004 Fam LR 2 (OH).

from her contributions in terms of domestic care. This was rejected by the court which did not accept that there was any clear identifiable advantage which derived from her identifiable contribution. Instead of calculating the financial value of 20 years of domestic care or attempting to assess the benefit of a well-run family to the ability of the husband to develop his business, the court looked instead to what would have happened if the wife had not taken on the role of homemaker. 'Clearly, if the pursuer had not been available to run the house and care for the children, other help would have had to be employed'.[74] Instead of assessing the cost of this employed help to the husband, the court took the view that if the wife had not been available it would have been because she was pursuing her career which in turn would have allowed her to bring in extra money to the family which could then have been used to pay for care, with the surplus being added to the family finances. In somewhat circular reasoning, the value of care given simply disappeared.

New stereotypes for old

Much of the focus of the work and family agenda has been on facilitating parents and other family members in maintaining and improving their access to employment. From the feminist calls of the 1970s for wages for housework to more recent public dispute about tax free childcare and 'stay at home mums', the issue is the same – childcare and domestic work remain undervalued and often invisible within economic policy and political debate. Working parents may be given short-term concessions at work in order to facilitate their caring responsibilities but long term it is their participation in paid employment which is really valued. Caring, traditionally, has had its place within the family, but as the focus shifts to facilitating participation of both men and women in paid employment throughout the life cycle, there is a risk that care will become increasingly invisible there too. The 1985 Family Law (Scotland) Act favours a clean financial break on divorce with limited scope for ongoing maintenance payments between ex-spouses. This system of family law assumes an employment model of equal opportunities and easy combination of work and care, which for many remains more an aspiration than a reality. Family law assumes that a spouse will have been able to combine work and family or at least be able to re-enter the labour market relatively easily when support within the family is no longer available.

Equal treatment, equal pay and shared parenting are all works 'in progress' and while change is happening, we should be wary of the headlines. It is easy to be impressed by the volume of reform and the extent of provision

---

74 Ibid. 9.

in employment law for family rights and to believe that work-life balance is within reach. Looking only at the statutory framework of financial provision on divorce, it is similarly credible that, within three short years of readjustment, a financially dependent carer will have returned to an independent worker but continuing evidence of the 'motherhood penalty'[75] makes it clear that such a view would be naïve. Moves are afoot to transcend the market/family dichotomy but '[...] care, human interdependence, and reproduction are only slowly and hesitantly coming out of the shadows of private life'[76] and we should remember that challenging divisions and dualisms requires the inclusion and equalisation of both sides, not the domination of only one. Within the narratives of diversity and choice, a new ideal lurks: the outdated characters of male employee and female carer are perhaps being replaced by a new, gender-neutral role model – the worker/carer; the individual with work/life balance; the person who has it all.

Bibliography

Articles and books

Barrett, Michele and Mary McIntosh. *The Anti-social Family*. Verso: London, 1982.
Busby, Nicole. 'Divisions of Labour: Maternity Protection in Europe.' *The Journal of Social Welfare and Family* 22:3 (2000), 277.
Busby, Nicole. *A Right to Care? Unpaid Work in European Employment Law*. (Oxford: Oxford University Press, 2011).
Charlesworth, Sara. 'Managing Work and Family in the "Shadow" of Anti-discrimination Law'. In *Work, Family and the Law*, edited by Jill Murray, *Special Edition, Law in Context* 23:1 (2005), 88 at 95.
Collier, Richard. 'A Hard Time to Be a Father? Reassessing the Relationship between Law, Policy and Family (Practices),' *Journal of Law and Society* 28:4 (2001) 520.
Eekelaar, John and Maclean, Mavis. *Maintenance after Divorce*. Clarendon Press, Oxford, 1986.
Fox, Bonnie. 'Women's Double Work Day: Twentieth-century Changes in the Reproduction of Daily Life.' In *Hidden in the Household: Women's Domestic Labour under Capitalism*, edited by Bonnie Fox. The Women's Press, Ontario, 1980, 184.
Freedland, Mark. 'From the Contract of Employment to the Personal Work Nexus,' *Industrial Law Journal* 35:1 (2006).
Gavison, Ruth. 'Feminism and the public/private distinction,' *Stanford Law Review* 45:1 (1992).
Geist, Claudia. 'The Welfare State and the Home: Regime Differences in the Domestic Division of Labour,' *European Sociological Review* 21:1 (2005), 23.

---

75 See, e.g., the recent TUC analysis: *Women who become mothers before 33 suffer a 15% pay penalty*. Available at www.tuc.org.uk/economic-issues/equality-issues/women-who-become-mothers-33-suffer-15-pay-penalty-says-tuc (accessed 14 March 2016).
76 Rubio-Marin, 'The (Dis)establishment of Gender,' 816.

Giddens, Anthony. *The Third Way*. Cambridge: Polity, 1998.
Gilligan, Carol. *In a Different Voice: Psychological Theory and Women's Development*. Cambridge, MA: Harvard University Press, 1982.
Herring, Jonathan. *Caring and the Law*. Oxford: Hart, 2013.
Hobson, Barbara, Ann-Zofie Duvander and Karin Hallden. 'Men and Women's Agency and Capabilities to Create a Work Life Balance in Diverse and Changing Institutional Contexts.' In *Children, Changing Families and Welfare States*, edited by Jane Lewis. Cheltenham: Edward Elgar, 2006.
Lewis, Jane. 'The Decline of the Male Breadwinner Model: Implications for Work and Care,' *Social Politics* 8:2 (2001).
Mair, Jane. 'Maternity Leave: Improved and Simplified?' *Modern Law Review* 63 (2000), 877.
Meehan, Elizabeth M. *Women's Rights at Work: Campaigns and Policy in Britain and the United States*. London: Macmillan, 1985.
O'Donovan, Katherine. *Sexual Divisions in Law*. Weidenfeld & Nicolson, 1985.
Olsen, Frances E. 'The Family and the Market: A Study of Ideology and Legal Reform,' *Harvard Law Review* 96:7 (1983), 1497.
Rubio-Marin, Ruth. 'The (Dis)establishment of Gender: Care and Gender Roles in the Family as a Constitutional Matter,' *International Journal of Constitutional Law* 13:4 (2015), 787.
Sevenhuijsen, Selma. 'A Third Way? Moralities, Ethics and Families: An Approach through the Ethic of Care.' In *Analysing Families: Morality and rationality in policy and practice*, edited by Alan Carling, Simon Duncan and Rosalind Edwards, 129–44. London: Routledge, 2002.
Tronto, Joan C. *Moral Boundaries: A Political Argument for an Ethic of Care*. New York: Routledge, 1993.
Weldon-Johns, Michelle. 'From Modern Workplaces to Modern Families – Re-envisioning the Work-family Conflict,' *Journal of Social Welfare and Family Law* 37:4 (2015), 395–415.

Reports and official publications

Commission Communication on Europe 2020 A strategy for smart, sustainable and inclusive growth COM(2010) 2020 final, Brussels, 3.3.2010. Available at http://eur-lex.europa.eu/LexUriServ/LexUriServ.do?uri=COM:2010:2020:FIN:EN:PDF (accessed 28 July 2016).
European Foundation for the Improvement of Living and Working Conditions *Second European Quality of Life Survey: Overview* (Luxembourg: Publications Office of the European Union, 2009), ch 3. Available at www.eurofound.europa.eu/sites/default/files/ef_publication/field_ef_document/ef0902en_7.pdf (accessed 14 March 2016).
European Foundation for the Improvement of Living and Working Conditions, *Third European Quality of Life Survey – Quality of life in Europe: Families in the economic crisis*, (Luxembourg: Publications Office of the European Union, 2014). Available at www.eurofound.europa.eu/sites/default/files/ef_publication/field_ef_document/ef1389en.pdf (accessed 14 March 2016).
Council of the European Union Conclusions, *Women and the Economy: Reconciliation of work and family life as a precondition for equal participation in the labour market,*

2 December 2011, 17816/11 SOC 1050. Available at http://ec.europa.eu/justice/gender-equality/files/concil_conlusion_pl2011_en.pdf (accessed 14 March 2016).

European Commission Roadmap, *New start to address the challenges of work-life balance faced by working families*, August 2015. Available at http://ec.europa.eu/smart-regulation/roadmaps/docs/2015_just_012_new_initiative_replacing_maternity_leave_directive_en.pdf (accessed 14 March 2016).

Fairness at Work, White Paper, Cm 3968, 1998.

Mair, Wasoff and Mackay, *All Settled?*, 2013. Available at www.crfr.ac.uk/assets/MinutesofAgreement20131.pdf (accessed 14 March 2016).

Modern Workplaces Consultation. Available at www.gov.uk/government/consultations/consultation-on-modern-workplaces (accessed 14 March 2016).

Opinion Matters, *Shared Parental Leave: Public Attitudes*, 2015. Available at www.gov.uk/government/uploads/system/uploads/attachment_data/file/394623/bis-15-32-shared-parenting-leave-public-attitudes.pdf (accessed 14 March 2016).

Scottish Law Commission, *Aliment and Financial Provision*, Memorandum No 22, Vol. 1, Edinburgh, 1976.

The Role of Men in Gender Equality – European strategies and insights; prepared for European Commission, DG Justice – Unit D2 Gender equality Contract ref no VC/2010/0592, (Luxembourg: Publications Office of the European Union, 2013). Available at http://ec.europa.eu/justice/genderequality/files/gender_pay_gap/130424_final_report_role_of_men_en.pdf (accessed 14 March 2016).

Cases

Adams v Adams 1997 SLT 144 (OH)
Cahill v Cahill 1998 SLT (Sh Ct) 96
Coyle v Coyle 2004 Fam LR 2 (OH)
Dekker v Stichting Vormingscentrum voor Jonge Volwasenen Plus [1990] ECR I-3941 (ECJ)
Dougan v Dougan 1998 SLT (Sh Ct) 27
Tele Danmark A/S v Handels-og Kontorfunktionaerernes Forbund I Danmark [2001] ECR I-6993 (ECJ)
Webb v EMO Air Cargo (UK) Ltd [1993] 1 CMLR 259 (ECJ)
Wilson v Wilson 1999 SLT 249 (OH)

Chapter 12

From obedience to initiative? Precarious work and changing subjectivities in labour law discourse

Marjo Ylhäinen

Introduction

The changes in the societal conditions of late capitalism, including the changes in working life, have led to debates on the adequacy, justification and efficiency of labour law regulation; labour law, according to most commentators, is in crisis.[1] In recent years, this debate has been affected by the broader public discussion on the crisis facing the economic system as a whole.[2] The debate has often focused on the differentiation that has developed between various modes of employment, including the rapid increase of atypical forms of work. Many have argued that these new forms severely challenge the way in which labour law is supposed to operate and even the fundamental ideas justifying this field of law.[3] The labour law regulation has been criticised for protecting only those employees who have permanent and full-time contracts and making employment of this kind a norm, the standard employment relationship (SER).[4] This standardisation of employment also presumes a bilateral contract between employer and

---

1 See for example the following collections: Guy Davidov and Brian Langille (eds.) *Boundaries and Frontiers of Labour Law*, (Oxford and Portland: Hart Publishing, 2006), Guy Davidov and Brian Langille (eds.), *The Idea of Labour Law* (Oxford: Oxford University Press, 2013).
2 Daniel Vaughan-Whitehead (ed.), *Work Inequalities in the Crisis, Evidence from Europe* (Cheltenham: Edward Elgar, 2011). Marie-Ange Moreau, 'Introduction' in *Before and After the Economic Crisis. What Implications for the 'European Social Model'?* ed. Marie-Ange Moreau (Cheltenham: Edward Elgar, 2011), 8–9. Adkins, Lisa. 'Out of Work or Out of Time? Rethinking Labor after the Financial Crisis,' *South Atlantic Quarterly* 111.4 (2012), 629–30.
3 See for example, Harry Arthurs, 'Labour Law after Labour,' in *The Idea of Labour Law*, eds. Guy Davidov and Brian Langille (Oxford: Oxford University Press, 2013), 13–29; and Alan Hyde, 'The Idea of the Idea of Labour Law: A Parable,' in ibid., 88–97.
4 See also Ann Christensen, 'Protection of the Established Position. A Basic Normative Pattern,' *Scandinavian Studies in Law* 40:2000, 290–1.

employee.⁵ The feminist critique has gone further by pointing out that the SER also represents a typically masculine way of working.⁶

This chapter explores the ways in which the assumptions underlying SER spring from the very construction of labour law as a special legal field, whose historical aim has been to mediate between certain contradictory interests and which, by the same token, has institutionalised particular representations of its central ideas.⁷ At the same time, these representations are construed as productive; they feed back into the discourse, thus forming new discourses connected to the founding ideas of labour law, i.e. labour law as doctrine.⁸ The theoretical framework – critical discourse analysis will be followed by the introduction of the particular discursive context relevant to the analysis: the changes in working life and the doctrinal structure of labour law.⁹

The chapter will proceed as follows. After an introduction to the analysed case material and to the theoretical framework, the cultural context of case analysis will be presented briefly, offering a glimpse of the societal change and the doctrinal structuration of labour law. This contextualisation is followed by a summary of an analysis of legal texts, mostly judgments, written by Finnish judicial bodies. These are studied in order to find out what kind of representations of the practice of labour (work, business) and the subjects participating in it (employer, employee) are created and reproduced in the discourses of labour law. The analysis will focus on the subjectivity of the employee, which will be discussed on two levels. First, I shall outline how the employee is created as a subject in legal texts which address precarious work. Second, I shall trace the formation of the employee's subjectivity as it concerns the subject of the employer in the practices of work and business. The discourse of the legal texts not only reflects legal regulation and its interpretation but also reiterates the notion of the typical employee. The employer and the employee emerge as a particular pair of subjects, informed and shaped by the images attached to the conditions of business.

---

5 Nicola Countouris, *The Changing Law of the Employment Relationship: Comparative Analyses in the European Context*, (Hampshire: Ashgate Publishing, 2007), 25, 38–9; Guy Davidov, 'Re-Matching Labour Laws with their Purpose' in *The Idea of Labour Law*, eds. Guy Davidov and Brian Langille (Oxford: Oxford University Press, 2013), 184–7; Leah F. Vosko, 'Precarious Employment and the Problem of SER-Centrisim in Regulating for Decent Work' in Sangheon Lee and Deirdre McCann (eds.), *Regulating for Decent Work: New Directions in Labour Market Regulation* (Chippenham: Palgrave MacMillan, 2011), 60–2.
6 Adkins, 'Out of Work or Out of Time?' 622–3, Leah F. Vosko, *Temporary Work, The Gendered Rise of a Precarious Employment Relationship*, (Toronto: University of Toronto Press, 2000), 160.
7 See Countouris, *The Changing Law of the Employment Relationship*, 17–25.
8 The analysis that is presented here is based on my doctoral thesis.
9 Norman Fairclough, *Critical Discourse Analysis: The Critical Study of Language*, (Harlow: Pearson Education, 2010).

The doctrinal foundations of labour law can be seen to build on the aim of balancing two opposed ideas: the need for the employee to be protected set against the employer's operations and business as the economical basis for the paid work that needs to be secured.[10] The main argument this chapter puts forward is that what often gets formulated as a problem of the SER and precarious work understood as atypical ways of working is better understood as a rupture in the correspondence between the regulative measures and ideals of labour law and the manner of production, which has changed significantly in recent decades. While the analysis is profoundly Finnish in terms of both the empirical material it draws upon and the doctrine of labour law, the broad lines of development addressed here are familiar to most Western welfare societies.[11]

The theoretical framework and material for the case analysis

Critical Discourse Analysis (CDA)

In the approach I have adopted, the notion of law is that of a special kind of social practice, one that both reflects and reproduces the meanings of its societal context, a world as both already institutionalised and objectified, and yet continuously re-objectifying and re-institutionalising itself. The theoretical starting point pinpoints law's role as part of the construction of society; it refers to discourse as something that creates and upholds established viewpoints and ideologies, the ways of constructing reality and meaning giving. On the other hand, in this broad sense, discourse is something that transforms and modifies those ideologies and concepts that make the world meaningful.[12] Law participates in this process but on the other hand the objectified structures channel what kind of discourses are possible and which of the competing discourses emerge as dominant. In other words, law is an institution, a mediator between the social phenomena of formation and social action. As such it is conditioned by the social formations (e.g. the way that political and economic systems are organised) but is not mechanically determined by those formations. There is a dialectical relation between formations, institutions and action.[13]

---

10 Otto Kahn-Freund, *Labour and the Law* (London: Stevens [for] the Hamlyn Trust, 1972), 52; Klare, Ken, 'The Horizon of Transformative Labour and Employment Law' in *Labour Law in an Era of Globalization. Transformative Practices and Possibilities*, eds. Joanne Conaghan, Richard Michael Fischl and Ken Klare (Oxford, Oxford University Press, 2002), 4.
11 Robert Castel, *From Manual Workers to Wage Laborers*, trans. Richard Boyd (London: Transaction Publishers, 2003), 336–40.
12 Fairclough, *Critical Discourse Analysis*, 58–9, 65–7.
13 Ibid. 30, 40.

On the first level, the theoretical framework channelling the analyses is the juridical framework, which first recognises and qualifies the questions as specifically legal questions and then provides the solutions to these questions through the institutionalised practice of interpretation. During this interpretative process a whole world gets recreated, a world which features specific surroundings of business and the practice of normal work, from whose surroundings the specific pair of subjects – the employee and the employer – are generated. The framework conditions how work and business as the central operational environment are described and what can be said about the employer and employee as the central subjects in these texts. In this sense 'discourse' refers to law as a special kind of institution, law as speech, as a certain language community.[14] In this language community, certain rules condition speech, the range of possible meanings and chains of meaning-makings. These rules which govern the ways of speaking are understood as something that frames and conditions the possibilities of meaning giving. They are objectified in the sense that this framework appears self-evident.[15] This objectified framework imposes the conditions of legal discourse. A certain amount of objectification of the operational context of law is necessary in order to distinguish legal discourse from other discourses and for it to be recognised as legal. The conditions embedded in the framework do not, however, consist in any natural, necessary or universal conditions. They are historically contingent and embedded in those significations that they are given in any particular moment in time. The legal framework sets boundaries for the creation of images and discourses, and limits their scope of operation.

The juridical framework that conditions the creation of discourses is connected to the wider context, the context of the legal tradition in labour law, which constitutes the second level of the theoretical framework. This tradition is a crystallisation of the established and routinised ways of expressing and describing the legally relevant facts in labour law cases in general. It offers an inside view on the regularities of traditional labour law thinking and is a conceptualisation of the legal thinking in this field, one shared by scholars and practitioners alike.[16]

---

14 Ibid. 42.
15 Ibid. 428–9. Jay L. Lemke, *Textual Politics: Discourse and Social Dynamics* (London: Taylor & Francis, 1995), 33–5.
16 See Pierre Bourdieu, 'The Force of Law: Toward a Sociology of the Juridical Field,' *Hastings Law Journal* 38:5 (1986), 830–1, Pierre Bourdieu, *Practical Reason: On the Theory of Action* (Stanford: Polity Press Stanford University Press, 1998), 7–9, 25. Pierre Bourdieu and Loïc JD Wacquant, *An Invitation to Reflexive Sociology* (University of Chicago Press, 1992), 137–8 and Pierre Lamaison, 'From Rules to Strategies: An Interview with Pierre Bourdieu,' *Cultural Anthropology*, 1:1 (1986), 111–12.

The cultural level of legal doctrine consists of the history and tradition, the historical composition of the ideological choices and emphases that created labour law as a special field of law. In general, the level of culture refers to representations that maintain different kinds of classifications, practices and traditions.[17] Moreover the discourses of precarious work reflect these historically developed choices. The cultural level is, on the other hand, a reflection of the historical construction of the development of the welfare state and its relation with industrialisation, the very formation that has conditioned the development of labour law.[18] The cultural level therefore reflects the conditions of production that prevailed in the past. The discourses found within the legal texts of precarious work are therefore a construction that both reflects and reconstructs the context of legislation, its cultural context as labour law doctrine and the ideologies behind it, and work as part of the formation of the welfare society, the third level of the theoretical framework.

Owing to its institutionalised and objectified character, law represents a relatively permanent tradition. In both their form and their content, judgments reflect that tradition. They are guided by previous judgments (especially those setting precedents), legislation and other relevant sources of law.[19] The analysis of the texts, the creation of images and the formation of discourses in these texts are conditioned not only by the legal framework of interpretation but also the ideologies on the cultural level and the premises set up by the formation of the welfare state and its primary way of work as paid work.[20]

The empirical material for the analysis

The empirical material of the analysis consists of three types of legal texts: 14 judgments of the Finnish Supreme Court (from the years 1980–2012); 14 judgments and two pronouncements from the Finnish Labour Court (from the years 1981–2014); and nine pronouncements from the Finnish Labour Council (from the years 1998–2010).[21] The texts were selected according to two criteria: First, I wanted to study texts that have significance for their part in the legal interpretation of labour law e.g. representative because of

---

17 Fairclough, *Critical Discourse Analysis*, 438–9.
18 Castel, *From Manual Workers to Wage Labourers*, 303–15; Countouris, *The Changing Law of the Employment Relationship*, 17–25, 16–18.
19 Bourdieu, 'The Force of Law,' 831–2, 845.
20 Castel, *From Manual Workers to Wage Labourers*, 336–8.
21 The Labour Court in Finland resolves matters of interpretation on questions concerning collective agreements. The Labour Council gives a non-binding opinion on matters of interpretation of health and safety regulation, such as the Working Hours Act. Both bodies have tripartite composition.

their institutional weight (and so representative in that sense). The legal texts selected are therefore presumed to have had an impact on juridical thinking and legal interpretation. However the selection covered all cases during the time periods in question and the cases were not selected on the basis of the normative importance of any individual case. The material that has been analysed here consists therefore of legal texts that have institutional import and bear relatively great weight where juridical interpretation of the paragraphs in question here are concerned.[22]

Second, the material is meant to be illustrative of legal texts representing precarious employment. In the Finnish context, precariousness has usually been debated in terms of fixed-term contracts. In addition, the main legislative tool in trying to cope with the uncertainty attached to precarious work and the problems of uncertainty (precarious society and the so-called precariat) has been the restriction of the fixed-term contract. The other signs of precariousness in working life, such as questions that concern outsourcing and its implications for employment contracts, the differentiation of contracts and the question of the independent worker do not come up in such legal texts that have a special status in juridical thinking, such as precedents.[23] The idea of 'the changing factory', the elements of changes in working time and workplace, are also signals of precarious work, which therefore affected the choice of materials for analysis.

In Supreme Court and Labour Court cases the subject matter is whether there has been a lawful reason to conclude a fixed-term contract on employment or not. In the Finnish legislation this means that the dispute concerns the nature of employment, i.e. whether or not it should be considered permanent. In the judgments of the Labour Court, the question of lawful

---

22 In the Finnish judicial system, precedents of the Supreme Courts are considered secondary to legislation, and as sources of the law they are not considered as binding as precedents in common law jurisdictions. Nevertheless, the normative weight of the precedents of the Supreme Court and their impact on the interpretation of the law can be considered strong. However, this is not the case with the decisions of the Labour Court or the pronouncements of the Labour Council. The purpose of including in the research material decisions of such disparate normative weight was to include all cases that deal with precarious work. The material therefore pinpoints the chronological uniformity of the subjectivities and their connections to certain images of work and business that were present in all cases that were analysed. The material reflects how legal institutions across the legal field construct subjectivities in the legal texts that they produce.

23 Freeland argues that these situations can be systematised in three different kinds of demutualisation of the risks; vertical demutualisation changing risk-sharing between employer and employee, horizontal from the collective of workers to individual worker and diagonal where the employing functions are transferred away from the original employer. Mark Freeland, 'Regulating for Decent Work and the Legal Construction of Personal Work Relations,' in *Creative Labour Regulation. Indeterminancy and Protection in an Uncertain World*, eds. Deirdre McCann et al., (Hampshire: Palgrave MacMillan, 2014), 77–8.

dismissal of those in permanent employment is also raised in several cases where the contract has been denounced permanent by the court.

In the pronouncements of the Labour Council, the juridical question was whether the Working Hours Act was applicable. The interpretation in the analysed cases deals with work that was carried out beyond the employer's premises and there was a dispute over whether the employer could control the work. This part of the analysed material highlights the presuppositions that underlie the labour law, presuppositions which posit certain kinds of working conditions that serve as preconditions for the protection of an employee.

Finally, a word about the limitations of the analysis provided here. The legal interpretation of the cases is not the focus here and as such the outcomes of the cases and pronouncements have been disregarded in the analysis. The material is analysed purely on a textual basis and no attention has been paid to whether it is the employer's or employee's representatives that have argued the case, nor whether the arguments presented in the texts form part of the court's reasoning or not. The analysis aims solely to determine what kind of discourse and understandings are generated by the texts. Furthermore, the choices that the courts make when selecting their arguments (and to what degree they inform the final judgments and pronouncements) form no part of the analysis.

The context of culture; social change and law

The crisis in labour law – late capitalism and changing manner of production

The precarious condition of contemporary society is a contested and much debated notion and discussed in a variety of contexts. While the notion of 'precarisation' and the derivative term 'the precariat' may indeed be theoretically insufficient and vague, I will use the term here in order to point out the departure from the issue of precariousness as a question of precarious work per se.[24] The societal change from which this analysis arises was neatly captured by Alain Ehrenberg as change from a society whose norms are based on guilt and discipline to one whose norms are based on responsibility and initiative.[25] Observing the gradual decrease in the degree of stability in employment relationships, Ehrenberg describes the development

---

24 Beatrice Appay, 'Precarisation sociale et restructurations productives', in Beatrice Appay and Annie Thebaud-Mony (eds.), *Precarisation sociale, travail et sante*, IRESCO, 1997, 514–15, 518–19.
25 Alain Ehrenberg, *The Weariness of the Self: Diagnosing the History of Depression in the Contemporary Age* (Montreal, Ithaca: McGill-Queen's University Press, 2010), 9.

in France: 'The means of regulating and dominating the workforce were based less on blind obedience and more on initiative: responsibility, ability to evolve and create projects, motivation, flexibility and so on'.[26]

The 'changing working life' is understood as a change in the operational environment of labour law e.g. a change in the manner of production.[27] The manner of production is understood as something that is situated between the operational environment and the employee. The manner of production is the way that work is organised as part of the production process. It consists of the methods of work, the ways to control work, the ways in which working hours are organised and the ways of passing on information and communicating in the working environment. The manner of production is also tied up with productivity aims or at least with assumptions about work productivity.[28] The change in manner of production means a change where the process of material production based on routines and repetition is replaced with a rapid process of producing the immaterial, cultural capital, based on communication and action between individuals. This change also means that even the value of material goods is measured in terms of immaterial values, the significations that are attached to it. But change is also about the running down of the 'factory' i.e. the one spot where all the necessary actions that relate to producing material goods takes place. In this sense, the change in organising the production means an expansion in outsourcing less essential functions.[29]

The factory, viewed both as a historical entity and a metaphor, is something that connects the idea of subordination and the force of united workers as a collective that safeguards parity; equality between the employer and the collective of employees. It is both the place of subordination and the place where power is united.[30] As many studies in recent decades have noted, the factory has lost its centrality as a place of production. Work has lost its disciplined and controlled nature, which was part of the continuous

---

26 Ibid. 184.
27 Adrián Goldin, *The Subjective Weakening of Labour Law*, in *Boundaries and Frontiers of Labour Law*, edited by Guy Davidov and Brian Langille (Oxford and Portland: Hart Publishing, 2006), 109–31, 113–15.
28 Richard Sennett, *The Corrosion of Character: the personal consequences of work in the new capitalism*. New York: Norton (1998), 20, 63. 71.
29 Jeremy Rifkin, *The End of Work* (Winnipeg: Social Planning Council of Winnipeg, 1996), 15–45; Eve Chiapello and Norman Fairclough, 'Understanding the new management ideology: a transdisciplinary contribution from critical discourse analysis and new sociology of capitalism,' *Discourse & Society* 2:13 (2002), 163; Luc Boltanski and Eve Chiapello, *The New Spirit of Capitalism*, trans. Gregory Elliott (London: Verso, 2007), 220–2, 444–5; Raija Julkunen, *Uuden työn paradoksit (Paradoxes of the New Work)*, (Tampere: Vastapaino, 2008), 90–4.
30 Countouris, *The Changing Law of the Employment Relationship*, 27–8.

process of material production. Instead it becomes communicative.[31] In this sense precarious work is something that is in connection with being human, being an individual subject. Precarious work is strongly attached to the individual and individual faculties and one's value in the labour market depends on the ability to constantly hone one's individual competitive edge.[32]

The doctrinal structure of labour law

The history of the regulation of work shows that regulated work has always had some attachment to the degree to which the worker is dependent.[33] Notably in the history of modern labour law, it is the degree of independence that characterises the regulated type of work.[34] In other words, the worker becomes a subject in need of protection only when his actions are neither free nor independent, but dependent on someone else who has the power over action and the power of control. Protection is about preventing the abuse of that power; its ordering as well as its control.[35]

I shall briefly sketch the development of Finnish labour law doctrine here, pinpointing some of the essential characteristics of labour law. The development of industrialisation formed the background for the development of labour law in all European countries, albeit at slightly different times. There were systematic differences in the development of labour law and the purview of the legislation was different. The doctrinal development at the initial stage of labour law, especially in Germany, drew attention to the status of the worker, class relations and the worker's economic dependence on the employer as the key elements of the employment relationship and labour law, although the conceptual origins were derived from civil law. In Finland, however, there was a certain urge to differentiate labour law from social law, and especially from social policy aims, and to clearly position labour law as part of private, not public, law. Nevertheless what was common for the development of labour law was the departure from the master–servant relation

---

31 Paolo Virno, *A Grammar of the Multitude: For an Analysis of Contemporary Forms of Life*, trans. Isabella Bertoletti, James Cascaito and Andrea Casson (New York: Semiotext (e) 2004), 51. See Boltanski and Chiapello, *The New Spirit of Capitalism*, 456–7.
32 Boltanski and Chiapello, *The New Spirit of Capitalism*, 456, 465; Jean-Philippe Deranty, 'Work and the Precarisation of Existence,' *European Journal of Social Theory* 4:11 (2008), 453–4.
33 Luca Nogler and Udo Refner, 'Introduction: The New Dimension of Life Time in the Law of Contracts and Obligations, The Historical Contribution of Employment Law to General Civil Law: A Lost Dimension?' in *Life Time Contracts: Social Long-Term Contracts in Labour, Tenancy and Consumer Credit Law*, edited by Luca Nogler and Udo Reifner (Hague: Eleven International Publishing, 2014), 32–3.
34 See also Goldin, 'The Subjective Weakening of Labour Law,' 112.
35 Kahn-Freund, *Labour and the Law*, 5, 17.

towards a relation based on contract.[36] In Finland this development was carried out by accentuating positive law, with legislation as the starting point for establishing coherence in this new field of law.[37]

From the point of view of legal doctrine, the most important parts of the employer's determining position, the employer's prerogative, are the right to direct and conduct work and the right to conduct business e.g. the right to take care of the economic interests.[38] The right to lead and conduct work is both an abstract characteristic of the employment relation and a concrete right to give orders and organise the working process.[39] Business decisions, by contrast, are mostly an expression of the employer's business freedom but the employment relationship is exposed here in two particular regards: at the moment of entering into a contract with a person and then when ending it. The most obvious connection between business decisions and the employment relation comes up when the decisions lead to collective redundancies.[40]

Both the right to direct work as an abstract right and the right to make business decisions are matters that blur the employment relationship. The first is peripheral to labour law in the sense that in order to fulfil the legally essential elements of the employment relation, this abstract right has to be considered. The right to conduct business is peripheral in the sense that it only partially reflects the employment relation, as it is mostly the indirect effect on the exercise of that power that is of essence. It affects the employer–employee relationship only indirectly. The concrete right to give orders, on the other hand, is at the core of the employment relationship in the sense of legal doctrine because the degree to which it is invoked is directly connected to the control of work and therefore to the degree of independence.

The freedom of contract and the freedom of business are both elements in the construction of labour law doctrine and function as its ideological background. They mark the boundaries of labour law by suggesting an outer limit to the idea of the protection of the employee. The contradictory elements, on the one hand the idea of protecting the employee and on

---

36 Luca Nogler, 'The Historical Contribution of Employment Law to General Civil Law: A Lost Dimension?' in *Life Time Contracts: Social Long-Term Contracts in Labour, Tenancy and Consumer Credit Law*, edited by Luca Nogler and Udo Reifner (Hague: Eleven International Publishing 2014), 279–319, 281–4.
37 Arvo Sipilä, *Suomen työoikeuden käsite ja järjestelmä sekä suhde sosiaaliseen lainsäädäntöön (The Concept of Finnish Labour Law, Its System and Relation to Social Law)* (Helsinki: Kauppalehti Oy:n kirjapaino, 1938).
38 Simon Deakin, 'Conceptions of the Market in Labour Law', in Ann Nummahuser-Henning and Mia Rönnmar, *Normative Patterns and Legal Developments in the Social Dimension of the EU* (Oxford and Portland: Hart Publishing, 2013), 149–51.
39 Countouris, *The Changing Law of the Employment Relationship*, 30–1.
40 Ruth Nielsen, *Employers' Prerogatives: In a European and Nordic Perspective* (Copenhagen: Handelshøjskolens forlag, 1996), 17.

the other the urge to fulfil the needs of the employer in order to secure his business, are embedded in the doctrine of labour law. The traditional thinking in labour law doctrine emphasises the protection of the working subject while the matter of the commencement and the termination of a period of employment are in the end left to the realm of business and economy.

Discourses of precarious work

The discourse of dependent work

The mainstream discourse that emerges in the analysed texts, is the discourse of dependent work, which is hegemonic in nature in the sense that it reflects the traditional line of thinking in labour law and the presumptions it entails. This discourse presents us with a narrative of the worker – the employee working as subordinated object in the normal environment under the control of the employer. The connection to this kind of subjectivity forms a precondition of the need for protection.

The discourse of dependent work builds on the tension between work that is done in a fixed-term contract as against a permanent contract. This tension can be observed in the texts analysed. The precariousness of work is described as oddities or unusual characteristics of work in comparison to something that is normal in work and working. It imposes what is embedded in the ideas of regulated work and protected subject. It is natural to work for one employer, who controls your work performance and orders the way in which the work should be carried out.

In this discourse, work itself as well as working conditions form an essential part of the preconditions for protection. The employee's subjectivity is created in opposition to the employer within the context of continuity; as regularity in work performance and similarity of duties. The regularity of work is measured by the alleged continuity either in working time or in terms of subsequent employment contracts.[41] Continuity is constructed in the descriptions of work for example by emphasising the sameness of tasks, although there have been many employment contracts or many titles under which the duties have been performed.[42] Regularity is present also in the

---

41   KKO 1996:105. KKO 1993:70. TT 4987–137. TT 2004–42. KKO 2012–2.
42   TT 1993–60. TT 2008–15. KKO 1995:14. KKO 2012:10. TT 2004–42. KKO 1996:105. TT 2009–34. TT 2002–2. The emphasis on the similarity of working tasks in the analysed legal texts is especially interesting if one compares it to the context of permanent employment. In this context change in an employee's duties have no relevance regarding the continuity of the employment relationship. This picture only strengthens in cases where there is a risk of termination of employment due to collective redundancies. There the employer has an obligation to offer work instead of dismissing the employee. The obligation is extended, not only to similar tasks to the ones that the employee has had before, but also to tasks that the employee could do if retrained.

act of work itself as a regular, continuous way of performing work in regular manner, without interruptions or breaks while working.[43] Besides the tension between regular-irregular and similar-different, the place of work has also significance while assessing the nature of working. The idea of the 'factory' is clearly present in the analysed texts. It includes the question of the employer's chance to supervise work in a special working place but moreover the permanency of the working place is used as an argument to confirm the factual permanent nature of the employment relationship.[44] The employer's business remains invisible in this discourse. The lack of the mention of normal, routine or regular business reflects traditional thinking in labour law, which in its premises of protection, ignores the business aspect, with its strong emphasis on the employer's sole authority.

It is natural and normal that the work, its task and duties reoccur in as similar a manner as possible and that the working conditions consist of a permanent lengthy employment in premises that are owned and controlled by the employer.[45] In the discourse of dependent work the employer is the one that exercises power, for better or worse. Work done by the employee forms part of the employer's business, as a natural, regular, continuous process. The normative pattern of work that should be fulfilled represents what is determined or generally agreed to be normal, the kind of work that is recognised for its place in a hegemonic structure. This normalised work is constructed in the tension that precarious work creates and is constructed through this tension. The employee as a subordinated subject is constructed within the practice of normal employment.

Given the impact of the legal framework that preconditions the context of analysis of the discourse, it can be argued that the discourse of dependent work reflects the images behind the regulative measures. The images of the working object, controlling subject and regular work are embedded in labour law. And it is in this sense that the discourse of dependent work is the hegemonic discourse of labour law. The normative pattern of work that should be fulfilled represents what is determined or generally agreed to be normal, the kind of work that is recognised for its place in a hegemonic structure. This normalised work is constructed in the tension that precarious work creates and is constructed through this tension. The employee as a subordinated subject is constructed within the practice of normal employment.

The discourse of business

The hegemony of the discourse of dependent work is challenged by the discourse of business. The point of reference in this discourse is the challenge

---

43 TN 1419–06. TN 1429–08.
44 KKO 1996:105. TT 2004:42, TT 2006–69.
45 Countouris, *The Changing Law of the Employment Relationship*, 34–5.

that it posits for the central elements of the discourse of dependent work. The ideas of normal work in a normal working environment and the assumptions that underlie their very existence are jeopardised.

Whereas the discourse of dependent work has its ideological background in traditional labour law thinking, pinpointing certain features of employee, employer and work, the discourse of business is mainly rooted in the central ideas of contract law. This connection emphasises labour law as the stepdaughter of contract law and its principles and is attached to the ideology of liberalism. And the connection leads us to the margins of labour law thinking, especially to the original idea of contract law and the idea of freedom to contract. Here the idea of freedom to contract prevails rather than the idea of the protection of the weaker party. The prevalence of the discourse of business has two points of departure: at the contractual beginning of the employment relationship and at the point where the employment is about to be terminated. These points of departure make up the periphery of labour law thinking where the employer's prerogative prevails.

Unlike in the discourse of dependent work, where business is left almost unspoken, clearly in the discourse of business it would have the main role. It is intertwined with work in a way that makes it difficult to draw a line between business and work. In this discourse, the employee's subjectivity is constructed through action and responsibility.[46] The employer is a victim of changing circumstances, which are coercive, compelling, and indisputable.[47] This image of the employer has its ideological background in the historically constructed division where the emphasis is on the employer's responsibility and use of power in the realm of labour law, accentuating the company's business administration and management that falls outside the realm of labour law.

The discourse of business draws attention to the boundaries of labour law – the outsourcing of the economic regime. This is a consequence of the ideology of economic liberalism that creates the conditions where labour law thinking flourishes. In this fringe area, the no-man's-land between the idea of protection of the employee and the power to make decisions of an economic character, an image of the vulnerable employer, victim of the market forces which override his (or sometimes her) powers comes into play.[48] The lack of a mighty employer, the operator of power and the active subject of employment wipes out the uneven relationship, leaving no room for the subordinated employee.

Business, which is left outside the discourse of dependent work, takes the place reserved for the protection of the employee in the discourse of

---

46 KKO 1995:159. TT 1982–191. KKO 2008:29.
47 KKO 1995–13. TT 2004–42.
48 KKO 1988:9. KKO 1996–105. TT 2006:29.

business. But the business that has this quality of becoming a major issue in the discourse is not the usual, regular or ordinary business that the employer practises. It is, in one way or another, exceptional. It might be built on the employee's work, it might not fit into the core of the employer's functions or then there is a crisis of business.[49] This is a moment where the normal process of production becomes unpredictable, rapidly changing and precarious. This moment, where the changes in business override the protection of the employee, is also embedded in the labour law doctrine. It is precisely the changes in the working environment, in a market-led economy that promote themselves as the natural, self-evident and legitimised place of giving up the idea of protection of the employee. This legitimisation of changing circumstances creates an entry point for the precariousness of work and society, a point where the traditional protection, focusing on the protection of established position, has no answers.

The obedient employee: a subordinated but skilful subject

In the discourse of dependent work the employee's subjectivity is created in equivalence with the idea of protection. The traditional emphasis of the protection of the working subject is especially notable in the pronouncements of the Finnish Labour Council. The legal framework here pinpoints the protection of the employee who works under control. The regulation of working time is bound to controlling the methods of work and the work performance, which are closely tied to a special working place. The employer's right to direct and conduct work, the employee's duty to obey orders, the controlled working time and employee's lack of power are typical elements in the construction of the employee's habitus as a subordinated subject.

For example, in a Finnish Labour Council case there are opposing perceptions as to the control of the working time, which reflect the tension between the employer's power to control and the objectified position of the employee. The employee's duty to notify the employer about their working hours, especially the commencement and termination of the work, is at issue.[50] In another case, the duty to report and the indirect control of the employer is likewise present as the main factor indicating the lack of independence of the employee. The indirect control is due to the employee's task performance, where the controlling subject is not the employer but a client.[51]

Sometimes the employee is represented as a subordinated subject in what would appear to be neutral descriptions of the facts when entering into an

---

49 KKO 2010–11. TN 1349–98. KKO 1996–105.
50 TN 1419–06.
51 TN 1429–08.

employment contract. In these Finnish Supreme Court cases the verbs used to describe the conclusion of contract indicate a subordinate position.[52] The employer's active role is by contrast emphasised. And similar emphases on the employer's role as an activator can be found in certain judgments of the Labour Court.[53] On the other hand, the Labour Court seems more sensitive to the supposed parity of employer and employee when making the employment contract and the choice of verbs here is more likely to be even.

The employer's use of power and the subordinated employee is also represented by directly referring to orders that the employee must obey. In these descriptions the employee is someone who is called to work, someone receiving different kinds of notices and information about changes in working tasks or changes in the payroll system.[54] The employee is sometimes repressed in such actions that demonstrate the employer's attempt to evade the law that should be protecting the employee.[55] One of the elements in the structuring of the employee's subordination occurs when the employer is accused of exceeding the limits of the use of power. When the use of power is arbitrary or disloyal the subordinated employee is under pressure or is forced to obey. These representations are often attached to descriptions concerning the termination of the employment. The suppressed employee is the object of the employer's use of power.

The picture of a subordinated object is accomplished by the skills they either have or might have. The expertise or proficiency of the employee usually comes up in connection with the description of duties. In Labour Court cases in particular, the employee's skills and expertise are described. These are cases where the legal framework of the conclusion of a fixed-term contract is accompanied by the legal framework of the termination of a permanent contract on financial and production-related grounds. This brings in the necessity to evaluate the employer's obligation to offer alternative suitable work and hence this legal framework requires the evaluation of the skills of the employee and the tasks that she could conduct.

The evaluation of the employee's skills and capabilities alters the picture of the subordinated employee. A good employee is defined in connection to the tasks performed. The employee has the correct kind of skills and meets the needs of the employer.[56] The employee might also be evaluated as a less valuable worker due to deficient or tangential skills and capability of carrying out only routine tasks. The employee with poor skills is dispensable and the lack of skills form a justified ground for dismissal. The

---

52 KKO 1995:13. KKO 2008:29.
53 TT 1985–2. TT 2006–69.
54 TN 1349–98. KKO 1996:105. TT 2006–69.
55 KKO 2008:29. TT 2008–41.
56 KKO 1995:54. TT 2008–15.

connection between the individual's capabilities on the one hand and the requirements of the individualised duties on the other creates the image of the good employee. The subordinated employee is sometimes evaluated by their skilfulness relative to employer's general needs, a need for a workforce as a collective of productive means. In this scenario, the employee, a good worker, is constructed as a potentially valuable part of such a workforce, one that the employer needs, especially in times of redundancies.[57]

The employee showing initiative: the autonomous and active subject

In the discourse of business, the central preconditions for the realisation of protection with the traditional ideas of the subordinated subject have been elided. The image of the employer, victimised by insuperable circumstances and market forces, is a necessary image for giving up the idea of protecting the weaker party.[58] It justifies the alleged necessary and inevitable changes in the manner of production that leave the employee outside the workforce. And this is exactly the point where prioritising production over the protection of the employee is reconstructed. The modified, and, from the labour law point of view, unusual type of business that is characterised by discontinuity and rupture, opens up a space where the identity of the employee is not defined by suppression but rather by autonomy and responsibility. And here, in the discourse of business, another subjectivity of the employee is created.

This autonomous and active subject is for the most part determined through the freedom of choice. This is especially visible in the judgments of the Supreme Court. Freedom of choice comes up in such questions of interpretation that are connected to the demarcation of dependent and independent work. In these cases there are several conclusions of employment contracts between the same employer and employee over a longish time period.[59] The distinctive feature in these cases is that working has been relatively irregular, and the number of both working days and working hours have varied substantially.[60] The legal framework in these cases is therefore connected to the question whether the commitment to work has been of a binding nature throughout the whole time-period, regardless of the interruptions. The employee's freedom to choose the occasions of work is decisive here.[61]

---

57 KKO 1995:13. TT 2006–64.
58 KKO 1995:14. KKO 1995–13. TT 2004–42.
59 KKO 1996–105. TT 1987–73. KKO 2011–73.
60 TT 2004–42. KKO 1980 II 84. TT 2006–42.
61 KKO 1980 II 84. KKO 1995.159.

Freedom to contract, which is manifested in the analysed material as the freedom to choose the party to contract, the right to decide one's place of work and working time, as well as the right to withdraw from a contract, are all components that generate the employee as an autonomous and active subject.[62] Freedom of choice in this context is defined as freedom to choose whether to enter into an employment contract as well as the ability to influence the degree of one's commitment to work.[63] The consequence of exercising one's freedom to choose is characterised by an obligation to tolerate the negative outcomes of one's denial.[64]

Moreover the autonomous subject is created through the evaluation of the degree of independence. Partly due to the legal framework within which the texts are produced, the significance of the degree of independence becomes especially evident in the pronouncements of the Finnish Labour Council.[65] However this assessment serves not only the evaluation of the degree of employer's control, but it also tends to expand into the evaluation of the work as business. When employee's work and employer's business coincide, employee's duties, responsibilities, roles, and the self-organised work represent not only the way that the employee works, but simultaneously the manner of production, the way in which the employer's business is organised.[66] The amalgamation of business and work is evident also in services where the business typically consists of the work-performance.[67]

The autonomous and active subject is no longer in the subordinated position where her work-performance is controlled by the other party of the contract. This autonomous subject actively promotes her own interests and is aware of the legally relevant facts that for example might function as the reasons or justification regarding the termination of the contract.[68] The active role of the employee is also constructed through an assessment of the economic rationality of the employee's actions. As an active subject, the employee is looking for her own best interest and aims to maximise and secure her economic interests.[69] The subject's awareness and consciousness, refers to the legal framework of the rationally acting legal subject. This subject is also responsible for her own actions and omissions.[70] The active, independent and self-possessed employee is not in need of protection and has therefore no use for the status of an employee.[71]

---

62 KKO 1995:159.
63 KKO 1980 II 84.
64 KKO 1980 II 84. KKO 1995:159. TT 1982–191. KKO 1993:70.
65 TN 1419–06. TN 1367–00.
66 TN 1432–09. TN 1349–98.
67 KKO 2010–11.
68 KKO 1990:54. KKO 1996:105.
69 KKO 1993:70.
70 TT 1981–43. TT 2009–34.
71 KKO 1995:159. KKO 1993:70.

Conclusions: the changing identity of the employee

By analysing specific types of legal texts, this chapter has critically explored some of the founding ideas of Finnish labour law as well as the unfolding dynamics of these foundations when the manner of production and social surroundings, both material and symbolic, change. The analysis has teased out discourses which define, first, the central object of this legal discipline, namely the social practice called work, and the contractual sphere where terms concerning this practice may be privately arranged by the parties. Second, and intertwined with these discourses defining work, the analysis identified discourses that produce and reproduce the subjects of labour law – the employer and, especially, the employee. This pair of subjects emerged in correspondence with the discursive shifts in what constitutes definitions of work. On the one hand, the subject pair of obedient subject and directing subject came about as part of the discourse of normal work, where the employee's subordinated position was balanced by the classical protective mechanisms of labour law. On the other hand, the negotiating pair of subjects came about as part of the business discourse, where the employee is viewed as an economic agent roughly on a par with the employer.

The line of development from strictly controlled forms of work carried out by obedient workers towards autonomous workers and flexible modes of work is crystallised in the image of a run-down factory. I pointed out above the resemblance to Alain Ehrenberg's diagnosis that the norm of contemporary society is based on responsibility and initiative. Indeed, one might ask if this in fact will lead to new ways of commodifying the personality and identity traits of the individual. It is no longer enough that the employee offers their skills to the employer: their character and personal qualities should be made available too. While the empirical material analysed here does not directly support such conclusions, what it does reveal are the structural limitations of labour law to adequately address the consequences of such a shift.

Bibliography

Adkins, Lisa. 'Out of Work or Out of Time? Rethinking Labor after the Financial Crisis,' *South Atlantic Quarterly* 111:4 (2012), 621–41.

Appay Beatrice. 'Précarisation sociale et restructurations productives.' In Beatrice Appay and Annie Thebaud-Mony (eds.), *Précarisation sociale, travail et sante.* IRESCO, Actions scientiques federatives 1997, 509–54.

Arthurs, Harry. 'Labour Law after Labour.' In *The Idea of Labour Law*, edited by Guy Davidov and Brian Langille, 13–29. Oxford: Oxford University Press, 2013.

Boltanski, Luc and Eve Chiapello. *The New Spirit of Capitalism*, trans. Gregory Elliott. London: Verso, 2007.

Bourdieu, Pierre. 'The Force of Law: Toward a Sociology of the Juridical Field,' *Hastings Law Journal* 38:5 (1986), 814–53.

Bourdieu, Pierre. *Practical Reason: On the Theory of Action.* Stanford: Polity Press, Stanford University Press, 1998.
Bourdieu, Pierre and Wacquant, Loïc JD. *An Invitation to Reflexive Sociology.* Chicago: University of Chicago Press, 1992.
Castel, Robert. *From Manual Workers to Wage Laborers,* trans. Richard Boyd. London: Transaction Publishers, 2003.
Chiapello, Eve and Fairclough, Norman. 'Understanding the new management ideology: a transdisciplinary contribution from critical discourse analysis and new sociology of capitalism,' *Discourse & Society* 2:13 (2002), 185–208.
Christensen, Ann. 'Protection of the Established Position. A Basic Normative Pattern,' *Scandinavian Studies in Law* 2000, 40: 285–324.
Countouris, Nicola. *The Changing Law of the Employment Relationship: Comparative Analyses in the European Context.* Hampshire: Ashgate Publishing, 2007.
Davidov, Guy. 'Re-Matching Labour Laws with their Purpose.' In *The Idea of Labour Law,* edited by Guy Davidov and Brian Langille, 179–89. Oxford: Oxford University Press, 2013.
Davidov, Guy and Langille, Brian (eds.). *Boundaries and Frontiers of Labour Law.* Oxford and Portland: Hart Publishing, 2006.
Davidov, Guy and Langille, Brian (eds.). *The Idea of Labour Law.* Oxford: Oxford University Press, 2013/2011.
Deakin, Simon, 'Conceptions of the Market in Labour Law'. In *Normative Patterns and Legal Developments in the Social Dimension of the EU,* edited by Ann Nummahuser-Henning and Mia Rönnmar. (Oxford and Portland: Hart Publishing, 2013), 141–59.
Deranty, Jean-Philippe. 'Work and the Precarisation of Existence,' *European Journal of Social Theory* 4:11 (2008), 443–63.
Ehrenberg, Alain. *The Weariness of the Self: Diagnosing the History of Depression in the Contemporary Age.* Montreal, Ithaca: McGill-Queen's University Press, 2010.
Fairclough, Norman. *Critical Discourse Analysis: The Critical Study of Language.* Harlow: Pearson Education, 2010.
Freeland, Mark. 'Regulating for Decent Work and the Legal Construction of Personal Work Relations'. In *Creative Labour Regulation. Indeterminancy and Protection in an Uncertain World,* edited by Deirdre McCann et al., 63–84, Hampshire: Palgrave MacMillan, 2014.
Goldin, Adrián. 'The Subjective Weakening of Labour Law'. In *Boundaries and Frontiers of Labour Law,* edited by Guy Davidov and Brian Langille, 109–31, Oxford and Portland: Hart Publishing, 2006.
Hyde, Alan. 'The Idea of the Idea of Labour Law: A Parable.' In *The Idea of Labour Law,* edited by Guy Davidov and Brian Langille, 88–97, Oxford: Oxford University Press, 2013/ 2011.
Julkunen, Raija. *Uuden työn paradoksit (Paradoxes of the New Work).* Tampere: Vastapaino, 2008.
Kahn-Freund, Otto. *Labour and the Law.* London: Stevens [for] the Hamlyn Trust, 1972.
Klare, Ken. 'The Horizon of Transformative Labour and Employment Law.' In *Labour Law in an Era of Globalization. Transformative Practices and Possibilities,* edited by Joanne Conaghan, Richard Michael Fischl and Ken Klare, 3–33. Oxford, Oxford University Press, 2002.

Lamaison, Pierre. 'From Rules to Strategies: An Interview with Pierre Bourdieu,' *Cultural Anthropology*, 1:1 (1986), 110–20.
Lemke, Jay L. *Textual Politics: Discourse and Social Dynamics*. London: Taylor & Francis, 1995.
Moreau, Marie-Ange. 'Introduction'. In *Before and After the Economic Crisis. What Implications for the "European Social Model"?*, edited by Marie-Ange Moreau, 1–37. Cheltenham: Edward Elgar, 2011.
Nielsen, Ruth. *Employers' Prerogatives: In a European and Nordic Perspective*. Copenhagen: Handelshøjskolens forlag, 1996.
Luca Nogler and Udo Refner, 'Introduction: The New Dimension of Life Time in the Law of Contracts and Obligations.' In *Life Time Contracts: Social Long-Term Contracts in Labour, Tenancy and Consumer Credit Law*, edited by Luca Nogler and Udo Reifner, 1–72. Hague: Eleven International Publishing, 2014.
Nogler, Luca. 'The Historical Contribution of Employment Law to General Civil Law: A Lost Dimension?'. In *Life Time Contracts: Social Long-Term Contracts in Labour, Tenancy and Consumer Credit Law*, edited by Luca Nogler and Udo Reifner, 279–319. Hague: Eleven International Publishing, 2014.
Rifkin, Jeremy. *The End of Work*. Winnipeg: Social Planning Council of Winnipeg, 1996.
Sennett, Richard. 'The Corrosion of Character: The Personal Consequences of Work in the New Capitalism.' New York: Norton (1998).
Sipilä, Arvo. *Suomen työoikeuden käsite ja järjestelmä sekä suhde sosiaaliseen lainsäädäntöön (The Concept of Finnish Labour Law, Its System and Relation to Social Law)*. Helsinki: Kauppalehti Oy:n kirjapaino, 1938.
Vaughan-Whitehead, Daniel (ed.). *Work Inequalities in the Crisis, Evidence from Europe*. Cheltenham: Edward Elgar, 2011.
Virno, Paolo. *A Grammar of the Multitude: For an Analysis of Contemporary Forms of Life*, trans. by Isabella Bertoletti, James Cascaito and Andrea Casson. New York: Semiotext (e) 2004.
Vosko, Leah F. 'Precarious Employment and the Problem of SER-Centrisim in Regulating for Decent Work.' In *Regulating for Decent Work: New Directions in Labour Market Regulation*, edited by Sangheon Lee and Deirdre McCann, 58–122. Chippenham: Palgrave MacMillan, 2011.
Vosko, Leah F. *Temporary Work, The Gendered Rise of a Precarious Employment Relationship*. Toronto: University of Toronto Press, 2000.

List of Cases

KKO 1980 II 84. 19.8.1980 Supreme Court of Finland
KKO 1990:54. 3.5.1990
KKO 1996:105. 6.9.1996
KKO 1993:70. 25.5.1993
KKO 1995:14. 13.2.1995
KKO 1995:159. 27.9.1995
KKO 1996:105. 6.9.1996
KKO 2012:2. 11.1.2012
KKO 2012:10. 24.1.2012
KKO 1988:9. 5.2.1988

KKO 1995:13. 13.2.1995
KKO 1996:105. 6.9.1996
KKO 2008:29. 19.3.2008
KKO 2010:11. 17.2.2010
KKO 2011:73. 3.10.2011
KKO 2012:10. 11.1.2012
KKO 2012:10. 24.1.2012
TT 1981–43. 10.4.1981 Labour Court of Finland
TT 1982–191. 31.12.1982
TT 2004–42. 25.5.2004
TT 2006–69. 18.8.2006
TT 2008–15. 12.2.2008
TT 2009–34. 29.4.2009
TT 2002:2. 29.1.2002
TT 4.1.1985
TT 1987–173. 22.12.1987
TT 2002–2. 29.1.2002
TT 2006–42. 18.5.2006
TT 2006–29. 4.4.2006
TT 2008–41. 18.3.2008
TT 2006–64. A:22.6.2006
TN 1419–06. 30.11.2006 Labour Council of Finland
TN 1429–08. 10.4.2008
TN 1349–98. 7.5.1998
TN 1367–00. 8.6.2000
TN 1432–09. 26.2.2009

Chapter 13

Human dignity mediated

Personhood, humanity, and the logic of property in law and bioethics

Ukri Soirila

Introduction

Rapid developments in science and technology – particularly in biotechnology – have, during the last couple of decades, radically challenged many of our basic assumptions about human ontology, subjectivity and personhood. This has also caused pressure on the basic categories of our legal thought which continue 'in the secular world the tradition based on the separation of the individual and spirit',[1] or things and persons.[2] The developments have created novel risks, such as exploitation of life in biocapital, but also new possibilities to rethink some of our outdated legal assumptions which all too often have led to paradoxical and exclusionary outcomes.

In this chapter, I focus on the prevailing legal solution to the novel bioethical questions, namely the concept of human dignity. Even though human dignity has no doubt been used as an important balancing tool against some of the threats posed by biotechnology, I argue that its use leads to very conservative answers to novel bioethical questions and hence tends to block opportunities to think legal subjectivity otherwise. This is so especially because the dominant usages of human dignity fall back on the same old logic of property that Roberto Esposito has claimed to have dominated philosophical and legal thought at least since ancient Rome.[3]

The chapter consists of three main parts. First, I introduce briefly Esposito's thought on the distinction of persons and things and the logic of property that he claims to have kept legal thought in stasis for the past two millennia – to the detriment of the body, which has been mostly excluded from legal categories. Second, I discuss how recent developments in science

---

[1] Joseph Vining, 'Dignity as Perception: Recognition of the Human Individual and the Individual Animal in Legal Thought', in *Understanding Human Dignity*, ed. Christopher McCrudden (OUP/British Academy, Proceedings of the British Academy Vol. 192, 2013), 574.
[2] Roberto Esposito, *Persons and Things: From the Body's Point of View*, 1st edn. (Cambridge; Malden, MA: Polity, 2015).
[3] Ibid.

and technology have challenged the logic traced by Esposito, and thus opened avenues for the entry of the excluded 'body's point of view'. Further, I highlight some attempts to rethink subjectivity and life that these developments have evoked in philosophy. Finally, I study the concept of human dignity as the prevalent legal solution to these novel issues, focusing especially on the two dominant usages of the concept, and suggest that the usages are not capable of accommodating the aforementioned philosophical views.

One last note before I move to the first main section. While I draw inspiration from Esposito, this is not a chapter on his thought. Rather, I simply use one very specific idea of Esposito – taken, admittedly, somewhat out of the context of his impressive oeuvre – as a springboard to the main topic of the chapter, namely the use of the concept of human dignity in the bioethical discourse.[4]

Persons, things, and the excluded body

In his recent work, Roberto Esposito argues that our legal and philosophical thinking has, at least since Roman law, been based on a strict distinction between persons and things – a distinction that is the outcome of a long disciplinary process. As Esposito writes:

> A watershed divides the world of life, cutting it into two areas defined by their mutual opposition. You either stand on this side of the divide, with the persons, or on the other side, with the thing: there is no segment in between to unite them.[5]

Hence, the legal world is primarily based between two poles: persons, which are defined by the fact that they are not things, and things, which are not persons. Between these, there is only void. To quote Esposito again, '[the] very entity the law deals with, if not an action, is either a person or a thing, according to a simple, clear distinction – a thing is a non-person and a person is a non-thing'.[6]

The relation between the two is, further, one of 'instrumental domination', in the sense that things exist to serve persons. A thing is often not perceived as something that *is*, but more as something that someone *has*: something that belongs to a person. Things are about value and, potentially,

---

4 For a more comprehensive discussion on Esposito's thought, see for instance, Peter Langford, *Roberto Esposito: Law, Community and the Political* (Abingdon, Oxon; New York, NY: Routledge, 2015).
5 Esposito, *Persons and Things*, 2.
6 Ibid. 16–17.

exchange.⁷ Moreover, one's personhood is closely linked to owning things. While I cannot go deeper into Esposito's theory of biopolitics, community, and immunity here, property is, according to Esposito, one of the key immunising constructions through which we try to protect our identities from falling into the void at the heart of any community by separating ourselves from others.⁸ Ownership plays thus a key part in a person's presence in the modern political community.⁹ To cut things short, 'whoever possesses things enjoys the status of personhood and can exert his or her mastery over them'.¹⁰ Ultimately, the legal world is built around a logic of property. In this sense, then, Esposito's analysis of law comes, in certain parts, close to (post-)Marxian thought.¹¹ As Michael Hardt and Antonio Negri write, for example, '[i]n the dominant line of European thought from Locke to Hegel, the absolute rights of people to appropriate things becomes the basis and substantive end of the legally defined free individual'.¹² Legal subjects are those that own property and who thus possess rights.

This means also that, by logic, every human being is not necessarily a person. As Esposito points out, no one was a person all their life in ancient Rome. And since then, too, some groups of people have throughout history been excluded from full personhood, be they slaves, women, coloured people, children, or whatever.¹³ To be sure, a lot has changed since the times of ancient Rome, and even since the peak of slave trade. But even now, the notion of person is not entirely reducible 'to that of the biological substance it designates'. Rather, in *Third Person*, Esposito argues that even today personhood relies on 'a sort of excess, of a spiritual or moral character, that makes more of the "person", yet without letting it coincide completely with the self-sufficient individual of the liberal tradition'.¹⁴ Similarly, although coming from a completely different theoretical background, Joseph Vining

---

7 Ibid. 81–85.
8 Roberto Esposito, *Communitas: The Origin and Destiny of Community* (Stanford, Calif.: Stanford University Press, 2010); Roberto Esposito, *Immunitas: The Protection and Negation of Life* (Cambridge; Malden MA: Polity, 2011); Roberto Esposito, *Bíos: Biopolitics and Philosophy* (Minneapolis: University of Minnesota Press, 2008).
9 See further Matthew Stone, 'Roberto Esposito and the Biopolitics of Property Rights', *Social & Legal Studies* 24:3 (2015), 381–98.
10 Esposito, *Persons and Things*, 17.
11 On Marx's view of the relation between rights and private property, see Karl Marx and Arthur Kemp, *On the Jewish Question*, 1st edn. (CreateSpace Independent Publishing Platform, 2014); Karl Marx and Sankar Srinivasan, *Critique of Hegel's Philosophy of Right*, trans. Andy Blunden (CreateSpace Independent Publishing Platform, 2015).
12 Michael Hardt and Antonio Negri, *Commonwealth* (Cambridge, MA: Belknap Press, 2011), 13.
13 See also Joseph Vining, 'Dignity as Perception: Recognition of the Human Individual and the Individual Animal in Legal Thought,' in Christopher McCrudden (ed.) *Understanding Human Dignity* (Oxford University Press/ British Academy, Proceedings of the British Academy Vol. 192m 2013), 581.
14 Roberto Esposito, *Third Person: Politics of Life and Philosophy of the Impersonal* (Cambridge, UK: Polity Press, 2012), 70–1.

writes that the notion of an individual is always seen in connection to a specific body, whereas a person may be embodied but does not have to be.[15] Hence, from whichever perspective we approach the issue, there is always a rift between the personal subject and human being,[16] irrespective of whether the predominance is granted to the biological or the rational.

What is left without adequate reflection in this division of the legal world to persons, on the one hand, and things owned by those persons, on the other, is, according to Esposito, the body. Indeed, although various powers have always competed over ownership of human bodies, the body has never been adequately defined legally. As the body does not really fit in the category of persons, or the category of things, it oscillates constantly between the two, at times part of the person and at other times reduced to the level of a thing, but never really fitting in either category.[17] Oftentimes the body is equated with the person, but this also means that when this is not the case, it tends to immediately become a thing – as is often the case with body parts, for example. In any event, the logic tends to lead to unanswerable paradoxes, enabling both very conservative and very exploitative situations.

The bioethical challenge and post-humanist theory

The old logic of law, traced by Esposito, has, however, recently been put under increasing pressure. The most visible challenge to the old logic is posed by rapid development in science and technology, including genetics, cloning, all kinds of implants, printings and xenotransplantation. In the words of the US President's Council on Bioethics:

> we have entered upon a golden age for biology, medicine, and biotechnology. With the completion of (the DNA sequencing phase of) the Human Genome Project and the emergence of stem cell research, we can look forward to major insights into human development, normal and abnormal, as well as novel and more precisely selected treatments for human disease.[18]

These developments challenge the old logic of law in at least three ways. First, new biotechnologies radically challenge the distinction between

---

15 Vining, 'Dignity as Perception: Recognition of the Human Individual and the Individual Animal in Legal Thought', 582.
16 Esposito, *Third person*, 11–13.
17 Esposito, *Persons and Things*, 99–100.
18 President's Council on Bioethics, Beyond Therapy (New York: Dana Press, 2003), 5–6, quoted in Roger Brownsword, 'Human Dignity, Human Rights, and Simply Trying to Do the Right Thing', in *Understanding Human Dignity*, edited by Christopher McCrudden (OUP/British Academy, Proceedings of the British Academy Vol. 192, 2013), 345.

human and non-human, making the border between the two porous and untraceable. As Johanna Zylinska writes, '[i]n biotechnological processes living and non-living elements exist in intimate couplings and associations which imply a design that disallows both the notion of life as something entering a machine in order to animate it, and the notion of technology as something added post-factum to the original living entity'.[19] These technologies therefore reveal our kinship with all kinds of material forms.

This alone is, however, not necessarily enough to challenge the person-property dichotomy, as personhood is explicitly something non-material – social or political, in opposition to merely biological. However, the distinction between the person as something socially constructed (or alternatively transcendental and given) and bodies as merely biological entities is also becoming blurred as 'the centrality accorded to the soma, to the flesh, the organs, the tissues, the cells, the gene sequences, and molecular corporeality',[20] changes how we understand ourselves as human beings. It is now increasingly understood that we cannot make a distinction between some rational part of ourselves and our bodies.[21] Moreover, Nikolas Rose writes, '[o]ur bodies have become ourselves, become central to our expectations, hopes, our individual and collective identities, and our biological responsibilities'.[22] Our bodies are therefore no longer something we master – that is to say, things – but an important part of who we are, socially speaking.

Finally, it has become increasingly difficult to allocate bodies as property of this or that person. To quote Rose again, '[c]ontemporary genetics is beginning to operate in a flattened world, a world of surfaces rather than depths. In the developing explanatory schemas of postgenomics, the genetic code is no longer thought of as a deep structure that causes or determines, but rather as one set of relays in complex, ramifying, and nonhierarchical networks, filiations, and connections'.[23] The social circulation pushes bodies outside the logic of persons and things and into the sphere of common.

Related to this biotechnological challenge to the old logic of law is a shift in power relations. Partly because of the aforementioned developments, and partly for other reasons, bodies have become a matter of competing interests. As Rose notes, biology is no longer destiny but opportunity. Now

---

19 Johanna Zylinska, 'Is There Life in Cybernetics? Designing a Post-Humanist Bioethics', in *Deleuze and Law: Forensic Futures*, edited by Rosi Braidotti, Claire Colebrook and Patrick Hanafin (Basingstoke; New York: Palgrave Macmillan, 2009), 119.
20 Nikolas Rose, *The Politics of Life Itself: Biomedicine, Power, and Subjectivity in the Twenty-First Century* (Princeton, NJ: Princeton University Press, 2006), 105.
21 Muireann Quigley, 'Property in Human Biomaterials – Separating Persons and Things?', *Oxford Journal of Legal Studies* 32:4 (2012), 659–83.
22 Rose, *The Politics of Life Itself*, 105.
23 Ibid. 130.

that life is understood and engineered at the molecular level, biopolitics has become a matter of optimisation. As '[a]lmost any vital element can, in principle, be freed from its ties to cell, organ, organism, or species, set free to circulate and to be combined with any other',[24] the question becomes, what are human beings in the optimal state – a biopolitical question *par excellence*.

All in all, then, these developments have created problems that the old categories of philosophy and law are not well-equipped to answer. Now that molecular elements of life are available for new forms of mobilisation, control, and connections, 'life itself has become open to politics'.[25] For example, the distinction 'between that which is not human and that which is human can no longer do the work that is required to resolve bioethical issues [for] that distinction is itself what is at stake in the politics of the contemporary bioeconomy'.[26] On the one hand, this has created new threats, risks, and power disparities. Perhaps the most obvious risk is that life has become open to new forms of exploitation in the form of biocapital: life and bodies as matter (not just labour force) can now be harnessed into a commodity for profit.[27] Further, they can be branded and, through creating new connections, turned into intellectual property.[28] As Donna Haraway writes, the creation of legally branded molecular databases that make the human genome available for the advancement of industry means that the taxonomic type of Man has become 'Man the brand'.[29] On the other hand, however, these developments also create new possibilities. In Esposito's mind, the excluded body's point of view could dismantle the knot that the logic of property and the person/thing distinction have created. For it is the body that unites our individual and collective experiences: bodies are what we have in common, and can therefore turn around the immunising and exclusionary logic on which law has for too long been based.[30] The new biotechnologies have made this more obvious than ever, as 'people who at one time appeared as individual monads may now house inside themselves elements that come from other bodies and even inorganic materials'. As Esposito continues, '[t]he human body has thus become the flow channel

---

24 Ibid. 16.
25 Ibid. 15.
26 Ibid. 39.
27 Rosi Braidotti, *The Posthuman* (Cambridge; Malden MA: Polity Press, 2013), 63.
28 For a legal analysis, see Chamundeeswari Kuppuswamy, *The International Legal Governance of the Human Genome*, 1st edn. (Routledge, 2009).
29 Donna Haraway, *Modest_Witness@Second_Millennium.FemaleMan_Meets_OncoMouse: Feminism and Technoscience* (New York: Routledge, 1997), 74.
30 On the complex relation between 'common' and 'immune', on which Esposito's thought is based, see Esposito, *Communitas*; Esposito, *Immunitas*; Esposito, *Bíos*.

and the operator, certainly a delicate one, of a relation that is less and less reducible to a binary logic'.[31]

Indeed, some innovative attempts to rethink life and subjectivity otherwise in the new situation already exist in philosophy. Especially interesting for me is the lineage of thought that, moving from Spinoza and Nietzsche through Deleuze, Guattari and Foucault all the way to present day, could perhaps be called neo-vitalist and anti-humanist. This kind of thought allows us to overcome the dialectical oppositions represented by the person/property dichotomy, and to understand matter as vital and self-organising – a perspective that is crucial for approaching the new mind-body interactions created by neural sciences and biotechnologies. For example Rosi Braidotti has been developing a notion of nomadic subjectivity, or subjectivity always in the state of becoming, which aims to take into consideration the complexities related to technological progress and multiple belongings, on the one hand, and posthuman theory with its focus on interconnections between self and (often non-human) others, on the other. Especially attractive in Braidotti's approach is that she does not base her theory of interconnectivity on shared vulnerability, but on 'an affirmative bond that locates the subject in the flow of relations with multiple others'.[32]

These kinds of ideas are admittedly incredibly difficult to introduce within legal thought. Nevertheless, jurisprudence, too, has during the last couple of decades started to slowly open its doors to the body. As Esposito writes, laws dealing with transfusion of blood and organ harvesting introduced *bios* into law and 'broke the exclusive relationship between body and individual, making the body a sort of collective good'.[33] A particularly interesting project has, however, been the attempt to declare the human genome common heritage of humanity. This is so at least if the project is not viewed from the perspective of sanctity of life, but rather as a 'transfer of the body from the sphere of the proper to that of the common',[34] in which case it seems, at least at first sight, to challenge approaches that aim to push body towards the logic of private property.

It should be noted that the approach based on the notion of common heritage of humanity has never managed to fully break through, however. Even the UNESCO Universal Declaration on the Human Genome and Human Rights, which has often been hailed as a milestone for the approach, states in its Article 1 that: 'The human genome underlies the fundamental unity of all members of the human family, as well as the recognition of

---

31 Esposito, *Persons and Things*, 4.
32 Braidotti, *The Posthuman*, 50.
33 Esposito, *Persons and Things*, 104.
34 Ibid. 105.

their inherent dignity and diversity. In a symbolic sense, it is the heritage of humanity'.

Thus, even in this non-binding declaration, the human genome is recognised as common heritage of humanity only in the *symbolic* sense, in the fear of intervening too much with intellectual property rights, even though the Declaration does stress that any research of human genome should benefit the humankind as a whole.[35] Although the attempts to push the human genome towards common heritage of humanity continued also after the Declaration in the work of UN Sub-Commissions,[36] it seems that a more intellectual property rights focused approach has nevertheless emerged as the winner.[37]

The age of human dignity

Instead of the doctrine of common heritage of humanity, then, the preferred legal solution for balancing private and common interests in issues dealing with biotechnology has been the application of the human dignity principle. Human dignity has of course played an important role in Western constitutional theory since it was not only mentioned in the key post-Second World War human rights documents but also made the guiding principle of all law in Article 1 of the German Constitution, thus producing, according to some theorists, a constitutional shift from liberty to dignity.[38] Yet, the fact that it has rapidly become the primary framework for dealing with issues of life and death bioethics is a more recent phenomenon. The new prevalence of human dignity in bioethics is reflected for example in the 2005 UNESCO Universal Declaration on Bioethics and Human Rights. As Kuppuswamy comments, human dignity features in the Declaration as the running theme that is used as a justification and rationale for principles put in place to protect human rights and that may contrast scientific freedoms.[39] Similarly, the Council of Europe Convention on Human Rights and Biomedicine declares in its Article 1 that 'Parties to this Convention shall protect the dignity and identity of all human beings and guarantee everyone, without discrimination, respect for their integrity and other rights and fundamental freedoms with regard to the application of biology and medicine'.

---

35 Kuppuswamy, *The International Legal Governance of the Human Genome*, 28.
36 Ibid. 35–7.
37 See generally Kuppuswamy, *The International Legal Governance of the Human Genome*.
38 Alexander Somek, *The Cosmopolitan Constitution*, 1st edn. (Oxford: Oxford University Press, 2014), 9; See, however, also Samuel Moyn, *Christian Human Rights* (University of Pennsylvania Press, 2015) for a somewhat different view.
39 Kuppuswamy, *The International Legal Governance of the Human Genome*, 30–1.

Considerations of human dignity are highly important, of course, and an important counterforce to bioeconomy. Yet, the problem is that the answers given to biotechnological problems by bioethics, applying the human dignity principle, have been rather conservative, drawing mainly from the old humanist tradition. Most importantly, instead of following the possibilities opened by post-humanist theory, the human dignity approach seems to, as I will argue in what follows, rely on the old logic of law detected by Esposito. Indeed, the roots of human dignity can be found in the aristocratic concept of *dignitas*, which is part of the same Roman law tradition that Esposito constantly refers to. Roman social life was fundamentally based on honour, which was linked to the office that an individual held, meaning that *dignitas*, deriving from office, not from the individual human being, was conceived to mean 'elevated position or rank'.[40] *Dignitas* was therefore not attributed equally to everyone, but was instead used as a term of distinction and applied to few only. Hence, in this usage, far from being an intrinsic and inalienable attribute, *dignitas* could be gained and lost. It was a relational concept that not only entailed certain powers but also certain duties to behave accordingly to one's rank.[41] As Oliver Sensen writes, 'the sense in which something is elevated over something else [had] to be specified with each usage of "dignity".'[42] In the same way, then, as rights of individuals depend on the notion of personhood, which is something separate from the biological entity human, *dignitas* was also linked to something that was somehow separable from the individual.

A lot has changed from the times of ancient Rome, of course, and indeed almost all commentators would agree that the logic of *dignitas* has been flipped on its head in the contemporary notion of human dignity. Some argue that there is a radical break between *dignitas* and human dignity, and that it does not therefore make sense to discuss the two together at all,[43] whereas others hold that the two notions are linked but that human dignity has become so egalitarian that it has been completely purged from the

---

40 Teresa Iglesias, 'Bedrock Truths and the Dignity of the Individual', *Logos: A Journal of Catholic Thought and Culture* 4:1 (2001), 120–1.
41 Ibid.; Rieke Van Der Graaf and Johannes Jm Van Delden, 'Clarifying Appeals to Dignity in Medical Ethics from an Historical Perspective', *Bioethics* 23:3 (2009), 155; Michael Rosen, *Dignity: Its History and Meaning* (Cambridge, MA: Harvard University Press, 2012), 11–14.
42 Oliver Sensen, 'Human Dignity in Historical Perspective: The Contemporary and Traditional Paradigms', *European Journal of Political Theory* 10:1 (2011), 75–6.
43 Sensen, 'Human Dignity in Historical Perspective'; Paolo G. Carozza, 'Human Dignity and Judicial Interpretation of Human Rights: A Reply', *European Journal of International Law* 19:5 (2008), 931–44.

problematic aspects of *dignitas*.⁴⁴ I would slightly disagree with both views, however.

To be sure, human dignity is, as some critics argue, a vacuous concept from an analytical point of view,⁴⁵ and thus capable of being used for myriad purposes and with myriad consequences. Yet, in practice the usage of human dignity is strongly dominated by two traditions which seem, at first sight, diametrically opposite, but which are connected, I argue, by a similar logic of operation as the one in Esposito's genealogy of persons and things. On the one hand, human dignity is often used to further the liberal idea of autonomous individuals. This is exemplified for example by a decision of the former President of the Israeli Supreme Court, Aharon Barak, in which he stated that: '[at] the center of human dignity are the sanctity and liberty of life. At its foundation are the autonomy of the individual will, the freedom of choice, and the freedom of man to act as a free creature.'⁴⁶ This notion of dignity is therefore used to immunise the individuals against such things as unwanted medical treatment, affirmative actions, and so on, and to protect freedom of choice, when it comes to abortion, for example.

On the other hand, there is a more communitarian, obligation-creating usage, where human dignity is conceived as something coming from elsewhere rather than linked to the autonomy of the individual, and hence used to negotiate the relation between the individual and the community. This usage is exemplified for instance by the French *Senanayake* case,⁴⁷ dealing with a blood transfusion given to a Jehovah's Witness in a critical condition, in which the Court decided that the operation could be carried out even against the wish of the patient and his wife, as the Court was of the opinion that:

> the notion of human dignity is *not* synonymous with autonomous freedom. It encompasses an *objective* dimension, founded in the belonging of the individual to *humanity*, and leads to giving a greater importance,

---

44 James Q. Whitman, 'On Nazi "Honour" and the New European "Dignity"', in *Darker Legacies of Law in Europe: The Shadow of National Socialism and Fascism over Europe and Its Legal Traditions*, by Christian Joerges, Navraj Singh Ghaleigh and Michael Stolleis (Oxford; Portland, Or: Hart Publishing, 2003), 243–66; For a somewhat more complex view, see Jeremy Waldron, 'Dignity and Rank', *European Journal of Sociology/Archives Européennes de Sociologie* 48:2 (2007), 201–37.

45 Ruth Macklin, 'Dignity Is a Useless Concept', *British Medical Journal* 327 (2003), 1419; Mirko Bagaric and James Allan, 'The Vacuous Concept of Dignity', *Journal of Human Rights* 5:2 (2006), 257–70; See also Christopher McCrudden, 'Human Dignity and Judicial Interpretation of Human Rights', *European Journal of International Law* 19:4 (2008), 655.

46 *The Movement for Quality Government in Israel v The Knesset* [2006] IsrSC 61(1) 619, 685.

47 *Senanayake et Donhoy*, Cour administrative d'appel de Paris, 9 June 1998.

whenever a human value is at stake, to the universal standard over singular preferences.[48]

Here, as in other cases using a similar notion of dignity, the concept is therefore used to justify restrictions on the autonomy of individuals, for example regarding medical practices, prostitution, peep-shows, or even working in dwarf-throwing events.[49] These two traditions are certainly not the only possible uses of dignity, but they are the dominant ones, as well as the ones that have been in play in the most important transnational cases dealing with bioethics, as demonstrated by Roger Brownsword.[50] And while these two approaches seem completely opposite, they are united by the fact that they share – despite the counter-arguments of most proponents of human dignity – a similar logic of operation with the ancient notion of *dignitas*.

Obligation-creating usage of dignity and the apparatus of humanity

Stéphanie Hennette-Vauchez has shown this link between *dignitas* and human dignity in an insightful manner with regard to the obligation-creating usage of dignity. Even though human dignity is extended to all humans, Hennette-Vauchez emphasises that, just like *dignitas*, it operates by introducing a third element between the individual and human dignity. As Hennette-Vauchez writes, 'it can be argued that the notion of humanity has been used as a mediator between the individual and human dignity',[51] and that '[a]s an abstract concept that has to do with eternity and intemporality, humanity may well be described as deposited within each and every one of us', yet still remaining, as eternal and intemporal, 'unchallenged by individual disappearances'.[52]

This is clearly visible in the French and German case law, both of which are full of references to absolute and objective values. Human dignity is therefore seen in these legal cultures as a quality of the entire human

---

48 M. Heers, conclusions, C.A.A. Paris, 9 June 1998 (1998) 6 Revuefranfaise de droit administratif, 1231–42, cited in Stephanie Hennette-Vauchez, 'When Ambivalent Principles Prevail: Leads for Explaining Western Legal Orders' Infatuation with the Human Dignity Principle', *Legal Ethics* 10 (2007), 202–3.
49 *Manuel Wackenheim v France*, Human Rights Committee, Communication No 854/1999, U.N. Doc. CCPR/C/75/D/854/1999 (2002).
50 Brownsword, 'Human Dignity, Human Rights, and Simply Trying to Do the Right Thing', 349–53.
51 Stéphanie Hennette-Vauchez, 'A Human Dignitas? The Contemporary Principle of Human Dignity as a Mere Reappraisal of an Ancient Legal Concept', SSRN Scholarly Paper (Rochester, NY: Social Science Research Network, July 1, 2008), 21, http://papers.ssrn.com/abstract=1303427.
52 Ibid.

species, rather than that of a single individual. The best illustration of this view is, according to Hennette-Vauchez, the French *Benetton* case.[53] The case dealt with Benetton's controversial advertisement campaign which consisted of photographs that 'were used [and] represented body parts that were tattooed "HIV Positive"'. Outraged AIDS patients' associations sued Benetton and the company was found to have crossed the limits of its freedom of expression in using 'degrading symbol[s] of stigmatization' which injured 'the dignity of people who implacably suffer in their flesh and soul' by 'provoking or accentuating at their expense a phenomenon of exclusion'. What Hennette-Vauchez emphasises regarding this case is the technical fact that the petitioners in this case actually had no link whatsoever with the controversial photographs: they had not posed in the pictures, nor were they linked to Benetton in any way. The Court could have therefore easily found the case inadmissible on the basis of lacking *locus standi*. Yet it decided to choose otherwise and 'judged that the petitioners' sole membership of humankind constituted a sufficient ground for their course of action'. As one commentator notes:

> the patients' [associations] had argued that the photographs excluded them from the community of humans. In other words, they did not place their action on the grounds of private life, but on that of humanity. Hence this double consequence: on the one hand their demand became perfectly admissible for they only claimed to be recognized as members of humanity, and on the other hand, dignity prevailed over freedom of expression.[54]

In this construction, then, the relation of life, in all its complexity, and the apparatus of human dignity, is mediated through another apparatus, namely humanity. As Hennette-Vauchez writes, '[i]n many instances, the principle of human dignity has served to ground obligations of the individual towards a higher instance of humanity, or towards the parcel of humanity of which he is a repository but not a proprietor'.[55] In this particular sense, the apparatus does not differ from the archaic Roman notion of *dignitas*, which was attached to human life only through the office that an individual held.

Further, the construction also implies that even though human dignity applies to all humans, some humans are still less human because of their desires that go against some objective humanity. In a way, then, the

---

53 Cour d'Appel de Paris, 28 May 1996, (1996) *Recueil Dalloz*, 618.
54 B. Edelman, 'La dignité de la personne humaine, un concept nouveau', (1997) Recueil Dalloz, 185, cited in ibid., 23.
55 Stéphanie Hennette-Vauchez, 'Human Dignity in French Law', in *The Cambridge Handbook of Human Dignity: Interdisciplinary Perspectives*, by Marcus Düwell *et al.* (Cambridge: Cambridge University Press, 2014), 371–2.

construction protects humanity against the animal within each of us. We are protected against outside violence but also against the darkest parts of ourselves. And if we cannot control this animal side, our humanity is at stake. Hence, for example in the dwarf-throwing case, where the applicant wanted to maintain his job being tossed around by the customers of a disco, the Court, in aiming to protect the dignity of the applicant, also unintentionally implied that the whole existence of the applicant was somehow less dignified that that of others. Similarly, the choices of prostitutes or peep-show actresses are not truly human. Hence, the apparatus maintains the rift detected by Esposito within each of us between an animal that has to be controlled and some other element that is something more than our biological existence.

Rights-founding usage of dignity and the apparatus of person

I agree, then, mostly with Hennette-Vauchez's analysis of the obligation-creating usage of dignity and its links to *dignitas*. I reject, however, her optimism regarding the other common usage of human dignity, namely a rights-founding one. In contrast to what Hennette-Vauchez writes, I will argue in what follows that this conception of human dignity has just as much in common with the ancient version of *dignitas* as the obligation-creating one. For in this version, too, the link between human dignity and concrete human life is mediated through another apparatus, just like *dignitas* was mediated through the office one held in ancient Rome.

In the case of the individualistic, autonomy-based usage of the apparatus of human dignity, the external apparatus mediating the relation between human dignity and human life is that of personhood. As the mainstream liberal view on human rights and human dignity in all its contradictions goes, every person has human rights because of her inherent dignity, while at the same time she has a right to dignity because she is a person. This formulation is of course a tautology that compromises the entire foundation of the more metaphysically oriented liberal take on human rights and human dignity.[56] Yet, what is more important for my purposes in this section is that whichever way the liberal formulation of human dignity is turned, it always relies on personhood. Thus, for example the preamble to the UN Charter reaffirms international belief in 'the dignity and worth of the human person', and the common preamble to the two International Covenants on human rights declares that human rights 'derive from the inherent dignity of the human person'. In this framework, then, attributing

---

56 See Waldron, 'Dignity and Rank', 203–4; Audrey R. Chapman, 'Human Dignity, Bioethics, and Human Rights', *Amsterdam Law Forum* 3:1 (2013), 8.

dignity to a being attributes personhood – or, attributing personhood attributes dignity – which then leads to autonomy.

Here we find, then, in an even more pure form than in the obligation-creating usage of human dignity, the same logic detected by Esposito between the personal and the animal. As long as human dignity operates through personhood, the key question obviously becomes whether and when a being can be considered a person. To claim our rights, we must first enter into the realm of personhood and manage to remain in it.[57] Further, as the apparatus of person is based on 'the assumed, continuously recurring separation between person as an artificial entity and the human as a natural being, whom the status of person may or may not befit', it again and again creates zones of indistinguishability at its borders, meaning that 'to experience personhood fully means to keep, or push, other living individuals to the edge of thingness'.[58]

Esposito traces, following the analysis of the legal historian Siegmund Schlossmann, the origin of the term 'person' both to 'mask 'and 'face', and to events in which the two merged into each other; first in theatre where the actor who in interpreting his role moulded himself until the mask and the wearer 'corresponded in every detail', and second in death rituals where 'death masks of wax were molded directly on the face of the deceased' with the consequence that 'in the face of death it was no longer the human being who donned a mask, but the mask that was incarnated in the human body, to the point of constituting its most authentic expression'.[59] If we take, then, this idea of mask, and combine it with the never-ending need to trace the borders of the person, it can be suggested that the human dignity-personhood decision-making apparatus seems to operate by attributing this or that entity a mask that includes them under the legal realm.

Unsurprisingly, then, with this usage of human dignity, we find again all the unanswerable paradoxes created by the distinction between persons – and consequently legal subjects – and things. Indeed, there is strong disagreement about who or what exactly human dignity should extend to in legal practice and theory.[60] It is commonly held, for example in bioethics inspired by the work of Peter Singer,[61] that human dignity covers only rational, sentient persons. At the other end of the spectrum, dignity has been extended also to non-human entities, including companies, and even

---

57 Esposito, *Third person*, 2–4.
58 Ibid. 9–10.
59 Ibid. 74–5.
60 Nick Bostrom, 'Dignity and Enhancement', in *Human Dignity and Bioethics: Essays Commissioned by the President's Council on Bioethics*, 1st edn. (S.l.: US Independent Agencies and Commissions, 2008), 176.
61 Peter Singer, *Practical Ethics*, 3rd edn. (New York: Cambridge University Press, 2011); Peter Singer, *Rethinking Life and Death: The Collapse of Our Traditional Ethics*, Reprint edition (New York: St. Martin's Griffin, 1996).

to alligators. In the *Let the Animals Live v Hamat Gader Spa Village* case, dealing with man–alligator fights, involving for example forcibly opening the alligator's jaw and tumbling the animal by grabbing its tail, Cheshin J stated that 'I find no justification for inflicting pain and anguish on a helpless animal solely for the purpose of entertaining an audience. Such an act is simply immoral and we should not allow it. The animal is a helpless creature, much like a helpless minor. Neither of them can protect themselves, or claim their insult, or regain their dignity.' As Cheshin J concluded, 'I do not know if the alligator itself feels humiliated when the human wrestler hold its tail, tumbles it back and forth, turns it on its back, and so forth, as if it were a lifeless rag doll. However, this I know – that the acts inflicted by man on alligator, were they to be inflicted on man, would be considered humiliating and oppressing.'[62]

Between these two poles – alive, sentient persons versus alligators or non-human entities – there are countless battlefields. Israeli courts have extended human dignity also to the dead, stating that 'an individual's death does not put an end to the state's duty [...] to protect him from assaults on his human dignity'.[63] Yet the status of the foetus is probably the one raising most debates, being granted human dignity by some courts and explicitly refused that status by others.

I want to emphasise that I am not arguing that these effects are all unwelcomed – this would be to take a very conservative stance on many fundamental questions of life: a stance I would feel very uncomfortable with. Nevertheless, it is important to note two things about this practice. The first is the way the relation between the apparatus of human dignity and human life is mediated through another apparatus, namely that of personhood. Not only does the apparatus of human dignity therefore operate in a similar way as the ancient apparatus of *dignitas*, but it seems to also follow the logic of law traced by Esposito The second issue worth noting is that this human dignity-personhood apparatus can be employed to create caesura between life that enjoys protection, and life that does not, or life that must live and life that can be allowed to die. In other words, it is important to point out the exclusionary logic through which these apparatuses function, resting as they are on the need to push some form of being – for example animals,[64] but also the body and sometimes even some human beings – to the edge of thingness, with *potentially* (though certainly not necessarily) disastrous effects.

---

62 *Let the Animals Live v Hamat Gader Spa Village Inc* (1997), IsrSC, 1648/96, cited in McCrudden, 'Human Dignity and Judicial Interpretation of Human Rights', 708.
63 *Jerusalem Community Jewish Burial Society v Kestenbaum* (1992) IsrSC 46(2) 464, cited in Erin Daly, *Dignity Rights: Courts, Constitutions, and the Worth of the Human Person* (Philadelphia: University of Pennsylvania Press, 2013), 43–4.
64 Peter Singer, *Animal Liberation*, 2nd edn. (Pimlico, 1995).

Conclusion

If the possibility opened by biotechnology and new theoretical innovations is, then, that they push us to think of legal categories and legal subjectivity otherwise, by challenging the notion of the human subject as a 'skin-bound sovereign', and by forcing us to take note of the complex interconnections between the self and others, including non-human others, and of the notion of body not as property, but as a common that unites us, it does not seem that the dominant traditions of human dignity are equipped to help in realising this possibility. As argued above, both of the seemingly opposite usages are united by the fact that they rely, following the logic of the archaic notion of *dignitas*, on a third element that mediates between life in all its complexity and human dignity. In the case of *dignitas*, this element was office, and in the case of human dignity it seems to be humanity or personhood. In this sense, the usages rely on a similar logic as that traced by Esposito, based on a separation of persons and things – a separation that exists not only in relations between human and other entities but also, and more importantly, within human life and within individual human beings.

It is partly this rift that novel theories of subject, such as that of Rosi Braidotti's, for example, aim to bridge. Braidotti's theory of nomadic subjectivity is specifically designed to fit our 'post-human condition', as it is based on the notions of a constant state of becoming and complex relations with multiple others. As such, it has room for creative, imagining subjects, without falling back on any kind of binary or immunising logic. Yet, the dominant logic of human dignity does not have room for such subjectivities. In its obligation-creating form, it falls back on some 'objective' notion of humanity, which creates a status quo and blocks any processes of becoming, turning difficult bioethical questions into a 'plan for the successful running of the pre-decided programme'.[65] And in the right-founding form, it tends to rely on the notion of personhood with exactly the same exclusionary and immunising consequences as in Esposito's genealogy of the *dispositif* of person.

Considering the analytical emptiness of the concept of human dignity, it might be possible to create novel usages of the concept, more fitting for the new challenges posed by biotechnology and more capable of taking into consideration post-human ethical considerations. But the notion of dignity comes with so much baggage that it might be more beneficial to come up with a completely new way of approaching contemporary challenges. In any event, the solution has to be one that does not try to hide the moment of decision involved in any bioethical problem, but instead allows creative and imaginative decisions and the creation of novel subjectivities.

---

65 Zylinska, 'Is There Life in Cybernetics? Designing a Post-Humanist Bioethics', 138.

Bibliography

Bagaric, Mirko and James Allan. 'The Vacuous Concept of Dignity,' *Journal of Human Rights* 5, no. 2 (2006): 257–70.
Bostrom, Nick. 'Dignity and Enhancement'. In *Human Dignity and Bioethics: Essays Commissioned by the President's Council on Bioethics*, 1st edn., 173–207. S.l.: US Independent Agencies and Commissions, 2008.
Braidotti, Rosi. *The Posthuman*. Cambridge; Malden MA: Polity Press, 2013.
Brownsword, Roger. 'Human Dignity, Human Rights, and Simply Trying to Do the Right Thing'. In *Understanding Human Dignity*, edited by Christopher McCrudden, 345–59. OUP/British Academy, Proceedings of the British Academy Vol. 192, 2013.
Carozza, Paolo G. 'Human Dignity and Judicial Interpretation of Human Rights: A Reply,' *European Journal of International Law* 19:5 (2008), 931–44.
Chapman, Audrey R. 'Human Dignity, Bioethics, and Human Rights,' *Amsterdam Law Forum* 3:1 (2013), 1–12.
Daly, Erin. *Dignity Rights: Courts, Constitutions, and the Worth of the Human Person*. Philadelphia: University of Pennsylvania Press, 2013.
Edelman, Bernard. 'La dignité de la personne humaine, un concept nouveau.' *Recueil Dalloz* 23 (1997), 185.
Esposito, Roberto. *Bíos: Biopolitics and Philosophy*. Minneapolis: University of Minnesota Press, 2008.
Esposito, Roberto. *Communitas: The Origin and Destiny of Community*. Stanford, Calif.: Stanford University Press, 2010.
Esposito, Roberto. *Immunitas: The Protection and Negation of Life*. Cambridge; Malden MA: Polity, 2011.
Esposito, Roberto. *Persons and Things: From the Body's Point of View*. 1st edn. Cambridge ; Malden, MA: Polity, 2015.
Esposito, Roberto. *Third Person: Politics of Life and Philosophy of the Impersonal*. Cambridge, UK: Polity Press, 2012.
Haraway, Donna. *Modest_Witness@Second_Millennium.FemaleMan_Meets_OncoMouse: Feminism and Technoscience*. New York: Routledge, 1997.
Hardt, Michael, and Antonio Negri. *Commonwealth*. Cambridge, MA: Belknap Press, 2011.
Hennette-Vauchez, Stéphanie. 'A Human Dignitas? The Contemporary Principle of Human Dignity as a Mere Reappraisal of an Ancient Legal Concept'. SSRN Scholarly Paper. Rochester, NY: Social Science Research Network, July 1, 2008, http://papers.ssrn.com/abstract=1303427. Last retrieved 22 May 2014.
Hennette-Vauchez, Stéphanie. 'Human Dignity in French Law'. In *The Cambridge Handbook of Human Dignity: Interdisciplinary Perspectives*, edited by Marcus Düwell, Jens Braarvig, Roger Brownsword and Dietmar Mieth, 368–74. Cambridge: Cambridge University Press, 2014.
Hennette-Vauchez, Stéphanie. 'When Ambivalent Principles Prevail: Leads for Explaining Western Legal Orders' Infatuation with the Human Dignity Principle,' *Legal Ethics* 10 (2007), 193.
Iglesias, Teresa. 'Bedrock Truths and the Dignity of the Individual,' *Logos: A Journal of Catholic Thought and Culture* 4:1 (2001), 114–34.
Kuppuswamy, Chamundeeswari. *The International Legal Governance of the Human Genome*. 1st edn. Routledge, 2009.
Langford, Peter. *Roberto Esposito: Law, Community and the Political*. Abingdon, Oxon; New York, NY: Routledge, 2015.

Macklin, Ruth. 'Dignity Is a Useless Concept,' *British Medical Journal* 327 (2003), 1419.
Marx, Karl, and Arthur Kemp. *On the Jewish Question*. 1st edn. CreateSpace Independent Publishing Platform, 2014.
Marx, Karl, and Sankar Srinivasan. *Critique of Hegel's Philosophy of Right.* Translated by Andy Blunden. CreateSpace Independent Publishing Platform, 2015.
McCrudden, Christopher. 'Human Dignity and Judicial Interpretation of Human Rights,' *European Journal of International Law* 19:4 (2008), 655–724.
Moyn, Samuel. *Christian Human Rights.* University of Pennsylvania Press, 2015.
Quigley, Muireann. 'Property in Human Biomaterials – Separating Persons and Things?' *Oxford Journal of Legal Studies* 32:4 (2012), 659–83.
Rose, Nikolas. *The Politics of Life Itself: Biomedicine, Power, and Subjectivity in the Twenty-First Century.* Princeton, NJ: Princeton University Press, 2006.
Rosen, Michael. *Dignity: Its History and Meaning.* Cambridge, MA: Harvard University Press, 2012.
Sensen, Oliver. 'Human Dignity in Historical Perspective: The Contemporary and Traditional Paradigms,' *European Journal of Political Theory* 10:1 (2011), 71–91.
Singer, Peter. *Animal Liberation.* 2nd edn. Pimlico, 1995.
Singer, Peter. *Practical Ethics.* 3rd edn. New York: Cambridge University Press, 2011.
Singer, Peter. *Rethinking Life and Death: The Collapse of Our Traditional Ethics.* Reprint edition. New York: St. Martin's Griffin, 1996.
Somek, Alexander. *The Cosmopolitan Constitution.* 1st edn. Oxford: Oxford University Press, 2014.
Stone, Matthew. 'Roberto Esposito and the Biopolitics of Property Rights,' *Social & Legal Studies* 24:3 (2015), 381–98.
Van Der Graaf, Rieke, and Johannes Jm Van Delden. 'Clarifying Appeals to Dignity in Medical Ethics from an Historical Perspective,' *Bioethics* 23:3 (2009), 151–60.
Vining, Joseph. 'Dignity as Perception: Recognition of the Human Individual and the Individual Animal in Legal Thought'. In *Understanding Human Dignity*, edited by Christopher McCrudden, 573–90. Oxford University Press/British Academy, Proceedings of the British Academy Vol. 192, 2013.
Waldron, Jeremy. 'Dignity and Rank,' *European Journal of Sociology/Archives Européennes de Sociologie* 48:2 (2007), 201–37.
Whitman, James Q. 'On Nazi "Honour" and the New European "Dignity"'. In *Darker Legacies of Law in Europe: The Shadow of National Socialism and Fascism over Europe and Its Legal Traditions*, by Christian Joerges, Navraj Singh Ghaleigh, and Michael Stolleis, 243–66. Oxford; Portland, OR: Hart Publishing, 2003.
Zylinska, Johanna. 'Is There Life in Cybernetics? Designing a Post-Humanist Bioethics'. In *Deleuze and Law: Forensic Futures*, edited by Rosi Braidotti, Claire Colebrook and Patrick Hanafin, 117–41. Basingstoke; New York: Palgrave Macmillan, 2009.

List of Cases

Cour d'Appel de Paris, 28 May 1996, (1996) Recueil Dalloz, 618
Jerusalem Community Jewish Burial Society v Kestenbaum [1992], IsrSC 46(2) 464
Let the Animals Live v Hamat Gader Spa Village Inc [1997], IsrSC, 1648/96
Manuel Wackenheim v France, Human Rights Committee, Communication No 854/1999, U.N. Doc. CCPR/C/75/D/854/1999 (2002)
Senanayake et Donhoy, Cour administrative d'appel de Paris, 9 June 1998
The Movement for Quality Government in Israel v The Knesset [2006] IsrSC 61(1) 619

Index

accommodation of family: employment law, and, 217–19
advance care planning, 156–9
age of human dignity, 260–3
ageing: significance of, 146
apparatus of humanity: obligation–creating usage of dignity, and, 263–5
apparatus of person: rights–founding usage of dignity, and, 265–7
Arendt's children, 123
Aristotle: justice and ethics, on, 172–3, *politics*, 42–9
attributes of personhood and belonging in legal thought, 4–18
autonomous and active subject, 247–8
autonomy: elder care, and, 146–70, individual and relational accounts 147–9
autonomy and relationality, 15–18

ballot box: purity of, 55–62
belonging: realms where constructed, 140
belonging and identity, 10–13
Benhabib, Seyla, 174
best interests of child, 123–45; intersectional analysis, 141–2, politics of belonging, and, 136–41, post–humanist theory, and, 256–60
biotechnology, 253–70
border of belonging, 131–6
Botswana, 193–213; administering estates of deceased persons, 205–6, cultural markers, 195, differential status of women in family networks, 210–12, empirical data, 195–6, field transfers to women and men, 204–5, gendered identities, 199–200, inheritance, 197–9, land, 194, land certificates, 202–6, past constraints on women's access to property and land, 197–9, personhood and property, 193–213, redefining formal land based jurisdiction, 201–2, re-evaluating personhood, 210–12, regulating administration of land under customary tenure, 200–2, research location, 195–6, residential transfers to women and men, 203–4, shifting parameters of customary law, 202–6, shifts in inheritance practices, 206–10, sociocultural dimensions, 197–9, transfers between related parties, 204
breadwinner, 214–31

capacity, question of, 147–8
care relations: care theory, 149
care theory, 149
caring relations, 13–15
changing manner of production, 238–40
child: best interests, 123–45
childhood: citizenship, and, 127–31
children as rights-holders, 129
children voting, 62–6; capacity, 63–4, electoral exclusion, 62, harm in, 63–4, problem with, 64–6
citizenship, 8–10; childhood, and, 127–31, identity factors, 128
citizenship test: best interests of child, and, 123–45
civic virtue, 66–8, disenfranchisement, and, 56–60

Committee on the Rights of the Child, 129
constituent people, 72–83
constituted electorate, 72–83
constitutional moment, 72
context of culture, 238–42
creating the citizen, 86–9
criminal disenfranchisement, 53–71
Critical Discourse Analysis, 234–8
cultural level of legal doctrine, 236

dementia, 146–70; borderline capacity, 153–6, clear incapacity, 156–9, definition, 149–50, full legal capacity, and, 150–3, home intervention, and, 164–6, precise level of capacity, 152, respecting autonomy, 149–59
dependency: question of, 131–6
dichotomy of market and family, 216–17
disciplinary identity, 139–40
discourse of business, 243–5
discourse of dependent work, 242–3
discourses of precarious work, 242–8
disenfranchisement, 53–71; civic virtue, and, 56–60, criminal, 53–71, electoral incapacitation, as, 61–2, political capacity, and, 53–71
disruptive voting, 55–6

elder care, 146–70
elections: between self-interest and civic virtue, 55–62
electoral shenanigans, 72–83
employee showing initiative, 247–8
employment law: accommodation of family, and, 217–19
Equality Act 2010, 106
ethical response, 175–7
ethics: role in human rights law, 171–90
ethics in law: human rights, and, 172–5
ethics of alterity, 171–90; symbiosis, 180–1
ethics of care 171–90; family relations, and, 177–80, symbiosis, 180–1
European Court of Human Rights: intersections, 181–7
expectation of work: family law, and, 219–21

families, identity and belonging, 193–213
family: concept of, 131–6

family law: expectation of work, and, 219–21
family relations: human rights, and, 177–80
family reunification: best interests of child in, 123–45
Family Reunification Directive, 136
fictive bearer of rights, 3–4
full legal capacity: dementia, and, 150–3

Gender Recognition Act, 106, 107
gender variant individuals in UK law, 106–10
gendered identities: Botswana, 199–200
genderqueer in UK law, 105–32, *Corbett* judgment, 107–8, history of sex, and, 113–14, identity, idea of, 112–13, insufficiency of current laws, 105–32, legal subject, 111–20, post–operative transsexuals, 109, regulation of relationship between sex and gender, 114, regulatory practices of gender formation, and, 112, scope of protective measures, 109–10, self–determination, and, 110, using Butler's work to critique, 110–20
genuine enjoyment test, 133–4
geriatric chair, 166–7

hegemonic forms of belonging, 135
Hesiod: *Works and Days*, 32–5
home intervention: dementia, and, 164–6
Homer: *Iliad*, 35–42
homemaker, 214–31
human dignity, 253–70
human rights: ethics in law, and, 172–5
human rights law, 171–90
humanity, 253–70

identities and intersections, 3–24
immigrant family reunification, 130
immigration: control by state, 136
infringement on rights of child, 131
integration into Finnish society, 138

juridical framework, 235

Kantian notions of ethics, 173

labour law, 232–52; changing subjectivities 232–52, crisis in, 238–40, doctrinal foundations, 234, doctrinal structure, 240–2,

empirical material for analysis, 236–8, from obedience to initiative, 232–52, material for case analysis, 234, opposed ideas, 234, precarious work, and, 232–52, theoretical framework, 234
land certificates: Botswana, 202–6
language skills, 137–8
late capitalism, 238–40
law and bioethics, 253–70
lawfulness of restrictions, 160–3
legal subject, 111–20
logic of property in law and bioethics, 253–70

modern families, 217–21
modern workplaces, 217–21

narratives of belonging and integration, 125
new conceptions of personhood, 23–4
new stereotypes for old, 228–9

obedient employee, 245–7
obligation–creating usage of dignity: apparatus of humanity, and, 263–5
offenders: political capacity, and, 66–8, problem with voting, 68
other, the, 171–90

P., C. and S. v the United Kingdom, 185–7
personhood, 253–70
personhood and property: Botswana, 193–213
personhood, property and contribution, 21–3
persons, things and the excluded body, 254–6
place of care: work/family balance, and, 222–8
police: nature of, 85
political capacity, 53–71; disenfranchisement, and 53–71, offenders, and, 66–8
political parties: dissolution of, 90–1
politics: dissensus, and, 84
politics of belonging: best interests of child, and, 136–41
politics, power and subjectivication, 19–20
porous state, 72

post–humanist theory: bioethical challenge, and, 256–60
principle of protection, 151

queer recognition: quest for, 116–17

reciprocity of affection, 178
recognising 'the different' subject 20–1
relational autonomy, 148–9
relationship of dependency, 134–5
restrictions on freedom: autonomy, and, 159–67, definition, 159–60, dementia, and 146–0; examples, 163–7, lawfulness, 160–3, right to have rights, 123–4
right to participate, 153–6
rights–founding usage of dignity: apparatus of person, and, 265–7

Saramago, Jose: *Seeing* 72–83
S.H. v Austria, 182–4
social change and law, 238–42
social class: meanings, 127
speech, 29–52; ancient subject of, 29–52, ethical criticism of, 35–42, humans defined by, 42–9, social criticism of, 32–5, what is wrong with, 29–32
standard employment relationship, 232–52
stereotypes, 214–31; outdated, 214–15
subjectivity, 5–8
substituted decision–making, 156–9
supported decision–making, 153–6

traditional ethics of justice, 179
transnational families, 131–6
Turkish citizen subject, 84–101; cabinets, 93–5, creating, 86–9, dissolution of political parties, 90–1, streets, 95–7

value of care, 226–8

work/family balance, 222–8; place of care, and, 222–8, practical challenge, 223–5, value of care, 226–8, who cares, 225–6
works/carer, 214–31

X and Others v Austria, 184–5